NEO-SLAVE NARRATIVES

Neo-slave Narratives

Studies in the Social Logic of a Literary Form

Ashraf H. A. Rushdy

New York   Oxford
Oxford University Press
1999

Oxford University Press

Oxford   New York
Athens   Auckland   Bangkok   Bogotá   Buenos Aires   Calcutta
Cape Town   Chennai   Dar es Salaam   Delhi   Florence   Hong Kong   Istanbul
Karachi   Kuala Lumpur   Madrid   Melbourne   Mexico City   Mumbai
Nairobi   Paris   São Paulo   Singapore   Taipei   Tokyo   Toronto   Warsaw

and associated companies in
Berlin   Ibadan

Copyright © 1999 by Oxford University Press, Inc.

Published by Oxford University Press, Inc.
198 Madison Avenue, New York, New York 10016

Oxford is a registered trademark of Oxford University Press

Library of Congress Cataloging-in-Publication Data
Rushdy, Ashraf H. A., 1961–
Neo-slave narratives : studies in the social logic of a
literary form / Ashraf H. A. Rushdy.
p. cm.   (Race and American culture)
Includes bibliographical references and index.
ISBN 0-19-512533-9
1. American fiction—Afro-American authors—History and criticism.
2. Slaves in literature. 3. Literature and society—
United States—History—20th century. 4. American fiction—
20th century—History and criticism. 5. Afro-Americans—
Intellectual life—20th century. 6. Influence (Literary, artistic, etc.)
7. Afro-Americans in literature. 8. First-person narrative.
9. Slavery in literature. 10 Literary form.
I. Title. II. Series.
PS374.S58 R87   1999
810.9'353—dc21   98-27667

Epigraph on page v copyright © 1980 by Lucille Clifton.
Now appears in *Good Woman*. Published by Boa Editions, Ltd.
Reprinted by permission of Curtis Brown, Ltd.

1 3 5 7 9 8 6 4 2

Printed in the United States of America
on acid-free paper

For Anna Amal Rushdy
and Alex Ashraf Rushdy
and in memory of their
Great-Grandmother Shogheih Yazdi

in populated air
our ancestors continue
i have seen them
i have heard
their shimmering voices
singing.
                    lucille clifton

Acknowledgments

First and foremost, I would like to thank my students who have helped me in thinking through the problems I raise in this book, my colleagues who inspired me with their example, my friends who both prodded me when I was too slow in writing it and sustained me before, during, and after, and my family who has provided me with the kind of love and succor that gives life meaning.

Space does not permit me to name all the students, especially those enrolled in my seminar on "Contemporary African American Narratives of Slavery" for the past seven years, whose thinking, conversations, and written work forced me to reconsider, to clarify, to modify, and sometimes to cling more stubbornly to many of the arguments I make in this study. Among that group, though, I would be remiss if I did not name: Michelle Berkeley, Casey Brown, Taylor Bynum, Kia Coleman, Johnny Cook, Lauren Elmore, John Emerling, Tamekca Faria, Tucker Foehl, Mark Gerber, Catherine Griffin, Makeda Mays, Stacy Morgan, Shani Mott, Patrick Rayner, Melanie Roberson, Angie Rodgers, Raquel Rodriguez, Shanti Roundtree, Chotsani Sackey, Crystal Scott, Christina Sharpe, and Ayana Webb.

While Wesleyan University has provided me with generous sabbatical leaves and financial resources that allowed me to complete this work, I am most thankful for the colleagues at Wesleyan I have had the privilege of working with. Space, again, prohibits me from mentioning all, but I would like especially to thank the following members of the English Department and the African American Studies Program: Christina Crosby, Mickey Davidson, Ann du Cille, Cynthia Horan, Gertrude Hughes, Indira Karamcheti, Jeff Kerr-Ritchie, Maureen Mahon, Richard Ohmann, Gayle Pemberton, Joel Pfister, Renee Romano, Kate Rushin, Richard Slotkin, and William Stowe. The Center for African American Studies at Wesleyan has been a home to me, and I would like to thank Ginny Gumz, and, especially, Georgie Leone, who have made it such a warm and wonderful place.

My friends, some of whom are colleagues, some former students, all dear to me, have given me encouragement, solace, and their unyielding affection. I thank former students and now warm friends David Derryck, Josh Guild, Cheryl Jones, Elisabeth

Nevins, Leigh Raiford, Natalie Stone, and Nadine Wilmot. I thank Ben Jackson, who has been a friend who also happens to save me from computer crises. Krishna Winston has been a model of kindness and solicitude. Cheryl Myers and Monique Sulle have been terrific friends who have alternately kept me up late at night and loudly wondered when my book was coming out. I am deeply grateful to Khachig Tölölyan for his consistent support, his neighborliness, and his capacious intellect. Jan Willis shared with me her profound knowledge of Buddhist traditions, a manuscript family history that proved as important to my work as it was inspiring to me, and numerous meals and wonderful conversations. It has been a delight to know Erness and Nathan Brody, whose wit, wisdom, and hospitality have enriched my life. Susan Hirsch has been a genuinely radiant presence who patiently listened to me, generously gave me references, thoughtfully shared with me her own work, and made the past seven years so much the better and happier for her friendship.

I could not have written this book without the limitless patience of the Interlibrary Loan staff at Olin Memorial Library. Librarians at the Schomburg Library and at the Moorland-Spingarn collection at Howard University have kindly helped me during research visits to those historic and invaluable sites of African American history. The first research for this study was undertaken when I was awarded a research grant from the Social Sciences and Humanities Research Council of Canada and the last proofreading done when I was a research fellow at the National Humanities Center in North Carolina; I am grateful for both fellowships. I would also like to thank four people who read various drafts of this work and saw merit in it when it was still far from meritorious. William Andrews, Joseph Skerrett, Cheryl Wall, and Joe Weixlmann have been personally kind to me and continue to provide me with models of professional magnanimity.

I would like to thank the editors who allowed me to reprint materials first published in different form in the journals *African American Review, Narrative, Arizona Quarterly,* and an anthology entitled *Criticism On the Color Line: Desegregating American Literary Studies.* I have greatly enjoyed working with the editors at Oxford University Press: Susan Chang the acquisitions editor, Shelley Fisher Fishkin and Arnold Rampersad the series editors, Robert Milks the production editor, and Ilene McGrath the copyeditor. I would also like to thank the anonymous readers for Oxford University Press for their helpful and informed comments. I would like to thank Shani Mott for helping with proofreading and indexing.

As always, I would like to acknowledge my deepest love for my family, my mother and father, my brother and his family, my Aunt Nabila, and my Uncle Mohsen and Aunt Felicity, and to express my gratitude for their constant encouragement, unqualified support, and invigorating interest in my work. This book is dedicated to my niece and my nephew, who have brought a joy to my life I can find nowhere else. Finally, I would like to thank and to find solace in the memory of my grandmother, my Taita.

Contents

NEO-SLAVE NARRATIVES

Master Texts and Slave Narratives

Race, Form, and Intertextuality in
the Field of Cultural Production

In the 1960s a set of intellectual and social conditions associated with the civil rights and Black Power movements generated a change in the historiography of slavery. This convergence of an intellectual change in the academic study of the American past and the social movements of the decade, especially Black Power, in turn, affected the fictional representation of slavery from the late sixties to the present. African American fiction in general has undergone a virtual renaissance since the sixties, assuming new importance in the literary canons and curricula of educational institutions, and consistently receiving important cultural awards. Within this large and diverse body of fiction authored by African American writers has emerged a large and diverse body of fiction about American slaves and slavery, beginning with Margaret Walker's *Jubilee* in 1966, John Oliver Killens's novelization of the film *Slaves* in 1969, and Ernest Gaines's *The Autobiography of Miss Jane Pittman* in 1971, along with the wildly popular and critically successful *Roots* of Alex Haley in 1976 and Toni Morrison's *Beloved* in 1987, and culminating in 1994 with Caryl Phillips's *Crossing the River,* J. California Cooper's *In Search of Satisfaction,* Louise Meriwether's *Fragments of the Ark,* Barbara Chase-Riboud's *The President's Daughter,* and Fred D'Aguiar's *The Longest Memory.*

I will be focusing here on one particular form of the contemporary narrativity of slavery, what I call "Neo-slave narratives," that is, contemporary novels that assume the form, adopt the conventions, and take on the first-person voice of the the antebellum slave narrative.[1] By studying together Ishmael Reed's *Flight to Canada* (1976), Sherley Anne Williams's *Dessa Rose* (1986), and Charles Johnson's *Oxherding Tale* (1982) and *Middle Passage* (1990), I am able to explore in some detail the social logic of the literary form of the Neo-slave narrative: its origins in the social, intellectual, and racial formations of the sixties, its cultural politics as these texts intervene in debates over the significance of race, and its literary politics as these texts make statements on engagements between texts and between mainstream and minority traditions. After delineating the social conditions within which the specific literary form of the Neo-slave narrative emerged by analyzing the political and academic de-

bates of the late sixties regarding the cultural politics, I will define how those original debates have been sustained through a specific kind of intertextuality in the
Neo-slave narratives produced during the seventies and eighties.

Between 1966 and 1968, there occurred a distinct shift both in the current social movements and in the intellectual trends in the American historical profession,
signaled by the emergence of the Black Power movement and the rise of New Left
social history. The New Left, especially the student workers affiliated with the Student Nonviolent Coordinating Committee (SNCC) and the Economic Research and
Action Project (ERAP) of Students for a Democratic Society (SDS), watched as poor
people, African American people, and students themselves assumed charge of their
lives by forcing changes in the policies of state agencies, prompting the national government to create and enforce new legislation, and creatively redefining the function
of those institutions meant to provide all citizens with social and educational services. Seeing the traditionally disempowered affect the policy- and decision-making
practices of the state forces, the New Left workers and those sympathetic to their
mission, many of whom were historians, began to appreciate how "history" was
made not solely by the imperial powers of a nation but also by those without any
discernible institutional power. Seeing history made from the "bottom up," New Left
social historians began to study it from the bottom up, changing not only the agenda
of research projects (witnessing the rise of labor and working-class history, women's
history, and ethnic studies) but also the methodologies and resources employed to
discern the past. The study of American slavery was invigorated by a renewed respect for the truth and value of slave testimony, the significance of slave cultures,
and the importance of slave resistance, all ideas that had briefly informed a flurry of
studies by historians and cultural workers in the Old Left in the thirties.[2]

In 1967, in the midst of these changing strategies for political reform and shifting ideas about the historical representations of slavery, William Styron published
what was perceived by the white literary establishment to be the first novel adopting
the formal conventions of the first-person antebellum slave narrative, the first novel
to be written "from the slave's point of view," *The Confessions of Nat Turner.* In 1968,
Black Power intellectuals challenged Styron's novel on a series of issues: its representation of a nonheroic slave rebel, its presumption of assuming the voice of a slave, its
uninformed appropriation of African American culture, its deep, almost conservative allegiance to the traditional historiographical portrait of slavery, and its troubling political message in a time of emergent black empowerment. Inspired by the
developments of the late sixties—the explosion of ghetto rebellions starting with
Watts in 1965, the call for "Black Power" during the 1966 Mississippi March Against
Fear, the emergence of black political and social organizations like the Lowndes
County Freedom Organization and the Black Panther Party, and the evolution of
new black cultural formations—the Black Power intellectuals and "paraintellectuals"
represented a novel force in American public discourse.[3] They opened up new discussions regarding the relationship of art to society, the meaning of cultural expertise
and appropriation in a multicultural country, and the function of a new discourse on
slavery in a time of emergent revolutionary black nationalism.

The shift from the civil rights to the Black Power movement, the evolution from
consensus to New Left social history in the historiography of slavery, and the devel-

opment of a Black Power intellectual presence in the dialogue over Styron's *Confessions of Nat Turner* constitute the moment of origin for the Neo-slave narratives. From the social, historiographical, and intellectual change in the sixties emerged the four Neo-slave narratives of the seventies and eighties: *Flight to Canada, Dessa Rose, Oxherding Tale,* and *Middle Passage.* The social logic of the Neo-slave narrative form is twofold: first, the form evolved from a change in social and cultural conditions in the late sixties; second, later deployments of the form have engaged in dialogue with the social issues of its moment of origin. Believing that no form "*loses* its ancestry," that the form "whistles and hums with this history" of its origins even as it accumulates new meanings "in layers of tissue as the form evolves," the authors of the Neo-slave narratives engage in an extended dialogue with their own moment of origins in the late sixties and early seventies.[4] All four novels raise and meditate on the issues developed out of the debates over the historiographical representation of slavery, the meaning of Black Power, and the significance of Styron's *Confessions*—these form the cultural conditions from which the novelists generate their materials. This study, then, is largely concerned with tracing how a specific literary form emerged and evolved in response to developments in the public sphere.

The authors of the Neo-slave narratives of the seventies and eighties are concerned with the politics of the sixties for several reasons. For one thing, they were part of that generation that was generally living out the legacy of the sixties, a phenomenon some cultural critics have termed "the Sixties-within-the-Eighties." According to Peter Collier and David Horowitz—two neoconservatives who have repudiated the radical political work they performed in the sixties—this phenomenon is both nostalgic ("a generation fondly recollecting a turbulent youth in the tranquility of its middle years") and avowedly political, since they believe that the "growing interest in the Sixties coincides with a renaissance of the radicalism that was the decade's dominant trait and is now being used to jump-start the Next Left." While there is a certain nostalgia in each of the Neo-slave narratives, there is also a critical examination of those issues, movements, and outcomes of the sixties. Each author of the Neo-slave narratives being explored here began writing in the sixties when each first became enamored of and then disenchanted with the politics of Black Power. Reed and Johnson were both participants in and then refugees from the Black Arts Movement when they were actively writing in the 1960s. Williams was an early theorist of the Black Aesthetic (in her 1972 critical work, *Give Birth to Brightness),* and she began writing the inchoate version of *Dessa Rose* in 1968 as a direct response to Styron's *Confessions of Nat Turner.* These authors are in dialogue with the sixties, then, because that epoch in American life constitutes their formative experience as writers and citizens. Their attitude toward the sixties is neither a reactionary disavowal of a turbulent decade nor a nostalgic reverie of a youthful paradise lost. Moreover, while it cannot be said of these three writers that they are nostalgic about the sixties as a way of generating a newer Left, certainly all three do produce a determined exploration of particular Black Power issues—especially the politics of property, identity, and violence—as a way of commenting on the failures of the New Left and articulating their hopes for whatever comes next.[5]

The Neo-slave narratives are also engaged in the sixties because that decade saw the formation of a contemporary discourse of slavery. Historians developed new methodologies and generated new visions of America's antebellum past. Cultural workers produced new fiction and poetry about slavery; Styron's *Confessions of Nat Turner* became the sixties' most representative novel probably because its subject was slavery. Social scientists began to use terms from the historiography of slavery to develop often conceptually facile portraits of what they termed the "black psyche." Civil rights workers, and, later, Black Power advocates, increasingly used the discourse of slavery to describe social conditions and political processes in the sixties. Gaines's *The Autobiography of Miss Jane Pittman*—the first Neo-slave narrative produced by a writer of African descent and a novel Gaines started writing in 1968— exemplifies the links between slavery and the sixties by having its protagonist live out both epochs, by showing the personally experienced connection between the slavery into which Miss Jane Pittman was born and the civil rights movement to which she devotes her final energies.[6] The difference between *The Autobiography of Miss Jane Pittman* and the later Neo-slave narratives is that the later novels make more allusive reference to the sixties and more explicitly focus on the politics of literary history and canon formation.

What is particularly interesting, and gives rise to this study, is the fact that the authors chose to employ the literary form of the antebellum slave narrative while developing their arguments about the political and cultural legacy of the sixties. Why did each of them write in the form of the antebellum slave narrative? After all, no African American author had used this form in the known history of the black novel. And how did this choice emerge from the cultural and racial politics of the sixties? I suggest that there are at least two profoundly important reasons Reed, Johnson, and Williams chose to adopt the conventions and strategies of the antebellum slave narratives, to write in the voice of fugitive or manumitted slaves—in other words, to produce Neo-slave narratives.[7]

First, they wished to salvage the literary form of the slave narrative from what was generally thought of as its appropriation in the sixties. This, after all, was the decade in which two white authors wrote novels that assumed the "slave's point of view" (Styron and Daniel Panger in *Ol' Prophet Nat,* also published in 1967, in which Nat Turner writes his reflections on the revolt in the margins of a Bible). The Neo-slave narratives make sometimes implicit, sometimes explicit comments about white appropriations of the slave's voice and challenge white authors who attempt to contain and regulate the first-person representation of fugitive slaves. In this way, the authors of the Neo-slave narratives are able to comment on cultural politics in America, especially the politics of canonization and the issue of appropriation in American cultural history. In this act of recuperation, the authors of the Neo-slave narratives were replicating the acts of the fugitive slaves who had originally written slave narratives in order to assert the authority of their experience—sometimes against the will and machinations of their abolitionist editors, always against the prevailing national sentiments regarding the testimony of people of African descent. Moreover, by using a form of writing that had been excluded from the academic study of slavery for so long, the authors of the Neo-slave narratives were able to make a critical comment about the historiographical tradition whose often romanticized representation of slavery was enabled by the exclusion of firsthand African American perspectives on the "peculiar institution."

Second, the writers of Neo-slave narratives wished to return to the literary form in which African American subjects had first expressed their political subjectivity in order to mark the moment of a newly emergent black political subject. The connections between antebellum America and the sixties were compelling, for the sixties were years when "race occupied the center stage of American politics in a manner unprecedented since the Civil War era," a decade marked by "intense conflict where the very *meaning* of race was politically contested."[8] Here is where the authors of the Neo-slave narratives were most engaged in developing an understanding of the relationship between cultural forms and cultural formations, between the forms literary texts assume and the intellectual assumptions behind social formations about race in America. The authors of the Neo-slave narratives raise questions concerning the possibility for subjective knowledge within a predetermined form of writing, especially as regards the construction and dismantling of "racial" identity. They ask questions about and demonstrate the process through which a historical subject constitutes itself by employing or revising a set of ideologically charged textual structures. They develop arguments about how contemporary racial identity after Black Power should be mediated through a reconstruction of the first form in which African American subjectivity was articulated—the slave narrative. They discuss the costs and presumptions involved in a modern author's adopting the voice of a fugitive slave and employing the literary form of the antebellum slave narrative. Most important, they ask what it means for a postmodern author to negotiate and reconstruct what is essentially a premodern form, one in which "race" was both a presupposition of authenticity for the author and yet a necessary absence for the primarily white, northern readership.

Finally, contemporary works that explore the power relations in the field of cultural production, that query the creation and recreation of race, and that self-consciously draw on the properties of intertextuality would of necessity situate their examination in terms of the sixties, for the sixties saw the emergence of world-historical political movements that created new social subjects, raising anew questions about race and racial identity, literature and literary history, texts and intertextuality. The empowerment of the "official 'natives' of the third world" and the "inner colonized of the first world"—"'minorities,' marginals, and women"—caused a "transformation of the cultural sphere" as postcolonial and Black Power intellectuals questioned the established canons and traditions. Responding to this cultural crisis, European and American theorists developed new models dispensing with the literary "work" as a product drawing significance from its insertion into a tradition, and promoting the "text" as a "commentary on other texts" in a "seemingly arbitrary fashion," an unstable project in which "basic 'intertextual' references become random, an *ad hoc* constellation which forms and dissolves on the occasion of each new text."[9] The sixties, then, constitute the formation of the political subjectivity of minorities, the reformation of the cultural sphere, and the transformation of the concept of the text within the project of intertextuality. To begin our exploration of a model for intertextual relations accounting for the complex interplay among literary texts, social processes, and cultural imperatives, showing how literary form contributes to and is partially derived from the processes of racial formation, we need first to determine the place of the field of cultural production within the field of power.

Master Texts and Slave Narratives: Refiguring the Field
of Cultural Production

Pierre Bourdieu defines the "field of cultural production" as "a separate social universe having its own laws of functioning independent of those of politics and the economy." Although the field of cultural production exists within the "field of power"—the sphere where politics and the economy are more direct determinants (homologous to the infrastructure)—the field of cultural production nonetheless has its own "specific laws of functioning." To speak of a field of cultural production "is to recall that literary works are produced in a particular social universe endowed with particular institutions and obeying specific laws." The field of cultural production is not simply a more complex way of describing the historical milieu or the social context of a literary text. It is itself a "veritable social universe where, in accordance with its particular laws, there accumulates a particular form of capital and where relations of force of a particular type are exerted." While the laws differ from those of the field of power, since the capital assumes a symbolic form and the force is less evidently material, the field of cultural production is nonetheless intricately *within* the field of power, embodying the same "power relations between classes" found in the "surrounding field of power" and containing struggles that are "never completely independent of external factors." While it is within the field of power, the field of cultural production is emphatically not a reflection of that field; it functions rather like a "prism which *refracts* every external determination," demographic, economic, or political, "according to the specific logic of the field." What happens within the field, especially in terms of formal innovations—"the logic of the development of works" —is a result of that refraction as textual strategies occur "through struggles for specific stakes, themselves produced by the struggles."[10]

The most important element of Bourdieu's model for our purposes is his emphasis on the specific ways a given society's political forces exert themselves in a refracted way on the formal innovations in the field of cultural production. Demonstrating how the dynamics within the sphere of literary production are refracted versions of the class struggles and the modes of circulating power in the larger society, Bourdieu is critical of those who deny the role of social forces in the field of cultural production—the Russian formalists, for instance, who affirm "that all that is literary can be determined only by the prior conditions of the literary system"—as well as those who simplistically view the "relationship between the social world and works of culture in terms of *reflection*" instead of acknowledging the refracted form that "external determinants" take when they are translated into the field of cultural production.[11] Providing us with a method for exploring the effects of this dynamic struggle on the formal production of literature, and specifically on the creation and sustaining of distinct literary forms and intertextual relationships within the field of cultural production, Bourdieu is likewise critical of a formalism that believes "defamiliarization" within a literary "system" constitutes the "fundamental law of poetic change" or a reflectionist model of mimesis, like that associated with the later Georg Lukács, in which the forms of certain works reflect the economic order in which they were produced.[12] Having posited a "relational" system in which cultural workers are situated in differentially empowered positions ("the consecrated artist" and the *"artiste maudit,"* for example) and in which "one can only understand what happens [in the relational system] if one locates each agent or each institution in its relationship with all the others," Bourdieu proposes an entirely relational mode of reading cultural works. Within the field of cultural production, one does not relate the "individual biography to the work of literature," or relate the "'social class' of origin to the work," or produce a practical critical reading of the internal intricacies of the individual work, or even situate the given work into a tradition and perform an "intertextual analysis" of it. Instead, we have to do "all these things at the same time," producing readings that develop an interrelated set of significances of the biographical and political subjectivity of the author and the formal and intertextual subject of the text.[13]

Bourdieu's model of the field of cultural production helps us better understand the general dynamics in American literary studies and the specific dynamics in the literary representation of slavery. When we translate Bourdieu's model from France to the United States—from the *homo academicus* of Gallic grounds to the *homo Americanus* of native grounds—we will find his theory adequate only in the way any social theory of European origins is useful to an American case; that is, we need to accent class-based categories with race-based analyses. In the United States, the field of cultural production certainly refracts the political and economic determinants of the society at large, but it is also a field fissured in a fundamental way along racial lines. This division was caused mostly by the segregationist impulses in the Anglo-American academy from the time of the emergence of American literary studies in the twenties through to the sixties; but it is also partially the result of some African American literary critics who responded to exclusion by employing the strategy of minority literatures in other colonized countries and constructing a separate literary tradition.[14] In the case of African American intellectual history, the strategy of forming separate traditions and canons was sporadically employed in the forties and fifties and urgently deployed in the sixties, particularly with the institutionalization of Black Studies programs in the late sixties. Recently, though, there has developed a countervailing impetus to halt the construction of countertraditions and to use this moment of general crisis to explore more thoroughly the potential for developing new modes of arranging analyses of the production of literary art and the construction of racial difference. Recent studies have challenged the idea of "tradition" in African American letters, arguing for less naturalized, more discontinuous and historicized sets of readings of those texts that putatively make up such a "tradition."[15] They are in the minority, though, because their work emphasizing the role of the social in the production and organization of the textual has gone unheeded. Too many scholars still pursue research agendas premised on the putative autonomy of the field of cultural production and publish work in which they assume rather than question the existence of distinct literary traditions.

This is the case because often scholars negate the question of power in the field of cultural production, not attending to the dynamic inequities in the institutional production, promotion, and reception of literary texts authored by white and black authors in the United States. The kind of work that better enables us to perform a comprehensive reconfiguration of literary production requires us to attend to the issues of power, and the differential in access to it, that not only exist within and beyond the literary traditions of specifiable groups in America but also directly affect the internal organizations of the distinct literary traditions. The issue of "difference" is not abstracted from social relations; it is a product of them. Moreover, we also need to account for power differential in our reconsideration of how texts within and between literary traditions dialogically engage with each other. We need to return the social to the literary when we explore how authors establish intertextual relationships with their predecessors as part of the strategy of revisionist striving for canonicity. Such an analytical method should prevent us from succumbing to the allure of a stable literary tradition, instead provoking us to search out the determining forces behind the impetus for constructing "traditions." Since the "function of traditions" is to create the illusion of "unity out of disunity and to resolve, if not make invisible, the social contradictions or differences between texts," our job as scholars of minority literatures should be to expose rather than perform that function.[16]

The political atmosphere of the 1980s, though, with rising right-wing attacks on affirmative action and premature calls for a color-blind polity, led inevitably to cultural projects aimed precisely at masking those contradictions that cultural workers in the 1960s had so brilliantly exposed. Just as the Reagan administration defined its political agenda largely in direct repudiation of the "sixties," a term right-wing politicians used to codify a seamless monolith of permissive liberalism they anathematized in the process of formulating a series of reactionary policies aimed at dismantling the social programs and civil rights legislation of the Johnson administration, so did conservative intellectuals seek to resist what they variously saw as the "fraying" or the "disuniting" of American culture by calling for "an all-embracing, revamped national literary history." Progressive scholars' fears that the new American literary histories published by Columbia and Cambridge University presses could possibly represent the "danger that two decades of innovative rethinking will not be consolidated so much as contained" were not unwarranted. After all, the conservatives who entered the so-called "canon wars," people like William Bennett, Lynne Cheney, and Allan Bloom, were not only vociferous but also politically empowered and very well funded; they were also quite successful. At the end of the decade, there was a "reactionary self-congratulation (a kind of collective sigh of relief)" in the academy at the incipient "move toward a return to the traditional library of English and American texts."[17]

Meanwhile, the gains made between the original ruptures in the sixties and the calls for harmony in the eighties were minimal. The one-volume Norton anthology of American literature that was used throughout the seventies contained the work of one African American author, who occupied the last two pages of the 1,906-page volume. The new Norton anthology published in 1979 included seven African American writers, taking up 70 of its 1,925 pages. The two-volume Norton anthology published in 1989 contains the work of twenty-one African American writers, amounting to 310 of its 5,242 pages. While the increase was consistent, in no anthology did African American writing represent more than 5.9 percent of the total. Black writers fared even worse in other spheres of the publication industry, as their works quickly went out of print during the eighties. When Toni Morrison appeared on the cover of *Newsweek* in 1981, for instance, "two of her four books were out of print and unavailable for classroom use." Moreover, where the work of African

American writers was available—in the Norton anthology, for instance—it was still not taught. Scholars of African American literature noted that their colleagues specializing in American literature would often reject the opportunity to teach any African American authors because they thought themselves inadequately trained for the task and because these writers were being taught in black literature courses anyway. Ironically it turns out that one of the perverse effects of "opening up the curriculum to black authors has been to preserve the traditional canon."[18] Not only has the opening up of new fields of minority literature served to maintain the traditional canon, but that act of preserving the canon has also affected the ways the texts produced within minority cultures get read. The result has been a considerably vexing problem in the production of knowledge about African American literature.

When we turn our attention to the local scholarly gestures that form the precondition for the construction of literary histories—that is, those acts of scholars detecting the precursors and influences of canonical authors on those candidates for later canonization—we see how the power differential in American society has already been at work in defining African American cultural production. Witness how many black novelists have first received widespread public notice as writers who "echoed" white writers, most commonly William Faulkner. Toni Morrison began an interview with John Edgar Wideman by reading a critic's commentary that compared Wideman's language to Faulkner's. "I can't think of anything more *lovely* than to be compared to Faulkner on the one hand," Morrison mused, "but comparisons are difficult. . . ." She asked Wideman to comment on what was going on "underneath" the comparison. Admitting that it was flattering to be placed in what he called "damn good company," Wideman nonetheless firmly believed that it was necessary for African American writers to dismiss the gesture of comparison when it was offered as a means of validation (just a way of getting one's "entitles") since "nothing ever comes out of that except a kind of dependency, except a kind of marginality." Wideman suggested a different course of action. Here one needs to examine the presuppositions of the claim that there is a mainstream tradition apart from the black tradition. "Just as much as they do their authenticating," he says, "we have to do our authenticating." The "next step" a critic must take after asserting that both Wideman and Faulkner employ an American language is to look at where Faulkner got *his* language. Once we start that search, Wideman concludes, we will discover that Faulkner is "part of an American tradition that includes the black voice, black sermons, black preaching."[19] Wideman, then, is not influenced by Faulkner, nor is he a filiation of a Faulknerian literary line, but rather someone like Faulkner only in drawing on the same resources and materials of a multicultural American heritage.

On several occasions, Morrison has herself declared that she writes literature that is "irrevocably, indisputably Black, not because its characters were, or because I was, but because it took as its creative task and sought as its credentials those recognized and verifiable principles of Black art." Her novels are "legitimatized by their own cultural sources and predecessors." Her work, then, is "irrevocably, indisputably Black" because of its cultural specificity. Her "choices of language," her "reliance for full comprehension on codes embedded in black culture," her attempt to achieve "immediate co-conspiracy and intimacy" and thereby establish a communal-choral sensibility in her reader, and her desire to "shape a silence while breaking it" all attest to her overarching aesthetic imperative to "transfigure the complexity and wealth of Afro-American culture into language worthy of the culture." Yet literary critics have approached Morrison's art, and the art of other African American writers, without a sufficient knowledge of and respect for the cultural imperatives defining African American literary production or much concern for the works exhibiting and transforming those principles over the course of two and a half centuries. Instead, they see in Morrison only what they are trained to see in any literary production, and they therefore believe she is influenced by those writers on whose works they were trained and whose aesthetic principles form their canons of evaluation. Morrison has long made the case that although "black writers ply their trade out of a multiplicity of intersecting traditions," they get classified by their alleged lines of literary influence from white American or European authors. "I am not *like* James Joyce," she asserts; "I am not *like* Thomas Hardy; I am not *like* Faulkner."[20]

Morrison and Wideman are forced to deny these apparent affiliations and filiations because too many critics have taken for granted that the hegemonic culture must exert its influence on the cultural practices of the minority, whose cultural productions can then be best evaluated by applying to them the hegemonic culture's aesthetic standards. Bringing with them little or no knowledge of African American cultural imperatives, critics read Morrison as if she belongs *only* to a mainstream Eurocentric literary tradition, concluding that her verbal inventiveness is Joycean, her comic-tragic examination of shifting rural and urban populations Hardyesque, and her treatment of the historically haunted present of American race relations Faulknerian. Not denying that her work may contain elements of Joyce, Hardy, and Faulkner, Morrison nonetheless insists that its cultural matrix is somewhere else, a somewhere else that gets denied when "the hard work of analysis is deemed too hard, or when the critic does not have access to the scope the work demands." Debates over the canon, as Morrison concludes, are always premised on cultural clashes in which political interests are inherently vested.[21]

The project more likely to lead to the end of separate and unequal literary traditions, then, is one that acknowledges the power differential in cultural exchanges and situates "difference" as a categorical distinction based on and masking social inequities.[22] Such a project would question the motives behind the construction and reconstruction of literary traditions, examining the processes and politics of canonicity. This project first requires us to expose and then dispense with the belief that institutions of literary production and evaluation are autonomous and free from the material interests and practices of the society in which they operate. Attending carefully to the complex interplay between cultural productions and the political situations encompassing them, we must relate cultural texts to "larger institutional and structural battles occurring in and across societies, cultures and economies," tracing how these texts describe or intervene in the operations of power and authority in the public sphere.[23]

We can best examine the specific ways the field of power affected the field of cultural production in the emergence of the Neo-slave narrative, by analyzing the process through which a set of social conditions and political events in the sixties prompted a change in the historiography of slavery, which, in turn, directed cultural workers in their representations of slavery. Because a generation's historiographical work is a response both to the political crises from which it emerges and to the professional and institutional arrangements within which it is produced, the state of historical study provides the best indicator of the concerns of a given cultural moment. The historical profession after World War II was demonstrably responding to a series of international developments. It was also responding in more direct ways to the social and political conditions in the United States as they reflected those international developments. Because the historical profession's work serves as an "essential litmus of social values and cultural change" of a given generation, we can best appreciate "the ideological imperatives of the . . . historical moment" of the sixties by tracing the transition from a dominant, hegemonic discursive formation about slavery to an emergent and contested discourse on slavery.[24]

Derived loosely, perhaps heretically, from Foucault's theory of "archaeology" as a way of discerning the relationship between an intellectual discourse and the "nondiscursive systems" adjacent to it, a "discursive formation" is a convergence of statements and events in the intellectual, social, and political fields, governing the representation and representability of a subject.[25] A discursive formation governs the production of knowledge about history by creating conditions in which historians can make specific propositions about a given subject because it has already delimited the field of inquiry, established certain forms and kinds of evidence as valid, and promoted the belief that this field and that evidence are the only sound means of pursuing knowledge about the subject. A discursive formation coalesces during a period of ferment and assumes a hegemonic form during periods of relative stability, which is also when it most actively forgets its social origins. When it has assumed its hegemonic form, as was the case with the complex of ideas about slavery by the end of the fifties, the discourse determines and limits the field of study for the given subject. At the same time, however, when the society enters a period of renewed flux, as happened in the sixties, an emergent discursive formation arises to challenge the hegemonic one. Unlike the hegemonic one, the emergent discourse responds to specific and immediate changes in the public sphere and actively contests the hegemonic discourse by reflecting directly on its social origins.

The next chapter demonstrates how the hegemonic discourse on slavery was fissured when progressive historians and Black Power intellectuals raised topics—especially the central topics of property (cultural and real), identity (issues of voice and the question of racial subjectivity), and violence (as strategy for revolution and historical act of resistance)—to show the links between the past and the present, between intellectual enterprise and social movements. The third chapter goes on to show how the major cultural debate of the decade, involving the prototype of the Neo-slave narrative, was fundamentally premised on the confrontation between the hegemonic and emergent discursive formations.

So far, I have defined how particular literary and extraliterary factors—the inequities in the field of cultural production, the creation of and dynamic between dominant and emergent discursive formations in the historical profession—help us define the particular historical moment during which the Neo-slave narrative form emerges and with which later deployments of that form engage. I now need to develop a theory explaining the specific mode of engagement by which later Neo-slave narratives enter into that cultural conversation comprising literary and extraliterary issues. The cultural conversation occurs within the field of cultural production but is nonetheless a refraction of the struggles in the social order within which that field is situated. In order to appreciate the importance of the representational strategies and specific literary forms assumed by oppositional texts, we need to generate a theory of how authors engage the social text as well as previous literary texts, a theory that accounts for how texts evoke the cultural conditions of their formal origin as well as their predecessors in that form.

Toward a Theory of Intertextuality

If we argue that texts are not simply products of aesthetic imperatives, or embodiments of concerns defined by a tradition, but rather cultural products emerging from and contributing to a specific social condition, we cannot think of them as engaged with each other in an act of revisionism based on one author's influencing a later one or borrowing from an earlier one. We need to redefine the concept of intertextuality so that it does not mean only the relationship between one text and another, a relationship in which a later text parodies, supplements, or subverts an earlier text, but also, and, more important, the ways texts mediate the social conditions of their formal production. To read intertextually is to discern how a given text creatively alludes to and possibly rewrites a predecessor text, evokes the political dynamic in the field of cultural production, and inscribes into that dialogue its concerns with the social relations in the field of power. Moreover, in the case of oppositional works like the Neo-slave narratives, authors do not strive for canonization by situating their texts in relation to a canonized text, but rather skeptically query the very process of canonicity and the appropriative gestures involved in that process; and they do so by reflecting on the social origins of the problematic they define and circumscribe.

When Julia Kristeva coined the term *intertextuality* in 1966 while introducing French readers to the theories of Mikhail Bakhtin, she defined it to mean the internally conflicted makeup of any given text as a "trans-linguistic apparatus." Intertextuality meant studying a given literary text made up of "several utterances, taken from other texts," within "(the text of) society and history," and defining the "specificity of different textual arrangements by placing them within the general text (culture) of which they are part and which is in turn, part of them." When Kristeva first imagined the dynamics of intertextuality, then, she argued that the practice of reading intertextually involved the act of placing the literary text within "the historical and social text."[26] Kristeva's theory of intertextuality is a radical departure from earlier forms of "influence" or "revisionist" studies, an enterprise in which scholars explored the direct relationship between two texts within a given "tradition," asking in what ways one author was influenced by another or what meaning should be ascribed to the process by which one text rewrote another. It is also a theory premised on a different political vision than "influence" studies which evolved out of the convergence of "mid-eighteenth-century interest in originality and genius," the rise of the nation-state, the spread of imperialism, and the creation of national literatures. In the hands of its comparativist practitioners, and in their most chauvinistic moments, influence studies became a form of "discovering parallels between the literature of two nations" and put to the service of "a crude cultural imperialism." Bakhtin's work appealed to Kristeva because of its political potential. "Dialogical" novels exist as social spaces containing a mixture of different languages, ranging form the statist and hieratic to the demotic and carnivalesque. Such novels were not agents in a central colonizing process, but rather internally multicultural products (living "essentially on the boundaries") attesting to the active negotiations occurring between empowered and disempowered, oppressors and oppressed, citizens of the metropole and subjects of colonization. For Kristeva, then, intertextuality was born of "an anticolonialist resistance to the concept of hegemonic influence."[27] Kristeva's theory is especially appealing because it allows us to focus on the social forces that condition the relationships between (and within) texts.

Unfortunately, Kristeva's promising theory of intertextuality was absorbed into the previous practice of revisionist and influence studies and thereby rendered less challenging to that practice. In dictionaries of narratology and semiotics, "intertextuality" is often defined as the "relation(s) obtaining between a given text and other texts which it cites, rewrites, absorbs, prolongs, or generally transforms and in terms of which it is intelligible."[28] In critical practice, intertextuality is often the study of a Freudian "anxiety of influence," a telling of "the story of intra-poetic relationships" paralleling the oedipal family romance in the son-poet's desire to kill the father-poet; or a feminist revision of the family romance in which the woman author actively seeks out a *"female* precursor who, far from representing a threatening force to be denied or killed, proves by example that a revolt against patriarchal literary authority is possible." The study of minority literatures is likewise based on textual revisionist or "signifyin(g)" relations, "links in an extended ebony chain of discourse," in the active construction of a separate literary tradition; or black feminist revisions of these "largely adversarial and parodic" relations, positing instead black women writers' "non-expropriating refigurations of precursorial texts," and finding "inspiriting influences" in the "intertextual relations among black women writers."[29]

In all these cases, the premise governing the work is that intertextuality describes the ways a literary text engages with an earlier literary text. That is not to say that these reading strategies have not been useful, indeed enormously so in opening up suggestive new terrain for readers. Literary theorists and critics have produced remarkably enlightening readings of given texts and, at times, brilliant elucidations of the relations among a set of texts. It would be dishonest and ungracious for us not to acknowledge the fact that a generation of readers has benefited from the labors of these critics. It would be unforgivable for those of us who work in African American literature to deny the importance of Henry Louis Gates's concept of "Signifyin(g)" or Mae Gwendolyn Henderson's of "speaking in tongues," or to underrate the brilliance of Deborah McDowell's and Michael Awkward's work in drawing our attention to the dialogical connections among a set of writings that have altered the disciplines within which we teach and study them. Nonetheless, these models do depart from Kristeva's original attempt to argue for understanding the literary text as an active agent within the social text, which I would argue is a yet more promising premise for formulating a theory of intertextual relations.

Recently, scholars drawing on and furthering Raymond Williams's insight that literary studies should view "cultural production as social and material," that literary texts are "powerful examples of the way a culture thinks about itself, articulating and proposing solutions for the problems that shape a particular historical moment," have reformulated theories of intertextuality based on the social and political location of literary texts. Proposing models for a "political intertextuality," a "histotextuality," or an "intertextuality of history," these critics have developed a "flexible concept of intertextuality that examines the clashing and blending of texts from the biographical, literary, and cultural records," challenging any "naive textualist or formalist assertions of the total separation of art from the world." Scholars of African American literature have produced models of "inter(racial)textuality" that avoid appeals to positivist racial presence or a stable racial subjectivity (of author or reader), arguing instead that an "intertextual reading would discover racial meaning in the play of difference and would read the production of racial difference as constitutive of, rather than reflecting, social identities."[30]

These new developments in the study of intertextual relationships serve us exceptionally well as we begin to generate a theory of intertextuality that adequately accounts for the refractions of politics in the field of cultural production. Such a theory of intertextuality must account for the power differential between various groups occupying diverse positions in the field of cultural production—producing either master texts or slave narratives—while equally respecting that slave narratives (and Neo-slave narratives) do not only "react" or "respond" to master texts, but actively engage both specific literary texts and the social conditions from which they emerge. It seems abundantly clear that Hortense Spillers has best broached these several subjects in the most compelling and suggestive way, and her rigorous writings and stunning readings provide us with a viable concept for developing a serviceable theory of intertextual relations between "mainstream" and "minority" discourses and traditions.

Since the mid-eighties, Spillers has been imaginatively demonstrating how minority writers in the Americas are deeply concerned with the concepts of "originality" and "appropriation," with defining the power differential in national cultural affairs and creatively employing forms that complicate the relationship between master texts and slave narratives. Because minority writers "must pit themselves against texts written long before," their works exhibit the "peculiar tensions established between a priority and a succession," a prohibitive condition for these authors not only because of the psychic effects of having predecessors (the "anxiety of influence" of poets "burdened by the sense of the past"), but also because of the social effects of a minority writer's having to respond to a mainstream writer's work situated in a canonical tradition maintained by its acts of positive exclusion and its premise of ignoring the power differential in the field of cultural production. In order to establish that the "politics of culture are not solely made by the logics of domination," oppositional literary texts articulating the subjectivity of the excluded and disempowered must show how "tradition" is a "critical fable intended to encode and circumscribe an inner and licit circle of empowered texts." In order to destroy this fable and dismantle the sense of "tradition" it has produced, we need to see how these texts form another kind of "tradition"—one emerging from a "matrix of literary *discontinuities*." An analysis of "literary discontinuities" would excavate the hidden voices of a literary tradition, expose the acts that go into premising a tradition on excluding certain voices, and discover the formal innovations minority writers have made in their resistance. The "pentimento" and the "palimpsest," for instance, two strategic genres New World minority writers employ for disrupting homogeneous narratives of "America," act as screens or canvases that carry "traces of preceding moments that alter the contemporaneous rendition, making the latter both an 'originality' and an 'affiliated,' or the initiation of a new chain of signifying as well as an instance of significations already in intervened motion."[31] By exploring how minority writers develop new forms of writing that challenge conventional terms of chronology and affiliation, Spillers is able to discern how these writers produce radical revisions of the national narratives that stabilize and reify the kinds of identities necessary for the maintenance of national traditions.

The concept of discontinuity provides us with a model of intertextuality neither premised on the construction of literary canons and traditions, nor concerned solely with defining the relationships between autonomous literary texts. The discontinuity describes the various directions to which a given literary text projects itself. The texts explored in this study are engaged in dialogue not only with specific literary texts, but with an ethos; not just with another novel, but with the discursive formation from which another novel emerged. A novel, especially a historical novel, is the product of several interrelated impulses: the historiography of the subject it purports to represent, the social and cultural conditions from which it emerges, and the literary form it adopts and the literary "tradition" into which it is potentially subscribed. An intertextual reading should determine the meaning of a novel emerging from and in dialogue with these impulses. The intertextual relationship is discontinuous because the fictional text is not establishing a coherent relationship between itself and a predecessor text; rather, the fictional text is engaged in a complex dialogic negotiation with the various spheres that together form the cultural moment of its production. Even when it is involved in an explicitly marked dialogue with another text, particularly one sharing the same form, it is nonetheless also engaged in a dialogue with that earlier text's being situated in its own social moment.

In this study, the intertextual relationship is also discontinuous because all four Neo-slave narratives situate themselves as belated participants in an earlier cultural conversation. Although these novels appear in the relatively conservative seventies and eighties, they engage in the issues raised during the heated, transitional period when the social movements and the historiographical debates of the sixties had not yet been respectively derailed and resolved. These novels engage in those formative debates for various reasons—some nostalgically, some with a revisionist desire, and some with an eye toward defining the conditions of future debates about racial, cultural, and academic politics. Taken as a whole, though, their concerted effort to establish themselves in a relationship of discontinuous intertextuality with the earlier cultural moment is also a means of challenging the very processes and racial dynamics of canonicity. Formally adopting the conventions of the antebellum slave narrative, the Neo-slave narratives comment on the cultural politics of the late sixties by situating themselves in that original dialogue surrounding the social origins of the Neo-slave narrative form, that historical moment in literary history when American intellectuals debated the political significance of representing the slave's voice in a work of fiction.

Each of the Neo-slave narratives is generated as a challenge to what Styron's *Confessions of Nat Turner* represents in American literary politics. For Styron's novel, despite its apparent form as a Neo-slave narrative, was a master text. All the publishing strategies and marketing events surrounding the publication of Styron's *Confessions* were aimed at asserting its place as a canonical text in the field of cultural production. *Harper's* paid "more to Styron ($7,500) than to any other author in its 117-year history" for permission to print a 50,000-word excerpt from the forthcoming novel. The Book-of-the-Month Club set a "house record for a novel" by paying Styron $150,000. Three years before the novel appeared, New American Library paid Styron $100,000 for the paperback rights. When the paperback edition did appear, it boasted on its cover the "Pulitzer Prize Winner of the Year" and "An All-Time Best Seller," a novel that was not only a "triumph," in the words of the *New York Times* reviewer, but also the "most profound fictional treatment of slavery in our literature," according to the quoted excerpt from C. Vann Woodward's *New Republic* review. In sum, then, Styron's book was not only "the most controversial novel of its tempestuous decade," but also a novel actively promoted to achieve canonical status as a master text in the field of cultural production.[32]

The Neo-slave narratives of the seventies and eighties revisit the debate over Styron's novel and raise anew those persistent issues of cultural appropriation, racial subjectivity, and the politics of canon formation. It is important to emphasize that the relationship between the Neo-slave narratives and Styron's novel is not one of response or reaction; their relationship is not one of dependency in the way parodic texts are dependent on their host texts. Rather, the relationship is one in which the Neo-slave narratives return to and reassess the cultural moment behind the production of a literary text. Not only does each author comment on and attempt to redefine the function of literary parody as a form of articulating grievances against the literary establishment, but each also attends to the politics behind the field of cultural production. In other words, each of the Neo-slave narratives explores the differential politics in the field of cultural production by examining the social origins of the field of cultural production. These are intertextual relations that are discontinuous.

Likewise, it is crucial to note that the Neo-slave narratives of the seventies and eighties assume the form of the antebellum slave narrative not as a way of imitating Styron, but rather as a way of intervening into the cultural, historiographical, and intellectual debates surrounding Styron's novel. They adopt the first-person voice of the fugitive slave to contest acts of cultural appropriation like Styron's, but they revise the conventions and topics of the slave narrative to assert the importance of that form of testimony to the historical profession and they revisit the slave narrative to demonstrate the connection between "cultural *forms,* the various sorts of textuality and subjectivity most closely related to human agency" and "cultural *formations,* the organizations, processes, and overdetermined conjunctures that bear most significantly on political life."[33] And the cultural formation most fully involved in their work has to do with the construction and reconstruction of race.

Racial Formation and Literary Form

The moment of origin for the Neo-slave narratives was also a crucial moment of transition in the contemporary meaning of "race" in America as intellectuals actively promoted the idea that race was a cultural construction neither inflexible nor implacable. Although arguments about race as a socially constructed category have a fairly long history, we tend to think of them as products of our postmodern sensibility, which they are only partly. It is true there is nothing new in the (recent) pronouncement that we need "another view of race, in which the concept operates neither as a signifier of comprehensive identity, nor of fundamental difference, . . . but rather as a marker of the infinity of variations we humans hold as a common heritage and hope for the future," but it is equally true that there is something dramatically new in a contemporary, postmodern insistence on "the *performative* aspect of race," or in thinking of race as a "plastic process subject to the macro forces of social and political struggle and the micro effects of daily decisions," as something "to some extent volitional."[34] Nonetheless, it is important to remember that responses to scientific racism have usually emphasized the idea of race as contingent, even if those earlier writers did not think of it as "performative" or "volitional." In fact, the intellectual conversation over the concept of race might be diagrammed as a debate between those advocates of scientific racism who respond to epochs of social upheaval by arguing for a conservative notion of race and those progressive writers who respond to scientific racism by arguing for the contingency of race.

Although scientific racism has been in decline since the beginning of the twentieth century, there have been periods throughout the century when individuals and schools of thought have attempted to resurrect the idea that biological inheritance could explain intellectual endowment and cultural differences. In response to the Great Migration, the influx of immigrants from Southern Europe, and the racial violence following World War I, writers like William MacDougall, Charles Davenport, Madison Grant, and Theodore Lothrop Stoddard produced works in the 1920s urging the government to formulate policies curtailing immigration from certain parts of the world in the interest of eugenics, and generally lamenting the passing of the great white race. So, too, in response to the civil rights and Black Power movements, writers like Arthur Jensen, William Schockley, and Hans Eysenck produced studies in 1969 purporting to show the innate, biological basis of intelligence. One of the foundational points subtending the work of these scientific racists is that races are stable and originally pure entities. The progressive scholars who answered scientific racism—especially Franz Boas before World War II and the anthropologists and geneticists who compiled four statements by the United Nations Educational, Scientific, and Cultural Organization (UNESCO) on race after World War II—stressed the fact that there is "no such thing as hereditary racial purity," that races are "not stable, immutable entities, but undergo changes due to domestication, selection, mutation, and other environmental influences." As the first UNESCO statement most forcefully put it in 1950, the major divisions of the species homo sapiens—Mongoloid, Negroid, Caucasoid—are not the same in the present as they were in the past, are certain to change in the future, and are based on "dynamic, not static" biological processes.[35]

Recently, progressive writers have focused more on the social contingency than on the evolutionary mutation of race, trying to understand "race as an unstable and 'decentered' complex of social meanings constantly being transformed by political struggle." Michael Omi and Howard Winant have used the term *racial formation* to describe the theory that "emphasizes the social nature of race, the absence of any essential racial characteristics, the historical flexibility of racial meanings and categories, the conflictual character of race at both the 'micro-' and 'macro-social' levels, and the irreducible political aspects of racial dynamics." Since the "meaning of race is defined and contested throughout society, in both collective and personal practice"—during which process "racial categories are themselves formed, transformed, destroyed and reformed"—it makes sense to think of racial formation as the "process by which social, economic and political forces determine the content and importance of racial categories, and by which they are in turn shaped by racial meanings." It is important to note that the process is one in which racial meanings and political forces are interrelated, each affecting the other. Not only do political structures form and mobilize racial categories, but the "crafting of an ethnic identity among different racial and ethnic groups" also constitutes these groups' attempts to "restructure America's public and political culture."[36]

For our purposes here, then, it makes sense to examine closely the texts on the cultural terrain where personal and collective practices get articulated, particularly those texts that assume a markedly racialized form in order to make a statement about racial formation. The Neo-slave narratives are exemplary texts for this purpose since each of them is not only a productive articulation about racial subjectivity but also a critical analysis of the intellectual mobilization of the concept of race. They are, in other words, both participants in and reflections on the process of racial formation. In this way also, they are engaged in the legacy of the sixties, which in some crucial ways can be said to be the decade that saw both the most concerted mobilization of political and cultural apparatus in the attempt to dismantle the "racial state" as well as the initial attempts to discern the systematic processes through which racial categories are formed and deployed in the interests of the racial state.[37]

Recent intellectual work recognizes that the late sixties saw a significant shift in thinking about race. In an article "periodizing" 1968, Kobena Mercer noted how important that year was to the evolving postwar attitudes toward race, pointing out that the "historical rupture or break from a classical to a modern regime of truth with regards to the representation and signification of race" depended on the debiologizing of race as a "transcendental signified" and on the new developments in the "black struggles" as African American intellectuals "subverted the signification of difference" that had been rooted in and helped recreate the "subjection and oppression" of people of African descent. The year 1968 was a crucial one in the process because it marked a strategic and ethical change in the black struggles of the sixties, a development following the 1965 Watts rebellion and the 1966 call for Black Power. It was also around this time that we saw a resurgence in scientific racism as a reactionary intellectual response to political developments in America and abroad; and, simultaneously, the response of progressives to the basic tenet of scientific racism, the putative stability of race as a scientific category. As but one example of this changing intellectual climate, witness the fact that Winthrop Jordan concluded his magisterial 1968 study, *White Over Black,* with a "Note on the Concept of Race" in which his major point was that "races are neither discrete nor stable units but rather . . . plastic, changing, integral parts of a whole which is itself changing."[38]

Between about 1965 and 1968, this intellectual debate became an integral part of the black movements themselves. Some black organic intellectuals contested or repudiated the ideas of liberal environmentalism and asserted a kind of cultural essentialism, arguing that race is a complex of cultural heritage, socioeconomic political experience, and biological makeup (sometimes internationalist in focus, as in Pan-Africanism and the rainbow coalition of the later Malcolm X, sometimes fiercely nationalist, as in some strains of black cultural nationalism). Other black organic intellectuals saw the rise of "ethnicity"—especially nationalist assertions of black ethnic identity—as problematic, counterproductive, and "socially and politically dangerous." They chose rather to extend the tenets of postwar liberal environmentalism, often in an antifoundationalist way, by arguing that race is completely a social construction. They chose to emphasize the contingent nature of race and the processes behind racial identification. Arguing that the "Black experience is a process," Black Power intellectuals maintained the need for "dynamic rather than static paradigms" to understand this "process of the creation of a new people." At the same time, black intellectuals radically historicized the creation of "Negroness" as a social and political phenomenon arising in a specific world-historical context. Asserting that the "American Negro . . . is an Anglo-Saxon invention . . . hatched in the brave New World" as a "rationalization for the colonializing of three-quarters of the earth's people," they ask: "Who will uninvent the Negro?" The answer was that African Americans would, and it would be done by those who explored race itself as a social construct with its own political history. "Nature created no races," wrote John Henrik Clarke. "Nature created people and people did not refer to themselves as belonging to a race until the rise of the colonial system and of the slave trade concurrent with that system."[39]

We can see, then, that intellectuals within the black social movements in the sixties created a significant dialogue about racial formation. While the dialogue is one version of a larger debate about race extending back to the middle of the eighteenth century, it is, more pertinently, a dialogue about race as a historically formed social construction through the course of the twentieth century. It was initiated anew in the sixties because the Black Power movement created a new black social subject. What was especially pertinent about the debate is that black intellectuals drew connections between the emergence of this new subject in the late sixties and the invention of the old black subject in the course of the slave trade and slavery. That debate is still with us and it is still largely governed by the same terms that arose in the sixties.

At a recent conference on "Race and Racism" at Skidmore College, for instance, Orlando Patterson noted that the sixties marked a shift in intellectual thought about race traceable to the rise of a form of cultural nationalism that still fissures black communities today. The postwar view that "insisted that race as a biological factor is not important, that race is primarily a social phenomenon constructed by people with certain belief systems" was "broken up" in the course of the sixties. Following such public spectacles as the Clarence Thomas–Anita Hill hearings, black intellectuals noted that it was "clear that the time for undiscriminating racial unity has passed," one arguing that the Thomas-Hill hearings constituted nothing less than the "remarkable dissolution of the national black identity." Once again, the spectacle of a newly emergent black political identity caused some to reflect on the history of slavery. At the

Skidmore conference, Jim Sleeper maintained that the Thomas-Hill hearings meant that "the culture of slavery is dead, because no longer do whites bring to such an event the expectation that race will be the dominant motif. It evaporated before thirty million people." Unwilling to see "race" as something having to do with how white people view black people (and also unwilling to think of "race" as something that inheres only to nonwhite peoples), Barbara Fields disagreed, arguing that there has "never been a way of identifying Afro-Americans in this country apart from their identification as a class." "That's how you knew who Afro-Americans were, people who are slaves, or how you know who they are now, people who are descended from slaves. There's no way you can separate those two identities."[40]

The Neo-slave narratives of the seventies and eighties enter this specific intellectual debate over race, especially as the debate plays itself out in discerning the relationship between the history of slavery and the social significance of contemporary racial identity. The Neo-slave narratives take up the issues raised by the anthropological idea of race as a performed and regulative social category, question the politics proscribing cultural crossing, and develop statements on the liberating effects that come with acknowledging the pliability of racial identity. At the same time, though, the authors of the Neo-slave narratives of the seventies and eighties articulate the problems that arise when intellectuals focus on the performance of social identity without considering the role of power and the effects of powerlessness in these performances. They do so, first of all, in the materials that each narrative explores, in the stories they tell, and in the kind of intellectual debates they raise. Just as the "ethnic autobiographies" of the seventies and eighties explore how "ethnicity is something reinvented and reinterpreted in each generation by each individual," the Neo-slave narratives, as part of the same intellectual moment and cast as fictional autobiographies, also articulate their concerns about the contingency of race and racial identity.[41] However, they also note the limitations on free play in the invention of racial identity by assuming the form of the antebellum slave narrative—a form that is creatively resistant to master texts and that also highlights the relative powerlessness of its author.

Moreover, since literary forms or genres "present a tension between tradition and performance, between past instances of the genre and the instance at hand," and since genre itself is "determined by the social formations from which it arises," the Neo-slave narratives immediately raise questions about the connection between slavery and postmodern black identity, between the moment when the first slave narratives were produced and the moment the Neo-slave narratives appeared.[42] In other words, they make that connection not only in their content but also in their form, since they adopt the conventions, gestures, and voice of the antebellum slave narrative in order to play with, partially dismantle, and partially demonstrate the implacability of that original identity—of slave. They also raise questions about the political and cultural legacy of the sixties, since they are addressing issues raised in the academic debate over slave testimony, contributing to the dialogue over Styron's novel (the prototype of the Neo-slave narrative form), and reflecting on the most recent shift in the intellectual debate over the social meaning of race.

2

Toward 1968

The Discourse in Formation

In the course of the sixties, American historians, social activists, and organic intellectuals contributed to the creation of a new discourse on slavery that shaped, and
continues to shape, the options of cultural workers representing American chattel
slavery. Three broadly defined topics emerged as particularly significant: *violence,
property,* and *identity.* These three topics assumed a prominent place in this new discourse on slavery because they so effectively demonstrated the connections between
the political climate of the sixties and the long-term effects the institution of slavery
had on American social life. Let me state at the outset that these topics which appear
to be enduring themes of what some might call "universal" importance are rather
specific points of reference for locally significant debates that best illustrate the mobilization of social forces in American public opinion, historical writing, and cultural
production during and since the sixties. This is not to deny that these topics have
had earlier lives in previous historical debates, or even that those earlier debates
helped shape the new discourse on slavery. It is to say, though, that these topics assumed the place they did within the new discourse on slavery because they emerged
from specific social conditions in the political movements of the sixties and helped
form the intellectual coordinates of the historiographical and cultural debates of the
decade.

The topic of violence, for instance, is certainly not germane only to American
life in the sixties and the slave experience in the antebellum period. Like narrative,
violence is transcultural and transhistorical as a practice and a conceptual category.
Nonetheless, we can understand violence as an issue in the emergent discourse on
slavery only if we look at the concrete events and intellectual debates in the moment
when the discourse is being formed. Although acts of racial violence were not new
to the South in the mid-fifties, having steadily declined but not become obsolete
since the national antilynching campaigns of the early 1890s, several lynchings in
Mississippi in 1955—the shooting of George W. Lee and Lamar Smith while they
were attempting to exercise their voting rights, and the brutal murder of Emmett
Till—constituted a novel moment in the history of racial relations in the South.

First, it was clear that the most recent wave of lynchings was related to the *Brown* decision of the previous year. Southern newspaper editor Frederick Sullens had proclaimed that "human blood may stain southern soil in many places because of this decision," and the murders of Lee, Smith, and Till bore out the truth of his threat. Second, these acts of racial violence were met with an energetic black resistance, utilizing the apparatus of the national media. The field secretary of the National Association for the Advancement of Colored People (NAACP) Medgar Evers made the lynching of Emmett Till a national event that eventually "set off a worldwide clamor and cast the glare of a world spotlight on Mississippi's racism." The NAACP published a booklet in November 1955, entitled *M is for Mississippi and Murder,* that directly affected political discourse around racial violence. Apparently responding to such pressure, the incoming governor of Mississippi, James P. Coleman, felt compelled to declare in his inaugural address in January 1956 that "the great overwhelming majority of the white people of Mississippi are not now guilty and never intend to be guilty of any murder, violence, or any sort of wrongdoing toward anyone."[1] At precisely the same time, of course, Martin Luther King, Jr., was theorizing, and the African American citizens of Montgomery were practicing, a deliberate and strategic form of "nonviolence," thereby creating the political and intellectual conditions for a decade-long debate between the proponents and critics of nonviolence in the civil rights movement, a debate that directly and indirectly affected the study of slavery in the sixties.

Indeed, one could say that the social violence of the sixties affected the historical study of the nation's past as a whole and helped shape the decline of consensus historiography and the rise of New Left social history. One of the features of consensus historiography that John Higham found objectionable was that historians tended to mute "classic issues of social justice" and gave little attention to the persistence of "violence in American life." This intellectual climate led to what one historian calls the "awkwardness and embarrassment surrounding the study of slavery in the early 1950's." By the late fifties, though, there was a significant change with the publication of Kenneth Stampp's *The Peculiar Institution* in 1956 and Stanley Elkins's *Slavery* in 1959. While Stampp emphasized the violence that slaves committed in their acts of resistance, Elkins drew an elaborate portrait of the relentless physical and psychic violence of the slave system itself. Both historians were aware of how their work reflected the developing civil rights movement, of how historians writing about slavery in the midst of the new black freedom movements were involved with "both present and past."[2] By the late sixties, historians not only would produce a spate of new historical work on American slavery but would have an entirely different attitude about the study of slavery and the role of violence in maintaining and destroying the system; and that history would be informed by a resolutely sixties sensibility toward violence.

With the rise in ghetto revolts in the mid-sixties, the development of a violent vanguard in the New Left in the late sixties, and a heightened perception of the pervasive police violence of the entire decade, it was widely recognized that violence was a fact of historical importance for the study of the nation's present politics. The year 1968 saw the simultaneous publication of the *Kerner Report of the National Advisory Commission on Civil Disorders* and the *Walker Report to the National Commission on the Causes and Prevention of Violence.* It was also becoming absolutely clear that violence was one of the most pronounced features of the nation's political past. The following year, at least three new anthologies and documentary histories of violence in America appeared: Hugh Davis Graham and Ted Robert Gurr's *The History of Violence in America,* Allen Grimshaw's *Racial Violence in the United States,* and Thomas Rose's *Violence in America: A Historical and Contemporary Reader.* It was also becoming obvious that the violence of the nation's past was directly connected to the present. The Rose anthology made the connection implicit not only in its subtitle but also in the organization of its three sections—the second entitled "Violence in American History," the third "Violence in the Sixties." Also the development of Black Power as a philosophy founded on the ruins of the strategic nonviolence of the early civil rights movement led to a new recognition of the pervasive violence of American society and foreign policy and a renewed respect for the violence of slavery. When Graham and Gurr set out to demonstrate and evaluate the "historical antecedents" to the "contemporary American experience with violence," the first item they listed in documenting the "individual and collective violence that troubles contemporary America" was "the psychological residues of slavery."[3]

This comment appeared at virtually the same time as John Henrik Clarke, John Oliver Killens, Vincent Harding, John A. Williams, Lerone Bennett, and a host of other Black Power-inspired cultural workers were contesting William Styron's representation of Nat Turner as a man who shrank from performing acts of revolutionary violence against the system that enslaved him and his people.[4] The topic of violence, then, became a part of the new discourse on slavery through a specific set of events and debates, a complex process involving political activists who engaged in sometimes violent resistance to the institutional violence of American political life, historians who recognized the connections between the nation's past instances of violence and its present turbulences, and cultural workers who reflected or challenged representations of what they considered rampant or revolutionary violence in artistic texts.

Likewise, the topic of property was incorporated into the emergent discourse on slavery through another, related set of events and debates. For one thing, historians and authors of government reports on ghetto revolts usually used the phrase "damage to property" as one part of their political definition of "violence." More important, however, property was an ascendant issue in the early civil rights movement because the struggle for civil rights in America has always been a struggle to define the limitations of property rights. Freedom fighters in the very first campaigns of the civil rights movement demonstrated their solid understanding of that fact. The 1960 sit-ins, for instance, provide a perfect example of the "definitive movement style" of the New Left because the sit-ins involved individuals acting collectively in a uniquely pragmatic way. They did not petition the government authorities or ask the store owners to allow them to sit down. They sat. "Instead of saying segregation ought to stop, they acted as if segregation no longer existed." Participants in the sit-ins and the freedom rides felt that their activity "inspired us to build a new image of ourselves in our own minds," creating a new "vision of freedom" inseparable from "the concrete day-to-day conditions that determine the quality of our lives."[5] In other words, to change current conditions, they performed their activities as if they were already living in the society they wished to inhabit, a society holding civil rights to be more important than property rights and therefore resolving any conflict between them in favor of broader civil and narrower property rights.

So, too, with the topic of identity. The early civil rights movement was based on the premise of an American identity that some, notably African Americans, could not fully assume because of racist pressures in the system, and that if the racist pressures could be reduced or eliminated, all citizens would be fully American. The civil rights movement's consistent and widespread call for integration was founded on the belief that equal access to national resources would promote equal sensibilities about national identity. By the late sixties, in response to the obvious failure of American institutions to meet these demands, the Black Power movement challenged these premises, dismantled the idea of a stable or transcendent American identity, and generated a new sensibility of empowerment through assuming a racial subjectivity.

Just as the events and debates on violence in the sixties had created the possibility for historians to reexamine America's slave past with a greater focus on the violence done by and to the system, so too did the events and debates on property and identity help mobilize new historical research programs. The topics of property and identity together were clearly important for the study of slavery, since slaves were "chattels personal," that is humans who were both persons and property. For the most part, earlier American historians had dealt with the slaves as if they were solely property, a labor force constituting the engine of an agricultural system. Toward that end, historians from Ulrich Phillips to Stanley Elkins denied the truth value and purposely excluded the testimony of former slaves from the historical record. With a new focus on slavery as a complete social system, though, came a reevaluation of slave autobiographies, interviews, and expressive culture. Slaves were property with social identities, and it was now necessary for historians to examine not only the records that gave data on the profit and labor productivity of slavery but also those records attesting to the personality and cultural productions of slaves. Although historians had made occasional calls for histories of slavery to incorporate the testimony of slaves throughout the twentieth century, especially in the thirties, the sixties saw the most concerted and ultimately successful assault on those historians who had denied and excluded the testimony of slaves from the historical record.[6]

In general, the work of historians in the sixties was energized by the political and social events of the decade and mobilized by the emergent discourse on slavery. Sometimes this influence was implicit in the presupposition the historian brought to his or her task. It is not hard, for instance, to see how the topic of identity changed the focus of historians from Kenneth Stampp, who had articulated the liberal environmentalism of the mid-fifties in his declaration that "slaves were merely ordinary human beings, that innately Negroes *are,* after all, only white men with black skins, nothing more, nothing less," to Eugene Genovese, who articulated the militant mood of Black Power in the late sixties in his declaration that "slaves, as an objective social class, laid the foundations for a separate black national culture." The topic of property in the new discourse likewise affected historians' examination of the past. Arguing that Reconstruction failed only because "political change was not reinforced by economic change," Staughton Lynd noted that the mistake Congress made was "to set up a stool with two legs—Negro suffrage and a Federal presence—which needed the third leg of economic revolution in order to stand by itself." In this 1965 article, written while the House debated the Voting Rights Act, it was difficult to tell which President Johnson's Congress Lynd was talking about: Andrew or Lyndon. Often, historians explicitly stated their indebtedness to the new discourse on slavery, as did Lynd when he praised contemporary studies on Reconstruction that consciously bring the present to bear on their exploration of the past, especially those "reflecting the Southern student movement and its demand for Federal intervention."[7]

Although they are by no means the only topics of value in the emergent discourse on slavery, the topics of violence, identity, and property serve us exceptionally well in defining the relationship among the social movements, the academic study of slavery, and the cultural debates over representations of slavery in the sixties. In order to delineate the process through which the emergent discourse on slavery was formed, locate the intellectual debates in which it participated, and define the social conditions to which it responded, I will first, describe the academic, intellectual terrain on which the emergent and the dominant discursive formations met; second, show the direct effects the social movements of the sixties had on the emergent discourse on slavery by demonstrating how historians responded to the promptings of the organic intellectuals within the civil rights movement; and, finally, discern how the emergent discursive formation was completed and then mobilized in an interactive relationship between historians in the academy and intellectuals in the Black Power movement. This emergent discourse on slavery was largely formed between 1959 and 1968, and it is not only the intellectual and cultural backdrop to the important 1968 debate over William Styron's *Confessions of Nat Turner* but part of the very debate itself and, therefore, part of the social origins of the Neo-slave narratives.

From Consensus to Dissent: The Intellectual Context of Stanley Elkins's *Slavery*

A brief reception history of Stanley Elkins's *Slavery: A Problem in American Institutional and Academic Life* (1959) will help us trace the direct and indirect effects the social movements of the sixties had on the study of slavery in the American academy. There are three reasons we need to focus on Elkins's *Slavery*. First, Elkins provides us with a key text at the transitional moment between the demise of consensus and the rise of New Left social history. In fact, Elkins did his graduate work under the supervision of Richard Hofstadter, one of the major, if not *the* major, exemplar of consensus history; he also wrote his dissertation between 1952 and 1958, key years in the evolution of consensus historiography. Published in 1959, the year Jonathan Weiner gives for the beginning of what he calls the "crisis in American history," *Slavery* also appears at the very moment when the political movements outside the academy created the conditions for an intellectual revolution within the academy. Second, those historians who were the beneficiaries of the social movements and the intellectual revolutions of the sixties persistently focused on Elkins. While it is certainly true that Elkins's *Slavery* was "less a cause of the scholarly investigations into slave behavior and slave life than a convenient target for those whose concerns and perspectives arose out of the zeitgeist of the late 1960s," it is equally important to note that those scholars *did* focus on Elkins, and they did so because they felt his work representative of precisely that school of historiography whose premises and dictates they wished to contest. Finally, Elkins's study quickly assumed a prominent place in the textual practices of social scientists and cultural workers who wanted a historical explanation for contemporary social conditions. Indeed, the book deeply influenced the authors of two of the most controversial texts to emerge from the sixties. *Slavery* became "the most vigorously contested book yet written about the subject" largely because it was used to buttress the Moynihan Report, which some have called the "most refuted document in American history," and, most important for our purposes, it was made to serve as a supplemental text to Styron's *The Confessions of Nat Turner,* "the most controversial novel of its temptestuous decade."[8]

Elkins's work is important, then, because it represents a point of transition, focus, and controversy in the formation of a new discourse on slavery during the sixties. By examining the reception history of *Slavery* in detail, we can discern what effect the early civil rights movement had on historians meditating anew on the wisdom of the abolitionists and the Radical Republicans during Reconstruction. We can also better appreciate how the emergence of ethnic studies disciplines in northern institutions of higher education and the contemporaneous development of New Left historiography caused historians to debate the forms of evidence ideally included in historical work that purported to examine history "from the bottom up." In other words, by following the various stages in the critical reception of *Slavery,* we will be able to assess the changing sociopolitical climate of America and, more specifically, to trace the formation of a discursive complex about slavery between two distinct climates of opinion.

The social and intellectual climate of the 1950s, when *Slavery* was conceived and written, was one of shifting reaction to the legacy of the New Deal and accommodation to the cold war. Daniel Bell argued that the "basic political drift of the former Left intelligentsia in the United States in the forties and fifties has been anti-ideological—that is to say, skeptical of the rationalistic claim that socialism, by eliminating the economic basis of exploitation, would solve all social questions." Moreover, "expanding opportunities for intellectual employment," the "acceptance of the Welfare State," and the cold war sentiment against Soviet Russia led these intellectuals to question "the populist basis of American radicalism" and to perceive "political conflicts of the fifties, such as McCarthyism" as more "fruitfully explained by sociological concepts such as 'status anxiety' than by the more conventional notions of class or interest group conflicts." These formerly or residually leftist historians produced what later critics would call "neoconservative" or "consensus" or "counterprogressive" historiography. Although they shared a tendency to reject the duality of life the progressive historians favored, particularly the duality of "haves versus have-nots," while emphasizing "unities over conflicts," believing that materially things just were not all that bad in America, and writing history that eschewed any kind of reformist or revolutionary action, the consensus historians were nonetheless a heterogenous group, some of whom at least framed their analyses of consensus in a Marxist cast. Indeed, two of the three most famous and arguably representative consensus historians employ "the idea of consensus as a framework for analysis" in a way not intrinsically conservative at all. Both Richard Hofstadter and Louis Hartz present the idea of an American consensus, a "common climate of American opinion," in order to criticize it. Only the reactionary

Daniel Boorstin celebrated the perceived consensus without much reflection. Only his books, "apologia for his disillusioned conservatism," fit the caricature of consensus history as neoconservative history.[9]

Nonetheless, both Hartz and, especially, Hofstadter have long been considered consensus historians and accordingly labeled political conservatives. Hofstadter is one of the intellectuals listed among those who represent the "changes in intellectual temper" of the fifties, and his 1948 book *The American Political Tradition and the Men Who Made It* is usually considered "one of the originals in the counter-Progressive school, maybe *the* original," a book that "clearly helped establish a new dominant view" of neoconservative history. Hofstadter himself thinks otherwise. He sees in that book a lingering residue of the radicalism that had inspired him to join the Communist Party in March or April 1938 when he was a graduate student at Columbia, quietly easing himself out of the party in February 1939, before breaking off his affiliation entirely after the signing of the Nazi–Soviet nonaggression pact in August 1939. Upon completing *The American Political Tradition*, Hofstadter wrote a letter to Merle Curti, describing the authorial tone of the book as "disgruntled, critical, [and] alienated," and the book itself as "slightly—tho not very much—to the left." Although by 1953 Hofstadter admitted in a letter to Curti that he had "grown a great deal more conservative in the past few years" (adding his hope that his "conservatism is libertarian in its basis"), he was yet unwilling to revise his opinion of his then five-year-old book. In a communication to the *Journal of the History of Ideas* in 1954, he dissented from the opinion of another historian who claimed that *The American Political Tradition* was a distinct contribution to consensus history.[10]

Although Hofstadter was willing to credit consensus history with rediscovering the "complexity" of the American past missing in the previous generation of progressive historians, as he did in a 1956 *Commentary* review, he nonetheless saw consensus history as "transitional" and a "corrective" tendency rather than a viable school. "In one form or other," he asserted, "conflict finally does remain, and ought to remain, somewhere near the center of our focus of attention." Arthur Schlesinger was careful to note the crucial differences between Hofstadter's thinking and that of more conservative historians, arguing that "Hofstadter perceived the consensus from a radical perspective, from the outside, and deplored it; while Boorstin perceived it from the inside and celebrated it." When, in 1969, Schlesinger sent Hofstadter a draft of this essay surveying Hofstadter's work, Hofstadter wrote "Thank you" in the margin opposite this sentence; he was, as his former student Eric Foner notes, never "entirely comfortable with the consensus label." In his 1967 preface to the Hebrew edition of *The American Political Tradition,* Hofstadter declared his "serious misgivings . . . about what is known as consensus history," and in his 1968 *The Progressive Historians* he added that his own "assertion of consensus history in 1948 had its sources in the Marxism of the 1930's." The consensus now is that Hofstadter was not a consensus historian, because he "never devolved into the uncritical celebration of the American experience that characterized much 'consensus' writing," but he rather "introduced the concept of consensus more to condemn than to praise it."[11]

This was certainly the understanding of Hofstadter's students, including Stanley Elkins, who also believed *The American Political Tradition* was not conservative but rather "a radical venture, owing more than a little to Marxist influences." In an ironic parallel between the career of student and supervisor, Elkins's book would also be perceived as the work of a consensus historian. Throughout the sixties, critics of *Slavery* argued that it contained the "inarticulate major premise of the consensus school generally, that power in society properly belongs to the businessmen who already have it," that it was in fact "one of the highpoints of the New Conservative scholarship of the 1950s."[12] Like his supervisor, Elkins did not easily fit into the framework of consensus history. *Slavery* might possess some of the characteristics of consensus histories, having little sympathy for "spontaneity" and "effervescence," but it is certainly not guilty of being bland, ignoring social justice, or not attending to the violence in American life. While it mutes conflict in proposing a counterfactual supposition of how the Civil War could have been avoided had there been stronger institutional support systems, it also demonstrates the fissures in American institutional life. One of the most perspicacious critics of consensus historians, John Higham listed Elkins among those who produced the "best scholarship of the 1950's" because they "struck the tragic note" and demonstrated the instability of the American past, praising him especially for discovering the "disastrous erosion of all institutional authority" in the first half of the nineteenth century. While one may agree with Higham's liberal reading of Elkins's achievement, one can also make the case that Elkins's criticism of the erosion of American institutions is remarkably conservative. Calling Elkins "ideologically conservative," Genovese predicted *Slavery* would win a popular hearing since his "defense of institutionalism and rejection of radical solutions to social problems" would strike a resonant chord with the times. But the times, as the Bob Dylan song goes, they were a'changin'. And Elkins's book may be interesting to future historiographers primarily because it was a product of that change.[13]

The book itself, as it was written in 1959, was divided into four chapters (two more historiographical chapters would be added to the third edition in 1976). From these four chapters there emerged three distinct theses, each of which would be thoroughly discussed in the next decade. The first thesis was that a comparison of Latin American and North American slave systems would demonstrate the especially "closed" nature of the latter; aligned to this thesis was Elkins's belief that legal statutes provided meaningful gauges for determining the nature of a given slave system. The second thesis was that the "closed" slave system produced a personality type of the "Sambo," a slave who was "docile but irresponsible, loyal but lazy, humble but chronically given to lying and stealing" (this is the main and most widely discussed Elkins thesis).[14] The basis of this thesis was Elkins's belief that a historian need not consult certain kinds of testimony and his understanding that there was a paucity of slave rebelliousness in the United States. The third Elkins thesis was that the abolitionists of the American antislavery movement were products of transcendentalism (itself a result of the failure of American institutional life in the 1840s and 1850s) whose enterprise was thwarted by their romantic rebelliousness and their failure to channel their energies through the proper institutions. Each of these three theses would come under close scrutiny in the course of the sixties. Also during these years there emerged a growing concern over Elkins's failure to use slave testimony, a concern in the ascendant between 1968 and 1970. By the end of the sixties the discipline of history had undergone a dramatic intellectual change. In tracing the reception of *Slavery,* not only can we discern the dismantling of a dominant and the formation of an emergent discourse on slavery, but we can see precisely how the social movements of the 1960s directed and mobilized that discursive formation.

Sambo in the Streets: The Movement and the Scholars, 1958–1968

Elkins presented the first fruits of his doctoral dissertation at the Ninth Newberry Library Conference on American Studies on May 3, 1958. After he gave a paper entitled "Slavery and Personality"—essentially the third chapter of his book, then in the process of being published by the University of Chicago Press—eighteen scholars gathered in the Librarian's Office to discuss with Elkins the first public appearance of what would become known as the "Elkins thesis." Even before the book Genovese would call "the most vigorously contested book yet written on the subject" of slavery was even published, its thesis was subject to a critical inquiry. It was the first but certainly not the last time Elkins was forced to defend his views. The book excited so much attention because it was provocative, made seemingly indefensible general statements, employed an unconventional methodology, and seemed relatively unconcerned about the traditional kind of scholarship informing the study of slavery from James Ford Rhodes to Kenneth Stampp. Moreover, because it ranged so broadly over a series of American themes, institutions, and heroes, it was sure to raise the ire of more specialized historians. Elkins's unfavorable comments on the abolitionists came under attack by historians of abolition. Elkins's discussion of Brazilian slavery came under attack from students of Brazilian race relations and Latin American slavery. Finally, and most significantly, Elkins's treatment of the American slave as a "Sambo" figure came under the scrutiny of those who agreed with him but wished to argue that slavery everywhere in the world created a slavish personality, and also those who disagreed with him and thought he had misconstrued the personality of the American slave because he had downplayed the role of resistance in U.S. slave history. It was a book many disagreed with, most thought incomplete, all found suggestive.

It would be truly an understatement to note that Elkins published his book at a crucial juncture in American political and intellectual life. Even in the relatively quiet Librarian's Office in the Newberry Library, it was obvious to these historians that history was being made elsewhere. There was a great deal to be learned from a comment Jules Zanger had made at this conference. Criticizing Elkins for not realizing that "Sambo" was a role and not a personality structure, Zanger noted as one pertinent example of "Sambo-as-role" the "astonishment and even outrage which white families in Montgomery, Alabama, were reported to have felt when they discovered that their servants, so obsequious in the white home, seemingly so content with their servile condition, were walking to work in protest against racial segregation on buses." Since this example provided us with "ample evidence that the white Southerner today is continually fooled" by the "Negro's actual nature and attitudes," might Elkins not imagine that slaves would also have fooled their masters into thinking them "Sambos"? From the vantage point of 1958, Zanger could intimate that what had happened three years earlier in Montgomery, what had happened the year before in Little Rock, what was happening all around the Newberry Library and throughout the United States was evidence of a changing social terrain. Of course, African Americans have always actively resisted slavery and segregation; the attempt to dismantle segregated schools did not begin after *Brown;* the attempt to desegregate public carriers and transportation systems did not begin in Montgomery. What was new, though, was that for the first time this concerted resistance to the status of second-class citizenship was a nationally broadcast phenomenon.[15]

A large part of what happened to *Slavery,* and subsequently to the study of slavery, was that historians, some prompted by the media coverage of the social movements of the sixties and others by their own involvement in those movements, formed what Jonathan Weiner describes as a "new generation of scholars, a new intellectual community" who responded to the "civil rights and antiwar movements" by developing a "critique of, and an alternative to, the ways American history had been constructed." The "civil rights and antiwar movements gave participants an experience of making history from below" and an "appreciation of the popular capability to challenge elite domination." The fact that African Americans and students, not especially empowered social groups, were able to produce a viable political opposition to the state's domestic and foreign policies (and to make some political gains in that opposition) suggested to historians the need to reassess the paradigms by which they had previously understood how history was made. The second wave of New Left history appeared in this ferment, bringing with it to the American historical profession a new paradigm based on the belief that history was made through the "interaction of social groups holding power in different forms." As Jesse Lemisch most famously put it, since the protest movements had shown that history "can happen from the bottom up," it was imperative for historians to apply that lesson to their own subjects and to write "history from the bottom up." In this paradigm, the Montgomery bus boycott was both a source of inspiration for historians and a spur to their thinking about the experience of those groups whose voices had been rendered almost inarticulate in historical scholarship since the brief flurry of work produced by the Old Left in the thirties.[16] A reception history of Elkins's *Slavery* provides us with a barometer of the changing times, shifting attitudes, and the slippage and construction of contested discursive formations about slavery.

As I noted in the last chapter, historians operating within and creating an emergent discursive formation tend to reflect directly on the social conditions within which they are working, implicitly criticizing the silence of the dominant formation on the subject of its political embeddedness while explicitly situating their own work as part of a politically relevant intellectual enterprise. We can see this process at work in the reception of Elkins's book. At first, a very few historians falteringly groped for parallel situations in their own time to help explain the failings of Elkins's theses, as Zanger did in the Newberry Library conference, or as Nathan Glazer did in his *Commentary* review of the book when he reflected on present politics in order to criticize Elkins for failing to see the impossibility of institutional reform in the antebellum South. "If the South today resists with such fanaticism the integration of lunch counters, what is there to make us believe that it could have been moved by a challenge to the institution on which its whole life was based?" For the most part, though, there was silence about the political situation in which the book was initially received in 1960–1961. The historians reviewing the book overwhelmingly criticized it for the author's failure to consult the primary documentary sources, not for his failure to situate his study in terms of the current political climate.[17] Within a few short years, though, as the emergent discourse gained strength and advocates, these historians would develop different strategies for assessing the relationship between the study of the past and the present.

Historians would change their minds about this relationship because the organic intellectuals in the social movements of the sixties made compelling arguments for seeing the past as analogous to and a cause of present politics. In the early civil rights movement, both the African American and European American participants in the sit-ins of 1960, the freedom rides of 1961, the civil rights campaigns in Albany, Birmingham, Saint Augustine, and Selma between 1962 and 1965, and the Mississippi Freedom summer in 1964 felt that their political commitments and historical situation best paralleled those of the American abolition movement. Stanley Aronowitz noted that the motive for the northern version of Freedom summer—the summer of 1964, when the Economic Research and Action Program (ERAP) of the Students for a Democratic Society (SDS) went into, organized, and created freedom schools in Harlem, Newark, Baltimore, and Chicago—was the "unstated concept" that "whites could redeem themselves only by helping blacks to become free." Participants in the Mississippi Freedom summer campaign agreed. One anonymous participant noted that at the same time "you felt . . . you were . . . making . . . history," you also "found yourself." Another participant felt that aside from the "good I think we did, it was my personal salvation as well." Aronowitz correctly notes that this "adoption of the concept of responsibility" and the concomitant concept of personal fulfillment is related to and as old as American abolitionism. Howard Zinn, participant in and historian of the early life of the Student Nonviolent Coordinating Committee (SNCC), called the members of SNCC "the new abolitionists."[18]

Historians who affiliated themselves with the goals of the civil rights movement almost immediately responded to these social movements and their self-characterization. Writing in July 1962, Martin Duberman noted that his "generation's confrontation with segregation" forced many to "feel as strongly about the evil of that practice as the abolitionists did about the institution of slavery." Like the abolitionists, contemporary social activists "have scant faith in Southern voluntarism or the benevolent workings of time; patience and inactivity have not done their work." Duberman, like those participants in ERAP and the Mississippi Freedom summer, hoped that his generation's actions and sense of urgency came "from concern for the Negro rather than from a need to escape from some private torment of our own." Wishing to believe this about their own generation, contemporary historians became more willing to credit what they called "our historical counterparts" with "equally good motives." The process was already at work. Younger historians concerned about black civil rights, people "involved in a similar movement of social change" as the abolitionists, began "to take a new look at the abolitionists" and to develop a more favorable assessment of those antebellum "reformers and resistants." It is no small part of the legacy of the early civil rights movement that it inspired a reconsideration of that previously maligned historical group—American abolitionists.[19]

In the midst of the civil rights movement, historians began writing new, appreciative studies of the abolitionist movement, many of which appeared in 1964 and

1965.[20] These authors reflected on the fact that a major part of what determined a historian's research program was "the spirit of the times in which he lives"—and the time in which these historians were living echoed the times of the abolitionists, "an earlier movement of roughly analogous outlines." In an essay entitled "Abolitionists, Freedom-Riders, and the Tactics of Agitation," Zinn commented directly on how the current civil rights movement paralleled and furthered the political struggles of American abolitionists. The people most appreciative of the American reform tradition were those "marching historians" walking the highways of the nation in support of federal legislation guaranteeing African Americans civil rights. The 1965 march between Selma and Montgomery, for instance, "linked the academic community to the nation, the past to the present, the professors who were writing our history to the men who were making it."[21]

As more and more works began to draw the connections between "New Leftists and Abolitionists," historians began to see how both abolitionists and freedom movement activists were responding to a previous conservative regime (the post-Napoleanic era and the Eisenhower years) and how the "young radicals of the 1830's and 1960's" both shared an anti-institutional radicalism. "Institutions, not the human condition, must explain the origins of evil. 'Immediacy' replaced 'progress' as the catchword for change: immediate withdrawal from Vietnam, immediate emancipation for the slaves. Supreme faith in human possibility took the place of institutional gradualism." Those marching alongside the marching historians appreciated the revisionist histories they were hearing. Albert Turner, an African American who gave up a prosperous situation as a bricklayer to do voter registration work and who later became a leader of the Alabama chapter of the Southern Christian Leadership Conference (SCLC), realized he had been taught the "white man's history" in school. "Reconstruction was presented as a bad thing and the fact that there were Negro voters and Negro officials in the Alabama of the eighteen seventies was not mentioned." Now, with a new history offered to him, Turner saw that there was a great deal to learn about the past in relation to the present. "We know now that you can't change the political system from above. . . . The movement has got to be rooted in the people."[22]

Given Elkins's severe critique of the abolitionists and his profound faith in institutional reform, his book was certain to elicit a grave response from those who now saw fit to admire the abolitionists as prototypes of contemporary social reformers precisely because they were not gradualists hindered by institutional barriers. Indeed, in the first full-length critical study of Elkins's *Slavery*, Earl Thorpe severely criticized not only Elkins but also "gradualists" in general, while celebrating the work of those dissident radicals who attempt to reconstruct society from outside any "institutional framework." Within a few short years, this dramatic change in the social order—first in African American students with the sit-ins, freedom rides, and civil rights campaigns in the rural and urban South, and then in white students with their participation in ERAP projects and Freedom summer, and finally in historians reflecting on the past through a fresh lens of contemporary political activism—would affect the readership and the reception of Elkins's *Slavery*. The first phase of scholarship responding to Elkins's work—the conferees at Newberry and the reviewers—had taken up the issue of his representation of the slave's personality; the next phase dealt with Elkins's assessment of the abolitionists.[23]

The third phase in the reception of *Slavery* similarly reflected the changes in the civil rights movement. Whereas the revision of Elkins's views of the abolitionists had followed the relatively euphoric march of 1965, the revision of Elkins's view of slave resistance followed the long hot summer of 1967. The rebellion in Watts in 1965 and the call for Black Power during the March Against Fear in Mississippi in 1966 rent the already riddled fabric of the early civil rights interracial coalition. Both those events attested to the failure of years of struggling to overcome the fundamental inequities in political and economic power between blacks and whites in America. The Watts rebellion, as Black Power intellectuals pointed out, was a result of a legacy of frustration at failed reforms, at continued police and racist mob violence against civil rights workers and innocent bystanders, and it was, most of all, a result of the lack of social justice in the divided society the Kerner Commission would describe three years later. As the Watts rebellion in the summer of 1965 signaled the end of one era, Stokely Carmichael's call for "Black Power" in the summer of 1966 signaled the beginning of another. Gayle Pemberton recalls feeling "emotionally and psychologically drained" at hearing news of the rebellion in Watts; Henry Louis Gates recalls responding to Carmichael's evocative phrase by feeling "proud of being black" and excited in sensing the possibility for "a new communal identity."[24] Watts and Black Power form the crucial background to the long, hot summer of 1967, but their own background resides in the summers of 1964 and 1965.

At precisely the time when academics were responding to the early civil rights movement by producing newly sympathetic histories of American abolitionists, white northern volunteers arrived in Mississippi and demonstrated to the African American social activists just what was problematic about certain kinds of abolitionists. Many of these white students, "not so much color-blind as supremely desirous of *appearing* color-blind," were utterly insensitive to the traditions and cultural practices of the African American people of Mississippi. They also seemed to have brought with them the abolitionist belief in their presumed responsibility for the souls of those whom they would save. One black Freedom summer worker noted that while many of the whites were sensitive and not paternalistic, there were some "who just came in and wanted to take over. Their attitude was 'okay, we are here, your troubles are over. We are going to put your house in order.'" This paternalism was a result of the educational and social systems through which the majority of the volunteers had passed, and of the media that reproduced the ideology of those beliefs and that education. Some of the volunteers acted as if they "had come to believe the view put forth by the national media; that it was they who had come to save the Mississippi Negro." The government and the media also brought home to the African American freedom workers the fact that their lives were not nearly as important as those of the white children of privilege. The massive government-sponsored search for James Chaney, Andrew Goodman, and Michael Schwerner, two white men and one black man who disappeared early in the summer, was unprecedented, even though eight black civil rights workers had already been murdered in Mississippi earlier that year. Black freedom workers felt dismayed at the fact that although there had been "sixty-three people killed around the question of the vote before '64," all of whom were black, "national concern" was "aroused only after two white boys are missing." John Lewis, president of SNCC during Freedom summer, felt this was

shameful; Dave Dennis, CORE field director for Mississippi and one of the organizers of Freedom summer, became depressed and "really got tired, mentally tired of
the whole scene."[25]

That weariness became pervasive at the end of the summer when Lyndon Johnson thwarted the attempts of the Mississippi Democratic Freedom Party (MFDP) to
seat themselves as delegates at the Democratic Convention in Atlantic City.[26] To that
mental weariness was added renewed frustration when the summer of 1965 saw the
same governmental attention to the death of a white man and the same indifference
to the death of a black one. President Johnson twice mentioned the martyrdom of
the white Reverend James Reeb—at a press conference and in the famous "We Shall
Overcome" speech introducing to Congress legislation that would become the 1965
Voting Rights Act—but failed to mention the martyrdom of Jimmy Lee Jackson, the
black man whose death by a trooper's bullet (as Jackson was shielding his mother
from the trooper's blows) was, after all, the very reason for the commemorative
march from Selma to Montgomery in the first place. Both Martin Luther King and
Stokely Carmichael thought that "the failure to mention Jimmy Jackson only reinforced the impression that to white America the life of a Negro is insignificant and
meaningless."[27]

It was a series of such frustrating discoveries about the value of African Americans' lives and votes—or, rather, of blatant and repeated confirmations of these
long-suspected truths—that led to the long, hot summers from 1964 to 1967. By
December 1967, there had been four summers of urban unrest across the nation; indeed the summer of 1967 had been so violent that on July 28, 1967, following the
Detroit uprising, Lyndon Johnson appointed the National Advisory Commission on
Civil Disorders. According to the Kerner Report, there were at least ten "disorders"
in the summer of 1967. By others' estimates, and according to different definitions
of "disorder," there were at least 160 riots in the first nine months of 1967. Moreover, whereas the Johnson administration responded to the early urban uprisings
with liberal sympathy in trying to understand the sources of inner-city frustrations,
the administration responded to the 1967 riots with the more conservative attitude
of not "rewarding violence."[28] This was the beginning of the antiblack backlash, the
critical reappraissal of the Great Society programs, and the emergence of calls for
"law and order." In this heated moment in the sixties, Black Power was almost as
popular as it was misunderstood, the civil rights coalition dissolved, and militant
nonviolence almost wholly lost its appeal.

Whereas in the early sixties the comparison of the civil rights workers to abolitionists had provided a celebratory source of historical continuity to those white
people engaged in radical action on behalf of the black struggle for freedom, by the
mid-sixties they discovered, as had the abolitionists more than a hundred years earlier, that the people they were attempting to free had their own impulses and wished
to pursue their own political visions. Just as the white antebellum abolitionists
found out that the slaves were not always willing to have the form and essence of
their life stories dictated according to abolitionist patterns, nor were they content to
work within the same political programs espoused by the white abolitionist organizations, so did their modern counterparts in the mid-sixties discover that the black
freedom fighters also had their own sense of where the movement should go and
what goals and aspirations they should strive to achieve.

Although the fissures had been showing since 1963, it was clear to most of the members of SNCC by December 1966 that the "civil rights movement is not and never was our movement." These were the words of John Churchville, a staff member of the Atlanta Project. Churchville also compared the freedom movement to the abolitionist movement, although he had a distinctly different interpretation of the similarities. "This means that the civil rights struggle since slavery" has been "one of advancing our position as slaves, but not abolishing slavery." The only events that actually assaulted the system, he noted, were "the *revolts* during slavery and the *riots* now." He concluded his meditation by completing his comparison of contemporary urban uprisings with plantation revolts: "What would have happened if the field nigger had revolted and confiscated the master's land? What will happen when we . . . begin to assert ourselves as non-niggers and non-slaves?" What did happen, of course, is that the government spent a great deal more money fighting "crime" than it did fighting poverty (although, of course, it spent the most money fighting the Viet Cong). What also happened was that historians looked anew at their original assessment of the civil rights movement as a modern counterpart to nineteenth-century abolitionism. Historians who intially made the connection between the civil rights workers and abolitionists in the early sixties now began comparing Black Power advocates to abolitionists *and anarchists.* Historians also turned their attention to slave insurrections in order to see the connection between those slaves "engaged in counter-aggression in pre-Civil War days" and the black youth "exploding in ghettos one hundred years later."[29]

Prompted by the activists' sensitivity to slave resistance as analogous to contemporary urban rebellion, historians in 1967 and 1968 began to reassess two issues raised by Elkins. First, they took up the issue of resistance to slavery, a point Elkins had superficially explored and a phenomenon he denied in order to produce his thesis that the slaves who did not rebel against their enslavement had been infantilized by the forces of the slave regime. Second, they took a closer look at and challenged Elkins's thesis about that allegedly infantilized slave personality, producing their own readings of slave psychology based on more intimate knowledge of slave testimony and slave culture.

George Fredrickson and Christopher Lasch disagreed with Elkins's thesis that slaves had developed a "state of internalized dependency," suggesting that his argument did not "fit the facts of widespread intransigence, insubordination, and mischief-making." In many ways, Frederickson and Lasch were talking about contemporary resistance in the urban ghetto as much as they were talking about slave resistance on the rural plantation. As they put it, "[r]esistance to slavery cannot be established . . . without making an implicit analogy between Negro slavery and the struggles of free men, in our own time, 'to give dignity to human life' by resisting oppression." Indeed, the fourth section of their essay in which they list four types of resistance that are accommodationist rather than revolutionary seems prophetically to anticipate the Kerner Report's listing of the three types of "disorders" in the urban North of 1967. And when two years later, Lasch commented on the fact that "many of the intellectuals who talk of Black Power do not understand the difference between riots and revolution," it was hard not to hear the echoes of his and Frederickson's comments about slave resistance as a "pattern of intransigence which is hedonistic rather than political, accommodationist rather than revolutionary." They conclude their essay with a telling comment about the abolitionists' limitations. They admit that the "abolitionist lens distorted the 'horrible character' of slavery," only to add that the "picture of a docile and apparently contented bondsman was no more faithful to the reality it purported to depict." But this, they conclude, should not surprise us. "It is not often that men understand, or even truly see, those whom in charity they would uplift." With the call for Black Power interpreted as a call for black separatism, and SNCC's decision to act as an all-black organization crystalizing that interpretation, it was not difficult to see that the rupture between Garrison and Douglass was as poignant as it was resonant for the New Left.[30]

At the same time as some historians were arguing that slaves were not infantilized because they resisted their enslavement in acts of violence, others were arguing that slaves were not infantilized because they resisted their enslavement in acts of cultural production. In an article on "Slavery and Personality," Mary Agnes Lewis maintained that so long as there existed a "viable, self-perpetuating slave culture" competing with the "slaveowner's authority and significance," there was no possibility that the plantation represented a "closed system," since the slave community provided the slave with an opportunity to play roles other than the one demanded by the master. Lewis was one of the first scholars to assert the existence of a "slave culture" and one of the first consistently to cite the slaves' own documents as a way of showing the strength of their personality. In another path-breaking piece of scholarship, Sterling Stuckey also argued that slaves were not "reduced to the level of Sambos" because they "were able to fashion a lifestyle and set of values—an ethos—which prevented them from being imprisoned altogether by the definitions which the larger society sought to impose." In arguing for the fluid nature of the connection between this generation and past generations, Stuckey turned to slave folklore to show that what the slaves learned about "handling misfortune was not only a major fact in their survival as a people," but substantially important for "future generations of Afro-Americans in coping with a hostile world." While noting that some of the very "songs being sung in antebellum days are the ones Afro-Americans are singing in the freedom movement today," he also notes that the "singing movement" of Albany, Georgia, was giving way to the Black Power movement of Mississippi. That, too, he hints suggestively, can be found in slave folklore, such as a slave song he calls "the antebellum equivalent of today's 'burn, baby, burn.'"[31]

We can see, then, how the emergent discursive formation on slavery took shape as historians once again took up the initial insights of social activists and began to explore the connections between contemporary urban violence and antebellum slave revolts, between Black Power in 1965 and acts of black empowerment before 1865. Those who responded to Elkins focused on the effect of slave resistance on the personalities of slaves, as did those who focused on the slaves' cultural productions. In other words, while those who focused on the violence of the Watts rebellion sought out evidence of slave violence in the past, those who focused on the Black Power call for a new communal identity and a renewed sense of black pride sought out instances of and resources for slave personality in the past.

By the end of 1967, then, those historians who were writing in the wake of the New Left's call for a new social history were making three specific recommendations for the study of slavery. First, they emphasized the existence and then the strength of what they increasingly called "slave culture" and "slave communities." Second, they called on historians to reexamine the extent and significance of slave resistance. Finally, they heeded the call of New Left historiography and proposed to write the history of slavery "from the bottom up" by allowing the slave subjects to speak for themselves in their own testimony, folklore, and autobiographies. Each of these recommendations would become axiomatic features of slave history by 1970.

Precisely a decade after Jules Zanger had pointed to the events of Montgomery to show Elkins that whites did not always understand black people, to suggest to him that he might learn from the present how to understand the past, the full effect of the social movements of the sixties on historical scholarship was made patently clear. The discussion of a decade before was substantially different, the source of historical insights no longer solely the archives, and the terms of the debate no longer concerned only with the best way of perceiving the past. By the end of 1968, then, Elkins had been criticized for each of the arguments he had made, although it is also important to note that the criticism on the whole was far from coherent. His comparison of slave systems in North and Latin America was criticized for its reliance on legal statutes to explain social behavior, its failure to negotiate the effects of capitalist development on distinct slave systems, and its dependence on a false vision of current Brazilian race relations. His criticism of the abolitionists was dismissed with the claim that he had defined only one unrepresentative branch of abolitionists and underestimated the existence and vigor of the institutions within which the abolitionists labored. Because his own political ideology was reformist and not revolutionary, radical historians claimed he failed to see the radical impetus driving the abolitionists to forgo institutional reform. Finally, his critics dismantled his analysis of the slave personality, arguing that he had mistaken a posture made necessary by the delusions of white slavemasters for the reality of slave behavior and self-conception, while not sufficiently accounting for the countervailing resistance slaves exhibited and the sustenance provided the slaves in their communal life and cultural productions.

Most important, toward the end of the decade, critic after critic, more and more emphatically, made the case that Elkins's failure to employ the testimony of those whose personalities he was purporting to delineate was not simply a failure of neglect leading to some awkward generalizations but rather the substantial explanation for the one-sided portrait he drew. Exactly a decade after Elkins had been criticized by the participants at the Newberry Library conference for failing to consult the "records," he was criticized anew for failing to consult the "records." What had happened, of course, is that the "records" were no longer the same, and the "new" records became popularly available as publishing houses quickly produced editions of them. Arno Press published William Loren Katz's *Five Slave Narratives* (1968); Beacon Press issued Arna Bontemps's *Great Slave Narratives* (1969); the United Church Press released *God Struck Me Dead: Religious Conversion Experiences and Autobiographies of Ex-Slaves* (1969); Indiana University Press issued an American paperback edition of Charles Nichols's *Many Thousand Gone: The Ex-Slave's Account of Their Bondage and Freedom* (1969); Harper and Row published Gilbert Osofsky's edition of the slave narratives of Henry Bibb, William Wells Brown, and Solomon Northup under the title *Puttin' On Ole Massa* (1969); and Holt, Rinehart and Winston followed suit with the release of Norman Yetman's *Voices from Slavery* (1970).

Two years later, under the general editorship of George Rawick, Greenwood Press published the first nineteen volumes of the Works Project Administration interviews with former slaves, collectively entitled *The American Slave: A Composite Autobiography* (1972). Finally, the simultaneous 1972 publication of the first two books systematically employing slave testimony to produce a historical portrait of the peculiar institution—John Blassingame's *The Slave Community* and George Rawick's *From Sundown to Sunup*—signaled the first practical results of the restoration of slave testimony as historical evidence.[32]

After a decade of the Movement and a decade in the life of Elkins's *Slavery*, the critical discussion was indeed on substantially new ground, the historical insights emerging from radically different perspectives, and the research agendas directed toward a relatively unexploited but now popularly available set of primary materials. By 1970, it was clear that the debate had assumed entirely different proportions and set up quite different positions from which to argue. Witness the debate between Howard Zinn and Herbert Aptheker. While Zinn believed that the historian needs to use the narratives of fugitive slaves as a way of dispensing with "that elusive 'objectivity'" of conservative historical analyses and instead attempting to "report accurately all of the subjectivities in a situation," Aptheker argued that if "one wants to know what the institution of slavery was," one must "go to the slave, to those who endured it," because only there can one find "the *objective* picture of that institution." This was a far cry from the belief of Ulrich B. Phillips in 1929 that slave narratives "were issued with so much abolitionist editing that as a class their authenticity is doubtful."[33] The reputation of the abolitionists had been redeemed by 1964, the slave narratives they edited by 1970.

This change in the historical sensibility is directly related to the debate between those historians who attempted to defend a decaying discursive formation on slavery (based on ideas of docile slaves, documented by reference to planters' records and outdated sociological stereotypes) and the social activists, organic intellectuals, and progressive academics who helped establish an emergent discourse (based on ideas of rebellious slaves, documented by reference to slave testimony and newly recognized African American cultural traditions, and resolutely aware of the political situation in which it was formed and circulated).

Two other important things happened between 1967 and 1970 to affect the course of historical writing on slavery. First, following the publication of the paperback version of *Slavery* in 1963, there developed a widespread misreading of Elkins's main thesis. This misreading found its way into popular psychology texts, social commentary, government policy, and finally back into academic discourse by 1968. Second, William Styron published a novel in 1967 that posed as a piece of slave testimony, reflected a critical misreading of the slave community, and attempted to employ the Elkins thesis as an explanation for the most famous slave rebellion in the history of the United States. In the debate over Styron's novel in 1968 and 1969, historians and critics would add to the emergent discourse on slavery, which by 1970 would assume a regnant place in academic discourse.

The popular and widely circulating misreading of the Elkins thesis is important because it shows us some of the problematic tendencies in an emergent discursive formation, as well as demonstrating the process of circulation through which an emergent discourse becomes mobilized. After organic intellectuals pose a more fluid notion of the relationship between the the past and present politics—a crucial stage in the formation of an emergent discourse—some historians and sociologists who follow suit sometimes develop facile explanations for current social conditions by assuming an untroubled continuity from the past to the present, as if structurally changing institutions did not alter the means through which past conditions affect contemporary situations. In the case of the emergent discourse on slavery, historians, sociologists, psychologists, public commentators, and government functionaries misunderstood what Elkins was saying about institutional effects on personality development and assumed a seamless continuity from the institution of slavery to those institutions providing contemporary patterns of socialization and individuation for late twentieth-century African Americans.

Although Elkins thought he had made it clear that his argument about the slaves' infantilization was exclusively about people who were enslaved—that is, individuals were subject to infantilization only by the force of the "closed" institution of plantation slavery and only for the duration of the time they were in that "closed" institution—readers between 1963 and 1965 picked up another interpretation: that African Americans had become infantilized during slavery, and, to a lesser extent, remained so even in the "open" institutions of contemporary society. The widespread circulation of this misreading emerged with particular force in 1964 and 1965, following the remarkable popularity of *Slavery* after 1963. From 1959 to 1963, *Slavery* had sold at a rate of about 450 copies a year. When the paperback edition was released in the spring of 1963, the book averaged 25,000 copies a year for the next few years.[34] As I suggested above, scholars were returning to the issue of slave personality in 1967 partly because of the connections they were drawing between slave resistance and the conflagrations in the inner cities, but partly also because the Elkins thesis was circulating widely outside the academy.

A series of books published in 1964 and 1965 extended Elkins's analysis of slave personality to an analysis of the personalities of contemporary African Americans. Thomas Pettigrew devoted the first section of his *A Profile of the Negro American* to a discussion of "Negro American Personality," in which he used the Elkins thesis not only to explain the basic facts of the personality of one held in bondage, but also to suggest that "[s]trong traces of these effects of slavery . . . have persisted since Emancipation because of bitter poverty and the uprooted life of migrants far from home." Charles Silberman used Elkins's *Slavery* to argue that the "'Sambo' of Southern folklore . . . was a reality and to a considerable extent still is." A "hundred years after its abolition, Negroes are still bound by [slavery's] effects on their minds and spirits." In *The Southern Mystique,* Zinn likewise incorporated the Elkins thesis into his study, suggesting that the "Sambo" personality did not end with Emancipation but would be reversed by this final onslaught of militant activists in the South. Robert Penn Warren agreed, arguing that only in 1965 can one say: "Sambo's day is over." Even Ralph Ellison, who took exception to the Elkins thesis, calling it something "that passes for intellectual discussion," would make the assumption in 1965 that "the Stanley M. Elkins 'Sambo' argument" is an attempt to prove that "slaves had very little humanity because slavery destroyed it for them *and their descendents*" (my italics).[35] Also written in 1965 was the most famous text to employ the Elkins thesis, Daniel Patrick Moynihan's *The Negro Family: The Case for National Action*. In his chapter on the "roots of the problem," Moynihan agreed with Elkins that slavery in the United States was "the most awful the world has ever known," and, more important, it was also the most deleterious "in its lasting effects on individuals and their children." Like the other intellectuals employing the Elkins thesis in their work in 1964 and 1965, Moynihan also believed that Elkins had been arguing that African Americans carried with them the apparently inherited personality structure of slaves.[36]

By 1965, the Elkins thesis had been questionably interpreted and made a part of public and political discourse; by 1968, the misreading returned to and became part of academic discourse. Sociologist Roy Simón Bryce-Laporte and historian George Rawick both argued that Elkins was constructing the "Sambo" personality to fit "the slave and his descendents." Not pretending to explore the past as if it were an isolated set of events having no relation to the present, not reading books putatively about the past as if that is all they refer to, these scholars charged that "Elkins and his academic kin" have not only written a history of slavery but simultaneously produced a "sophisticated conservative defense of existing social relations."[37] In the academy, the study of the past was informing the present in much the same way that the politics of the present had inspired a revision of the past. This is a key gesture and a crucial moment in the emergent discourse on slavery in the shifting climate of the late sixties. It is precisely this circular interchange between past and present— between slavery and the Movement—that created the conditions for Styron to represent slavery as he did and for that representation to have the effect it had. Before turning to the debate over Styron's novel, the subject of the next chapter, we need to explore how the emergent discourse on slavery that was formed in the productive interaction between social movement and academic discussion was mobilized in new directions through the political rhetoric of Black Power.

Sambo No More: Black Power and the Topics of the Emergent Discourse

As we have seen, Elkins's critics persistently raised the topics of violence, identity, and property. This was so partly because Elkins generally dealt with these topics in his own way. He wrote about the violence of the slave system while denying the extent of the violence against the system; he developed a paradigm for analyzing the slave's personal identity, producing a troubling argument that the slaves essentially had no personality; and he wrote favorably with a Jamesian lyricism about the kinds of institutions that protected and were premised on property rights. Partly, though, the critics' pointed response and focus on these topics had less to do with Elkins than with the ways these topics were becoming more important in the social and intellectual climate of the sixties. The violent revolts in the ghettos during the long, hot summers helped historians clarify for themselves the potential of violence as a strategy for the oppressed and led them to explore slave revolts as incidents of violent resistance. The Black Power movement with its call for a new black or African American identity with a strong and consistent history not only challenged those simplistic sociological caricatures of black people as "victims" lacking personal and collective agency, but also created the conditions for and impelled historians to examine earlier moments of militant identity among antebellum African Americans. The civil right movement's lack of success in creating a revolutionary change in the relationship between property and civil rights also forced historians to see how the American past was fundamentally premised on a series of compromises in which those in power always acceded to the desires of the propertied class while ignoring pleas for substantial civil rights for the oppressed. Earl Thorpe, for instance, criticized Elkins as a "a staunch elitist and conservative" because Elkins believed in gradualism and institutional reform. Thorpe and the New Left generally favored people like "Socrates, Jesus Christ, and similar non-propertied idealists and reformers who worked largely outside of institutional frameworks."[38]

The three topics informed the study of slavery and thereby became major intellectual coordinates in the emergent discursive formation because they arose from the interaction of the academy and the streets, from the historians studying the past and the organic intellectuals of the social movements making the present. These topics assumed an even more prominent place in the emergent discourse because they also organized the production and reception of the intellectual and rhetorical strategies of the Black Power movement. Arguably the major impetus for the reassessment of the historiography of slavery in the late sixties, the Black Power movement and its organic intellectuals made the most significant contributions to the discursive formation by raising and negotiating these topics as socially and culturally relevant. Between 1966 and 1968, the Black Power movement was in a state of flux as its advocates and its critics attempted to define its position on precisely these three topics.

Almost as soon as Stokely Carmichael and Willie Ricks made a call for "Black Power" in Greenwood, Mississippi, on June 16, 1966, the media sensationalized the situation through what Vincent Harding calls "their vast image-creating (and image-destroying) techniques." *Time* magazine called Black Power a "racist philosophy" because it seemed to be "a philosophy of black separatism," while the *Saturday Evening Post* offered a barely veiled threat of white backlash. After initially deciding that it was a call to separatism, the press almost immediately decided that the phrase was also a call to violence. The press compounded whatever confusion the phrase inherently possessed by "harping on every connotation of violence and racism" while "minimizing the central call for ethnic unity." "When the cry of 'black power' burst upon the American landscape," wrote one journalist, "some observers ran for the hills or their shotguns, fearing it signaled the beginning of a racial war." The media strategy of representing Black Power as a violent, separatist philosophy had enormous ramifications. In a survey of Detroit residents in 1967, University of Michigan researchers discovered that almost 40 percent of the whites interviewed believed "Black Power" meant "black rule over whites." After the initial media frenzy tapered off, other publications such as the *Christian Science Monitor,* the *Boston Herald,* and *Newsweek* criticized the "many U.S. newspapers" that had hastily demonized and failed to examine more closely and thoroughly a "slogan that was ambiguous and undefined."[39]

The newspapers were not the only ones to leap to a conclusion about the meaning of Black Power. While the Congress of Racial Equality (CORE) endorsed Black Power at its national convention in Baltimore on July 1–4, 1966, the NAACP rejected it at its convention in Los Angeles on July 5–9, 1966. The president of the NAACP, Roy Wilkins, proclaimed in his address on July 5 that "[n]o matter how endlessly they try to explain it, the term 'black power' means antiwhite power." Black Power, he said, signifies "a reverse Mississippi, a reverse Hitler, a reverse Ku Klux Klan." Apparently much had happened in the two weeks since Carmichael and Ricks issued their call for Black Power to make it comparable to the Holocaust and a century of racial lynching. On the same day, and in a more temperate mood, President Johnson declared: "[w]e are not interested in black power, and we are not interested in white power, but we are interested in American democratic power, with a small 'd.'" In a speech to the NAACP convention the following day, Vice-President Hubert Humphrey called Black Power a form of "racism." At the same time, the executive director of the Urban League, Whitney Young, threatened to cut off ties with any group that "formally adopted black power."[40]

By this time, even the press took exception to the ways that government and organization leaders had so thoroughly condemned a concept and program yet to be defined. Two days after Humphrey's speech, an editorial in the *Christian Science Monitor* declared, with some measure of understatement, that "there tends to be a panicky overreaction to the slogan 'black power.'" The overhasty response of these leaders helped create a mood that made it virtually impossible for the public to appreciate the positive meanings in the concept of Black Power. Nonetheless, the major responsiblity for the public's perception of Black Power as a form of violent reverse racism lay with the media. Even Martin Luther King, who made the effort to discern the positive elements of Black Power, found fault with the term because it lent itself to media manipulation; he noted in particular the "implications of violence that the press had already attached to the phrase."[41] While correct in seeing in Black Power the end of nonviolence, the press was nevertheless wrong to assume that those groups no longer advocating nonviolence necessarily believed in violence. The opposite of nonviolence for virtually all the Black Power advocates was self-defense; even in the most extreme cases, the call for Black Power meant revolutionary violence, not racial violence as the press maintained.[42]

A few thoughtful commentators also pointed out that even if Black Power were a call to violence, that turn in the freedom movement would be only an inevitable response to the earlier violence of the white backlash in the South and the imperialist violence of the government's foreign policy. Given the nature of America's domestic and international aggression, some maintained that SNCC and CORE, the two foremost parties to claim Black Power, had "appropriately found their place in the midstream of a violence-prone culture." By the mid- to late-sixties, both historians and psychologists were researching the violent nature of American society and analyzing its effect on the formation of the New Left. Kenneth Keniston argued that violence formed the most important element of the socialization of the generation born after World War II, belated witnesses to Auschwitz, Hiroshima, and Nuremberg, cities whose names signified forms of horrific violence. This was the first generation to be exposed to the "violence of television, both as it reports the bloodshed and turmoil of the American and non-American world, and as it skillfully elaborates and externalizes in repetitive dramas the potential for violence within each of us." Exposed to the "*historical* violence of war, cataclysm, and holocaust," desensitized to representations of violence on television, this generation developed an abhorrent fascination with the *"psychological* violence of sadism, exploitation, and aggression." The political events of the sixties—assassinations, urban uprisings, continued labor–capital clashes, and the war in Vietnam—only reinforced the impression that America "despite its claims to peaceableness and justice, is in fact one of the most violent societies in the history of the world." Examining the civil rights and the anti-war movements, Keniston noted the paradox of having a "non-violent revolution" in a "violent world," pointing out the irony of activists who attempt to maintain their posture of nonaggression when each peaceful action elicits violent response from the racist and conservative forces of the society. "If we are to choose one issue as central to our time, one danger as most frightening, one possibility as most to be avoided and yet most fascinating, one psychological issue that both rationally and irra-tionally preoccupies us," he wrote in 1967, "it is the issue of violence," which, he concluded, "is to this generation what the issue of sex was to the Victorian world."[43]

In their preface to the anthology *American Violence,* the editors note that in a "time of unprecedented concern over American violence the value of a documentary reader on the history of our domestic violence needs little explanation." The public concern over escalating incidents of violence and the even greater rhetoric of vio-lence was not without its substantive reasons. For the members of SNCC, six years of nonviolent activity had exacted a heavy physical and psychological toll while pro-ducing minimal political gains. In the face of continued assault, SNCC was no longer willing to show the preternatural patience of Dr. King. The new SNCC presi-dent, H. Rap Brown, announced his belief that African American people had the right to defend themselves, adding, nonetheless, that he thought "the use of arms" unnecessary for black people to seize political power. In response to continued po-lice violence against student demonstrations, though, Brown began to use more heated rhetoric. At Cambridge, Maryland, Brown gave a speech the police felt was responsible for inciting the riot that followed a few hours later. In that speech, Brown apparently urged his listeners to take up arms against white society. "We are going to burn it down if we don't get our share of it," he announced.[44] Calls to vio-lence had become part of the rhetoric of SNCC workers, urban violence part of their strategy.

Nor was this turn to violent rebellion a phenomenon only in Black Power groups in the late sixties. For the white New Left, violence had also become a press-ing concern. Within SDS, violence was "endlessly talked about, feared, skirted, flirted with," constituting the organization's very "fantasy life." The events of the six-ties left the members of SDS convinced that violence was the "harsh currency of the twentieth century." It was becoming apparent to the New Left that what was hap-pening in the society was not an aberration but a logic of its history. The most vio-lent and ultimately self-destructive faction of the New Left, the Weathermen, had correctly read the climate of America. So, too, had SNCC. Violence, Brown pro-claimed, is "as American as apple pie," and Black Power was the inevitable culmina-tion of the "inescapable heritage of violence" to which African Americans were his-torically subject in the United States. Two sociologists looking at the urban rebellions as contemporary forms of slave uprisings argued that "[v]iolence is part of the American culture, it is not a subculture." Both those ghetto residents who rioted in 1965 and 1966 and those slaves who rose against their masters in the nineteenth century "believed in the American way." In "their use of violence," both slaves and ghetto dwellers "are and have been thoroughly American."[45]

Violence might have been thoroughly American for the New Left, but the theory of violence that the Black Power advocates found most appealing came from abroad. "Their Bible," wrote both Reverend King and Minister Eldridge Cleaver, "is Frantz Fanon's *The Wretched of the Earth,*" which sold 750,000 copies between 1965 and 1970. It would be difficult to overemphasize the American popularity of Fanon's idea of the cleansing effects of revolutionary violence. *Liberator* editor Dan Watts told reporters that they should read *Wretched of the Earth* if they wished to understand black youth in the ghettos, since "[e]very brother on a rooftop can quote Fanon." The members of the Atlanta Project, the black separatist wing of SNCC, were heavily influenced by Fanon's book. Their position paper written in the spring of 1966 drew heavily on Fanon, especially when they compared the situation of African Americans with the position of the colonized people in the Third World. In coordinating a staff educational program to train organizers in 1967, SNCC arranged for regular rap sessions about Camus and Fanon. So much had these thinkers become part of the assumed knowledge of the Black Power intelligentsia that Jack Minnis suggested that "people who do not read Camus and Fanon learn about them through conversation with those who have read." Fanon was held in equally high esteem in the Black Panther Party. Bobby Seale had read *Wretched of the Earth* six times before he introduced Fanon to Huey Newton. Once Newton read the book, he began to speak of black people as a colony in imperialist America whose only option out of their plight was revolutionary violence. "Only with the power of the gun can the Black masses halt the terror and brutality perpetuated against them by the armed racist power structure."[46]

In Fanon, the Black Power advocates found not simply a philosophy of the revolutionary uses of violence, nor only a theory of violence as what Fanon calls a "cleansing force" freeing the native from an "inferiority complex," replacing the native's "despair and inaction" with fearlessness and self-respect. Rather, what they also found in Fanon was a means of explaining the process by which a hegemony is established. Fanon insistently argued that the colonial world is ordered around persistent and structural violence, and that the identity of the native and the property structure of the colonizing force are both integrated products of a systemic violence. Violence orders "the colonial world, which has ceaselessly drummed the rhythm for the destruction of native social forms and broken up without reserve the systems of reference of the economy, the customs of dress and external life" of the native peoples. It was Fanon's genius to have defined the "violence with which the supremacy of white values is affirmed and the aggressiveness which has permeated the victory of these values over the ways of life and of thought of the native."[47] What Fanon showed, then, was that hegemonic cultural values, economic systems, and sources for personal identity were all founded on and instated by institutional violence.

It was just this diagnosis of the American social order that the Black Power advocates were making in the late sixties. In some cases, they noted the regularity and purpose of police brutality in the colonization of African Americans in the inner city. As Cleaver wrote in *The Black Panther* newspaper, "We do not claim the right to in-

discriminate violence. We seek no bloodbath. We are not out to kill up white people. On the contrary, it is the cops who claim the right to indiscriminate violence
and practice it everyday." Moreover, the police were not brutal by personal inclination or professional deformation; they were acting out of a set of social interests and
pursuing a coherent strategy. The case of Greensboro, North Carolina, provides a
paradigmatic example of the logic of police action against African Americans. In response to an emergent nonviolent Black Power movement in Greensboro, George
Dorsett, leader of the local Klan, called for a public effort to end the perceived violence of Black Power. "We don't believe in violence," he told a rally in Raleigh, "and
we won't have it if we have to kill every nigger in America." He incited acts of violence in Greensboro around a crisis in the housing issue. It was later discovered that
Dorsett was a paid FBI informer, whose work was to create a simulacrum of crisis in
order to produce a backlash by the white public and the police. In Greensboro, as
almost everywhere else in the nation, "government counterintelligence operations
seemed most effective in creating a specter of violence which then could be used to
justify massive counterviolence by other government agencies." This was part of the
colonial system of repressive violence Fanon helped Black Power advocates to discover. As Byron Rushing noted, he soon learned to perceive the police as "the occu-
pation troops in the black colony, free to beat, insult, shoot black natives with the
total, defensive, calculated, paranoiac support of the white administrators." If you
wish to know what the "mayor, governor, president, [and] bishop think of black
people," Rushing wrote, "[l]ook in the face of some dumb cop."[48]

In other cases, though, Black Power advocates acted on Fanon's more impres-
sive insight and worked to diagnose the more subtle institutional violence of the society that necessitated the counterviolence of radicals who would reconstruct the social order along more humane and less exploitative lines. Carmichael wrote that
although Black Power insists on the right to self-defense and would not rule out any
possible strategy for transforming the society, it does not advocate violence. The violence, he noted, exists in white American institutions. The cultural apparatus of the
society forms a "dictatorship of definition, interpretation, and consciousness" serving to denigrate African American history and identity. Carmichael spoke of the
need for Black Power advocates to "reclaim our history and our identity from the
cultural terrorism and depredation of self-justifying white guilt." As a critical ad-
mirer of Black Power, Harold Cruse also discerned what he called the "malfunction-
ing social organism" of American institutional life. Against its violent incursions into
African American life, he too advocated revolutionary resistance. He believed that
"violence enters the picture only to the degree that American (white) institutions resist the pressures towards social change exerted by the Afro-American social dynamic." Another sympathetic critic of Black Power, Dr. King, noted that the best reason to avoid violent retaliation against the American social order is precisely that the
order was founded on and maintained by violence, which King called the "inseparable twin of materialism."[49]

The National Committee of Negro Churchmen issued a statement in the *New
York Times* supporting Black Power for precisely the same reason. "We deplore the
overt violence of riots," they announced, "but we believe that it is more important to
focus on the real sources of the eruptions," namely, the "silent and covert violence

which white middle-class America inflicts upon the victims of the inner city." Interested in exposing the "organized violence" beneath a "false democracy," Tom Hayden denounced the "official violence" of the state while celebrating the Newark "ghetto response" to it. Making the distinction between "violence directed at you to keep you in your place and violence to defend yourself against that suppression," Black Panthers also claimed to be "opposed to violence—the violence of hungry children, illiterate adults, diseased old people, and the violence of poverty and profit."[50] From Fanon, then, Black Power advocates had gained not a means of justifying random acts of retaliatory violence but a theory through which to explain the systemic violence of American institutional life.

They also acquired a strategic vantage point from which they could see how African American subjectivity had been sacrificed at the altar of capitalist production, allowing them, then, to discern the interrelatedness of violence, identity, and property. In their discussions about identity, Black Power intellectuals counseled the need for a new and empowering "black consciousness" to offset the denigrated subjectivity instated by institutional violence. Carmichael and Hamilton, for example, counsel black people to assert their own definitions of themselves against the systemic damage done to black subjectivity in America, to recover their history from the academic project that denies the experiences of people of African descent in the New World and the Old, to reclaim their culture from those who appropriated or disclaimed its existence, and to create "their own sense of community and togetherness." Black Power consciousness consisted of "a sense of peoplehood: pride, rather than shame, in blackness, and an attitude of brotherly, communal responsibility among all black people for one another." The process began with an assertion of a new collective sense of selfhood and a reclamation of the legacy that identification symbolized. "From now on," they asserted, "we shall view ourselves as African-Americans and as black people who are in fact energetic, determined, intelligent, beautiful and peace-loving." Despite numerous disagreements among the pluralist, cultural nationalist, and revolutionary nationalist factions of Black Power, there remained a virtual unanimity regarding the value of Black Power's call for "psychological liberation and cultural identity." In fact, even those critical of Black Power saw the importance of the "black consciousness" aspect of it. Bayard Rustin, for instance, who maintained that Black Power was "positively harmful" for the civil rights movement, had to admit that "'black power' must be seen as part of the psychological rejection of white supremacy, part of the rebellion against the stereotypes which have been ascribed to Negroes for three hundred years."[51]

African Americans attested to the exhilaration of rejecting a circumscribed identity and embracing a newly liberating black subjectivity. When Carmichael announced the advent of Black Power, the "Negroes" in Henry Louis Gates's town became "Black people." He himself "got goose bumps just thinking about being *black,* being proud of being black," of participating in "an exciting and sincere effort to forge a new communal identity among a people descended from splendid ancient cultures. . . . We thought we had learned at last our unutterable, secret name, and that name was BLACK." Like Gates, Carolyn Rodgers went through a personal transformation at the onset of Black Power. She remembers being "a plain, Black, too-dark, nappy do-nothing hair girl / woman" until she heard the "proclamation," Black

Power's "declaration of beauty." Literally overnight, she says, she went from "super ugly Black to Super Black Beauty." So, too, in an essay entitled "I Learned to Feel Black," Jean Smith records her transformation from a "Negro citizen" to a "consciously black" person. Black Power, she wrote, was the other side of the coin of "black consciousness." What Black Power taught her was that the system through which she had previously identified herself and defined her ambitions was premised on her absence and degradation. Realizing this, she concludes that "Negroes must turn away from the preachings, assertions and principles of the larger white society and must turn inward to find the means whereby black people can lead full, meaningful lives. . . . We must become conscious that our blackness calls for another set of principles" derived from "our own experiences." Smith appreciates that the "black self that I am now" will have a difficult but worthwhile task in discovering the "best ways to work in this new, black world" she now inhabits. Such personal discoveries and conversions became so common that the psychologist William Cross systematized the various stages of what he called the "Negro-to-Black Conversion Experience" within a project he named a "psychology of Black Liberation."[52]

The psychology, of course, was not about individual self-assertion alone, but about establishing connections to an African American collective identity and claiming the legacy that identity entailed, "the culture and heritage of black Americans." In this aspect of Black Power, there was an emphasis on restoring what had been lost by those assimilationists who willingly sacrificed the specificity of African American cultural practices for the opportunity of a costly and ultimately failed effort at integration. The "essential difference" between integration and Black Power, wrote Carmichael, is that Black Power insists that the "racial and cultural personality of the black community must be preserved and the community must win its freedom while preserving its cultural integrity." LeRoi Jones called "cultural shame" the "last pure remnant of the slave mentality." Moreover, in this rejection of the assimilationist project and the concomitant reclamation of black culture, Black Power advocates emphasized authenticity, both cultural and personal. Black Power, noted Vincent Harding, means "emphasizing the existence and beauty of an authentic Afro-American culture." The term and concept used to describe this authenticity was "soul," a cultural style that couldn't be learned because, as comedian Godfrey Cambridge quipped, "no one can give you all those black lessons." Where "soul ideology" was most evident was in black music. Henry Dumas wrote a wonderful short story about three white musicians who attempt to play with a black band during a session intended for "Brothers and Sisters only." The sessions are segregated so as not to endanger the white listeners who are susceptible to the lethal vibrations of authentic African American music. The three white musicians force their way in and perish while listening to the music, which is described as being like "an atom stripped of time, black."[53] In Dumas's short story, authenticity was not difficult to discern; those who survived exposure to core black culture were authentic.

The other side of authenticity was appropriation. The white musicians in Dumas's story believe they are capable of playing the music of African Americans with more expertise and style than those with whom it originated. After one of them had sung blues at a civil rights rally in Alabama, either Mississippi John or Muddy Waters had given him an ambiguous compliment. (He didn't know who had given him the compliment because the two singers looked alike to him.) "Boy, you keep that up, you gwine put me back on the plantation." What would put the black singer out of business, or "back on the plantation," is not the beauty or the genuine quality of the white singer's efforts, but its marketability. Despite the compliment, the singer had to admit to himself that he had not "found the depth of the black man's psyche." When he was exposed to someone sounding that depth, he died. In another story about musical appropriation, Alice Walker drew a portrait of an anguished white musician who achieved fame and fortune as a singer of black songs that haunted him because he could never fully understand them. In the nonfictional world, LeRoi Jones called this form of appropriation "Stealing music . . . stealing energy (lives)" and transforming it into "White Music." The Rolling Stones and Beatles, for instance, "steals" and "minstrelizes," because black music is the only soulful music in the Western world. Their material success notwithstanding, Jones believes they have failed to achieve authenticity. "Minstrels," he concludes, "never convinced anybody they were Black either." Yet whites' desire to act black certainly did not diminish with the call for Black Power. Robert Blauner noted the "pathetic need of many young and not-so-young liberal and radical 'friends' of the Negro movement to feel that they, too, have 'soul.'" The "denial of Negro ethnicity," he concluded, "is the more serious form that white appropriation takes today."[54] Actually, it was probably a less serious and less deleterious form of cultural appropriation than those more material practices of the culture industries.

In discussions over Black Power, the issue of cultural appropriation was raised in terms of the issue of cultural and personal identity. Those who celebrated Black Power saw it as the essential element of a cultural and psychological rebirth for African Americans. According to Julius Lester, the "cry for Black Power has done more to generate black consciousness than anything else." It was important for African Americans to develop a "new cultural awareness" because this produced new individuals who no longer view themselves as "marginal." Instead, they are able to view themselves as participants in a vibrant culture whose practices and styles not only survived all attempts at forced disacculturation, but have also become virtually the solitary native-born American cultural forms. Part of the program of "cultural genocide" was precisely the systemic appropriation of African American cultural practices. At the same time that "whites were denigrating black culture, they were stealing it." Even critics of Black Power had to admit to the value of cultural affirmation as a means of offsetting and preventing cultural appropriation. While believing that in "our search for identity we must recognize this dilemma" that black and white Americans are "bound together in a single garment of destiny," Martin Luther King nonetheless also believed that white Americans committed what he called "cultural homicide" against African Americans. To offset this tendency either to ignore or to appropriate the black elements of American culture, King advocated "[p]sychological freedom [and] a firm sense of self-esteem." "This self-affirmation," King concluded, "is the black man's need made compelling by the white man's crimes against him. This is positive and necessary power for black people."[55] In other words, Black Power was making a rightful claim for cultural property. Even those who firmly continued to believe in integration clearly saw that African American cultural practices were subject to appropriation within the capitalist system of white America.

Ironically, it was precisely when the issue was property—cultural or real—that Black Power itself turned out to be most subject to appropriation. In spite of the best efforts of the black Left to argue that Black Power was a rejection of capitalism, which they diagnosed as the structure underwriting racism and colonial imperialism, conservative African American individuals and civil rights groups managed to produce a pro-capitalist version of Black Power. In their Black Power manifesto, Carmichael and Charles Hamilton were clear about the radical nature of their challenge to the status quo of the American social order. Black Power parties would form coalitions, even interracial coalitions, but they would not accept a platform or work with a group advocating institutional reform instead of radical reconstruction. "We do not see how black people can form effective coalitions with groups which are not willing to question and condemn the racist institutions which exploit black people; which do not perceive the need for, and will not work for, basic change." The sort of "basic change" they had in mind was a rejection of perhaps the most basic premise of the Constitution—what they called the "rubric of property rights." The black community, they write, "must insist that the goal of human rights" takes precedence over "property rights." Where absentee slumlords fail to provide adequate services and decent facilities in ghetto housing, they should be forced to forfeit their property to a black-run organization that would manage and collectively own the property in question. Elsewhere, Carmichael argued for a resolutely anticapitalist program of economic empowerment. The society we seek to build, he noted, "is not a capitalist one," but one in which "the spirit of community and humanistic love prevail." The Black Panther Party platform argued for a program of full employment and a guaranteed minimum income, but it also doubted that the capitalist system would provide either of these. They foresaw that the "means of production should be taken from the business men and placed in the community so that the people of the community can organize and employ all of its people."[56]

Even at sites where sympathetic groups sought to work within capitalist structures to empower the black community, Black Power advocates challenged the capitalist system. When he was invited to deliver a paper at a conference called by the Interreligious Foundation for Community Organization to discuss ways to develop the black community economically, James Forman declined the invitation since he believed "there could be no solution to the economic problems of black people within the framework of capitalism." Dorothy Dewberry of SNCC, one of the organizers of the conference, urged him to accept the invitation and advised him to speak on whatever he wished. What he chose to speak on not only shocked the conference but also provoked the interest of Attorney General John Mitchell and FBI Director J. Edgar Hoover, who both ordered the Justice Department to interview all the participants at the conference. Demanding reparations of $500 million to establish socialistically organized economic, educational, and cultural apparatus for black people, Forman also asserted that African Americans "must resist the attempts to make us capitalists." Instead, he advocated the building of a "socialist society inside the United States where the total means of production and distribution are in the hands of the State," a state run by "revolutionary blacks who are concerned about the total humanity of this world."[57] The left-wing faction of Black Power, then, was advocating the establishment of a socialist society and clearly working its way toward theorizing the basis for such a society.

At the Black Power conferences, however, the concept was adopted by right-wing factions to develop a defense of black capitalism. The first Black Power conference, in Newark in June 1967, was organized by black Republican Nathan Wright, and its concluding statement implied that Black Power meant getting a "'fair share' of American capitalism." The next conference, at Philadelphia in June 1968, was even less subtle in its statement that Black Power was equivalent to black capitalism. Critics began to take up the point the Black Power conferences raised. Believing Black Power not to be revolutionary save in its advocacy of "defensive violence," Harold Cruse argued that the "Black Power ideology is *not* socialistic in its economic and political orientation." Black Power, he maintained, is nationalistic and in its "economic and political ambitions . . . a *social reformist* ideology." Cruse compared Black Power to the economic philosophy of Booker T. Washington's Tuskegee machine. So, too, did the Kerner Commission, claiming that much of the Black Power "economic program, as well as their interest in Negro history, self-help, racial solidarity and separation, is reminiscent of Booker T. Washington." Sensing the shifting mood, Richard Nixon stated his belief that Black Power was a good thing because it meant "the power that comes from participation in the political and economic processes of society." He defined Black Power advocates as "entrepreneurs" in search of "a share of the wealth and a piece of the action." Since Nixon thought that "[m]uch of the black militant talk these days" was nothing more than an espousal of the "doctrines of free enterprise," he found it entirely consistent with his politics to claim support for "black pride, black jobs, black opportunity, and yes, black power." The *Wall Street Journal* praised the presidential candidate's stand; so too did Floyd McKissick and Roy Innis, signaling the beginning of CORE's shift to the right. As James Forman noted, Nixon performed the "supreme act of co-optation" in redefining Black Power as black capitalism. Nonetheless, Forman blamed mostly himself and other members of SNCC for not defining the term precisely, thus leaving the door open for "opportunists to define the term in any manner they chose." If SNCC and other Black Power groups on the left had been careful to produce a revolutionary definition of Black Power, then the "government and its Negroes might not have been able to co-opt the term."[58]

Although the term was co-opted, and the strategy of Black Power redefined, there appeared to be no clear victor between those on the right and those on the left. For some, Black Power was not a conservative economic program but rather a "challenge [to] capitalism, at least in principle," because the Black Power advocates were proposing to "replace white businesses with black *cooperatives.*" Black Power's call for *"collective* self-help" was not the same thing as "individualist petty capitalism on the one hand, or, on the other hand, a separate black economy." For others, Black Power was lacking in revolutionary impetus because it was a movement directed by and for the benefit of the "black petite bourgeoisie," using "petit bourgeois rhetoric" to advocate a conservative economic agenda. Beneath "the rhetoric of Black Power, black control and black self-determination," there "was a budding 'new' black middle class hungry for power and starving for status." The black conservatives, the "'new' black business, professional and political elites," heard the "bourgeois melody behind the radical rhetoric and manipulated the movement for their own benefit."[59] Like violence and identity, then, property was a site of contestation for the organic intellectuals of the Black Power movement, just as it had been for the civil rights movement of the early- to mid-sixties and for the academic study of slavery.

By 1968, at precisely the same time the public discourse stipulating that slavery was the major cause for present social relations returned to the academy, Black Power became the major impetus for academics working within the newly mobilized discursive formation. Asserting that the "recent upsurge of political awareness and participation has had an undeniable impact on historians" and has dramatically affected the study of slavery, academic historians hailed Black Power as a positive force on the emergent discourse. Reflecting on the developments since the New-berry Library conference, historians of slavery concluded that "the contemporary black struggle has clarified and illuminated many matters, rendering the discussion a very different one than the one begun nearly a decade ago." In his article "The In-fluence of the Black Power Movement on Historical Scholarship," Eugene Genovese noted that while the early civil rights movement had led historians to issue negative critiques of earlier "ideological nonsense," the Black Power movement was having a generally productive effect and lending itself to "a decisive turn in the understanding of our national experience and of the black experience."[60]

The other point Genovese makes is a larger one about how the writing of history and the living of it are dialectically related. Unlike those who would believe simply that they live in a climate of opinion of which their work is a reflection, or those who, with equal simplicity, believe that their intellectual productions form the climate of opinion in which they live, Genovese argues that politics and scholarship were as interpenetrative as any superstructural and infrastructural phenomena, as any set of material and intellectual conditions. The conjuncture of "material condi-tions" and "intellectual labors," or the "question of the effects of politics on scholar-ship," wrote Genovese, must "be understood primarily as the intersection of two de-rivatives of a common source that is at once political and scholarly." Scholarship, he suggested, is itself a "political force of considerable consequence."[61] So, also, as he realized in an intellectual debate that helped him reach this conclusion, is aesthetic cultural production. The debate that revealed the political force of aesthetic produc-tion to Genovese and to the sixties in general was the debate over William Styron's *Confessions of Nat Turner*—the same debate that focused on and in many ways re-solved the struggle between the emergent and dominant discursive formations on slavery, and the debate in which the three topics of violence, identity, and property played a prominent role in the contested definition of Black Power.

3

The Discourse Mobilized

The Debate over William Styron's
The Confessions of Nat Turner

William Styron's *The Confessions of Nat Turner* and John Henrik Clarke's *William Styron's Nat Turner: Ten Black Writers Respond* represent not only a novel and a book of literary criticism, respectively published in late 1967 and early 1968; rather, they together form a site of historical and cultural contestation at a crucial moment in the post–civil rights era. For one thing, Styron's novel, largely based on the hegemonic discourse on slavery culminating in the Elkins thesis, was a text cultural critics claimed "perfectly reflects the blind spots of past treatments of slavery." Moreover, Styron's decision to cast his novel as a first-person narration, using the conventions and forms of the antebellum slave narrative and in fact basing his book on a piece of slave testimony, raised deeply divisive issues of cultural expertise and appropriation. The emergent post–civil rights era black intelligentsia rallied itself around these interrelated issues of historical and cultural representation. African American intellectuals noted that "never before, at least not in our lifetime, had there been such defiant unanimity among blacks as during the controversy over Styron's treatment of Nat Turner." The controversy over Styron's novel marked a transitional point in the emergence of the Black Power–generation intellectuals, the "whole syndrome of the novel and the responses" to it marking an "important change in the American literary climate" and inaugurating the "new coming of age of the black literary intellectual."[1]

The debate over Styron's novel was also not only a "Black Power–era controversy," but a controversy in which Black Power was an issue, perhaps *the* issue, of the debate. Noting that this was "no ordinary literary squabble," the *New York Times* reviewer suggested that the Clarke collection's "assumption of a militant black audience" signified a change in American cultural politics. The terms in this "literary squabble" reflected the larger social conflicts in American domestic politics. It is worth noting, for instance, that the *New York Times* review of the Clarke collection was framed by three articles, one on Mayor John Lindsay's response to police guidelines in handling mass protests, a second on the Columbia University student takeover, and a third on the Urban League's decision to "back Black Power."[2] The news around the books was for many the subject of the books. On the whole, then, the debate between the novel's critics and those who defended Styron's artistic integrity is an interesting cultural phenomenon because it shows us the changing political climate of the late sixties, the mobilization of a new discursive formation on slavery, and the emergence of a new intellectual force in American public discourse.

These are all interrelated phenomena, though, and it is often difficult to distinguish among the strategies certain intellectuals used to defend Styron's artistic license, dismiss the critics' comments, and buttress the hegemonic discourse on slavery, since they often did all three things simultaneously. By looking at the entire debate, one can get a sense of how an empowered intelligentsia designates a certain set of materials as valid historical evidence (and thereby exludes others as invalid) at the same time as it distinguishes certain political positions as responsible and defines one intellectual position about access to cultural property as acceptable. While the question of what materials are acceptable for historical study gets resolved with fairly little commotion (slave testimony was granted "standing" by 1970), the issue of who is empowered to speak for a cultural tradition has not yet been resolved, nor has the issue of artistic license in a multiethnic society (and neither of these two issues will likely be resolved any time soon, mostly because their resolution will depend on a fundamental change in social relations rather than any realignment in the field of cultural production).

In discussing the instructive debate around Styron's *Confessions of Nat Turner,* I will be using three terms to describe those who intervened at various times: "reviewers" to designate those who wrote initial reviews of Styron's novel in 1967 or 1968; "critics" for those who wrote critical commentaries on the novel in 1968 (focusing mostly on the work of the critics in the Clarke collection); and "respondents" to designate those who wrote in response to *William Styron's Nat Turner: Ten Black Writers Respond* (particularly those whom Styron himself has persistently praised for their interventions on his behalf—Eugene Genovese, Martin Duberman, and Seymour Gross and Eileen Bender). The debate occurs in two phases, the first involving the black writers' critique of Styron's novel in 1968, the second the respondents' critique of the Clarke collection between 1968 and 1971.

The first section of this chapter delineates the dynamics of this dialogue, the miscommunications and significant ellipses that characterized the debate, discerning the strategies the respondents employed as they evaded the crucial points raised by the critics about access and control in the literary establishment, intellectual hegemons in historical study, and cultural propriety. For the critics, Styron's novel is part of a social project in which African American culture is both appropriated and denied its history. For them, the terms of the debate are political and historical. What racial stereotypes does Styron exploit from his reading of American social life? What configuration of historical understanding does he employ in his reading of the African American past? In what ways is the novel constructed around those contested topics (violence, identity, and property) that had formed the intellectual coordinates in the debates over the historical representation of slavery and the political strategies of Black Power? The second section explores Styron's representation of Nat Turner's identity as it is developed through the nexus of violence and sex. The third section examines how Styron appropriates a text of slave testimony by reading it through the filter of the hegemonic discourse on slavery. It also shows how the critics challenged this act of appropriation by dismantling the terms of that hegemonic discourse. The issues the critics raise about the hegemonic discourse have affected the study of slavery since 1968; the issues they raise about cultural appropriation have determined the trajectory of the Neo-slave narratives published since then. The final section argues that the critics set a paradigm for the Neo-slave narratives of the seventies and eighties by mobilizing the new discursive formation on slavery in the field of cultural production.

The Dynamics of the Debate: Critics and Respondents

Reviewers of Styron's novel hailed it as "the most profound treatment we have had of slavery in our literature. And the only one that tells the story from the slave's point of view." It was an intriguing use in 1967 of a phrase—"the slave's point of view"—that had been a stock abolitionist statement in prefaces to slave narratives in the nineteenth century, and was invoked in the first half of the twentieth century as a historiographical imperative by Mary White Ovington (1910 and 1918), W. E. B. DuBois (1918), Carter G. Woodson (1919), Lawrence Reddick (1937), B. A. Botkin (1944), Richard Hofstadter (1944), and Charles H. Nichols (1949 and 1959), before it became the singular concept around which the critique of the Elkins thesis coalesced between 1967 and 1970.[3] The novel came to be debated in the terms in which it was debated because Styron chose to write from the slave's point of view; the debate took on the tone it took because white intellectuals asserted that the only person who could write from a slave's point of view in 1967 was a white southerner. C. Vann Woodward concluded that the "rare combination of talents essential to this formidable undertaking" could not "have been found anywhere else." For Philip Rahv, "only a white Southern writer could have brought it off"; a black writer suffering from a complex personal, social, and political anxiety "would have probably stacked the cards, producing in a mood of unnerving rage and indignation, a melodrama of saints and sinners."[4] Responding to the presumptious arrogance of these reviewers, June Meyer (now June Jordan) noted that Nat Turner, "this object of attention, attack, and vast activity, cannot make himself be heard, let alone be understood" because *"he has never been listened to."* In general, she noted, black people "have been speaking as subjects, as first persons, as the only people we are." "Is anyone, is anyone white, preparing to listen?" Judging by the responses of the white intellectuals who first misrepresented and then attacked the black critics' comments on Styron's novel, the answer to that question was, no, the time for listening had not yet arrived, not in 1968, not then.[5]

The terms of the debate over Styron's novel were set early, then, and they were not the terms so many later commentators mistakenly argued them to be. Many scholars have mistaken the terms of the debate because they have replicated Styron's act of rewriting and attempting to contain the political and cultural resonance of black testimony. Examining how the respondents failed to listen to the charges leveled by Styron's critics will prove enlightening, because this cultural conversation—with its ellipses, gaps, and miscommunications—provides us with a model for discerning how in a shifting sociopolitical intellectual moment, such as the one following the development of Black Power, an empowered intelligentsia weilding a hegemonic discursive formation engages in only a peripheral dialogue with an emergent intelligentsia mobilized by an antithetical discursive formation. At the same time as the critics exposed the deepening fissures in the hegemonic discourse on slavery, the respondents struggled to buttress that hegemonic discourse, largely failing to appreciate that the critics were working with a different appreciation for the methods, resources, and means of understanding the history of slavery or that they were mobilizing a different and differently organized discursive formation. Likewise, mainstream media intellectuals proved unable to understand the terms and tenets posed by black cultural workers who valued a distinct set of cultural experiences that, they argued, produced a certain expertise not otherwise accessible. By diagnosing the respondents' misreadings of the critics' comments on historical methodology and cultural politics, we are better able to discern the resolute resistance African American cultural workers met as they attempted to constitute a new intellectual formation in American public discourse.

The respondents' first and most consistently employed strategy in discounting the Black Power intellectuals' work was to "characterize" the debate over Styron's novel by reading it in a certain way and trying to convince others that the debate took on certain permutations and exhibited a certain dynamic. They attempted to argue that the first phase of the debate consisted of an innocent white man beseiged by a group of ten intellectual thugs who resorted to mean-spirited ad hominem critiques of Styron himself. Almost immediately, the critics were accused of employing "tactical insult," uttering things that were "slanderous," and "ruthlessly and unfairly assault[ing]" Styron.[6] This initial characterization largely succeeded in producing a widespread belief among later scholars that the debate constituted what one recent critic calls an "attack by ten black writers" employing "invective and flammable rhetoric." At the same time, these same scholars utterly ignored the respondents' aggressive, insulting, and often racist language. According to the respondents, the ten black critics were "furious" (Fremont-Smith), "hostile" (Gross and Bender), "rhetorically violent and irrational" (Akin), "angry" and "bitter" (Durden), "hysterical" and "ferocious" (Genovese), and "infantile," "irrational," and "philistine" (Styron).[7] A rereading of this debate shows a completely and startlingly different dynamic. The respondents on the whole miserably failed to take up most of the major issues raised by the critics, since they did not listen to the critics but instead contested and repressed both the emergent discourse on slavery and the Black Power intellectuals who mobilized it.

The respondents suggested that the Black Power intellectuals (somewhat, though by no means completely, connected with the *Freedomways* editorial collective) lacked "objectivity" because of their race or commitments to Black Power. Arguing that the "black intelligentsia faces a serious crisis" because its "political affinities lie with the Black Power movement, which increasingly demands conformity, myth-making, and historical fabrication," Genovese contended that black intellectuals entangle history with present politics and thereby distort the "actual past" while creating some kind of "usable past." Liberal journalists covering the birth of Black Studies at historically white college campuses in the late sixties echoed this complaint as they charged black intellectuals with distorting history and creating myths to serve their narrow political agenda. As one of those journalists put it in an article, "Black History, Black Mythology?" "black history, taught by blacks to blacks, will be in constant danger of departing from historical objectivity and degenerating into mere anti-Establishment propaganda."[8] On the one hand, then, the respondents attempted to prevent the emergence of the post–civil rights African American intelligentsia by denigrating its political connections with Black Power, while on the other they attempted to conserve the hegemonic discursive formation on slavery by removing "history" from "politics" and claiming the existence of some mythical realm of "objective" history, created in intellectual spaces where, to use the journalist's categories, white history was taught by whites to whites. In neither case did the respondents ultimately succeed, but what is more interesting than their failure to repress the emergent Black Power intelligentsia or their failure to conserve the hegemonic discourse is the process by which they made the attempt, the rhetorical strategies they employed in that attempt, and, most of all, the nature of the contested space between the existent and the emergent intellectual formations.

The respondents also attempted to defend Styron's fiction and conserve the hegemonic discourse by misreading the critics' comments on the significance of Styron's "occasional omission or distortion of detail" in the "historical evidence." Maintaining that the "burden of the attack on Styron's book is the charge of historical falsification," the respondents argued that the critics' condemnation of "Styron's portrait as having no justification in the historical record" is ultimately wrongheaded since the critics themselves are unable to claim any "supposedly unassailable rampart of historicity." The issue raised by the critics, however, had much more to do with cultural representation than with historical accuracy, a point the respondents worked hard to miss. According to Gross and Bender, the "My" in the title of Vincent Harding's essay, "You've Taken My Nat and Gone," is meant to "refer to the 'real,' the 'true,' the 'historical' Nat Turner," even though Harding makes it absolutely clear that he is talking about cultural appropriation, not historical accuracy. He is claiming not that he occupies a transcendent place from which he can see the "real, true, historical" Nat Turner, but rather that Styron has produced a Nat Turner who is based not on any African American cultural traditions but only on "the whitened appropriation of our history." It is on the point of appropriation, including both the co-opting of Nat Turner's voice and the appropration of a cultural figure, that the critics level their most important and most ignored claim—the claim that what Styron produced was less a "meditation on history" than it was an appropriation of a slave's voice, a slave's life's meaning, and an important piece of slave testimony. Black critics maintained that the issue of "historical distortions" was peripheral; the "central problem" was that the "writing of Styron's book was a political gesture," an act of "cultural dominance" and "cultural imperialism."[9]

The "My" in Harding's title, like the "Our" in Charles Hamilton's title, "Our Nat Turner and William Styron's Creation," is not only about historical accuracy; it is about historians' unwillingness to investigate or value the cultural traditions of subject peoples. Of course, the pattern of historians' denying the value of slave testimony to the historiography of slavery suggests that the cultural tradition of slaves is precisely what historians have to deny in order to produce their historical work. Genovese, for instance, calls Harding's claim of an African American tradition regarding the life of Nat Turner a "pretense." Duberman is shocked to discover the black critics "*reduced* to citing" the "oral tradition" (emphasis added).[10] Having dismissed oral and questioned the existence of cultural traditions, having missed the point made by the critics about cultural appropriation, the respondents are finally able to miss and dismiss the critics' objection to Styron's portrait.

Let me offer two examples of the pervasive miscommunication in the debate. Each centers on an individual character—the first, Nat Turner's wife, an absence contested by the critics, the second, the exaggerated presence of Margaret Whitehead. In the first example, we see how the critics and respondents employed different strategies for reading a slave narrative, in the second how they differed in their reading of Styron's novel. In each case, we see how the critics and respondents were mobilized by distinct discursive formations affecting how they chose to approach slave testimony and deal with the distinctively New Left idea of slaves as the subjects of their own lives.

Because they failed to see what the critics were saying about the hegemonic forces determining Styron's rendering of history, the respondents wholly misunderstood what the critics were saying about those forces governing Styron's reading of a specific historical document, Thomas Gray's *Confessions of Nat Turner* (1831). Instead the respondents took the predictable tactic of denying the authenticity of Gray's *Confessions* and accusing the critics of overestimating the text's truth value, arguing that the "attacks on Styron's novel generally take it for granted that Thomas R. Gray was not much more than a recorder of Turner's words and that therefore his *Confessions* is a reasonably reliable source for our knowledge of Turner and his motives." According to the respondents, the black critics "have not pointed out that those confessions are themselves subject to challenge" and "seem to believe that the original confessions are Absolute Truth and that every account which deviates from them partakes of malignant intent."[11]

When we read the critics' own words, though, we find a far from uncritical assessment of Gray's *Confessions*. While referring to Gray's *Confessions* as the "primary historical document"—which of course it is both for historians of Nat Turner's revolt and for Styron himself, who called it the "single significant contemporary document concerning this insurrection"—the critics also point out what they call its "limitations": its "obviously spurious" sentences and its internal dynamic as a text "prepared by a white man hostile to Nat Turner and the cause he represented." The critics note that in order to take seriously Styron's own statement that he "rarely departed from the known facts about Nat Turner and the revolt of which he was the leader" ([xi]), they must go back to the text Styron called the "single significant document." "No other conclusion seems sensible," they write, "if one takes the basic historical document (Turner's own dictated *Confessions*) with the seriousness claimed by Styron." The critics read Gray's text so carefully, then, because they wish to determine how "incidents reported in the original *Confessions* and transformed by Mr. Styron's imagination are indicative of the pattern of interpretation throughout the book." In other words, they are reading for the intertextual absences and exaggerated emphases so that they can discern the significance of Styron's reading habits. None of the ten critics claims anything more for Gray's *Confessions;* they take the text seriously as Styron's primary document and they read it with an eye toward seeing what Styron systematically highlights or eliminates. This hardly seems uncritical and certainly not an indication of the critics' belief in Gray's text as "Absolute Truth."[12]

Having attempted to argue that Gray's *Confessions* is a text limited in historical value, if not spurious, and certainly not the "Absolute Truth," the respondents then curiously argue that Nat Turner's failure to mention his wife in Gray's *Confessions* is proof positive that he did not have one. The "evidence for Turner's alleged black wife is slim and not beyond challenge," notes Genovese. "The black critics make much of Turner's references to his grandmother and his parents" in Gray's *Confessions*. "How incredible, then, that he failed to mention his wife." In his interviews first and then later in public forums, Styron repeated Genovese's argument. In a 1968 interview, he noted that it is "incredible that he would mention his parents and his grandparents and not mention his wife." At the Southern Historical Association conference, Styron again marveled at this fact: "this is one of the amazing things about it. He mentions all the rest of his family, but mentions no wife." Gross and Bender chime in: "why if Turner had a wife did he not mention her in Gray? He mentions the rest of his family."[13]

In a letter to the *New York Review of Books,* Anna Mary Wells pointed out precisely why Turner would have no good reason to mention his wife to Gray. Drawing on Thomas Wentworth Higginson's account, Wells argues that Turner's wife was "tortured under the lash" in an effort to get her to "reveal the hiding place" of Turner's "secret papers." This fact provides "ample explanation of Turner's failure to mention her in his *Confessions,"* since Turner "hoped, no doubt, to spare her further suffering." Gross and Bender respond to Wells's perspicacious argument with remarkable imperspicacity. "Anna Mary Wells' explanation for Turner's failure to mention his wife in Gray's *Confessions* as an attempt 'to spare her further suffering' is extremely far-fetched since it assumes that Turner believed that no one knew he had a wife, which, considering the composition and size of the society in which Turner lived, is rather unlikely."[14] Gross and Bender's reasoning is more than a little suspect. If everyone in the society in which Turner lived would have known about his wife, then why precisely would Turner feel compelled to mention her? Wells's reason is hardly "far-fetched"; it is in fact very well founded.

On September 26, 1831, while Turner was still at large, the *Richmond Constitutional Whig* ran a story in which the reporter recorded that he had "in [his] possession, some papers given up by his wife, under the lash." Likewise, in the 1831 *Authentic and Impartial Narrative,* also written before Turner was captured, Samuel Warner wrote that "his wife was a slave, belonging to Mr. Reese, and it was in her possession after Nat's escape that his papers were found." Moreover, the scholar who has performed the greatest archival work on the Nat Turner revolt, Henry Irving Tragle, speculates that the author of the piece in the *Richmond Constitutional Whig* might have been Thomas R. Gray, the very author of the *Confessions.*[15] In other words, we can now more carefully imagine Turner's situation during his interviews with Gray. He is sitting with an individual who has in his possession Turner's own papers, which he possesses because he had whipped Turner's wife. What precisely do Genovese, Gross and Bender, and Styron want Turner to say? "I presume you know my wife, Mr. Gray?"

Finally, Styron and the respondents seem to think that Turner was operating without his own pressures in his interviews with Gray. Let us not forget that Turner was at large for eight weeks, during which time over 150 slaves and free blacks were murdered in cold blood by vigilante bands in reprisals for the insurrection. The newspaper reports were consistent in threatening that any future slave resistance would result in the extermination of the whole African American population. The *Richmond Whig* asserted on September 3, 1831: "Let the fact not be doubted by those whom it most concerns, that another such insurrection will be the signal for the extirpation of the whole black population in the quarter of the State where it occurs." The *New York Morning Courier and Enquirer* of September 17, 1831 also warned that "another such enterprise will end in total extermination of their race in the southern country."[16] Some of Turner's comrades had been ruthlessly murdered, others executed. His friends were shot in the streets and left hanging from trees. The furor surrounding his capture would have alerted him to the mood of the county. It was hardly a propitious time for Turner to mention his wife. Indeed, had Styron and the respondents read Gray's *Confessions* with more attention, they would have discovered that Turner does not mention anyone still alive. Everyone he mentions is already dead or presumed dead. That fact might solve the false mystery the respondents attempt to construct about why Turner would mention his grandmother and father and mother—all beyond the pale of life or of Virginia—and "fail" to mention his wife.

While the debate over Turner's wife demonstrates the ways the respondents misread slave testimony because they lacked the capacity to interpret the silences the social conditions of slaves forced them to inscribe, the debate over Margaret Whitehead and the role she plays in Nat Turner's sexual and political imaginary is significant because it demonstrates how the respondents misread Styron's novel by failing to see how the social inflects the artistic, how the field of power is situated in the field of cultural production.

The respondents argued that Styron should be praised for having the "courage to confront the depths of America's racial tragedy" and for seeing the "sexual dimension of the racial confrontation." They maintained that Styron's genius was to recognize Turner as a revolutionary leader who could make the people "see their oppression as flowing from a common social source and to help them to identify the oppressor." He revolted because he loved his people. "Had he not loved them, he would not have protested so much against their weakness in the face of oppression." Noting that Turner was sometimes wont to express this "love" in a curious way, such as referring to "my black shit-eating people [who] were surely like flies, God's mindless outcasts" (27), the respondents nonetheless felt that "[n]o revolutionary could be free of such feelings of hatred" for it is "essentially a hatred for the oppression rather than the oppressed." Therefore, Turner's "love for his people is also in the novel." Turner, they conclude, was motivated by his religious sensibility and his love for his people, not by his lustful infatuation for a white woman. "Styron does not, as some charge, make Turner's feeling for Margaret Whitehead the spring of his action. Nothing in the novel suggests anything so absurd."[17]

The critics, on the other hand, saw not only an author "immersed in a white-racist sexual fantasy" who has his black male protagonist persistently masturbate while obsessively fantasizing about white women, but an author who denies the revolutionary subjectivity of Nat Turner by having white women mediate Turner's relationship with God and his relationship with his community of enslaved African

Americans. Consider the scene on which the novel ends, as Turner stands in his jail cell awaiting execution. In his final statement on his life, Turner says that the only change he would make if he had the revolt to live over would be to spare "her that showed me Him whose presence I had not fathomed or maybe never even known." Only after he concludes this thought does he suddenly recall God's name (428). Readers more acute than Styron recognized that this statement belies everything his novel had hitherto represented about Turner's religiosity since "God had been a presence in Nat's life long before he met the girl."[18] What this scene tells us, though, is that Styron is intent on arguing that Turner's religious imagination is mediated by and ultimately beholden to Margaret Whitehead. The critics' reading of the novel likewise demonstrates how Styron uses Margaret Whitehead as precisely that force mediating Turner's love for his community, turning "Nat from hatred of his own people to a missionary effort to uplift." They point to the scene in which Turner first gazes hatefully at a group of black people—declaring to himself, "I hate them one and all"—before discovering "Margaret Whitehead, her dimpled chin tilted up as, with one arm entwined in her mother's, she carols heavenward, a radiance like daybreak on her serene young face." He then turns back with wet eyes to the group of black people, feeling "a kind of wild, desperate love for them" (104). In other words, the two forces that drive Styron's Turner to revolt—his belief in God, and his love for his community—are both mediated through Margaret Whitehead.[19] The novel, as the critics show, does suggest something so "absurd."

In the end, then, we see that this cultural conversation is thwarted because of the respondents' willful misreading of the critics. On several specific topics—the objectivity of history, the issue of cultural appropriation, the social forces determining reading strategies, the cultural expertise of lived experience, and the reading of either Gray's or Styron's *Confessions of Nat Turner*—the critics' comments were simply not heard. One might wearily conclude that this reaction is but another example of the literary critical enterprise at its worst (or, more cynically, at its most common). It seems to me, though, that this episode in cultural history—with its pervasive miscommunication and deliberate misrepresentation—reveals something else, namely the ways a dominant American intelligentsia attempts to resist the critique and ignore the emergent discourse offered by a newly organized subaltern intelligentsia. Indeed, the debate over Styron's novel constituted a primary site of contestation between the hegemonic and emergent discourses on slavery. While the respondents were arguing for the "objectivity" of history, the critics were showing how "white southern historical writing" was premised on the "distortion of black reality." While the respondents wished to assess Styron's achievement as the creation of an individual artist, the critics insistently demonstrated how the hypersexualized and largely dehumanized Turner that Styron represented was "the only one that could have possibly emerged from the framework" of immanent social stereotypes about contemporary black life and a discursive formation on slavery in the historical writing produced in the climate of those stereotypes. What the critics demonstrated, then, is that Styron had performed an act of cultural appropriation by reading the past, and reading slave testimony about the past, through the filter of a decaying discourse on slavery.[20]

We saw in the previous chapter how the emergent discourse was formed through the concerted actions and intellectual productions of historians of antebellum America and social activists of the sixties. We also saw how the topics of violence, identity, and property engaged the attentions of historians of slavery and Black Power advocates as the discourse was formed from 1960 to 1970. We can now see how those topics—those contested coordinates in both the historiography of slavery and the social movements of the sixties—occupy a significant place in the most important literary cultural debate of the decade.

Sex, Violence, and Identity in Styron's *Confessions*

By assuming the confessional mode, Styron raises questions about the sources of personal identity, specifically black revolutionary identity. His representation of Margaret Whitehead as the primary source of Nat Turner's religious and communal identity is problematic because he implicitly suggests that sexual lust is the primal spur to black revolutionary subjectivity and action. Turner has persistent sexual fantasies about white women, and these fantasies largely define his selfhood, religious sensibility, and political impetus. What is most problematic about Styron's text is the ways it reiterates the myth-making discourses of historical American racism. In arguing that a black male revolutionary defines himself through his phallus, and in insistently confusing political violence and sexuality, Styron reinforces the circulation of racist stereotypes, and his novel, therefore, sadly constitutes a regressive replaying of the national history of those stereotypes.

Although Styron insisted that at the "center of [his] approach to Nat Turner" was a "theological aspect," that Turner's "relationship with God seemed to be the central thing in [his] conception of the man," he thoroughly saturates Turner's religious piety with sexual imagery and largely represents it through sexual activity. Consider, for instance, the final scene of the book, which Styron says is meant to tell us the "story of his redemption." "How does he achieve redemption before he is executed, before he goes to his maker, so to speak?" As he sits in his jail cell, Turner feels the wind blow softly against his cheek and turns, seeking Margaret Whitehead's "breath." Feeling the "warmth flow into my loins and my legs tingle with desire," Turner yearns for her with his usual rage, pouring out his "love within her; pulsing flood." She "arches against me, cries out, and the twain—black and white—are one" (426). Turner will apparently "achieve redemption" by achieving orgasm. Reviewers questioned the wisdom of representing Turner's final religious epiphany as a "masturbatory fantasy," wondering whether Styron was making a comment about religion—one asked if "Styron had a lapse of taste or committed one of those unintentional puns" when he repeatedly used the biblical phrase "I come quickly" to describe Turner's recovery of grace—or capitulating to racist stereotypes of people of African descent.[21]

There are several points we need to raise about Styron's choice to channel Turner's religiosity through his sexuality. There might be some who think autoeroticism is an act that metaphorically captures the sensibility of religious agony (I do not, nor would I care to witness their public devotions). While masturbation is a good enough thing in itself, and an act whose representation can serve a variety of aesthetic and political purposes, it is neither what the historical Turner was doing on the eve of his execution nor a flattering representation of anyone facing death. In the original *Confessions,* on which Styron claimed to rely so much, Thomas Gray gives us a Nat Turner who dares to "raise his manacled hands to heaven, with a spirit soaring above the attributes of man."[22] Styron gives us a Turner who is not manacled, or whose manacles are not so prohibitive as to prevent a certain kind of motion, whose hands are not held quite so high or heavenward, and whose spirit and thoughts are clearly not intent only on heaven.

This final scene is not an isolated event, of course, since Turner had been an active masturbator throughout the novel. He was, however, not an equal opportunity masturbator, since it was always a white woman, *"always* a nameless white girl . . . with golden curls," who occupied Turner's mind on his Saturday masturbation ritual (173, my italics). The critics objected to this representation of a "man with a sex hang-up who goes out into the wilderness to meditate only to get a simple thing like freedom hopelessly confused with masturbation while having fantasies about white women" as a deep betrayal of the heroic Nat Turner of African American folklife.[23] Moreover, not only is Styron's obsessive representation of Turner's sexual fantasy life clichéd and demeaning, it also masks the political in his novel. The critics correctly noted that the sexual theme was an attempt to "escape the judgment of history embodied in Nat Turner and his spiritual sons of the twentieth century," that Styron reduced "the social to the personal," "institutionalized oppression to isolated acts of personal outrage," "history to sex."[24]

Consider, for example, two competing scenes in the carpenter's shop on the Moore plantation. In the first, Turner explicitly delineates the social relations in a protocapitalist system. As he meditates on the psychic effects of being commodified as chattel, realizing that he represents both a body of exploited labor yielding surplus value as well as a reproductive capital investment in "body and brains," Turner also talks about the pleasure he gets from a labor process that is unified and not alienating. It was "the greatest delight to me to be able to fashion the traps myself— box traps which I made out of scrap pine from the shop, sawing and planing the wood with my own hands, carving the pegs and the notched pins which tripped the doors, and uniting one after another of the miniature coffins into a single smoothly operating, silent, lethal assembly" (51). In the other scene in the carpenter's shop, Turner locks the door he himself designed and enjoys his "vision of the golden-haired girl with her lips half open" while he crouches masturbating and "panting in the pine-smelling sweetness" (173). In one scene, we get a marvelous description of the irony of an available nonalienating labor process operating within the utterly alienating social system of slavery. In the other, we get the reduction of history to autoerotic sex. In the same social space in which Turner gets pleasure from manufacturing, he also gets pleasure from masturbating. To judge by the majority of readers' responses, the more resonant scene is clearly the one in which Turner is expressing his frustrated sexuality. In placing two manual acts in a shared social space, having one explicitly political and another explicitly apolitical, Styron turns our attention from the social to the personal, from the collective to the individual, from the political to the sexual. And the reviewers did not read this as only a historical fiction, but as an "analogy for our times," that contemporary "black militants" also feel the same "great overwhelming obsession" to "jump into bed with Mister Charlie's daughter."[25]

Rather than sounding the "depths of America's racial tragedy" and the "sexual dimension of the racial confrontation," as the respondents argued, Styron was superficially repeating all the clichés of an older, and still residual racial-sexual politics, evincing a hardly subtle fascination with the stereotype of the black rapist and its corollary, the black penis. Consider those scenes when Turner imagines himself as a rapist of white women. At one point, as he rides beside her on the wagon, Turner smells Margaret Whitehead's "warm girl-sweat" and begins to think that he could "throw her down and spread her young white legs and stick myself in her until belly met belly and shoot inside her in warm milky spurts of desecration" (367). At another, he imagines himself raping Major Ridley's fiancé "with abrupt, brutal, and rampaging fury, watching the compassion melt from her tear-stained face as I bore her to the earth, my black hands already tearing at the lustrous billowing silk as I drew the dress up around her waist, and forcing apart those soft white thighs, exposed the zone of fleecy brown hair into which I drove my black self with stiff merciless thrusts" (264). Each imagined scene of rape follows a moment when the white women expressed their liberal sentiments—Margaret Whitehead voiced her opinion that "the darkies in Virginia should be *free*" (366), while Major Ridley's fiancé had on her face an imprint of "pity—pity wrenched from the very depths of her soul—and the sight of that pity, the vision of that tender self so reduced by compassion to this helpless state of sobs and bloodless clenched knuckles and scalding tears, caused me an irresistable, flooding moment of desire. And it was, you see, pity alone that did this, not the woman herself apart from the pity" (263–64).

Styron's point that a slave could respond to pity or any other form of condescension with violent rage is not a bad observation; represented differently, it could have been a complex and worthwhile one. Many reviewers and respondents felt the scene with Major Ridley's fiancé was especially well rendered, calling it "one of the finest episodes in the novel" and "a masterful portrayal of complex emotions of hate, lust, love and shame contending within a man's heart." The reviewers also noted that this "incident more than any other gives the motive for Nat's actions," that Turner's encounter with Major Ridley's fiancé is a "crucial moment in the story" providing us with what one reviewer called "a psychologically 'true' observation"—that, as Turner put it, "it was not a white person's abuse or scorn or even indifference which could ignite in me this murderous hatred but his pity" (267). The reviewer points out that this observation was "fresher some years ago when presented by James Baldwin and Malcolm X."[26] It was not only fresher when Malcolm and Baldwin made it, but substantially different.

Styron is not content to allow Turner to meditate on this observation, nor does he allow him to express it in any way other than through an imagined act of sexual violence. As if impelled by some strange logic, Styron has Turner follow each penetrating insight with an unsightly scene of forced penetration. He cannot feel hatred toward Margaret Whitehead or Major Ridley's fiancé without imagining himself raping either of them. Are we meant to understand that rape is the only way Turner has of expressing his philosophical insight? That implication, it seems to me, is bad enough. But Styron is not content to leave it at that. In each case, in the course of the rape Turner's penis becomes his "self." He tells us that he wishes to "stick myself" into Margaret Whitehead and to drive "my black self" into Major Ridley's fiancé. Over and over again, Styron shows us a Turner whose response to the world is to stick his penis in it. On the day the sun eclipses, Turner yearns to perform coitus with the universe. "I thirsted to plunge myself into the earth, into a tree, a deer, a bear, a bird, a boy, a stump, a stone, to shoot milky warm spurts of myself into the cold and lonely blue heart of the sky" (347). We surely cannot accept one respondent's comment on this description that "Nat's passion here is for Love—for communion and fulfillment in some meaningful way with some meaningful being or spirit."[27] Turner is just not that discriminating in his choice of what objects to commune with—some would seem dangerous, some uninteresting, and others difficult to imagine "plunging [oneself] into." And "Love" doesn't strike me as the governing emotion in Turner's mind at this moment. Love is what one senses Whitman feels for nature; and Turner just does not provide a compelling example of Whitmanesque *jouissance* here. The point, rather, is not what Turner may be feeling or the objects toward which he feels whatever he feels. The point, crudely made, is that Turner's way of being-in-the-world is quite literally, to come-in-the-world. For Styron, then, Nat Turner's penis plays an inordinately significant role, being practically the primary source of his identity and selfhood and the sole means he appears to have of communing with nature. Indeed, Styron makes Turner's whole body become phallic in its reactions, "hot and swollen" as he watches a white woman, and detumescent when he completes his final act of masturbation: "I faint slowly. My head falls toward the window, my breath comes hard" (265, 426).

Styron's representation is deeply troubling not only because it simplistically celebrates the phallus, but also because it precisely replays the history of the most damaging racist stereotypes. In *Black Skin, White Masks,* Frantz Fanon demonstrates how whites have "fixated" African men at the level of the "genital," arguing convincingly that the "whole mystique surrounding black sexuality arises from white colonialism, as both an outlet for the white man's fears and fantasies, and a justification for his brutality." The mythic constructions of the sexuality of people of African descent in the United States took on pretty much the same forms and betrayed identical motives as those of the English colonists who generated similar propaganda regarding the virility and promiscuity of black people. Colonial Americans only added to British constructions of African male sexuality the belief that black men lusted after white women. During times of interracial crises these constructions seemed to circulate more widely and carry greater political force. Following the Stono rebellion in 1739, a story went around about how leaders of a prior slave revolt in 1730 had confessed before their execution that they had each chosen the "wife, daughter, or sister" of a white master for a "future bedfellow." Although there is "no evidence that any Negroes in revolt ever seized any white woman for their 'own use,' even though rebellious slaves certainly had opportunity to do so during the successful insurrections in the West Indies and also at Stono in South Carolina," white men still insisted that slaves plotted conspiracies in order to gain access to white women. Historians conclude that the fears of black male "sexual aggression during periods of alarm over insurrection did not represent direct response to actual overt threat, but rather a complex of reactions in the white man." The "increasing white obsession with physical violation" in colonial America "must be taken as an integral part of the white minority's wider struggle for social control."[28]

Ninety years after the Stono rebellion, southern proslavery ideologues pursued a different strategy for mobilizing public opinion about people of African descent in response to a different set of material conditions and social relations. The lascivious slave of myth was largely replaced by the equally mythic docile slave. Historians noted that "open assertions of *permanent* inferiority [of black people] were exceedingly rare" prior to the 1830s. After 1830, though, following the rise of organized abolitionism in the North, the proposal by progressive legislators to abolish slavery in the Old Dominion during the Virginia legislative debates in 1829–1830, and especially in the aftermath of the Nat Turner revolt, such assertions flourished, as did their inevitable counterpart—the "stereotype of the happy and contented bondsman." Although many southern ideologues still maintained their belief in what one of them called the "native barbarity and savageness" of people of African descent, they supplemented that stereotype with the new stereotype of the "Sambo" figure, a mythic type serving "to channel genuine fears and anxieties" into less distressing forms of condescension.[29]

It was neither colonial nor Jacksonian America that saw the most mature development of the mythic construction of African American sexuality, of course. That happened in the period between Reconstruction and the turn of the century, when African Americans first exercised political and economic power and simultaneously suffered social domination in the form of internal colonization. Ida B. Wells was among the first, and she remains one of the most incisively insightful, to analyze the "relation between political terrorism, economic oppression, and conventional codes of sexuality and morality." In response to the minimal gains made by former slaves, the white South rose up with a brutal history of violence, justified by the myth of the black rapist in lusty pursuit of white women. Indeed, the mythical black rapist was the exemplary figure in the "broader sexualization of politics in the Reconstruction South." What was particularly striking about this myth of the black rapist is that it seemed so thoroughly to repudiate the myth of the docile slave, the "Sambo" figure emerging around 1830, and to reconfigure the mythic slave rebel of the mid-eighteenth century. What appears to be contradiction, though, is actually the "oppositional logic underwriting the representational structure of black male images in nineteenth- and twentieth-century United States culture, a logic in which the discourse of sexual difference—from feminized docility to hypermasculanized phallicity—comes to play a primary significatory role." Whether it is docility or phallicity, the referent is always an indicator of the "unconscious formation of white masculinity."[30]

The same oppositional logic dictates Styron's choices, and the same formative discourse of white masculinity directs his representation of Nat Turner. He offers us portraits of either docile slaves or slaves who wish to perform violent rapes against white women. The male slaves in Styron's *Confessions* stand at two opposite poles, from the docile Hubbard, who represents "some grotesque harbinger of all in black folk gone emasculate forever" (363), to the exorbitantly libidinous Will, whose desire to murder is exceeded only by his desire to "get me some of dat white cunt too" (377). Standing between these two poles is Nat Turner, who dreams of rape, is represented as a walking phallus, and thinks of his place in the world in terms of his penis. Styron's representation of Turner in a condition of almost perpetual desire for white women, in a state of fantasy about raping white women, betrays precisely that complex of anxieties marking each stage of the mythic construction of the black male oscillating between docility and phallicity. By showing us what a slave revolutionary thinks about, Styron is replicating the stereotypes of those early colonists and post-Reconstruction ideologues. By incorporating these myths without attempting to disrupt them in any meaningful way, Styron suggests that whatever revolutionary violence slaves perform toward gaining liberty is motivated by libidinous desire for white women. Styron not only reverts to an atavistic mythic construction of the black rapist, but also perpetuates a dangerous misperception about the phallus.

By representing an African American male whose fantasies of violence revolve around his penis, Styron validates an instrumentalist theory of rape and celebrates the symbolic power of the male sexual organ. A few years after Styron's book appeared, Susan Brownmiller published her highly celebrated book, *Against Our Will,* in which she promoted an uninflected theory of an unhistorically specified patriarchal rape culture premised on the idea that "men rape because their penises possess the objective capacity to be weapons, tools, and instruments of torture." Her critics, notably black feminists, noted that Brownmiller's admittedly important book also constructed arguments "pervaded with racist ideas." Moreover, as other critics have pointed out, Brownmiller's theory of rape tends to support rather than contest the "quasi-invincibility of the male body." Of course, it is not scholars like Brownmiller who created that myth, nor is it important books like hers that do the most to recreate it. It is rather actively or unreflectingly masculinist discourses that perpetuate that myth. Police manuals, for instance, "often neglect to mention male genitalia when they designate the vulnerable points of a potential rapist's body," a neglect that perpetuates "the myth of the unassailably powerful penis." The way to dismantle that myth is to emphasize the "fragility" and the "vulnerability of male genitalia." As Richard Dyer has reminded those who need reminding, "penises are only little things (even big ones) without much staying power, pretty if you can learn to see them like that, but not magical or mysterious or powerful in themselves, that is, not objectively full of real power." We need to perform more such revisionist readings of the physical property upon which the symbolic power of the phallus is founded. Lynne Segal has brilliantly deciphered the "inner contradictions of 'masculinity'" by pointing out that while "on the one hand its symbol, the phallus, stands for adult human power and worth, on the other hand it is physically tangible only as a piece of biological equipment men share with rats, bats and every other higher vertebrate male."[31]

What is so exacerbating about reading the *Confessions of Nat Turner* is that Styron seems compelled by some weird but not hard to discern social force to retreat from his best insights into a grotesque and uncomplicated representation of the black phallus. His own writing elsewhere and, more important, his own novel suggest that he knows better. In a digression in a 1963 review, he had noted that the "concept of 'the white Negro'"—one aspect of which is the "caricature" of a "sexual carnivore of superhuman capacities"—is "preposterous" and nothing more than the product of "lampoons and vulgarizations" of African American culture, arising from "an imaginary notion of Negro life," and the product of a social "wish fulfillment." His representation of Reverend Eppes—the slave owner who asked Turner whether it was true that "a nigger boy's got an unusual big pecker on him" and then spends the better part of the summer trying to get into his slave's pants—is a devastating satire on those whose fascination with the black phallus impells them to master those they believe its possessors (237). Styron might well have modeled Eppes on a character in an anecdote James Baldwin could have told him.

Baldwin reported that once when he was in the South in the early days of the civil rights movement, one of the "most powerful men" in the state—a man who could "prevent or provoke a lynching" with one phone call—started to reach for Baldwin's penis. "With his wet eyes staring up at my face, and his wet hands groping for my cock, we were both, abruptly, in history's ass-pocket." Baldwin found it frightening because it was such an abject moment. As "my identity was defined by his power, so was my humanity to be placed at the service of his fantasies." This was a powerful man whose efforts could save or destroy lives. "Therefore, one had to be friendly: but the price for this was your cock." After a brief digression tracing this pathological situation back to slavery in America, Baldwin concludes that "it is absolutely certain that white men, who invented the nigger's big prick, are still at the mercy of this nightmare, and are still, for the most part, doomed, in one way or another, to attempt to make this prick their own."[32] Styron's representation of Eppes, whose desire for his slave's penis is at war with his desire for his slave's domination, is a brilliant example of this dynamic (239–40).

Despite this insight, which shows his refined sense of what directs and motivates white men's thinking when it comes to black men's penises, Styron's Turner still manages to think of his relationship to the world in terms of his plunging penis-first into it. Despite being able so finely to distinguish between the bodily woman he imagines raping and the emotion that enrages him—"pity alone . . . did this, not the woman herself apart from the pity"—Styron's Turner is apparently unable to distinguish his selfhood from his penis, nor to understand that there are other ways to commune with nature than to "plunge myself into it" and "to shoot milky warm spurts of myself into" it. (The lesson to be learned here is not to eat liver when you visit the Portnoy's, and not to go camping with Nat Turner.) Despite the various communications and visions Styron's Turner has with God, only an act of masturbation allows him to recall the name of his Savior. In each instance, it is Turner's penis that centers his activities toward others, his understanding of himself, his relationship with nature, and his hopes for heaven. Styron's representation is a gross measure of Turner's manhood, an exceedingly uninteresting sense of selfhood, and a not very refined or realistic sense of penishood. He would have done well not to celebrate the phallus with quite the eagerness he shows and to recognize that penises are, after all, only small and not particularly meaningful physical items. In other words, they are not things around which to construe selfhood, with which to commune with the natural world, or through which to achieve redemption and a place in the supernatural world.

In offering us a portrait of a black man who defined his identity around his penis while fantasizing about raping white women, Styron essentially rehearses the *topoi* of the mythic Reconstruction-era black rapist. Of course, at the heart of all mythic constructions of black male sexuality resides the mythic construction of black female sexuality. Images of black women as "hot constitution'd ladies" have consistently served to justify slavemasters' raping of slave women or to explain the excessive lust of black men infected by the libidinousness of their mates. As Angela

Davis points out, the "inseparable companion" to the "fictional image of the Black man as rapist" is the "image of the Black woman as chronically promiscuous." This nation was as true of the propaganda circulated in the 1870s as it was a century later in the early 1970s, which saw the "resurgence of racism" accompanied by a "resurrection of the myth of the Black rapist" and a recrudescence of the myth of the "oversexed-black-Jezebel."[33]

There are only two black women in Styron's *Confessions of Nat Turner,* each of whom represents an aspect of the myth of black female sexuality. The first is a "plump doxy," a kitchen maid "with a rhythmic bottom and round saucy eyes," who has the distinction of being the sole black woman of Turner's masturbatory fantasies. She is also the most sexually aggressive, "thrusting" her "glossy brown midriff" at Turner, "wheedl[ing]" him with offers of *"honeycomb, sweet pussy,"* while grinding her hips in his face. Called "every nigger boy's Saturday piece," this black woman represents the unholy temptation of unrestrained sexual license ("my Bible availed me none"), and explains the kind of lust exhibited by Turner, whose overwhelming desire following his fantasy of this black woman is to "penetrate" the flesh of "a young white woman," and Will, whose murder of white women takes on the appearance of rape, as he stands between his victim's "thrashing, naked thighs . . . in stiff elongate quest like a lover" (346–47, 390).[34]

The second black woman is Turner's mother, Lou-Ann Turner, who represents the inherently rapable black woman, the female equivalent and etiological cause of the black male rapist. The respondents wholly neglect both these black women. Although she is raped by the Irish overseer McBride, the respondents still claimed "there are no instances of rape in Styron's book."[35] This ignorance and omission are symptomatic of a more general social problem, in which public intellectuals and cultural commentators on American society discount the significance of violence done against African American women. We may call this attitude the "Bessie Mears phenomenon." Bessie Mears is the "other woman" Bigger Thomas murders; the Bessie Mears phenomenon is the remarkable absence of Bessie Mears in the critical discussion of *Native Son.* To look at the secondary literature on *Native Son,* one would not know Bessie Mears existed, that she and she alone was raped in the novel, that she and she alone suffered a willful and premeditated murder at Bigger's hands. It would be impossible, however, to find a single study of Wright's novel that omitted Mary Dalton, the white woman Bigger accidentally murders and is wrongly suspected of raping. The spectacle of a white woman's being raped or murdered by a black man is of such social import that the rape or murder of an African American woman becomes essentially absent, negated. As Margaret Whitehead is to Mary Dalton, so is Lou-Ann Turner to Bessie Mears.[36] In Styron's *Confessions,* so much attention goes to the way Margaret Whitehead is raped in Turner's imagination that it is hardly surprising to discover Lou-Ann Turner's actual rape is ignored.

Having said that, let me add that a reading of the scene in Styron's novel makes one wish Styron had not attempted to deal with the issue of a slave woman's being raped. What he ought to have done is simply said that Turner's mother was raped, an act that affected Turner enormously. He is successful when he has Turner refer to "the near-drowned yet lingering and miserable recollection of my mother in a drunken overseer's arms" (194). He is also successful when he informs us that

McBride has been fired because of his "lecherous ways." He is less successful when he resorts to euphemism—the "Irishman's encounter with my mother"—and suggests that McBride "never dared to approach her again" because he was "perhaps daunted by her basic unwillingness" (175). Where Styron is not only unsuccessful but in fact horrifically misguided is in actually attempting to represent the rape itself. As Nat Turner plays underneath the elevated house, he hears his mother singing a spiritual: "Bow low, Mary, bow low, Martha, / For Jesus come and lock de do', / An' carry de keys away." He then hears McBride enter the house and his mother resist him: "'Gwan outa here,' my mother cries. 'Gwan away! I ain't havin' no truck with you!' Her voice is shrill, angry, but edged with fear, and I can no longer understand the words as she moves to another part of the room above" (146). Rushing up to the edge of the house, Turner hears his mother say something "insistent, still touched with fear, but her voice is blotted out by the man's grumble, louder now, almost a roar" (147). He moves into the house just in time to see McBride holding the broken neck of a brandy bottle "like a dagger at [his] mother's neck" with one hand and fumbling at her clothes with the other. As he watches, Turner hears his mother's voice change: "a shudder passes through my mother's body, and the moan is a different moan, tinged with urgency, and I do not know whether the sound I hear now is the merest whisper of a giggle ('Uh-huh, aw *right*,' she seems to murmur)." He continues watching as "her brown long legs go up swiftly to embrace his waist, the two of them now joined and moving in that . . . strange and brutal rhythm" (147–48). Pleased with himself, McBride gives the field hands the rest of the day off, while, Lou-Ann Turner resumes her sweeping and her spiritual—"For Jesus come and lock de do' / An' carry de keys away"—in a voice "gentle, lonesome, unperturbed and serene as before" (150).

What precisely is Styron saying by showing us a slave woman who enjoys her rape to the extent of achieving orgasm and embracing her rapist? Or who resumes her singing and sweeping as if nothing had happened, her voice not even betraying a hint of the brutality she has just suffered? Albert Stone hardly succeeds in persuading us that McBride's rape of his mother provides Turner with his future "violent revulsion against both [black and white] cultures and the sexual basis on which they often conflict and relate." What would Turner find repulsive when his mother is represented as *enjoying* the rape? Rather, as both black reviewers and black critics noted, Styron's depiction is meant to prove that since the "incident has not troubled her" the "[r]umors about Negro women are true; they are more licentious than white women." Indeed, this representation of a woman who "enjoys being raped" is another way "Styron dehumanizes every black person in the book."[37] If this were an isolated incident in the novel, we might simply turn away, nauseated no less, but willing to ascribe to Styron yet another lapse in judgment (a serious and troubling lapse, to be sure).

But this is not an isolated scene; this confusion is arguably the very lynchpin of Styron's *Confessions of Nat Turner*. When he reflects from afar on the rape, it remains a rape, an act of violence; when he depicts the rape, the act of violence becomes an act of sex. It is quite simply Styron's fatal mistake, the error governing his reading of the social fabric of America, the error thoroughly directing and overdetermining his reading of Gray's *Confessions*. Here we get to the heart of what the critics say is wrong with Styron's work. Styron used troubling, vicious stereotypes from the ideological fabric of American society to produce a hypersexualized Nat Turner whose ideas about violence took on sexual forms, and an equally hypersexualized Lou-Ann Turner who feels acts of violence against her body as sexual expression. This hopeless confusion between sex and violence is something that plagues Styron's text, and, again, arguably against his own better judgment. In a spring 1968 symposium on "Violence in Literature," Styron commented on the social confusion of what he called the "cliché" linking "sex and violence." Violence, he noted, "is not like sex at all; it's quite the opposite. It's antipleasure."[38] Yet, when he represented a black woman being raped, when he represented a black rebel in the process of articulating his revolutionary sensibility, he could not avoid falling into the very dangerous cliché linking violence and sex. Let me be clear: I am not doing anything so absurd as denying that violence is always filtered through the socially interrelated terrains of race and gender, or, more specifically, that violence possesses its own deeply disturbing erotics, as Robin Morgan has recently shown. Nor am I disputing Catherine McKinnon's point that in a society in which "violence against women is eroticized as it is in this culture," it becomes "very difficult to say that there is a major distinction between being assaulted by a penis and being assaulted by a fist, especially when the perpetrator is a man."[39] What I am saying is that Styron's conflation of violence and sex in his representation of black men and women follows precisely the contours of historical American culture, taking its shape from the specific, long-enduring racist discourses used to demean peoples of African descent.

To summarize, then, we see how Styron manipulates two of the topics that form important coordinates within the hegemonic and emergent discourses and in the contested space between them: violence and identity. He represents Nat Turner's search for identity—religious, communal, personal—by showing us a man completely obsessed with his sexuality, most often expressed in fantasies of violent sexual domination. Styron uses rape as a trope for the kind of violence Turner imagines himself inflicting most commonly, while representing a hero whose personal identity resides in his penis (which he refers to as his "self" on more than one occasion). Quite simply, then, Styron uses sex to mediate Nat Turner's identity and uses violence to represent his sexual sensibility. Sensing that Styron mistreated the topics of the discursive formation connecting the antebellum past and the social movements of the 1960s and that he parodied the way Black Power intellectuals were redefining those topics through and in service of an emergent discourse, the critics argued that Styron's representation of a Turner whose vacillating sense of racial identity resides largely in his hypersexuality and is persistently fixed on his penis, his portrait of a revolutionary hero whose sensibility about violently overturning the social order is mediated through fantasies of raping white women, was particularly noxious because it would be read by the white literary establishment as a comment about contemporary black freedom struggles. Their fears were well founded, since mainstream reviewers felt that Styron's portrait of the slave rebel who confuses violence, identity, and sex leaves the reader "to draw his own connections to the Black Power movements of today."[40]

The third topic, property, was also deeply implicated in the debate over Styron's novel. As we saw in the previous chapter, the topic of property, when it was not about the potential political economies available to Black Power, defined debates over issues of cultural property and cultural appropriation. In the debate over Styron's *Confessions of Nat Turner,* the topic of property was about both economics and cultural appropriation, although primarily the latter. More specifically, the debate concerned Styron as someone whose reading of a text of slave testimony was determined by the hegemonic discourse on slavery, and particularly about how a hegemonic discourse creates a reading strategy premised on and reproduces acts of appropriation. The issue, then, is with Styron not as a writer, but as a reader, not as an individual who *produces* potentially resistant or potentially reactionary cultural work, but as an individual who *reproduces* the constellation of ideas sanctioned by the hegemonic forces. In response to Styron's reading strategies, the critics offer more promising and more resistant readerly options. In both cases, Styron and the critics are intent not only on reading the text they are reading, nor only on promoting one reading strategy as superior to the other, but also on constituting a readership in support of their intellectual formation.

Reading Black, White, and Gray in 1968

Although they were published only about seven months apart, Styron's novel and Clarke's anthology are products of two distinct climates of opinion and represent two distinct readerships, distinct not because of the race of the readers but rather because of how the acts of reading recreate prevailing schemes of racial difference. I would argue that this moment of extreme conflict between white and black intellectuals in 1968 helps us see how an intelligentsia with a racially defined subjectivity endorses a reading strategy which, in turn, consolidates and recreates that racially defined subject position. I would like, therefore, to explore how two distinct readerships take up a specific text and offer two revisionary readings of that text. By examining material practices of reading, we are able to see how specific readerships are solicited and altered by a given conflict. In 1968, the text both Styron and the critics take up is "Nat Turner." Their diverse readings of that text raise several key questions. What are the determinants of reading? How much do ideologies of the contemporary social order direct a reader's practices? How much do residually influential historical precedents of reading (what I call "first readings") govern a reader's actions? I would like to explore these questions by examining how Styron and the black critics read the text of Gray's *Confessions of Nat Turner.* Although Gray's text is not the only contemporary account—there were newspaper reports, and Samuel Warner published a book on the Southampton revolt before Turner had been captured—it is the document that directly or indirectly has "provided the basis for most of what has been written, in both a fictional and a pseudo-historical sense, about the Southampton Revolt." It is also the text Styron repeatedly called "the single document that means anything."[41] I will begin with what are arguably the "first readers" of Nat Turner.

Gray's *Confessions of Nat Turner* is a text with a curious dialectic, a collaborative effort in which the two collaborators not only are unequally situated but are in fact opposed in their motives for producing the joint work. While Gray was intent on developing a portrait of an aberrant and contained revolt that was the "offspring of gloomy fanaticism," Turner was creating a self-portrait of a heroic and divinely led prophet. While Gray wished to know only the "history of the motives" for the revolt, Turner wished to use the opportunity of the interview to construct a history of himself. This is a crucial event in the history of African American self-representation, since Gray's *Confessions* contains the "first significant chronology of an African American life in southern literature." Because this text is based on a "diametric" or "antagonistic collaboration," we should think of "Nat Turner" as a "product of the dynamics of the text itself," examining where Gray attempts to contain and suppress "Turner's revolt by situating it within a description of fanaticism" and where Turner is able to assume a degree of subversive subjectivity when Gray suffers "a momentary lapse in the countersubversive regulation of his own language."[42]

One of those key moments in the text occurs when Gray collects himself to pronounce on the alleged dementia of his subject. "He is a complete fanatic," writes Gray, "or plays his part most admirably." Despite his stated goals of containing the revolt and preventing the spread of fear of future revolts among the citizens of Virginia and North Carolina, Gray cannot ultimately suppress his abiding suspicion that he has been an unwilling accomplice in the production of an image or idea Turner controls. He cannot finally say he understands the essential madness of this man. Turner could well be a consummate actor and Gray an unwilling director not fully in control of the production he is about to issue. Each time Gray attempts to offer a portrait of a singularly demented villain, he is forced to acknowledge the humanity and superhumanity of his subject. Wishing to impress his readers with the fact that Turner still bears "the stains of the blood of helpless innocence about him," Gray nonetheless cannot keep himself from commenting also on the fact that Turner is "clothed with rags and covered with chains." The body of Nat Turner, in other words, not only is a spectacle of guilt because it is stained with the blood of his victims, but it is also a commodified, ill-treated, and captive entity. Describing the "expression of his fiend-like face when excited by enthusiasm," Gray feels simultaneously impelled to note that Turner dares to "raise his manacled hands to heaven, with a spirit soaring above the attributes of man." In Gray's internally divided portrait, Turner's face may be demonic but his actions tend toward heaven. Although he began his narrative with the stated intent of laying to rest the "thousand idle, exaggerated and mischievous reports" which excite fear in the "public mind," Gray himself concludes his last look at Nat Turner with exactly that same fear he had set out to exorcise: "I looked on him and my blood curdled in my veins."[43] As a reader of Nat Turner, then, Gray is forced to attest to the ambiguity and the heroic nature of his subject. His madness might be a semblance, his religiosity might be sincere.

A year after Gray published his *Confessions,* Thomas Dew, professor of political law at William and Mary (later, president of the college), wrote what most historians consider the first book-length proslavery argument. Responding to the Virginia legislative debates of 1831–1832 concerning the future of slavery in the Old Dominion, Dew wrote a tract showing the prohibitive cost of emancipation, concluding that "the time for emancipation has not yet arrived, and perhaps it never will." At the very outset, Dew situates his text in relation to the Southampton revolt. As much as does Gray's *Confessions,* then, Dew's book employs a strategy of containment, of noting the aberrant nature of that insurrection and of showing the folly of pursuing a course of political action in any way conditioned by the aftermath of that revolt. He points out the foolishness of Virginia legislators' even choosing to debate the possibility of emancipation just six months after the revolt. "Any scheme of abolition proposed so soon after the Southampton tragedy would necessarily appear to be the result of that most inhuman massacre." Once slaves get the idea that their violent actions can lead to political changes, then in all probability, Dew notes, slaves will create more insurrections. Dew's major strategy is to show that the economics of emancipation make impossible any political program for it; his supplementary minor strategy, though, is to revise the popular understanding of the Southampton revolt and its leader. "Any man who will attend to the history of the Southampton massacre," he writes, will see at once that the revolt was the product of a "demented fanatic" and could have been prevented by one good white man. Had "Travis, the first attacked" woken up when Turner had the ax over his head and "shot down Nat or Will, the rest would have fled, and the affair would have terminated *in limine*." Dew was here exaggerating an idea the press had propagated as its containment measure. The *Richmond Whig,* for instance, asserted "that 20 armed whites would put to the rout the whole negro population of Southampton." According to Dew, that would have been nineteen whites too many.

Mostly, though, Dew is concerned with containing the character of Nat Turner, which he does in two ways. First, he castigates the representation of discontented slaves and those who offer those representations—the abolitionists in the Virginia legislature, those political malcontents who are "subversive of the rights of property and the order and tranquillity of society." What they do, Dew argues, is "commit the enormous error of looking upon every slave in the whole slave-holding country as actuated by the most deadly enmity to the whites, and possessing all that reckless, fiendish temper, which would lead him to murder and assassinate the moment the opportunity occurs." They are grievously in error, he claims, because slaves are servile, dependent, abject, and cheerful beings. The typical Virginia slave in his or her "[c]heerfulness and contentment" is the "most harmless and happy creature that lives on earth." He remarks on the "quiet and contentment of the slave who is left unemancipated." He notes that the slave has the "intellect only of a child" and ought not to be set free in the "infancy of his uninstructed reason." The slaves of a good master are "his warmest, most constant, most devoted friends." A "merrier being does not exist on the face of the globe than the negro slave of the United States." Writing the first proslavery tract in America, Dew produces the "Sambo" stereotype in response to the fear aroused by Nat Turner's revolt. The myth of the docile slave, then, emerged from a specific historical moment in response to the planter class's anxiety about Nat Turner.[44]

The second strategy Dew employs is to produce a reading of Gray's text that reduces or eliminates the ambiguity in Gray's own reading of Nat Turner. The Southampton revolt, writes Dew, "originated with a fanatic negro preacher (whose confessions prove beyond a doubt mental aberration)."[45] Gone is the suspicion that Turner might be acting, eliminated the speculation that Turner might have had cause for his revolt, removed beyond a shadow of a doubt the idea that Turner might actually have had communication with that heaven he sought with his manacled hands. In place of that ambiguity there is now a mentally aberrant preacher, nothing more.

To put it another way, Dew's reading strategy is to remove the "Gray" from the text and make it a "black" and "white" issue. These two first readings of Nat Turner, then, constitute the prehistory of the contemporary debate over Styron's novel. We can call the method of reading Nat Turner as an ambiguous heroic revolutionary the "Thomas Gray reading strategy," and the method of reading Nat Turner as an unambiguous religious fanatic the "Thomas Dew reading strategy."

Having before us the two contemporary, historically specific methods of reading Nat Turner, we can now turn to William Styron as a reader of Nat Turner. Since Styron presents himself as a reader of Gray's text, it is imperative for us to know what kind of readerly strategies he employs. The first thing we need to do is to examine his interviews both before and after the publication of *William Styron's Nat Turner: Ten Black Writers Respond;* this will give us a sense of Styron as a reader in relation to the two first readings of Nat Turner (the Gray reading and the Dew reading). Once we have determined how Styron represents himself publicly as a reader of Gray's text, we can examine how he realizes his reading strategies in the production of his novel itself. In the interviews he conducted before the novel became engulfed in controversy, Styron consistently does two things. First, he praises Nat Turner's intelligence and takes an almost quixotic view of *his hero.* Second, he suggests that the Margaret Whitehead connection is part of his reading of Gray's *Confession* and he takes an almost quixotic view of *his book.* Then in the interviews conducted after the controversy, he takes less quixotic attitudes toward his hero and his book. (By "quixotic" here I mean what Cervantes represented in his most famous character—a man unable to make too fine a distinction between himself and his reading, his life and his book.)

In a 1963 interview, Styron says that Turner was "an extraordinary man," a "man of heroic proportions." In a 1965 interview, Styron says that after he gave a reading at Wesleyan University, a student asked him whether someone like Nat Turner would think in the literary language Styron gave him. Styron responded sharply: "I had to tell him—I'm afraid it embarrassed him—that I found that question very condescending to Negroes." Turner, he insists, "was a very complicated man. . . . He was educated—not highly educated, but a man, I think, of some genius—and therefore one has to allow him a mode of expression which will take in these complexities." He adds that Turner's education "gave him a sense of his own worth as a human being." Indeed, Turner was "one of the few slaves in history who achieved an identity." Two things helped him imagine Turner. First, living with James Baldwin allowed him to conceive of "a black Negro, not a, you know, white Negro, but a black, black homely Negro" who possessed a sparkling intelligence. Second, he had to empathize with his hero to the degree of "turn[ing] myself into a unique slave." Once he accomplished this act of supreme sympathy, Styron assumed a quixotic relationship with Nat Turner: "If you start finding out about Nat, discovering things about Nat, well, of course, every passage, every chapter, every section is kind of a revelation both for yourself and for Nat."[46] It is not only impossible to discern whether Styron is talking about his fictional Turner or the historical Nat Turner; it is intriguing to find him talking about his fictional creation as a living being.

Now there is nothing unusual about that. Most novelists who talk openly about their creative impetus say that they not only inhabit their fictional characters, but they live with them. Few, however, so quickly turn on their characters and banish them from the house of fiction. In the interviews following the publication of the Clarke collection, Styron no longer talks about that heroic, intelligent, complex, educated man who was a "genius" of sorts. Instead, Styron now insists that "any intelligent person" who read the original *Confessions* would be "appalled," because the Nat Turner found there is "not very heroic looking at all." Indeed, the historical Nat Turner "was an almost insanely motivated religious fanatic" with a "deranged mind." As a writer, Styron asserts, "I took the perfectly legitimate liberty of humanizing this man, or monster, by giving him a rational revolutionary plan, plus other talents." No longer quite so confused about the space between the historical and the fictional Nat Turners, Styron notes that "the real Nat Turner as opposed to the one I created were and are two different people." Indeed, it is safe to say that Styron is no longer Don Quixote; he has become Dr. Frankenstein. "I," he intones, "I gave this man a dimension of rational intelligence which he most likely did not really possess." As recently as 1992, he suggested that in his "countless" readings of Gray's *Confessions* he had "early on" discovered that Nat Turner was "a person of conspicuous ghastliness," a "madman" who was "singularly gifted and intelligent," but "mad nonetheless." In the end he had to conclude that "on the record Nat Turner was a dangerous religious lunatic."[47]

The image one gets here is of Styron as an unstable reader, a reader whose whimsy and whose current politics direct how he publicly represents his reading strategies, and whose quixotic attitude toward his characters sometimes leaves him slightly confused about the difference between historical figures and fictional characters. The important point, though, is that Styron's unstable reading strategy is not arbitrary. What he does, in fact, is enact each of the two first readings of Nat Turner. He reads as Gray before the controversy and as Dew after it. In neither case does he betray his novel, though, because he wrote a book in which he exhibits both the sympathetic ambiguity of Gray and the rigid containment strategy of Dew. The difference, however, is that Styron did not use religious fanaticism as his "Dew point," but rather sexual obsession. As we have seen, the debate over Styron's novel is conducted around the figure of Margaret Whitenead, whom Styron makes the object of Turner's most violent sexual fantasies and his most troubling religious epiphanies. More important, Margaret Whitehead also constitutes the figure around whom Styron organizes his reading of Gray's *Confessions*. She is a historical figure present in Gray's *Confessions;* and in both Styron's mind and those of his critics, she is linked to an absence in Gray's *Confessions,* namely Nat Turner's wife.

In 1992, Styron used the occasion of the twenty-fifth anniversary of his novel to elaborate on how he read the absence of Turner's wife in Gray's text. In the "process of using the *Confessions* as a rough guide," he writes, "I was struck by the fact" that Turner never refers to a "woman in a romantic or conjugal sense." This "absence was quite significant and I had to use my intuition to guess at its meaning." His intuition led him to read that absence in terms of the presence of the one woman Turner murdered during the insurrection—Margaret Whitehead. Although at first he intended to make the relationship between Whitehead and Turner a relatively minor episode, he says he was "drawn irresistibly" to their relationship which he then explored more fully in the novel. According to his critics, Styron's omission of Turner's wife was deliberate since he used that absence to produce a sexually repressed black man constantly lusting after white women. As we saw earlier, both the critics in 1968 and later scholars have shown that not only is there abundant contemporary evidence attesting to the existence of Nat Turner's wife, but there are sound reasons for Turner's not wishing to reveal her existence to Thomas Gray. We also now know that Styron himself knew of the existence of Turner's wife, since he wrote in the margin of page 33 of his copy of William Drewry's *The Southampton Insurrection*—"Nat's wife: Fannie?"—while also speculating, on the margin of the front blank sheet of that book, whether "Nat has seen his wife seduced by Travis."[48]

One can hardly fault Styron for failing to read an absence in a text; so, although he knew of the existence of Turner's wife, his desire to remain faithful to Gray's *Confessions* must have prohibited him from mentioning her. That leaves us with the question of Margaret Whitehead. She is mentioned in Gray's text, and she is apparently the only person Nat Turner did kill. Styron's greatest achievement, it seems to me, is to have worked into the very fabric of his novel a reading of Gray's text in which the murder of Margaret Whitehead signifies Turner's love or lust. Styron repeatedly said that he based his reading of Turner's alleged lust or love on two crucial points: first, Nat Turner murdered only Margaret Whitehead, and second, "after that murder his insurrection seems to quickly run out of speed," "collaps[ing] internally once he has killed." In any case, he adds, "[t]hat's what my reading of the *Confessions* tells me." Fascinated by the fact that Turner murdered only one person, Styron argues that there "must have been—I say *must* have been because I have no proof, but I'm convinced—some kind of relationship between the two, and I think it was a very guarded sexual relationship." With that theory in place, Styron is left with no readerly options but to draw the conclusion he has already arrived at. "I can't explain otherwise the fact" that Turner killed only "this one girl, an eighteen-year-old girl who's the only nubile girl, so far as I can find out, killed during the insurrection."[49]

Unfortunately, Styron is mistaken in each of his premises. Margaret Whitehead was not the only young woman killed during the Southampton insurrection. The slave rebels also murdered a seventeen-year-old woman who was engaged to be married the following day. Moreover, as Lerone Bennett pointed out in regard to Gray's *Confessions,* there was a compelling reason Turner murdered only once. Nat Turner was "the *leader* of the Southampton insurrection" and "generals seldom kill." In Gray's *Confessions,* Turner himself explained his role in the revolt: "I took my station in the rear, and as it 'twas my object to carry terror and devastation wherever we went, I placed fifteen or twenty of the best armed and most to be relied on, in front, who generally approached the houses as fast as their horses could run; this was for two purposes, to prevent their escape and strike terror to the inhabitants—*on this account I never got to the houses, after leaving Mrs. Whitehead's, until the murders were committed,* except in one case. I sometimes got in sight in time to see the work of death completed, viewed the mangled bodies as they lay, in silent satisfaction, and immediately started in quest of other victims" (emphasis added). For the most part, as might be expected of "General Nat," Turner was directing rather than performing the sanguinary work of the revolt. Finally, there is hardly any warrant for suggesting that the revolt "runs out of speed" after Turner murders his one victim. After the rebels leave the Whitehead household, they are prevented from murdering more families only because the families to whose houses they go have already fled. Nonetheless, after Nat Turner kills Margaret Whitehead, the rebels do go on to kill 27 people. Since that number constitutes practically half the total killed during the Southampton revolt, it is absurd to say the revolt "collapsed."[50]

Despite his mistaken premises, or perhaps because of them, Styron's reading of Gray is interesting precisely because we learn a great deal from what Styron chooses to omit or highlight in his rewriting of Gray's *Confessions*. Consider how Styron represents the acts of violence Turner inflicts on the three people he attempts to murder: Joseph Travis, Mrs. Newsome, and Margaret Whitehead. In the first section of the novel, Styron quotes Gray's text on both of Turner's unsuccessful attempts. Styron has Gray read back to Turner the attempt on Travis: "it being dark I could not give the deathblow, the hatchet glanced from his head" (38). Gray also reads back the incident regarding Mrs. Newsome: "I took Mrs. Newsome by the hand, and with the sword I had . . . I struck her several blows over the head" (39). Yet in the third section, when Styron has Turner recall the events of the insurrection in his own mind, unmediated by Gray, these two events are vastly revised. On the initial attempt, Styron has Turner miss Travis "by half a foot, striking not Travis's skull but the headboard between him and his wife" (388). Then he has Turner miss a second time, the "outside of the blade glanc[ing] lightly from [Travis's] shoulder" (389). In the third section also, Mrs. Newsome disappears entirely and is instead replaced by two anonymous victims whom Turner fails to kill. He recalls that "two times when I had raised the glittering blade over some ashen white face, only to have it glance away with an impotent thud or miss by such an astonishing space that I felt that the blow had been deflected by a gigantic, aerial, unseen hand" (403–4). Styron's revision of Gray's version of the attempt on Travis's life is pretty easily explained; he wants to make Turner an irresolute and thoughtful individual for whom murder did not come easily. So he has him miss twice instead of once, and ensures that he never hits Travis on the head.

His decision to eliminate Mrs. Newsome is more complex. Not only did it serve Styron's purpose to have Turner fail to murder twice more instead of once, but it also allowed him to eliminate the only other woman Turner attempted to kill. It would indeed have proved difficult for Styron to include Mrs. Newsome, because his confusion between violence and sexual desire would not permit it. Let me explain what I mean by returning to an interview in which Styron demonstrates his readerly strategies. Because the original *Confessions* "are sketchy," he notes, he had "to read between the lines constantly" in order to achieve "the kind of insight I did." The insight is that "since Nat killed no one else, and he killed this beautiful girl, considered one of the belles of the county, the psychological truth was that Nat did not hate her. He loved her, or at least had a passion for her." To buttress this logic, Styron adds: "I believe this must have been true. I cannot prove it. I think that if there is any psychological truth in these insights, it partially lies in the fact that one often wishes to destroy what one most earnestly desires."[51]

What Styron seems not to notice is that he has twisted the connection between sexual desire and the desire to destroy. There clearly is some "psychological truth" in Styron's insight; what one does desire one sometimes destroys. But that is not what Styron argues in his reading of Gray's *Confessions*. His argument is that since Nat

Turner destroyed Margaret Whitehead, he must have desired her. Rather than arguing that one's desire sometimes results in violence to the desired object or person, he is arguing that Turner's violence signifies desire. In the one instance, violence is an aberrant effect of desire; in the other, desire is diagnosed through acts of violence. We know nothing about what Nat Turner felt for Margaret Whitehead. We know he killed her. From this information, that Nat Turner performed a violent act against her (because he happened to be in the right place at the right time, as Gray's *Confessions* show), Styron deduces that he desired her. Violence is interpreted as desire.[52] By removing Mrs. Newsome from the novel, Styron is able to maintain that Turner acted on his violent desire only with Margaret Whitehead.

· It is clear from Styron's statements in his interviews that Margaret Whitehead is the figure on whose presence he fundamentally bases his reading of Gray's *Confessions*. Indeed, one could say that Margaret Whitehead is nothing less than the figure Styron uses to inhabit and then appropriate Gray's *Confessions*. We saw that one of the ways Styron situates his novel in an intertextual relationship with Gray's is by quoting descriptions of Turner's acts from Gray's text in the first section of the novel and then rewriting those descriptions in an entirely different and more graphic way in the third section. This strategy of situating his novel intertextually in relation to Gray's *Confessions*, however, is only ancillary to Styron's most concerted strategy for appropriating Gray's text. The means Styron uses to appropriate Nat Turner and Gray's text is his exaggerated reading of Margaret Whitehead, which in turn is based on his confusion between violence and sexual desire.

Styron's fundamental representational strategy in that attempt is to appropriate Gray's *Confessions* and to place himself in Gray's stead as "Nat Turner's Last White Man." He does this first by giving his book the same title as Gray's pamphlet, then incorporating Gray's text into his novel. In the "Author's Note" introducing his *Confessions,* Styron calls Gray's text the "single significant contemporary document concerning this insurrection" ([xi]). He then prefaces his *Confessions* with Gray's own preface, entitled "To the Public" (xv–xviii). Finally, Styron exerts his energies in a concerted effort to situate *his* Thomas Gray (character) as *the* Thomas Gray (author), and *his* Confessions as a "dangerous supplement" to Gray's *Confessions*. He begins by having his narrator define the limits of the text of Gray's *Confessions*. When he is unable to respond to Gray, Styron's Turner thinks to himself: "I couldn't—not because there was no reply to the question, but because there were matters which had to be withheld even from a confession, and certainly from Gray" (34). He goes on to inscribe his very silence into the text. "It was impossible to talk to an invention, therefore I remained all the more determinedly silent" (35). Later, Turner will reinforce this skepticism: "I wondered just how much of the truth I was telling him might find its way into those confessions of mine that he would eventually publish" (393).

Styron also casts doubts on Gray's *Confessions* by suggesting the text was a collaboration and not simply the autobiographical musings of Nat Turner. When Gray reads back part of Turner's statement, Turner is confused about the voice: "His words (mine? ours?)" (37). At the same time, Styron insinuates that in his *Confessions* Turner is now telling the truth he was unable to tell Gray. Turner prefaces a description of his masturbatory fantasies with a Rousseau-like honesty: "I should tell it, even though it concerns a matter I would hesitate to dwell on had I not resolved to make this account as truthful as possible" (172). He refers to the text containing information not found in Gray's *Confessions* as "this account of my life" at the same time that he suggests that this is information he told Gray ("I told him. . . ," "as I told Gray") (247, 252). Toward the end of the third section, Gray returns to the scene, bringing with him the material text: "the folded paper notes to my confessions" (392). Again, Styron's Gray pretends to have information the historical Nat Turner never offered the historical Thomas Gray (394).

Finally, Styron has the character of Gray validate the text we are about to read by reading into it precisely the one point Styron used to read Gray's *Confessions*. Styron's Gray prefaces his reading of Gray's *Confessions* by suggesting that he will pause over the interesting facets of the text: "while I recite the entire thing out, there are a few items that I haven't gotten entirely straight in my own mind and I want you to clarify them for me if you can" (29). He pauses over two "items." The first concerns Turner's decision to murder a master he considered "kind" (33–34). The second concerns the fact that Turner murdered only once. Gray addresses Turner on what he insistently calls this "main" point: "the main point is this, which you didn't tell me in so many words, but which I'm going to bring out now by deductive reasoning, as it were. The main point is that in this whole hellish ruction . . . you, Nat Turner, were personally responsible for *only one death.* . . . How come you only slew one? How come, of all them people, this here particular young girl?" (36–37). Gray will repeat this "main point" in the courtroom as a way of explaining the motivation for Turner's rebellion.

When Gray addresses the court, he asks generally pertinent questions regarding Turner's motives—"How did it happen? . . . From what dark wellspring did it flow? Will it ever happen again?"—before offering the sole source of the answers to these queries: "The answer lies here, the answer lies in the confessions of Nat Turner" (83–84). The "confessions," of course, are the ones to follow, not the 1831 text. But that confusion between the two "confessions" is necessary for Styron to incorporate his major readerly interpretation into his novel through the mouth of Gray. Moreover, Styron's Thomas Gray has now become Thomas Dew. His purpose in addressing the court, he says, is "to demonstrate that the defendant's confessions, paradoxically, far from having to alarm us, from sending us into consternation and confusion, should instead give us considerable cause for relief" (84). Unlike Dew, however, Styron's Gray does not relieve public consternation by arguing that Turner is a religious fanatic. The public has no reason to fear, he says, picking up a copy of the confessions, because "Nat Turner was personally responsible for only one murder. *One murder*—this being that of Miss Margaret Whitehead" (84). The answer Styron's Gray offers for Turner's motivation centers entirely on the fact that Turner murdered only Margaret Whitehead, "a young girl in all her pure innocence." While the murder of Margaret Whitehead is itself "inexplicably motivated, likewise obscurely executed," Gray nonetheless intimates that it is clearly the lynchpin in understanding Turner. Styron's Turner himself will attest as much. As Gray's voice drones on in the courtroom, Turner suddenly recollects several moments he shared with Margaret Whitehead, noting each detail about her appearance, her smell, her words. In other words, both Gray in court and Turner in his mind make Margaret Whitehead the central figure in the drama about to unfold (88). While Gray refers to the second, third, and fourth sections of the novel as the "confessions of Nat Turner," which will answer his questions about motives, it is clear that the answer is the one given at the end of the first section. As Styron's Gray makes explicitly clear both to Turner himself in his reading of Gray's text and to the court that convicts Turner, the answer is Margaret Whitehead.

She is also the figure through whom Styron publicly revises and appropriates Gray's *Confessions*. Just as Styron had assumed a quixotic attitude toward his hero when he spoke about Nat Turner in his interviews, so, too, when he talks about the figure of Margaret Whitehead he tends to assume a quixotic relationship to his book. His early comments to interviewers suggest that he was in the process of interpreting Gray's text. In one interview, as I noted earlier in this chapter, he asserted his belief in a relationship between the two. In another interview, he suggested the same thing: "I believe this must have been true. I cannot prove it." When he was interviewed by George Plimpton, though, Styron was no longer interpreting Gray's text; he thought that his text had become the reality of Nat Turner's life. "Nat's feelings for her," he tells Plimpton, "were just as I described them in the book." Turner "was smitten by her, this paragon of the unobtainable, in some obscure and perilous way so that the killing of her was not only a matter of working out his frustration but possessing her soul and body as well."[53] In Styron's mind, then, Styron's *Confessions* became Gray's *Confessions*. The historical Nat Turner felt for Margaret Whitehead just what Styron's *Confessions* tells us he felt. In his public representation of his book, Styron was arguing that his novel was no longer a reading but an enactment of historical fact.

The ten black critics were absolutely correct, then, when they contended that Styron was deliberately misrepresenting an African American revolutionary hero and simultaneously appropriating the autobiographical document containing the written record of his life. Given the way Styron was representing his novel as being true to "the *known* facts," and given that historians were praising him for doing nothing less than producing an exact replication of Gray's text, it is no wonder the critics felt compelled to return to and produce a corrective reading of Gray's *Confessions,* insist on divorcing Styron's version of Nat Turner from Gray's version, and demonstrate how Styron uses Margaret Whitehead as the figure through whom he appropriates Gray and transforms Turner. The critics also raised a set of questions about the historiographical representation of slavery, racial politics in the field of cultural production, and the relationship between the social order and a literary text. They saw that Styron buttressed the failing but still dominant view historians took of American chattel slavery, while also indirectly but ruthlessly criticizing the Black Power movement. They also saw that the novel was being circulated and received as a master text in the white literary establishment. Their book was the first in a series of attempts by African American intellectuals to counter the effect of Styron's text by showing the failings of the hegemonic climate of opinion about slavery, asserting the cultural principles of Black Power, and directly contesting Styron's reading of Gray's *Confessions*.

William Styron's Nat Turner: Ten Black Writers Respond was not so much a reaction to Styron's novel as it was an exposition of the conditions that made the novel possible. At the same time, the Clarke collection was also a testament to the changing conditions in American intellectual and social life in 1968. Indeed, this remarkable volume was not so much a reflection of the changing social conditions of the late sixties as it was part of the shifting power relations in cultural affairs in this period. The writers in the Clarke collection not only defined the hegemonic forces directing Styron's reading of Gray's *Confessions,* they also determined the historical resources and materials necessary to disrupt that intellectual hegemon, including slave testimony, folklore, and oral reminiscences. In initiating a project respecting slave testimony, altering the historical debate over slavery, and creating the conditions for a new historiographical portrait of slavery, the Clarke collection also set the agenda for the later fictional representations of slavery appearing between the seventies and the nineties. The Clarke collection not only used slave testimony strategically in its own volume, but also had a noticeable effect on the study of slavery and the collection of materials for future study. Here, I can best specify that effect on historical scholarship by examining the immediate change in the collection of material on the historical Nat Turner in the aftermath of the controversy over Styron's novel.

The writers in the Clarke collection demonstrated how the complex of ideas operative in the hegemonic climate of opinion governed Styron's reading of Gray, insisting that Styron's reading strategy was deliberate (there is a "pattern in his distortion of the facts") and significant ("the pattern is meaningful"). They argued that Styron "forces history to move within the narrow grooves of his preconceived ideas" formed by the climate of opinion about slavery coalescing around the belief that slaves were docile (Elkins) and that their families provided no meaningful countervailing support against the destructive aspects of enslavement (Moynihan). The critics demonstrated how Styron deliberately pursued a reading of Gray's *Confessions* premised on these two theses by showing precisely where and why Styron misquoted Gray.[54]

At the beginning of the novel, after Styron's Gray tells Turner he is "going to read the whole thing [the *Confessions*] out to you here," he starts quoting liberally from Gray's text (29). In one instance, he reads out a passage about Turner's early life: "And my mother strengthened me in this my first impression, saying in my presence that I was intended for some great purpose" (31). In Gray's *Confessions,* though, the passage runs as follows: "And *my father and* mother strengthened me in this my first impression" (italics added). Whereas in Gray's text Nat Turner had referred to "my grand mother, who was very religious, and to whom I was much attached," Styron's Turner refers to "My mother, to whom I was much attached" (31). Styron has the grandmother die before Turner is born and he takes away her religiosity altogether. Whereas Turner tells Gray he grew up among slaves in his community who would often consult him when they pursued any "roguery," Styron has his Turner exhibit fairly thorough disgust with the field hands and nothing resembling respect or affection for other slaves (except Willis and Hark). Where Turner tells Gray he learned to read miraculously amid his family—given a book to stifle his crying, he starts spelling words to the "astonishment of the family"—Styron has the white Miss Nell teach Turner to read. In each case, Styron rewrites Gray's text so that Turner's family plays a less significant role. By eliminating Turner's father, negating the extended family, and diminishing the importance of an extended communal network, Styron produces what the critics called "a proper ADC slave family" and "a wretched precursor of the Moynihan report." The critics strenuously objected to this effort to read a text of slave testimony through the filter of the hegemonic discourse. That was what they called the "deliberate" distortion of Nat Turner's own account of himself, and that is why they, unlike some scholars, did not believe that "Styron's slight departures from the text of the original *Confessions* are beside the point."[55]

They also objected to the ways Styron employed Moynihan's own precursor, Elkins, whose main thesis Styron consistently praised. In a 1963 review of Herbert Aptheker's *American Negro Slave Revolts,* Styron gave his most complete remarks about Elkins's book. Comparing Aptheker's argument about the ubiquity of slave revolts with Elkins's contention of their absence, Styron concluded that Elkins's book was a "brilliant analysis" which produced an accurate portrait of what "must have been the completely traumatizing effect upon the psyche of this uniquely brutal system, which so dehumanized the slave and divested him of honor, moral responsibility, and manhood. The character (not characterization) of 'Sambo,' shiftless, wallowing happily in the dust, was no cruel figment of the imagination, Southern or Northern, but did in truth exist."[56] Despite his thorough admiration for Elkins, Styron did not produce a novel that is in any way a simple replication of the Elkins thesis. He portrays some slaves who were defiant, such as Nelson (who resisted his master's attempt to whip him), and others who were in the process of being transformed from "Sambos" into revolutionaries, such as Hark, whose response to spilling white blood was to feel himself no longer a "servant of servants" but rather a "killer of men" (100, 391). Although Styron created a few slaves who were sometimes able to shed their servile and infantile personalities, most of the slaves Turner meets are in some way or other deeply wrought variants of the "Sambo" character.

The critics found Styron's use of the Elkins thesis also part of the "pattern" of reading the African American past. Not only does Styron recreate the stereotype of "Big Black Sambo," but he actually has the effrontery to put the "Sambo thesis in Nat Turner's mouth."[57] After toying with the idea that a "Sambo" personality structure might be only an elaborate act, Styron's Turner concludes that it is truly the dominant personality structure of African American slaves. He notes that in the presence of white people Hark became "the unspeakable bootlicking Sambo"; the "very sight of white skin cowed him, humbled him, diminished him to the most fawning and servile abasement" (55, 57). Styron's Turner also insists Hark is *acting* as a "Sambo" in order to play a role that protected him, both before and after his transformation into a "killer of men." Treating Hark as "a necessary and crucial experiment," Turner sets out to "destroy that repulsive outer guise" of "Sambo" and nurture "the murderous fury which lay beneath" (58). At the end of his experiment, Styron's Turner recognizes that there might be slaves like Hark, slaves who possess an inner personality core that is not ultimately servile and infantile, while at the same time he is forced to acknowledge the "painful fact that *most* Negroes are hopelessly docile" (58, emphasis added). In the end, the majority of the slaves are not like Hark or Nelson but more like Hubbard, "some grotesque harbinger of all in black folk gone emasculate forever" (363).

What the critics objected to was that Styron utterly ignored the fact that his reading of slave personality-types was based on the strategy of containment employed by the proslavery polemicists in the aftermath of the Nat Turner revolt—that is, the myth of the docile slave was precisely the response of ideologues such as

Thomas Dew to the specter of Nat Turner. They pointed out that the "Sambo" ste-reotype was created amid particular social conditions attesting to particular class anxieties. If "the majority of slaves were inert 'Sambos,' broken in mind and spirit, as Styron's Nat suggests," then why did southern state governments fill the "official record with so many requests for federal troops to guard against insurrection?" By failing to recognize that the "Sambo" stereotype was created in the aftermath of the Nat Turner revolt as a means of controlling the ramifications of that revolt, Styron was unable to see "that antebellum southerners and their modern descendents had to believe that Sambo existed in order to deal with the contradictions of their own existence."[58] Both the "antebellum southerners" fearful of slave rebels and "their modern descendents" afraid of Black Power created stereotypes and dominant dis-courses to dispell and contain the forces they feared.

Having shown that Styron's reading strategy was governed by the dominant his-torical representation of American slavery and the political representation of con-temporary black family life, the critics then challenged what they considered Sty-ron's act of cultural appropriation. They issued that challenge by first showing how Styron misread the dynamic features of African American history and culture through the filter of an eroding discursive formation. Then, by appending to their own volume a significant piece of slave testimony, they criticized the methodologies of those historians who produced that discourse by denying the value of slave narra-tives to their historical work. They pointed out that Styron's Turner was a response to a certain political imperative and was founded on a reading strategy itself based on a certain set of historical statements that no longer possessed the validity they had assumed five years earlier. They insisted that the portrait of Turner that Styron drew was, like Thomas Dew's, based on the needs and demands of a white cultural imperative attempting to deny the meaning of slave resistance (in Dew's case) and the significance of contemporary Black Power politics (in Styron's).

Appending Gray's *Confessions* to their text as a way of returning the written his-torical record to public discourse so that people could see how Styron read and mis-read that remarkable piece of slave testimony, they also attested to the emergence of new, literary Nat Turners whose own voices, unlike Turner's, needed no Gray inter-mediary. They claimed in their text, preceding the one in which Nat Turner spoke for himself, that the Nat Turner representative of African American cultural life "still awaits a literary interpreter worthy of his sacrifice." The volume resonated with this point. Clarke introduced the volume by maintaining that "our Nat is still waiting" and Thelwell concluded it by stating that the history of Nat Turner "remains to be written." Immediately thereafter, as a guideline to what would be written, came the 25 pages of Gray's *Confessions*.[59] In this volume, Nat Turner was the eleventh black writer to respond. The critics challenged Styron's local reading of Gray and, more generally, addressed themselves to the climate within which Styron and other histo-rians read slave testimony.

The Discourse Mobilized

This debate in American literary history had significant ramifications, both immedi-ate, affecting the readerships that entered and emerged from it, and enduring, altering the scope of later American cultural representations of slavery (both historical and fictional). In other words, this literary debate, the site of contestation between historiographical schools, the terrain on which were defined the terms of cultural appropriation and the significance of a Black Power intelligentsia in the post–civil rights era, helped mobilize the emergent discursive formation on slavery. We can see in what ways this discourse was mobilized by examining how historians, social activists, organic intellectuals, and cultural workers read Nat Turner after Styron. On the one hand, Styron largely succeeded in appropriating Gray's text and making his novel the major intermediary for Nat Turner's life for the majority of readers who published their responses to the novel in the mainstream press. The white literary establishment received the novel with virtually unanimous acclaim, while historians like Woodward, Duberman, and Genovese validated it. As a sign of how completely Styron managed to appropriate Gray's *Confessions,* consider that Genovese presumed to change the title of Gray's text. Since "Styron's novel has the same title as that Gray gave to the original," he writes, "I shall refer to the latter as Turner's *Testimony.*" By giving Styron's book the title, Genovese indicates that the novel supplanted the original, and that device, one assumes, pretty well left Styron entitled to tell the story of Nat Turner. As another comment on how successfully Styron appropriated Nat Turner himself, we can cite the fact that in 1969 James Cone was compelled to add a caveat to his list of the heroes of black consciousness: "Nathaniel Paul, Daniel Payne, Nat Turner (not Styron's), Marcus Garvey, Elijah Muhammad, and Malcom X."[60] A final indication of Styron's successful appropriation of Gray's text is the fact that later historians of Turner's revolt would read Gray's *Confessions* through the filter of Styron's novel, attempting to answer the questions Styron posed to that text or to represent in an overdetermined fashion those features of Nat Turner's life that Styron eliminated.

Stephen Oates's essay on the Southampton revolt in the October 1973 issue of *American Heritage* is a case in point. On the one hand, Oates performs solid revisionist work in returning to the historical record what Styron removed from it or in correcting what he distorted. Oates insistently restores Nat Turner's family—in one paragraph he notes that "[b]oth parents praised Nat," that "[h]is mother and father both told him that he was intended for some great purpose," and that "Nat was also influenced by his grandmother." He also asserts the existence of Nat Turner's wife, Cherry. On the other hand, Oates feels compelled to respond to Styron's reading of Gray's *Confessions* by accepting the presuppositions Styron articulated through his fictional Thomas Gray. Oates probes into the reasons Turner did not kill more people, something he describes as a mystery: "a fatal irresolution? the dread again?" When he reads the description of Turner's three unsuccessful attempts at murder, he spends an inordinate amount of energy trying to explain Turner's failure, using intentionalist language to describe Turner's attempt on Mrs. Newsome's life— "evidently he could not bring himself to kill her"—instead of analyzing any connection between Turner's lack of success and the inutile weapon he was using. Because his attention is so preoccupied with a desire to answer Styron's question about Turner's failure to murder more, Oates is compelled to pursue his own misreading of Gray's text.[61] Some historians believed Styron to be faithful to Gray's account; others, contesting Styron's fidelity to Gray, felt bound to respond to those very questions Styron had posed to Gray's text.

A final sign of Styron's success is that he has been able to promote himself as the "origin" of the contemporary interest in Nat Turner and to convince others that he has the right to the title. In a letter responding to Oates's article, Styron claimed full responsiblility for the interest in Nat Turner exhibited by historians "happily engaged in the cottage industry I established." Through the years, he has continued to express wonder "at the bustling cottage industry which *The Confessions of Nat Turner* spawned during the subsequent years."[62] The critical and historical work on Nat Turner has been voluminous: two collections of materials, one edited by Eric Foner (1971), the other by Henry Irving Tragle (1971), as well as two casebooks, one edited by Melvin Friedman and Irving Malin (1970), the other by John Duff and Peter Mitchell (1971), and two historical studies of the Southampton rebellion, F. Roy Johnson's *The Nat Turner Story* (1970) and Stephen Oates's *The Fires of Jubilee: Nat Turner's Fierce Rebellion* (1975). (But there are also works published before Styron's novel appeared: F. Roy Johnson's earlier book, *The Nat Turner Slave Insurrection* [1966], and Daniel Panger's novel *Ol' Prophet Nat* [1967]; the trouble with "origins," of course, is that one needs to deny so much to establish them.)[63]

A more important point Styron neglects to mention, though, is that these later books also do what he failed to do, and precisely what his critics accused him of failing to do: consult the folk traditions of African Americans. In his collection of material pertaining to the revolt, Foner has sections on nineteenth-century African American historians' representations of Nat Turner, on literary and journalistic representations of Nat Turner in the 1880s, and on the centenary of his revolt in 1931, as well as a section on the contemporary "folk memory of Nat Turner." Tragle not only compiled all the relevant written historical material on the Southampton insurrection, but he also interviewed some 60 individuals regarding the folk tradition of the insurrection. After traveling to Southampton County in 1969 and interviewing both European Americans and African Americans living there, Tragle determined that it is "possible to say with certainty that Nat Turner did exist as a folk-hero to several generations of black men and women who have lived and died in Southampton County since 1831." Johnson added 35 pages of "new material provided by Black tradition and white tradition" to his second book on the Southampton revolt, drawing on "hundreds of folk tales," on William Drewry's interviews with 72 residents of Southampton County, and on his own interviews with an "even larger number of persons." In researching his book, Oates also traveled to Southampton County in the summer of 1973 in order to consult African Americans living there about the folk tradition of Nat Turner.[64]

These later writers and collectors took up the important point raised by Albert Murray in his review of Styron's novel and Vincent Harding in his critique of it. When Harding said that Styron did not use the "living traditions of Black America" (repeating Murray's point that Styron did not employ the insights from "Negro folk heritage"), Genovese took issue with the statement, arguing that "we have yet to be shown evidence that slaves and postslavery blacks kept alive a politically relevant legend of Nat Turner." Indeed, Genovese went so far as to call Harding's claim a "pretense" and argue that "if the existence of armed resistance to slavery is now generally appreciated, William Styron deserves as much credit as any other writer." In his response, Harding rightly took exception to Genovese's assumption of claiming to know "what is alive and well in the continuing traditions of Black America," and he raised the crucial issue of what Genovese meant when he used "we" so freely. There is "another 'we,'" writes Harding, "the black part of the pronoun, one might say," who live in the black tradition and who have a claim to be heard when stating a living knowledge about Nat Turner. Harding lists Frederick Douglass, Samuel Ringold Ward, Henry Highland Garnet, Harriet Tubman, and H. Ford Douglass as people who knew what it was to live with the "memory of Turner." He offers a succinct bibliography of black journals and materials that contained information about slave resistance well before it occurred to Styron to inform African American people of this tradition. And finally, Harding mentions the folklore, particularly the folklore passed on by "great-grandparents and grandparents," the folklore generated within families between generations.[65]

In another forum, held the day before Harding's rejoinder was published, in the panel discussion at the Southern Historical Association in New Orleans on November 6, 1968, Ralph Ellison informed William Styron himself that African American familial oral lore contained historical figures from slavery, including figures associated with slave revolts. "This record exists in oral form," noted Ellison, "and it constitutes the internal history of values by which my people lived even as they were being forced to accommodate themselves to those forces and arrangements of society that were sanctioned by official history." Encapsulating what the black critics collectively maintained, Murray, Harding, and Ellison inform their white would-be informants that there is another historical, living tradition, what Ellison elsewhere called "our familial past," providing a supplementary and often subversive version of the past contained in the "official versions."[66] The work produced on Nat Turner after the controversy over Styron's novel took seriously what Ellison, Harding, Murray, and the black critics in general were saying by researching the oral, the familial, and the cultural traditions in black America.

It is important to note how the critics' comments affected later work on Nat Turner, because they alert us to the fact that Styron was not completely successful in appropriating Gray's *Confessions*. While his novel may have conditioned some future readers of Gray's *Confessions* to pursue answers to those questions Styron thought worth asking, the Clarke collection was able to initiate another project, one of collecting and making public the folk heritage and unwritten history of African American cultural life under slavery. In retrospect, we can see that the project of collecting and publishing the oral testimony of ex-slaves and the descendants of ex-slaves changed the reading patterns of those who approached slave testimony for the next three decades. The critics argued that the "[e]vidence and materials concerning the slave culture and world view, although largely ignored, do exist," and the "reality of slavery" is to be found in the "testimony of the slaves themselves." What the critics argued in 1968 was also the centrally contested point in the debate over Elkins between 1967 and 1970.[67] In a large measure, it was the Clarke collection that opened up a new space and initiated a new interest in the resources available for those historians who wished to see slavery from the slave's point of view; and it was the debate over Styron's novel in general that determined the tenor of the historiographical debate in its final years in 1969 and 1970.[68] More important, the writers in the Clarke collection also demonstrated that reading is itself an activity governed by institutional and social forces.

Because it did that, the Clarke collection also had an almost immediate effect on the readership that had so highly praised Styron's novel. Consider, for instance, the altered strategies of two readers, a reviewer and a historian. In a *New York Times* review of Styron's *Confessions,* Eliot Fremont-Smith claimed that Styron's novel "resurrects" and "is based on" Gray's *Confessions.* Indeed, the novel "faithfully reflects the voice of the real Nat Turner as it comes through in the actual confessions." So thoroughly does he believe Styron's accuracy that he himself reads Gray's *Confessions* through Styron's eyes, thinking there are only two pertinent questions asked in Gray's *Confessions*—why did Nat Turner kill a kind master and why did Turner kill only once?—which are precisely the questions Styron put into his fictional Gray's mouth. In his *Village Voice* review of Styron's *Confessions,* Martin Duberman also believed Styron faithful to the historical record, arguing that Styron's "determination to be true to the past," his "insistence on historical authenticity" in paying his "scrupulous debt to the past," led him "to put aside his subjective vision, his own truth, in order to serve those twenty-odd scraps of paper we call Nat Turner's 'confessions.'"[69] Both readers believed that Styron produced the definitive reading of Gray's text. Once the Clarke collection entered public discourse to show that Styron was neither scrupulous in his debt nor so bound to Gray's text, readers had to reassess their reading strategies.

In those reassessments, Fremont-Smith and Duberman both denied the validity of the very text they had earlier praised Styron for reading and bringing to life. Fremont-Smith had to admit that Styron's reading of Gray was not definitive, that it was, in fact, a "characteristically callous white-liberal appropriation of a Negro hero for the purpose of containing and destroying his mythological potency." The "actual confessions" Styron had once rendered so faithfully now became one "myth" among several. Duberman, too, had to admit that the "original confessions" were "filtered through the eyes and words of a white man and therefore automatically suspect," adding that he had been "wrong in saying that Styron had kept scrupulously . . . to all the details of Nat Turner's original 'confessions.'" After noting that the black critics effectively showed how "Styron did change or omit a number of details in the confessions," Duberman implicitly admitted that the Clarke collection's intervention had caused him to question his own local acts of reading. Although he had read "those confessions so many times in the past," and had quickly reread Gray's text once again when reviewing Styron's novel, it took the critics' reading to show him how his own (and Styron's) reading strategies were determined by the social conditions forming the hegemonic climate of opinion in America in the mid-sixties.[70]

We can see, then, that the debate over Styron's novel helped mobilize the emergent discourse on slavery and transformed the cultural habits of an American readership. Historians began to gather materials from the folklore and oral traditions of African American heritage, thus altering the field within which slavery and slave resistance would be studied in the future. For instance, before 1968 Genovese had been extremely skeptical of the historical value of slave testimony; after 1969, after participating in the debate over Styron's novel, Genovese had a radical change of heart, began heartily to endorse the use of slave testimony, and reimagined the project he had been working on to reflect his new attitude. The product of that change was, of course, the 1974 massive and groundbreaking *Roll, Jordan, Roll: The World the Slaves Made.*[71] Other readers of Styron's novel began to question their own strategic placement, institutionally and socially situated to read in a certain, determined way. Following the debate of 1968, historians of American chattel slavery pursued the critics' point about slave testimony in a more systematic and concerted fashion, while readers of America's slave past learned to be vigilant about their own cultural location by bringing folklore and other forms of the oral tradition to bear on the subject of slavery. From these conditions would emerge the contemporary narratives of slavery, especially the Neo-slave narratives.

These intellectual realignments and conversions represent a broader shift in American society in the post–civil rights era, linked directly to the emergence of Black Power. That African Americans developed a newly empowered sense of black subjectivity and a renewed respect for black cultural practices and imperatives positively affected writers of contemporary narratives of slavery. Most contemporary authors would agree with Sherley Anne Williams that while the civil rights movement was important because it "gave would-be writers of new African-American histories and fictions the opportunity to earn financial security and thus the time to write," it was essentially "the Black Power movement that provided the pride and perspective necessary to pierce the myths and lies that have grown up around the antebellum period as a result of Southern propaganda and filled us also with the authority to tell it as we felt it." There were also crucial institutional factors that made possible this renaissance of black writing about slavery. In the late sixties, publishers and other cultural institutions opened up some space for African American writers. A *Newsweek* story in the summer of 1969, entitled "The Black Novelists: 'Our Turn,'" said there was a "black revolution" in literature, on which the publishing industry was quick to capitalize. Previously uninterested publishers began "scrambling to add black writers to their lists" in the late sixties. And, of course, with the development of Black Studies programs in northern, predominantly white universities between 1968 and 1969, there was a new demand for texts written by African Americans.[72]

The late sixties, then, saw a social change with the emergence of Black Power, an intellectual change with the development of New Left social history, and an institutional change with the opening up of new opportunities in publishing and teaching black-authored texts. These changes together formed the conditions that led to the renaissance of African American writing about slavery for the next three decades. It is not hard to see how the debate over Styron's novel played a large role in both signifying the need for and promoting those changes. The writers in the Clarke collection constituted the vanguard of the Black Power intellectuals who initiated the challenge to the "Southern propaganda" about American slavery. They also represented New Left social history in insisting on examining slavery "from the bottom up" by incorporating the testimony of slaves into the historical record. The Clarke collection also attested to the existence of an emergent new readership whom publishers would see as an opportune market, since one of the things reviewers repeatedly noted is that *William Styron's Nat Turner: Ten Black Writers Respond* addressed a new kind of readership and presupposed a militant black audience.

These social, intellectual, and institutional changes in American cultural life made possible the contemporary representations of slavery in African American writing. Addressing a readership alert to new historiographical work on the strength of slave communities and the importance of slave culture, a readership formed largely out of the debate over cultural propriety and appropriation, the authors of the seventies and eighties produced contemporary narratives of slavery that reflected and helped create a new climate of opinion about the American past, distant and recent. The Neo-slave narratives in particular insistently view slavery from the slave's point of view, raise issues regarding cultural appropriation, and reflect on their moment of origin in the Black Power movement. While Styron adopted the slave narrative form in his *Confessions,* he oscillated between the Dew and the Gray reading strategies. In contrast, the authors of the contemporary narratives of slavery in general, and the Neo-slave narratives in particular, employ oral productions that test the limits of and ultimately subvert the authenticity of any "official" history and challenge the presumed authority of those "first readers." These novelists establish a dialectic between slavemasters' oppressive literary representations and the slaves' own liberating oral witnessing of slavery, staging a struggle between a form of writing that would master and the practice of self-representation that would free the slave.

This changed attitude toward oral production—the collective folk heritage Murray advised Styron to consult, the generational folklore Harding defined, and the familial narratives to which Ellison attested—marks what might be the most important development in the narratives of slavery. With that development, the contemporary novelists signaled their departure from the reading strategies of Styron's generation. They would read absences in the historical record with more knowledge of how that record is compiled by acts of exclusion, with more of a sense of how the authority claimed by an official historical record is often a result of its ignoring or rendering mute the testimony of its exploited victims. They would attend more carefully to what is present in that existent record and not misread it through an overzealous desire to find in it what Murray calls the "folklore of white supremacy and the fakelore of black pathology."[73] Finally, they would supplement that record by incorporating into it the previously excluded testimony. They would transform the record and simultaneously reconstruct its readership. Following those brave critics of 1968, contemporary novelists of slavery have incorporated into their novels a sensibility about oral productions of knowledge that causes their own readership to distrust the borders of anything in black and white, and, in this particular case, in Gray.

So far, I have suggested that the debate among Styron, his critics, and his respondents helped initiate a new attitude toward the fictional representation of slavery by mobilizing a new discursive formation wrought out of the rise of New Left social history and the emergence of Black Power. It will be the burden of the next four chapters in this book to demonstrate how each of the Neo-slave narratives participated in that debate, particularly how they engaged in a dialogue whose terms were set by the writers in the Clarke collection. The Clarke collection is also responsible for the fictional treatments of slavery in the seventies and eighties in a more meaningful and direct way. In situating itself as the inevitable, corrective intertext to Stryon's text, the Clarke collection also irrevocably wed Stryon's *Confessions* to its historical moment, the era of Black Power. That intertextual relationship set the conditions and established the dialogic principles from which the Neo-slave narratives of the seventies and eighties would emerge. The Clarke collection played a fundamental role in establishing itself as the intertext to Styron's novel, situating both novel and intertext as symptoms of the emergent Black Power movement, and thus setting up the conditions that would govern the discontinuous intertextual relations the later novels would generate as they negotiated the historical moment when the Neo-slave narrative form first emerged, and signaled their entry into the dialogue, their participation in the discontinuous intertextual relationship, their meditation on the sixties.

The resolution to the debate over slave testimony is crucial to the development of the Neo-slave narrative for several reasons. First, the historical acceptance of slave testimony as a valid form of evidence about the past invigorated the movement toward writing fiction from a slave's point of view. Once the antebellum slave narrative was recuperated as a class of writing whose authenticity was not in doubt, this narrative form offered prospective novelists a new vehicle through which to explore the representability of slavery. Second, the fact that this debate was conducted *through* the debate over Styron's *Confessions* raised questions about a different kind of authenticity, about authorial prerogatives and the racial dynamics of American literary culture. The first debate was over the voice of the slave—the second over the voice of the novelist who would represent the slave; not only what the representation of slavery would be like, but who would do the representing. The issue was cultural appropriation.

In addition to contributing to the historiographical debate over slavery, the Clarke collection also proved invaluable for future fictional treatments of slavery as it came to represent the countervailing force to Styron's novel itself. When he listed those books produced through the "cottage industry" he felt he established, Styron attempted to suggest that one of them was *William Styron's Nat Turner: Ten Black Writers Respond*. His attempt to contain the Clarke collection as but another of those craft industry products his corporation spawned is belied by his ever-evident anxiety regarding that volume. He realized the Clarke collection was something new in American letters and represented a novel political force in American literary culture, that it constituted, in his words, "the first time in this country that an entire book was devoted to an attack on a novel." This was not an intellectual force he could dimiss or wish away, although he attempted to do both. Instead, he pretty well reconciled himself to the fact that the Clarke collection was going to be read alongside his novel. In fact, he was dismayed when he discovered that the Clarke collection had become standard reading for some Black Studies courses in which his novel had not been assigned. He was dismayed partially because he felt he was being slighted, but also because he had come to accept that the Clarke collection inhabited his text the same way he had inhabited Gray's text. Styron's later critics also support this consensus that the two books existed in a unique relationship, since virtually all these critics devote some portion of their criticisms of Styron's novel to discussing it in terms of the Clarke collection. It was their tacit understanding that the Clarke collection was the inevitable intertext to Styron's novel, that the reader should read Styron's novel "in conjunction with" the Clarke collection.[74]

What the Clarke collection did more than anything else when it established itself as the intertext to Styron's novel is irrevocably wed Styron's *Confessions* to its specific historical context. Later scholars have not found it easy to remove Styron's novel from the first site of its reception; they have first had to disentangle it from the controversy (which they claim was "local") before they could claim that Styron was truly dealing with the classical humanist themes of spiritual alienation, religious piety, or heroic self-discovery (which themes they claim are "universal"). Typically, these scholars argue that the black critics adopt "a sixties point of view" when they take "a social-political position on Turner" and claim "him as their own," while Styron "took an almost purely literary position, claiming him for both whites and blacks."[75] In other words, they want to deny that Styron's novel is a social product belonging to its historical moment of production and reception in order to transform it into a literary artifact.[76] Styron, too, attempted to divorce his novel from its social conditions, imagining the different reception his novel might have been accorded if it had been published in 1948, before "the anguish and the wrench of contemporary events caught us up," or if he had not been white, or if New Criticism were not then in decline and his work had been read as "an aesthetic object" instead of a social one.[77] In his efforts to salvage the reputation of his novel, Styron wants to escape history, race, and cultural politics, attempting to transcend precisely those political issues the black critics defined as the ways to understand and transform the field of cultural production situated in a fundamentally unequal society.

Styron's attempt to remove his novel from its political moment was doomed, though, not only because any attempt to escape history is futile, but also because the Clarke collection ineluctably fixed Styron's *Confessions* in its specific social milieu. In establishing itself as the inevitable intertext to Styron's novel, the Clarke collection situates Styron's *Confessions* as part of the very debate over Black Power. By 1968, Black Power had become not only the context for, but pervasively present in, the debates over the historical and cultural representations of slavery. Noting that Styron's novel was "no mere 'fiction,' but a cultural and social document" very much about "contemporary attitudes" toward the latest developments in the struggle for freedom in the late sixties, the critics explored and deplored its handling of those important Black Power topics of violence, identity, and property.[78]

The critics raised the issue of violence not only to question Styron's representation of a rebel ambivalent about committing physical violence against the body of his enslavers, nor only to criticize the ways Styron uses violence to represent the imaginary of interracial sexuality in the mind of a black man, but mostly to comment on the ways historical and fictional representations such as Elkins's and Styron's conspire to commit psychological violence against contemporary African Americans. Styron's text operates as a function of the "violence of representation," not the violence of contesting or resisting a social order, but rather a violence signifying precisely a "power struggle for the *maintenance* of a certain kind of social order." This was precisely the point of Styron's critics, that the novel was "a project of destruction involving the vitals of the historical personage named Nat Turner." Such a project of destruction served to disembowel not only one individual, but the heritage of an entire social group, constituting an attempt "to kill, to obliterate a complete historical and political tradition of black people."[79] The violence, then, was systemic and part of a long-term project of historic attempts to dismantle the integrity of black American social life. It was just this kind of systemic violence against cultural integrity and its effects that black consciousness was meant to contest.

Just before and immediately after the call for Black Power, African Americans started to use "Nat Turner" to signify revolutionary black consciousness. Malcolm X found Nat Turner an exemplary revolutionary since he did not preach "'non-violent' freedom for the black man." The editors of *Negro Digest* introduced their reprinting of Thomas Gray's *Confessions of Nat Turner* in the July 1965 issue of the journal by asserting that to "millions of American Negroes, then and now, Nat Turner, the insurrectionist, was a hero." Julius Lester noted the affiliation between the most famous African American slave rebel and the "angry children of Malcolm X," each of whom was potentially a "young Nat Turner." He repeated his point about the inner cities in the North. "Today we have our Nat Turners on the street corners of every ghetto." Harding referred to "Memories of Nat Turner" in the emergence of the Black Power movement, hoping that the time would not make it necessary for young revolutionaries to have to raise again "Nat Turner's rusty sword." Addison Gayle held up Nat Turner as a philosopher of action and an antecedent of Black Power who demanded "*destruction* of the oppressive apparatus not *coexistence* with it."[80]

In the discourse of Black Power, then, Nat Turner constituted a cultural property and a social identity for African Americans. Styron's representation of him and the rebellion he led was an act of appropriation of that cultural property. Harding considered the "whitened appropriation of our history" tragic because it signifies a "total negation of our power and our truth, indeed an ultimate betrayal of all creative power and liberating truth." What African American intellectuals need to do, he concluded, is reclaim that property and reconstruct the historical and fictional representations of slavery with cultural productions from "the bittersweet bowels of our blackness."[81] The other issue connected to the topic of property concerned a fundamental ambiguity in Black Power itself. For some Black Power advocates on the left, Black Power meant socialism and they espoused revolutionary reconstructions of the American social order, while Black Power advocates on the right argued for "Black Capitalism" and endorsed mild reforms and accommodation to the present American social order. What Styron did in his novel, according to the critics, is take the rebellious Nat Turner, who heralded and augured Black Power, and transform him into a conservative, almost reactionary figure. "Styron's Nat Turner" was what Thelwell, following convention, called a "house nigger" who thereby represented "the spiritual ancestor of the contemporary middle-class Negro."[82] Styron had taken the historical figure who had become resonant as a social identity for the revolutionary faction of Black Power and created him anew as a symbol of the conservative faction of Black Power.

Nat Turner, then, was an especially prominent part of the discourse of Black Power, and Black Power a dominant factor in the intertextual relationship between Styron's *Confessions of Nat Turner* and Clarke's *William Styron's Nat Turner: Ten Black Writers Respond.* This debate over the historiography of slavery, the cultural propriety of representing the "slave's point of view," and the issues and topics of Black Power constitutes the moment of origin for the Neo-slave narratives of the seventies and eighties. Products of the emergent discourse on slavery that values slave testimony, reevaluates slave personality, and respects the quality of slave resistance, the four novels discussed in the next four chapters adopt the same form of first-person representation of slavery that white reviewers believe Styron to have inaugurated and that the black critics believe Styron to have appropriated. Moreover, these novels not only take on the form of the Neo-slave narrative, but they also constitute acute reflections on the moment when that discursive formation coalesced and assumed a prominent place in the historiography of their subject. Each of the Neo-slave narratives published in the seventies and eighties would take up the issue of Black Power, partly because each of their authors came of intellectual age and started writing during the Black Power movement, but also because each employs a form whose prehistory is firmly situated in the era of Black Power. In short, these novels establish a discontinuous intertextual relationship with the moment of their formal origins.

4

The Possession of Resistance

Ishmael Reed's Flight to Canada

When the first of the Neo-slave narratives appeared in 1976, the "sixties" was be-coming an object of discourse, criticism, and ambiguous nostalgia, a process that began in the late sixties, gained strength in the early seventies, and flourished in the bicentennial year. There were good reasons both for the rise in nostalgia in the sev-enties and for the ambiguous character of that nostalgia. For one thing, the seventies was a pallid decade marked by political corruption, social indifference, and economic malaise, whereas the sixties, the early to mid-sixties at least, had been politically ide-alistic, culturally adventurous, and economically healthy. America, held metaphori-cally hostage by OPEC at the beginning of the decade, literally hostage by Iranian fun-damentalists at the end of the decade, in the seventies lost its leadership position in the world as the "American century" came to a close after only 28 years (1945–1973). Domestically, the decade was marked by social crises stemming from the ruthlessness of the Nixon administration (Kent State, Jackson State) and the political corruption leading to those crises (the invasion of Cambodia) and following them (Watergate). "It was the worst of times, it was the worst of times," *New West* magazine eulogized. Al-though the decade had its share of historically significant social events and cultural developments, to most people it was a time when "it seemed like nothing happened." In these conditions, then, it was hardly surprising for contemporary cultural criticism to become excessively nostalgic for the heady times of the civil rights movement, the New Left, and the counterculture.[1]

The seventies, however, was also a decade of political confusion, diffusion, and polarization, a time when those people Michael Harrington saw "moving vigorously to the Left, the Right, and the Center, all at the same time" could not and did not share in the ascendant nostalgic mood. Indeed, one of the characteristics shared by the emergent New Right and neoconservatives was their resolute antinostalgia for the sixties, by which they meant primarily the Democratic Party of Kennedy and Johnson whose left-liberal political economy they eschewed, the New Left activists of SDS and SNCC whose strategies for social transformation they deplored, and the zealots of the counterculture whose personal and communal values they found abhorrent. Echoing the growing conservative constituency and the corporate sector of the country, who criticized the 1960s as a "time of excess," what the 1975 Trilateral Commission called a "democratic distemper," the popular media of the seventies reveled in stories of sixties activists' "conversions." The *U.S. News and World Report* smugly reported that "many former radicals or dropouts have become entrepreneurs," while Morley Safer noted there was little "counter about the counterculture" of the seventies as he walked down Telegraph Avenue on *60 Minutes*. "Returns" were a staple item in the news, as activists associated with particular sites revisited those sites during the seventies, as Mario Savio did Berkeley and Mark Rudd Columbia. So, too, were stories of prodigal sons emerging from exile, as both Abbie Hoffman and Eldridge Cleaver did in 1975. Cleaver's story was especially prominent in the national media, much being made of the fact that he had found patriotism and religion while in exile. The former Black Panther Party Minister of Information, who used to speak of American "facism" in the sixties, now proclaimed that despite its faults "the American political system is the freest and most democratic in the world." The former member of the black separatist Nation of Islam became an evangelical Protestant who believed in "the limitless possibilities of the American dream." For neoconservatives like Daniel Moynihan and Norman Podhoretz, both of whom donated money and hosted fund-raising parties for Cleaver's defense fund, these stories were welcome news that what a 1977 issue of *Time* magazine called the "long hallucination of the 1960's" was finally over.[2]

For liberals and leftists, including the radical black journalists who called Cleaver a "Patty Hearst in reverse" and a "Bicentennial coon," these "media obituaries" were "partly expressions of wish, partly sighs of relief, and partly arguments against resurrection" of the sixties spirit. Inspired by the social quiescence of the seventies, the reactionary neoconservative mood of the times, and their own midlife crises, former sixties activists began to develop either a revisionist or an ambivalent nostalgia about this period of their lives and this epoch in American history. One study of the "sixties generation" noted that by the "mid-1970s, sixties revolutionaries felt compelled to reassess their fundamental beliefs about the potential for reform, free expression, and normal politics in the United States," generally abandoning "their revolutionary commitments" while preserving their identity as "radicals." While some were recovering from the sixties in various forms of therapy, echoing Carl Oglesby's sentiment that "the best part of the struggle was the surrender," others were either continuing their political work under less glamorous conditions or actively recharacterizing and then entering the "system" they had earlier opposed. Tom Hayden, as one famous example, ran for a seat in the U.S. Senate in 1976, proclaiming: "the radicalism of the sixties is the common sense of the seventies."[3] Among sixties radicals, America's bicentennial occasioned another kind of nostalgia for more recent origins.

In American fiction, too, the sixties was being figured anew as writers of various political persuasions attempted to portray the ambivalent nostalgia of the time. In her 1976 novel *Meridian,* for instance, Alice Walker gives us a compelling portrait of former civil rights workers who long for and are critical of the days of the southern civil rights campaigns at the very moment they seem destined to enter into petit bourgeois lives. Acknowledging that the "theme of the sixties" was revolution, but also certain that "all that is gone now," one of her characters spends his time "making a statue of Crispus Attucks for the Bicentennial," claiming that he is a revolutionary only insofar as "all artists are." Walker's representation of Truman Held's ambivalence—creating art simultaneously revolutionary and patriotic—captures the late seventies sensibility about the sixties. "It was a decade marked by death. Violent and inevitable." But it was also a decade marked by collective youthful energy and a social commitment no longer in evidence in the seventies. In the midst of what one historian called the "torpid, constricted climate of the seventies," the "sixties," an entity some were calling "less than an epoch but more than an episode," had become "the watershed of our recent cultural history."[4]

The year 1976 also marked the end of the Black Arts movement, the cultural arm of Black Power. Ceasing publication in 1976, *Black World,* the major journal of the Black Arts movement, issued key statements critical of the cultural values and literary production of the Black Power sixties. Nathan Hare noted that the "Black Movement of the 1960's grew introverted and turned upon itself," arriving at an "ultra-nationalism that was mystical, messianic and hence dysfunctional." The literature of that period, according to the even more blunt George Schuyler, was "crap" and "dribble." Just as the intellectuals of the Harlem Renaissance had done in 1935, so too the architects of the Black Arts movement renounced their earlier manifestos and statements on the function of African American artistic production. At the height of the movement in 1968, Larry Neal had strenuously argued that "the artist and the political activist are one," that the Black Power movement required a "new sense of literature as a living reality," that "Black literature must become an integral part of the community's life-style" instead of being an exercise in "dead forms." By 1976 he was arguing that "propaganda" did not allow the African American artist to "perform the highest function of his art: that of revealing to man his most enduring human possibilities and limitations," that the black artist had to be open to the "accumulated weight of the world's aesthetic, intellectual, and historical experiences," and that without a respect for "form" or "art as method" instead of "art as experience," art itself was "futile."[5]

Socially, politically, and culturally, the mid-seventies was a period of ambivalence, as some movements came to an end while others were being resurrected in a community of memory. In the midst of this revisionist social moment, with its shifting aesthetic values and right-leaning politics, Ishmael Reed published a Neo-slave narrative that took up the aesthetic, political, and social issues raised during the Black Power movement, negotiating anew those topics of violence, property, and identity that organized the sixties' debate over Black Power and the representation of American slavery in historical and fictional texts. *Flight to Canada* is important because it is the first Neo-slave narrative mobilized by the new discourse on slavery, appearing at a key moment when the "sixties" itself became an object of historical study and a subject of political debate, and representing a crucial statement in Reed's personal, political, and aesthetic development. In this novel, Reed makes some of his most considered comments about the literary politics of canonization and cultural appropriation, while also ambivalently figuring his responses to the social politics of Black Power. The novel, then, is part of the general temper of the mid-seventies in being critically nostalgic of the social movements of the sixties; but, more important, this Neo-slave narrative is also specifically in dialogue with the sixties and the cultural and political debates of that epoch in national life, because they constitute the moment of its formal origins.

I will here consider how Reed negotiates the Black Power politics of the sixties and the literary politics of the Neo-slave narrative form, first by examining his shifting attitudes toward the Black Power sixties, second by discerning in what ways *Flight to Canada* poses a dialectic between violence and property as it establishes itself as an active participant in a relationship of discontinuous intertextuality with the cultural debates of the sixties, third by discussing how Reed uses this dialectic to articulate his ideals and principles for a renewed social order, and finally by analyzing the methods by which *Flight to Canada* conceptualizes the constructedness and performativity of racial subjectivity as it intervenes into the hegemonic racial formation of the state.

Inside of History: Reed on the Black Power Sixties

Although it evolved in complex and not especially tidy ways, Reed's attitude toward Black Power politics went roughly from a position of engaged sympathy in the mid-sixties, to profound disaffection in the late sixties and early seventies, to reconciliation in the mid-seventies, to a renewed respect in the eighties and early nineties. It is important to trace Reed's evolving political views because his changing opinions on the successes and failures of the Black Arts movement and the social and cultural principles of the sixties allow us better to understand his somewhat ambiguous attitude toward Black Power at the time he was writing *Flight to Canada* in the mid-seventies, when he was somewhere between disaffection and reconciliation. By appreciating Reed's ambivalence toward the sixties, an ambivalence that was a national phenomenon in the mid-seventies, we can discern how Reed represents his appreciation and critique of the Black Power movement in a novel mobilized by the discourse on slavery created out of that social moment.

Although in the early to mid-sixties he had been loosely affiliated with those poets of the Umbra Workshop "who formed the aesthetic and intellectual wing of the Black Power movement," and he himself wrote poetry in those years sympathetic to Black Power, by the late sixties Reed was alienated from the Umbra poets and the Black Power advocates, about whom he wrote parodically and disparagingly, especially in *Mumbo Jumbo*, completed in January 1971, and *The Last Days of Louisiana Red,* completed in December 1973. In his nonfiction prose of the period he explains that he became disenchanted with Black Power because of the "jargon and political abstruseness about the political movement in the 1960s," and he became cynical when he "saw some of the militants picking up the habits of the oppressors." His primary animus was the Black Arts movement theoreticians and their liberal fellow travelers who attempted to control the aesthetic impetus of African American artists. He was relentless in his critique of what he called those "eastern-based black pseudo-Nationalists and white mundanists who in the 1960s sought to dominate Afro-American intellectual thought with their social realist position papers." He thought that an alliance of black nationalists and revolutionaries and white radicals and liberals promoted "rather dubious political programs" while controlling the

African American cultural apparatus (calling this alliance the "Axis" of American publishing). In *Mumbo Jumbo,* for instance, a "Negro editor" who works for a white publisher refuses to publish work that "lacked 'soul' and wasn't 'Nation' enough."[6]

By the mid-seventies, having lived through Nixon's presidency, Reed was beginning to see the value of what Black Power had stood for and what its advocates had accomplished. By 1973, he was praising black writers of the sixties for breaking away from the constricting traditions of the Christian Church, the following year was defending black poetry of the sixties as "a richer period in Afro-American writing than most thought," and by 1978 was celebrating the "tremendous independence and drive that happened in the 1960's." He began also to give a different spin to his own earlier commentary on Black Power. In a 1976 interview, Reed dismissed the idea that he had been caricaturing Angela Davis in *The Last Days of Louisiana Red,* and insisted that his work was "not an attack on the Panthers." While still critical of what he called those "sullen humorless critics of the Black Aesthetic movement," Reed was beginning to develop a nostalgic fondness for the Black Power movement as a set of collective actions and principles that not only altered the national scene but had far-reaching international implications. He was himself not immune from what he called the "sixtomania" sweeping the country in the mid-seventies, as he celebrated the "New Black of the 1960s" as "glamorous, intelligent, international, and militant."[7]

By the eighties, in the midst of the Reagan presidency, an epoch he called "selfish," a decade "meaner than a junkyard dog," Reed was wholeheartedly nostalgic for the Black Power sixties. Praising the black nationalists for "broaden[ing]" his "knowledge of black culture" during the "Second Renaissance" of the sixties, Reed also felt that his experience with the Umbra Workshop was important because it brought him into contact with "other black poets" and allowed him to become "acquainted with the techniques of the Afro-American literary style." And the Umbra Workshop, he noted with pride, was "instrumental in setting up the philosophy of Black Power." He praised the Black Panther Party for its role in changing Oakland from a "feudalistic fiefdom, controlled by a few families, to the twenty-first century multicultural city that it is becoming." Black Power, he wrote, "brought power to the people." Reed also began to appreciate that the sixties was not a time of restricted aesthetic principles but rather a time that opened up new canons and new fields of literary representation. When he addressed the PEN conference in 1986, he credited the social movements of the sixties not only with demanding political reforms but also with inspiring a "multiethnic revival in literature."[8]

In Reed's evolving politics, Black Power had been transformed from a movement without respect for the past, lacking a viable program of action, to a movement "inspired by black culture and politics" in a decade he regards as "the most thrilling and humanistic of this century." To gauge his changing sensibilities, we can compare his 1974 comment that the sixties was a "strident decade"—"The Decade that Screamed"—with his 1989 comment that only "cultural and political conservatives" believe the sixties to have been "a demonic decade." By the end of the eighties, Reed realized that the "decade that screamed" had been screaming something worthwhile and for a reason. Indeed, Reed was sounding like a Black Power advocate himself, criticizing the white "New Left, who sought to use the Black Panthers to foment a violent revolution," but who had "by the late seventies . . . joined the Reagan consensus, or had begun to wallow in a selfish consumerism."⁹ By the late eighties, then, Reed was explicitly criticizing a position he had held in the early seventies and which, I argue, he had begun substantially to revise in the mid-seventies.

What, then, is the politics Reed holds and envisions in *Flight to Canada,* which he wrote during the period of the most flux in his thinking about Black Power? Two articles he wrote in the summer of 1976 demonstrate his ambivalence. In one, published in *Antaeus,* Reed wrote approvingly of Amiri Baraka's comment that "it was necessary in the 1960s to call the white man a devil because many of us grew up thinking he was a god." In the other, published in the *New York Times,* Reed castigated those members of the Black Power literary establishment—he calls them the "Apostles of the Black Aesthetic"—for their failure to respect a writer's freedom to choose his or her own subjects and to deal with them in complex and not always celebratory ways. He claimed that Black Power writers' conferences served as little more than "tribunals where those writers who didn't hew the line were ridiculed, scorned, mocked, and threatened."¹⁰ But while sustaining his critique of the regulatory function of the Black Arts movement, Reed was also developing a more comprehensive analysis of the various hegemonic influences on the cultural scene. Consider, for example, Reed's critique of Black Power's disdain for the past endeavors of less sensationalistic African American social movements.

Reed persistently criticized Black Power advocates for failing to appreciate the extent to which previous African American cultural movements and political figures had also struggled to achieve the same social freedoms for which Black Power advocates were striving. Reed chastised those members of the "younger generation of Afro-Americans" in the sixties who falsely believed themselves "the first generation to fight back" and who therefore "viewed their ancestors with contempt," hoping that these militants would learn "that the 'black experience' is a galaxy and not the slave-pen many whites and blacks desire it to be." Reed articulated this sensibility in his poem "The Reactionary Poet." "If you are a revolutionary / Then I must be a reactionary / For if you stand for the future / I have no choice but to / Be with the past." The poem was published in his 1978 collection *A Secretary to the Spirits,* but it first appeared in an earlier version of *Flight to Canada.* In that shorter version of "Flight to Canada," Reed has his hero John Swell of the Porke Plantation (later named Raven Quickskill of the Swille plantation) write this poem as a response to his critics who didn't approve of his choice of subjects. "It's hard to be well-rounded in Emancipated," notes John Swell, because it is a "town with one philosophy and one style."¹¹

At the same time that he was criticizing Black Power advocates for their reluctance to appreciate the diverse political styles within the black community, their inability to accept the complex aesthetic values beyond protest fiction, and their unwillingness to revere cultural formations from the past, Reed was also wholly attentive to how the mainstream discourses of American public life were mobilized by and produced that "slave-pen" version of African American history and thereby provoked the "contempt" black militants felt for their ancestral heritages. As he notes in his "Black Power Poem," the "powers of old america" are not only political ("richard nixon edward teller billy graham") but are also driven by the cultural and media apparatus ("time magazine the new york review of books and the underground press") which "seem only interested in our experience's seamy side." When it comes to the subject of slavery, this apparatus manufactures public representations that promote the belief that "North American Blacks were docile" because they hide the truth about Gabriel Prosser, Nat Turner, and David Walker. So, while Reed criticizes Black Power intellectuals for their narrowness of vision, he also criticizes those participants in the discourses of "old america" who are largely responsible for creating that narrowness. And in the case of the discourse on slavery, those participants are Stanley Elkins and William Styron—one of whom, Reed notes, depicted slaves as "fawning, cringing, and shuffling darkies," while the other gave Nat Turner's revolt what he euphemistically calls an "inadequate Freudian interpretation."[12] In other words, Reed acknowledges how mainstream discourses on slavery effected the failures of some Black Power advocates to respect the past. In *Flight to Canada,* he not only continues this critique of the old discourse on slavery, but also inscribes his appreciation of those Black Power intellectuals who critically explore the discourse mobilized by the false and troubling version of the past culminating in the "Sambo" thesis and its literary articulation in Styron's novel. Consider that Raven Quickskill contributes poetry to a book whose title sounds suspiciously like that of the Clarke collection—*The Anthology of Ten Slaves* (63).

It is not surprising that Reed aligned himself, at least partially, with the Black Power intellectuals who attempted to establish a distance between two texts—Gray's *Confessions* and Styron's *Confessions*—in order to disrupt their intertextual relationship, since he himself was also involved in representing the costs of textual appropriation in *Flight to Canada*. Reed's novel is framed by successful or attempted acts of literary appropriation, beginning with Raven's meditation on the meaning of Harriet Beecher Stowe's "theft" of Josiah Henson's *The Life of Josiah Henson* and ending with Stowe's attempt to persuade Raven's fellow slave Uncle Robin to allow her to write his story for "Jewett Publishers in Boston" (8–9, 173–74).[13] Reed is not only saying that white writers appropriate black life stories for commercial gain (making "enough money on someone else's plot to buy thousands of silk dresses and a beautiful home"), but also that these writers define black subjectivity in the process. While making a lot of "Black money," Stowe also takes away Henson's "thing that is himself," since a "man's story is his gris-gris," his "Etheric Double" (8–9). Black lives are as subject to white power when they are written as when they are lived. Reed's insistence on defining acts of cultural appropriation—"When you take a man's story, a story that doesn't belong to you, that story will get you" (9)—continues the work of the Black Power intellectuals who had also claimed that Styron's use of Nat Turner constituted a "deliberate attempt to steal the meaning of a man's life."[14] Indeed, Reed is implicitly critiquing Styron's cultural appropriation by revisiting the analogous case of Stowe's act of appropriating Henson's narrative. He allusively makes the connection between Stowe and Styron by comparing "Uncle Tom" and "Nat Turner" as representatives of two distinct strategies for resistance, and by condemning white authors who use the lucrative profits from their books about black subjects to build themselves a "Virginia plantation in New England" (178, 9). This comment must have struck the Virginia-born Styron close to home in Roxbury, Connecticut.

Like the Black Power intellectuals who contributed to the Clarke collection, Reed was intent on salvaging models of heroic behavior from the African American past. Unlike them, though, he was intent not on celebrating Nat Turner by castigating Uncle Tom, but rather in complicating both the Nat Turners and the Uncle Toms. Reed returns to and rearranges those three organizational topics that mobilized the discourses on slavery and the political rhetoric of Black Power in the 1960s. Black Power advocates had produced reified portraits of Nat Turner as a militant who believed in revolutionary violence, eschewed property, and historically represented the best possible cultural identity for the new black subject; Uncle Tom, on the other hand, was someone who believed in the ethic of property ownership and material consumption, held firmly to the ideology of nonviolence, and represented the polar opposite to the new black subject.[15] In his 1976 novel, Reed worked out his own complicated resolution to this dialectic of Uncle Tom and Nat Turner, first by posing them as complex and not altogether contradistinct symbols of the relationship between property and violence, and then as figures who participated in distinct but interrelated ways in the process of racial formation in the post–civil rights era.

"Who's the Fool?": The Dialectic of Violence and Property

In order for us to appreciate the complexity of Reed's responses to Black Power and the sixties and therefore to understand his political vision in *Flight to Canada,* we need first to look at the way he establishes a dialectic between violence and property in the novel. Reed does this throughout the book, mostly by compiling a brilliantly eclectic set of allusions to a series of intertexts including Stowe's *Uncle Tom's Cabin,* Henson's *The Life of Josiah Henson, Formerly a Slave,* Edgar Allan Poe's *Fall of the House of Usher,* Samuel Cartwright's 1851 medical articles on "Diseases and Peculiarities of the Negro Race," and Styron's *Confessions of Nat Turner.* The issues raised in and through these allusions come to a head at the end of the novel when Reed poses two sets of questions that not only create a dialectic between violence and property but also inaugurate the writing of the text, forcing us to acknowledge that *Flight to Canada* is ultimately also an intertextual "reading" of *Flight to Canada.* The function of this "meta-intertextuality" has to do with Reed's argument about the articulation of a new black subject (which I will discuss in the final section). His insistence on creating a dialectic between violence and property, though, has to do with Reed's argument about the institutional conditions necessary for the formation of that black subject, with establishing the optimal arrangement of the social forces acting on that subject. Reed initiates this discussion at the end of his novel by having Uncle Robin ask a question about the alleged contradistinction of Uncle Tom and Nat Turner.

By invoking Uncle Tom and Nat Turner, Reed was responding to and participating in a historical dialogue among African American intellectuals in a debate between ideals of resistance and accommodation, between myths of slave docility and romances of slave resistance, between symbols of black messianism and black nationalism. Historically a resonant pairing with far more complexity than has been generally appreciated, the Nat Turner–Uncle Tom dialectic was especially apt for Reed's purpose because it not only gave him a way of articulating "two jarringly opposed symbols" of "two conceptions of the religion of the oppressed"—and religion and particularly oppositional religions constitute deeply important issues for Reed—

but also a way to situate his novel in the midst of the bicentennial dialogue about the sixties since that opposition in many ways marked the major shift in the sixties. As more than one historian has noted, while "the Uncle Tom tradition of turning the other cheek achieved undeniable importance in the passive–resistance tactics of the civil rights movement, the Nat Turner model soon began to provide a more acceptable self-image even for moderate and gradualist political activists."[16] And with the shift to Black Power in the late sixties, Nat Turner became the most salient model of political activity and social identity.

For Black Power advocates, Nat Turner was a cultural hero who served as an analogue and model for the Black Power movement, precisely because he "chose to gain freedom in the only way that freedom can be gained with honor—by wrenching it from the hands of the master through violence." It was the method that "hundreds of thousands of Nat Turners" living in "American society today" would also employ. Unlike those accommodationists who wanted only "an equality of rights which in no way implies a change of structure in the property system," the new Nat Turners wished to "destroy an oppressive system totally," dedicating themselves "to the elimination of the oppressive social and political apparatus, not in the interests of a few but in the interest of all." "No philosophy which does not demand change in the American power structure for the benefit of all the victims can be called revolutionary in any sense of the term. The Black Power proponent, like Nat Turner, realizes this fact." The name that Black Power advocates gave to those who believed in the fairness of the oppressive system and only wished to see a redistribution of resources rather than a revolutionary overthrowing of the system, those who had internalized majoritarian values about private property and capitalist enterprise, was "Uncle Tom."[17]

In the early seventies, Reed challenged the Black Power critique of "Uncle Tom." Arguing that "lots can be said for Uncle Toms," Reed noted that there was a Confucian equivalent to "Uncle Tomism"—"what they call taking abuse from the outside by preserving your inner light all along." His research for *Flight to Canada* showed him that those "blacks called uncle toms by liberals and missionaries" were admirable because they were able to overcome the "anti-business pyschology" instilled in slaves and develop an interest in the mainstream economy. Reed often but uneasily defends the property system of capitalism and admires those who strive to make it work more equitably. Living in America, living in a capitalist society, he believed, people of African descent should strive to abide by American values regarding consumption and accumulation. In a piece he wrote for *Black World* in 1972, Reed noted that those "who've tried to build a politics or culture based on the assumption that we're going to be here have been regarded as Uncle Toms. These 'judgment day' assumptions have been enervating and wasteful," he concluded.[18]

In the early seventies, Reed admired an Uncle Tomism representing property ownership, an integral identity, and nonviolence. By the mid-seventies, though, Reed was in the process of redefining his politics regarding the place of violence in social movements, the structure of property in capitalist societies, and the types of cultural identity a new black subject should be forming, showing himself to be more sympathetic to a revolutionary Black Power agenda, especially one calling for strategic violence against capitalist structures of property. At the same time, he did not wholly repudiate property ownership, nor did he castigate Uncle Tom as a woefully benighted figure. His politics are firmly "independent" (his own term), and his political economy is based on the belief that "we need some kind of socialism in this country, but at the same time we need the private sector." While insisting that America needs a "socialist base" guaranteeing "an adequate standard of existence" for all people, Reed also believes in what he calls *"real* free enterprise," noting that "in a capitalist country the primary demand should be equal access to the capital."[19] Articulating and experimenting with these ideas in *Flight to Canada,* Reed concludes the novel by setting up and then complicating the standard contradistinction between material possession in the figure of Uncle Tom and material resistance in the figure of Nat Turner.

Returning to the early version of "Flight to Canada," we can see how Reed was in the process of revising his representations of Black Power in the mid-seventies. In this earlier version, he represents Nat Turner in an entirely unsympathetic light. Some of the inhabitants of Emancipation City in the short story are survivors of "the Nat Turner skirmish," an insurrection John Swell describes as a political failure, something that "put heat on everybody and according to some postponed emancipation of Virginia slaves." Included in that "some" is Styron, whose Thomas Gray articulates the novelist's own beliefs that Turner "done more with your Christianity to assure the defeat of abolition than all the meddlin' and pryin' Quakers that ever set foot in Virginia put together." In one representation in the mid-seventies, then, Reed was giving us a Nat Turner emblematic of the inefficacy of revolutionary violence. Later, though, Reed would refer to Nat Turner as the "self-taught visionary who led a slave rebellion that people still talk about in Virginia." This transformation of Nat Turner from the misguided rebel responsible for delaying collective freedom to the visionary still celebrated in folk culture parallels Reed's changing vision of Black Power, and the social movements of the sixties generally.[20]

When he revised and transformed "Flight to Canada" into *Flight to Canada,* Reed edited out the unsympathetic references to Nat Turner. In the final version of the novel, he gives us one ambiguous reference to Nat Turner in Uncle Robin's penultimate speech:

> Yeah, they got down on me an Tom. But who's the fool? Nat Turner or us? Nat said he was going to do this. Was going to do that. Said he had a mission. Said his destiny was a divine one. Said that fate had chosen him. That the gods were handling him and speaking through him. Now Nat's dead and gone for these many years, and here I am master of a dead man's house. Which one is the fool? One who has been dead for these many years or a master in a dead man's house. I'll bet they'll be trying to figure that one out for a long time. A long, long time. (178)

The first thing to note about this passage is that the reference to Nat Turner is not necessarily an allusion to Styron's novel, although it is likely most readers of *Flight to Canada* would have seen it as at least a covert glance in Styron's direction as well as a reference to the prototype of the Black Power militant of the late sixties. This is an instance of a discontinuous intertextual relationship, that is, a text uses its pretext not only to comment on literary interrelationships but also to produce an excessive reading of both the "host" text and the social text. Here Reed uses Styron's pretext as a means of delineating his own multivalent version of Black Power.

At first glance, Uncle Robin seems to be suggesting not only that Nat Turner's insurrection was doomed to failure, but that it was flawed primarily because of its revolutionary impetus, because of Nat Turner's unwillingness to respect property ownership and the power accruing to material possessions. It would appear that Uncle Robin is celebrating his own accommodationist attitude in which he, although property, becomes propertied—"Property joining forces with property," as he puts it (171)—while at the same time he criticizes Nat Turner's revolutionary desire to eliminate those who defined him as property. A closer analysis of this passage and its context, however, reveals that Reed is using Uncle Robin's penultimate speech to pose a set of questions about the possibility for imagining a more dynamic relationship between violent and nonviolent revolutionary action and exploring an opportunity to configure a more subtle dialectic between material and spiritual forms of resistance—between an Uncle Robin who is possessed to rewrite a will that leaves him propertied and a Nat Turner who is possessed to act on the will to power, murder his master, and thereby destroy his status as property.[21]

Uncle Robin's penultimate question—who is the wiser, Uncle Tom or Nat Turner—needs to be placed in relation to his final question, the question with which he enigmatically concludes the novel. After pondering his wealth for a moment, Uncle Robin concludes his meditations with a set of questions about the death of Swille: "Who pushed Swille into the fire? Some Etheric Double? The inexorable forces of history? A ghost? Thought? Or all of these? Who could have pushed him? Who?" (179). The question is clearly important to Uncle Robin, since this series of questions constitutes his final statement in the novel. Immediately thereafter, we are informed that Raven has returned to start work on Uncle Robin's story, so these questions in a way inaugurate the writing of *Flight to Canada*. It is also important that these questions have answers, since the murder of Swille was the precondition for Uncle Robin's reworked will to take effect; without Swille's death, Uncle Robin would not be free or propertied. We can attempt to answer Uncle Robin's question by looking carefully at the scene in chapter 21 in which Swille dies. The chapter begins with a dialogue between Swille and a Union general revealing that Swille arranged the assassination of Lincoln because he "gave away all that property. All that property" (130). Swille's wife, who had just found out in the previous chapter that her son Mitchell the anthropologist was dead, when his ghost appeared to her in the form of the Congo crocodile that had eaten him, comes into the room with a gun aimed at Swille. After he manages to pacify and disarm her, the ghost of Swille's dead sister Vivian appears. The ghost of Vivian reminds Swille of their Poe-like necrophilic and incestuous relationship—"You'll never give me up, will you, brother? Out in my sepulcher by the sea"—and then backs him up into the fireplace, where he is consumed by the fire. "Fire grabs his coattails. Fire is hungry. Fire eats" (136). Robin rushes out of the room to where Pompey stands guard, tells Pompey to revive Ms. Swille, while he himself takes a very leisurely trip to the kitchen to get water to save his master (137). By the time he returns, Swille is dead and he is on his way to becoming the owner of all that property Lincoln had given away.

As well as being a Neo-slave narrative, then, *Flight to Canada* turns out to be an Edgar Allan Poe mystery and a plain old-fashioned whodunit. The critics attempting to solve the mystery and answer Robin's question—"Who could have pushed him?

Who?"—have offered three answers: Swille was killed either by Vivian's ghost, or by Mrs. Swille who takes on the "form of the ghost of his dead sister" as a ruse, or by both the ghost and Mrs. Swille.[22] I argue that neither the ghost nor the wife murders Swille. The mystery at the end of Poe's *The Fall of the House of Usher* is whether the "enshrouded figure" of Madeline Usher, who falls against her brother Roderick, bearing him to the "floor a corpse, and a victim to the terrors he had anticipated," is a ghost or the living body of the woman Roderick had attempted to bury prematurely. There is apparently no answer to the mystery, because the narrator flees and the house falls. The mystery of the fall of the house of Swille is not a mystery so much as it is a riddle. Reed himself suggests in an article on the tradition of "serious comedy" in African American literature that his work is based on reworking African American folklore into modernist and postmodernist forms. "If the slaves, for example, enjoyed riddles more than any other form," he writes, "then among my work would be whodunits with busy plots, and trickster endings."[23] *Flight to Canada* is just such a work, a Neo-HooDoo whodunit. Moreover, I think we get the solution to the whodunit in the novel's "trickster ending." Just after Robin asks "Who could have pushed him? Who?" Pompey, Uncle Robin's secretary and formerly Swille's butler, interrupts to tell him Raven has returned. We are told that Pompey, "as usual[,] has appeared from out of nowhere" (179). I suggest that Pompey, who appears literally as an answer to Robin's question, is the person who murdered Swille.

The problem with this solution is that Pompey is apparently not in the room when Swille is murdered—but that is a slight problem once we consider Pompey's peculiar talents. When we are first introduced to him just after Swille purchased him, we are told Pompey is so fast that he "can serve dinner before it's cooked, beats himself getting up in the morning so that when he goes to the bathroom to shave he has to push his shadow out of the way, and zips about the house like a toy train" (35). Uncle Robin also comments on Pompey's remarkable speed: "The boy's fast. He's so fast that some of the people are talking about seeing him in two places at the same time" (175). Pompey's supernatural speed, then, permits him to be both in the room when Swille is murdered and outside standing vigil by the time Robin encounters him a few seconds later. Pompey's other talents are also suggestive. He is a "a good voice-thrower" and an expert mimic who "can do impersonations." "He got the whole Swille family down pat. He can do all the men and women, *and the dead ones too*" (175, my emphasis). Moreover, Pompey has a room full of "all kinds of animal and reptile and bird masks." What we are meant to infer, then, is that Pompey is the one who appears to Ms. Swille as the ghost of Mitchell in the form of a crocodile and appears to Master Swille as the ghost of Vivian. He has their voices "down pat," owns the equipment to outfit himself as their spectral presences, and possesses the speed to push Swille into the fire and stand vigil outside the door within seconds. In other words, in the Neo-HooDoo whodunit that is *Flight to Canada*, we can say: the butler did it.

This discovery that Pompey murdered Swille should complicate our assessment of Uncle Robin's question regarding the distinct kinds of resistance—his own canny rewriting of the will or Nat Turner's insurrection. Uncle Robin becomes the "master of a dead man's house" because there is a "dead" man who died an unnatural death. A slave had to possess the courage and will to murder the master before Robin could possess the house according to the will. It will take a "long, long time" to figure out the answer to whether overt violence or covert cunning is the superior form of resistance, because there is no easy answer. There is ultimately a necessary dialectic between material forms of resistance such as violent action and spiritual forms of resistance such as religious possession. And that is true of both Nat Turner and Uncle Tom.

We need to recall that even Josiah Henson, on whom Stowe would model the meek and exceedingly sanctimonious Uncle Tom, whose narrative Reed is salvaging, and whose example Robin is here invoking ("me an Tom"), also considered murdering his master. Having been cheated out of his freedom and his money, Henson forms a plan of violent and immediate freedom: "I resolved to kill my four companions, take what money there was in the boat, then to scuttle the craft, and escape to the north." As he raises his axe to "strike the fatal blow," he is suddenly struck by the thought that he is about to commit murder. "'What! commit *murder!* and you a Christian?'" The voice causing him to desist is his own, but it appears to him to be another's. "All this came upon me instantly, and with a distinctness which made me almost think I heard it whispered in my ear; and I believe I even turned my head to listen."[24] When Stowe "borrows" Henson's narrative, she revises this scene so that Uncle Tom persuades Cassy not to act on her vengeful feelings. Her children sold from her, Cassy "resolved in her soul an hour of retribution, when her hand should avenge on her oppressor all the injustice and cruelty to which she had been witness, or which *she* had in her own person suffered." Unable to lift the axe because her "arms are so weak," Cassy attempts to get Uncle Tom to wield the weapon; he, however, refuses—"Not for ten thousand worlds, Misse!"—and concludes that they need to love their enemies.[25]

By inscribing into *Flight to Canada* the violent resistance of Pompey, Reed reinscribes into Henson's own narrative that dialectic of material and spiritual resistance Stowe had removed. Even the original Uncle Tom was willing to consider violence, Reed reminds us. Likewise, the other text Reed is implicitly parodying is Styron's *Confessions of Nat Turner.* Instead of the Turner whom Styron represented as a Christian zealot whose religious fantasies are confused with his sexual ones, Reed offers a partial portrait of another Nat Turner, one whose acts of violent resistance are sustained by African gods. Like Henson, Nat Turner heard voices. But those voices, in Reed's version, turn out to be more like Guede than Christ. Robin attests to the specificity of Nat Turner's religious life when he notes that "the gods were handling him and speaking through him." Not "God," but "gods." Just as Uncle Tom became revolutionary, so did Nat Turner become Neo-HooDoo. In this way, Reed revises Styron's "Atonist" text—that is, a text representing a "mind which sought to interpret the world by using a single loa"—that he had earlier parodied in *Mumbo Jumbo,* mocking the attempt of "writer Bilous Styronicus" to rewrite "Osirian history in a book called the *Confessions of the Black Bull God Osiris.*"[26]

With this representation Reed produces a revisionary reading of Stowe's and Styron's appropriative texts and simultaneously highlights the performative aspect of racial roles. Revising those master texts that appropriate slave narratives, he also exposes the dramatic flaw in the hegemonic racial formation's inability to appreciate how racial identities are performed. The racial formation Reed disrupts not only defines the social relations between those who have no "race" and those who are "en-raced," but also organizes the internal relations of those enraced groups. In the late sixties and early seventies, the hegemonic racial formation mobilized a dialectic between field slaves and house slaves, between radical revolutionaries and bourgeois accommodationists, between Nat Turner and Uncle Tom. Emerging with particular force in the late sixties, the conventional scheme had it that the "house Negro always looked out for his master . . . [and] loved his master more than his master loved himself. That's why he didn't want his master hurt." The field slaves, on the other hand, "hated their master," were rebellious, and physically resisted enslavement. As Malcolm X put it, if the master's house caught fire, the house slave would "try and put the fire out" while the field slave would "pray for a strong wind to come along." Arguing that the sixties was a decade characterized by what he calls "field nigger romanticism," Reed set out to revise these conventional and reified racial roles.[27]

First, in Reed's novel the field slaves are not so revolutionary that they resist the urge to become capitalist entrepreneurs. The field slave Stray Leechfield, for instance, does not just steal a chicken or two from Swille to supplement his meager diet. He steals thousands of chickens, sets up a poultry farm in the next county, underselling his rivals in "eggs, gizzards, gristles, livers" and "succulent drumsticks," and uses the profits to purchase a fully outfitted carriage (36). The house slaves, on the other hand, all engage in revolutionary action. The house slaves Pompey, Uncle Robin, and Raven turn out to be just as revolutionary in their willingness to perform violent acts against their master as any of the field slaves. Not only does Pompey murder Master Swille by pushing him into the fire (the fire that Malcolm referred to, perhaps?), but both Robin and Raven also attempt to kill their master. Raven puts "rat poison" in Swille's "Old Crow," which would have killed Swille had not a stray Confederate bullet shattered the bottle as he raised it to his lips, while Robin, an admitted "old hand at poisons," has been slowly killing Swille over a period of years by serving him Coffee Mate instead of slave mothers' milk (5, 30, 175). Moreover, unlike the house slaves Malcolm described, who would inform their masters of field slave rebelliousness, the house slaves in Reed's novel support the field slaves' acts of resistance. As Raven tells Stray Leechfield, the master "knew about the poultry" but the house slaves claimed that the inventory mistake was the fault of the "Texas calculator." "We covered for you all the time—made excuses for you and sometimes did the work ourselves that you were supposed to do" (73).

By producing a set of quite unconventional relations between house slaves and field slaves, Reed is revising our understanding of slave history as well as making his own important commentary on the Black Power politics of the sixties. For Black Power advocates did not eschew all apparent "Uncle Toms," believing that since "Uncle Toms suffered from cultural disorientation" they could be "cured" through "cultural reeducation." Nikki Giovanni, for instance, wrote to the potential revolutionary still hiding behind the mask of "Uncle Tom" that she wanted him "to reclaim yourself." In another poem, she asks: "Can you kill a white man / Can you kill the nigger / in you / Can you make your nigger mind / die / Can you kill your nigger mind / And free your black hands." Larry Neal praised Ben Caldwell's play *The Militant Preacher,* about how an "Uncle Tom preacher" mouthing "platitudes against self-defense" becomes a militant preaching "the gospel of the gun, an eye for an eye," celebrating Caldwell's ability to "twist the rhythms of the Uncle Tom preacher into the language of the new militancy." He also praises LeRoi Jones's play *Jello* for showing how "even Uncle Tom has a breaking point beyond which he will not be pushed," thus demonstrating that behind the "most docile Negro" one will find "a conscious murderer." And he concludes his own poem "Love Song in Middle Passage" with a representation of someone whose "uncle tom teeth brightly grin . . . while thrusting the blade into the beast-heart" of the oppressor.[28] Uncle Toms possessed revolutionary potential and could be potential revolutionaries.

Reed uses that conventional dichotomy of the sixties—Uncle Tom and Nat Turner—to show that those who seem to be Uncle Toms in their bourgeois values can sometimes turn out to be Nat Turners in their dedication to concerted and planned revolutionary action, including strategic violence. Those unsuspected house slaves not only supported the field slaves in their resistant theft of property and their escapes, but they exceeded them in their active use of violence. Of all the slaves to whom we are introduced on the Swille plantation, only one is so thoroughly devoted to the master that he fits the conventional description of a house slave; and that is Master Swille's illegitimate son and the overseer on the plantation, Cato the Graffado, who is "[s]o faithful that he volunteered for slavery, and so dedicated . . . to slavery, the slaves voted him all-Slavery" (34). Even the other figure whose devotion to slavery is beyond suspicion, Mammy Barracuda, physically pummels Mrs. Swille into southern ladyhood. With the exception of Cato, then, all the house slaves commit violence against the bodies of their masters and mistresses.

In situating violence, particularly violence against slavemasters, so centrally in his novel, Reed is contributing to the dialogue over political activism emerging from Black Power and the sixties debate over the inefficacy of nonviolence, participating in the debate over slave resistance in the discourse on slavery, and alluding to one of the basic features of Styron's novel (the confusion of violence and sexuality, which Swille the masochist exemplifies). Reed uses his representations of slave resistance to delineate his own historical and political vision of Black Power by showing us the relation between two forms of resistance. Flight, according to Reed, constitutes the slaves' "most subversive" act, because the fugitive slave "stole his own property." Murdering the master, on the other hand, constitutes another kind of "quiet technique" of altering the plantation economy through the use of "subtlety and cunning."[29] Whether it was stealing oneself or murdering a master, Reed suggests, the slave performed an act of violence against a distinct system of property. By demonstrating the connection between violence and property—whether systemic violence supporting ownership in humans or subversive violence against property and property holders—Reed was pointing out the flaws of the Black Power movement, correcting the lacunae in historical treatments of slave resistance, and constructing a new cultural economy.

Changing the Big House: From Peculiar to Cultural Institutions

From his earliest pronouncements on the function of his fiction, Reed has said that his art aims "to sabotage history" and that he wanted to conduct an ongoing "artistic guerilla warfare against the Historical Establishment."[30] In *Flight to Canada,* Reed takes on both the cliometricians who wrote revisionist histories of slavery in forums like the *New Republic* (150–51) and those historians with whose definitions of slave resistance he was in disagreement. The most important book of historical literature on slave resistance was Eugene Genovese's massive 1974 publication *Roll, Jordan, Roll,* which, incidentally, had the working title of *Sambo and Nat Turner.* For Genovese, every slave was potentially "Sambo" or "Nat Turner," often simultaneously exhibiting both "accommodation and resistance to slavery." What was important for Reed was Genovese's definition of two different forms of resistance: (1) "prepolitical," "apolitical," or "nonrevolutionary self-assertion," and (2) "political responses" to enslavement. Political responses included collective acts of violence or individual acts of flight, while apolitical resistance consisted of acts such as lying, stealing, dissembling, shirking duties, infanticide, suicide, arson—and murder. Genovese concludes his discussion of the dialectic between resistance and accommodation by placing slave religion as the "organizing center of their resistance within accommodation" because slave religion reflected the "hegemony of the master class" while providing the slaves with a "critical world-view" limiting the extent to which that hegemony invaded their psyches and their social relations.[31]

In *Flight to Canada,* Reed takes up several issues raised by Genovese concerning slave resistance. While agreeing with Genovese that flight constituted a form of political resistance, Reed questions Genovese's placing the murder of a master in the category of prepolitical resistance. According to Genovese, the "significance of slaves' murdering their master or overseers cannot be reduced simply to 'resistance to slavery.'" Even while granting that such action was significant because it defined the limits within which slaves were willing to acquiesce, Genovese concludes that such explosive action as murdering the master ultimately acted to reinforce the lesson of "acquiescence in the status quo." Since it was "an individual reaction to individual abuses," murdering the master was a form of protest that "set a model that reinforced the regime." The legal statutes of slave states seem to belie this reading, though. Although Brazil's Imperial Constitution of 1824 created more liberal slave codes, banning whipping and other brutal physical punishments, its 1829 Criminal Code nonetheless made the punishment for a slave's murdering a master beyond appeal, even appeal for imperial clemency. In 1835, the Regency of Dom Pedro Segundo reinforced this law by passing an "exceptional law" stating: "The punishment of death will be suffered by all slaves, male or female, who kill by any means whatsoever, give poison, gravely wound, or commit any serious physical offense against their master, his wife, his descendents or forebears who may be living in his company."[32]

Even in the antebellum and colonial United States, where conditions did not permit the kind of perpetual slave unrest found in Brazil, there was an accentuated attention to slaves who murdered. In the South Carolina Act of 1712, for example, all cases of slave crime called for the court—made up of magistrates and freeholders—to "diligently weigh . . . and examine . . . all evidences, proofs and testimonies" before passing judgment on the accused slave. In "cases of murder," however, the court was permitted to make its judgment on the basis of "violent presumption and circumstances."[33] These stringent legal codes against slaves murdering masters, of property doing damage to property owners, betrayed the underlying fear that the regime was combustible, that a sufficient number of "individual reactions to individual abuses" could overthrow the slave system. A slave who rose to murder a master was a slave who had clearly exceeded the definition of slave. Moreover, the murder of the master, unlike the murder of an overseer, was a direct challenge to the system of property transfer. The 1835 law of Brazil clearly defines the most heinous acts as those perpetrated against the possible heirs.

In order to make the case that violence against a master constitutes an important action against the system of property, Reed has to expose the connections among the social institutions of the state, tracing the alignment of legal to other hegemonic social practices to show how an act of violence creates a disturbance in the whole series of societal apparatus. He creates an allegory of master–slave relations by producing a carnivalesque scenario in which the master becomes an exaggerated figure embodying the body politic against which an act of violence begins to appear symbolic of an act of revolutionary insurrection. Finally, Reed also presents that dialectic between violent and nonviolent action he considered necessary for any singular act of violence to be effective by situating the murder of Swille within a supplementary political program, namely the acquisition and redistribution of property and the creation of new cultural apparatus.

Samuel Cartwright, the Virginia-born physician remembered primarily for the fourteen articles he published in *De Bow's Review* between 1851 and 1862—the most famous of which ("Diseases and Peculiarities of the Negro Race") Reed parodies in *Flight to Canada*—had insisted that slaves do not respect property rights and thus caused an escalating problem since their making off with their labor caused the price of cotton and clothing to rise. It is only by keeping the price of cotton low that the white "laboring classes having less to pay for clothing, [can] have more money to spend in educating their children, in intellectual, moral and religious progress."[34] Without the subordination of black labor, the evolution of white civilization becomes impossible. The murder of a master in these terms is assuredly a challenge not only to the plantation, but, by Cartwright's measure, to the foundations of human progress. Even as a challenge only to the plantation, though, such an act of violence still contains a resonant challenge to the political system on which slavery is based. In exaggerating the significance of the interactions between masters and slaves, Reed delineates an allegory of social relations which no less a figure than John C. Calhoun had attempted to describe in similar terms.

According to Calhoun, the "Southern States are an aggregate, in fact, of communities, not of individuals. Every plantation is a little community, with the master at its head, who concentrates in himself the united interests of capital and labor, of which he is the common representative. These small communities aggregated make the State in all, whose action, labor, and capital is equally represented and perfectly harmonized." Once we disaggregate Calhoun's image of the social contract of the nation and return to his definition of the State as an aggregation of plantations, we see that the plantation becomes a miniature state, and the murder of its master, then, becomes nothing less than a political assassination. Calhoun's major point is that the plantation system excelled the industrial because the master represents the "united interests of capital and labor." Where capital and labor are not unified in one person, Calhoun argues, we find those conflicts between social classes in Northern states and in European countries that make it "so difficult to establish and maintain free institutions."[35] Given Calhoun's argument about the importance of the master's representative status, then, the act of murdering a master becomes nothing less than a microcosm of national insurgency, promoting the essential conflict between labor and capital—a conflict that would, and historically did, destroy the plantation system. Reed's representation of Swille suggests he had something like this in mind.

Swille is not a Simon Legree who is nasty and brutish, but nothing more than a typically mean master. Swille is an economic, social, and political force representative of the history of the colonizing impetus of the United States. The Swille family has a history of being involved in colonization, slave-trading, and cultural appropriation. Easily the wealthiest man in America, Swille owns "fifty million dollars' worth of art," an accomplishment Lincoln thinks should permit Swille to *name* the Civil War (23). As he tells Lincoln, while the Confederate states are loyal to their own flag and the Union states to theirs, "everybody salutes *our* flag. Gold, energy and power: that's our flag" (38). Swille finances both sides of the Civil War, owns Fort Knox, controls the state's interest rates, and possesses *"objets d'art"* in his house exceeding the value of the United States Treasury (32, 31, 38). He even attempts to buy Europe (17), just as his father had lent England the money to buy Burma (127). He sends his anthropologist son to the Congo to "check for some possible energy resources" and to colonize the country. "We used to send priests," notes Swille, "but they were too obvious" (34). Swille, then, is not just a slavemaster; he represents and embodies the colonizing enterprise, both in America and abroad. He is referred to as "an empire unto himself" (86). The murder of a master like Swille clearly signifies a much larger revolutionary impetus than an individual act against an individual master; it seems more like the destruction of the imperialist impetus within a multinational corporation.

Nonetheless, Reed does not simply advocate random acts of violence, even violence against a figure symbolic of the country's genocidal history and economic wealth. He argues that any act of insurgent violence becomes revolutionary only when it is performed within a larger social program. This is also a discovery that Black Power advocates were to make around 1970. The instances of Black Power–inspired urban unrest in the mid-sixties were effective insofar as they alerted federal agencies to the plight of the inner cities. The riots in Rochester in 1964 and Los Angeles in 1965 forced the Johnson administration to undertake a series of socioeconomic reforms in the ghettoes of these two cities. The Office of Economic Opportunity (OEO), the Department of Health, Education, and Welfare (HEW), and the Department of Housing and Urban Development (HUD) "pumped significant amounts of funds into each of these cities in the immediate aftermath of the riot occurrence." Indeed, the Model Cities program of 1966 was a "direct response to the initial riots (especially Watts)." Within a year of the Watts riots, the Johnson administration had concluded that "massive federal aid will be necessary to prevent a recurrence of the riots." The violence was necessary, as Robert Weaver attested, because "race riots aroused conscience, or guilt, or fear that resulted *in action.*" These federal programs and policies were "clear-cut results of the initial black upheavals" of the early to mid-sixties and proved what "attention-getting, catalytic effects" domestic violence could produce, given certain conditions. Those conditions, however, were of short duration.

For one thing, the government response to Rochester and Watts did not contain reforms so comprehensive as to "bring about a major redistribution of power." For another, public sympathy changed quickly. By 1968, there was a discernible shift in public opinion and in the Johnson administration's commitments. The escalating war in Vietnam, obviously, took first priority. Even among domestic-policy makers, however, urban unrest no longer prompted the belief that the Great Societies programs were working or were necessary. By 1969, with Nixon in office and with "law and order" in the headlines, there was a concerted shift to the right and a concomitant decline in the funding of Great Societies programs. The Nixon administration responded to ghetto uprisings with "physical suppression" of what it considered "anarchistic" and "illegitimate violence." Nixon's attorney general John Mitchell followed the president's command that the primary response to urban unrest should be "immediate and decisive force." The Justice Department began heavy surveillance of black militants and Black Power groups. The most significant expenditures in the inner cities were no longer those made by OEO, HUD, or HEW, but rather the Law Enforcement Assistance Administration (LEAA), which spent millions of dollars on "local riot control, training, equipment, and intelligence apparatus." Even politically moderate African Americans talked about this military incursion into their neighborhoods in terms of "severe oppression and even concentration camps."[36]

Black Power advocates also began to sense that violence was no longer an effective political strategy. Seeking to supplement the political strategy of violence Nat Turner historically represented, some reacted to Eldridge Cleaver's calls for an "orgy of violence" with a concern that such violence was ultimately inadequate. When someone like Cleaver "accepts the gun and the world of the gun as the essential reality, he ceases to be an outlaw, and becomes what is infinitely worse, more American than Americans." Challenging what had earlier seemed to be the defining feature of Black Power's disagreement with integrationists—"the devotion of one to violence and the other to non-violence"—Black Power intellectuals now argued that a fair society was not predicated "upon the gun" but upon an economic, social, and cultural reconstruction.[37]

Reed also advocates the need for a supplementary program to create that fair society. The most obvious sign of the supplementary program is the fact that Reed is suggesting that the murder of Swille is not revolutionary unless there is someone like Robin to tamper with the will. Without the manipulation of existent legal structures for the transfer of property, the murder of Swille would only have left Virginia with one less slavemaster. By manipulating the legal system, Robin creates the conditions for a redistribution of property (and since Swille owns more property than anyone in America, Robin's sleight-of-hand does genuinely change the social fabric of the country). Nonetheless, the shifting of property from one possessor to another has little potential for social reconstruction unless the person now in possession of that property puts it to radical use.

At the end of the novel, Robin looks around him at the property he now owns and decides that he will not simply assume the rights and prerogatives Swille had taken as his birthright. Remembering his own status in life and recalling that the economic system had disempowered him and people like him—"it's us serfs who have to pay"—Robin decides against a life of obscene wealth. "I don't want to be rich," he concludes (179). His final thoughts on the property he has inherited seem to suggest that he will do what Thaddeus Stevens could not convince the Radical Republicans in the 1868 Reconstruction government to do—to take the property forfeited by the Confederate rebels according to the 1862 Confiscation Act and redistribute parcels of it among the poor whites and freedpersons. Although ambiguously stated, Robin's resolution—"I'm going to take this fifty rooms of junk and make something useful out of it" (179)—attests to his decision not to deploy his newfound wealth to produce more surplus value from the appropriation of labor, but to serve in some way those people whose labor has been appropriated by his former master.

The Black Power that Reed represents in the novel, then, is a strategic critical intervention based on an act of violence that would have been meaningless without a supplementary strategy for controlling the shifting of economies. For that reason, although he himself has been poisoning his master, Raven has to refuse the kind of random violence articulated by 40S, who rejects the transformative power of language for the power of guns: "you take the words; give me the rifle. That's the only word I need. R-i-f-l-e. Click" (81). Economic control, however, is only part of the social reform movement Reed figures in *Flight to Canada*. Both Raven and Robin dismiss the kind of hope articulated by Leechfield that economic reforms will answer the social dilemmas of peoples of African descent: "money is what makes them go. Economics. He's got the money he paid for me, and so that satisfy him. Economics" (74). As Robin tells Leechfield, one cannot buy one's way out of history; one cannot transform the position of a class of people without transforming the social relations that had previously defined some as slaves, others as masters (177). What Reed offers, instead of a politics based on violence and economic control, is a social movement founded on a rather more complex interplay among politics, economics, and, most emphatically, culture.

The critique of Black Power most closely resembling Reed's is that of Harold Cruse, whom Reed has praised on different occasions for helping give historical force to the issues the black intellectuals of the sixties faced. Like Reed, Cruse argued that Black Power was only a reformist movement insofar as "all purely economic and political reorganizations of any type in America can be only reformist movements." For Black Power to become revolutionary, Cruse argues, "other dynamic elements must be added to the economic and political combination." The total dynamic of a successful social movement must include "at one and the same time *a political, economic, and cultural movement.*" Focusing specifically on the cultural aspect of this synergistic movement, Cruse comments that a "truly and effectively radical" cultural movement must produce a "definitive critique of the entire cultural apparatus of America." It must, in other words, examine nothing less than the "politics of culture as expressed within the context of American intergroup status and relations in the cultural arts." That finally includes not simply an alteration in the superstructure but a change in the control of the cultural apparatus. "No one can hope to change America's cultural standards and values unless the proprietorship, the administration, and the uses to which the cultural apparatus are put, are changed to allow for more democratic social control."[38]

Following a similar set of imperatives, Reed saw that the cultural institutions of mainstream America were inimical to the best interests of black cultural workers.

Within what Reed calls "the literary politics operating in America today," "aesthetic brokers" use "words like 'quality' and 'standards' the same way John Dean used the word 'inoperative.'" "Big-time publishing" was still a "white sport," African American books were not effectively promoted, and the cultural scene and critical discourse prohibited the emergence of a genuine multiculturalism. Against this reality, Reed saw as ideal a situation where there would be "more independent publishing companies, more controlled by artists and writers." Artistic and economic control of "counter-institutions" would allow minority writers to produce positive images, which Reed feels are "subversive" in the ideological climate of the United States, and to engage in what he calls a "cultural revolution."[39]

In *Flight to Canada,* Reed inscribes his critique of mainstream American cultural apparatus as they affect people of African descent and promotes his vision of a comprehensive program for an effective social movement. Yankee Jack represents the present system of exploitation by those big publishing conglomerates who control "the American sensibility," deciding what Americans "see, read, and listen to" (150). Uncle Robin represents the imperative to alter that situation by establishing a more democratically controlled set of cultural apparatus. After an act of necessary political violence leaves him with the economic control of the Swille Castle, Robin sets out to produce a cultural revolution. Those "fifty rooms" Robin wished to make something "useful out of" become the residences for a kind of multicultural university, since Robin has invited fifty "[c]raftsmen from all over the South: blacksmiths, teachers, sculptors, writers" to occupy the castle (11). Not only has Robin thereby transformed the "dead man's house" into a set of cultural apparatus controlled through more democratic social means, but he has also fully committed himself to supporting the cultural workers who now have access to these cultural apparatus. When Harriet Beecher Stowe phones him from "the plush-carpeted walnut-wooded offices of Jewett Publishers in Boston" and offers to write his autobiography as a slave— "what it felt like being the house man of one of the most rich and fabulous men in the world"—Robin rejects her offer because he has offered the authorship of a different kind of narrative to Raven (173–74). Giving him the office space to do the work in the "big spacious rooms" of the whole first floor of the Swille Big House, Robin counsels Raven to produce a work that can not be appropriated (11).[40]

In building his theory of Black Power on a set of concerted and holistic programs for economic, social, and cultural freedom—a Reconstruction multiculturalism— Reed envisions a crucial and serial relationship among political violence, economic power, and administrative control over the means of cultural production.[41] Like the Black Power intellectuals, particularly those affiliated with the Clarke collection, Reed saw that there was a social violence in certain kinds of representations that African American cultural workers could answer only by establishing oppositional institutions and counterdiscourses. Since conventional discourses on slavery created by and in hegemonic cultural apparatus worked not only to delineate portraits of the past but also to comment indirectly on contemporary African American social life, it was crucial for black cultural workers both to dismantle the hegemony and to mobilize a new and enabling discourse progressively attuned to the new intellectual developments on the social construction of race. Like the Black Power intellectuals, Reed shows that caricatures of essentialized racial identities are the creations of American institutions used to stabilize inequitable social relations and sanction acts of cultural imperialism. His Neo-slave narrative is ultimately a critique of those disempowering identities, those acts of cultural appropriation, and the institutions that make them possible.

Toward a HooDoo Practice: Identity Politics and Literary Form

While partially disagreeing with, and partially complicating, the Black Power intellectuals' statements regarding the politics of violence and property, Reed wholeheartedly agrees with their statements on the institutional forces determining the relationship between race and readership, their insistence on seeing literary texts as discontinuously engaged with a present social moment, and their strategic responses to acts of cultural appropriation. He follows their lead in challenging traditions of historical writing about American slavery, demonstrating that the absence of slave testimony leads to flawed and politically disempowering historical representations of African American peoples. He shows how "reading" is a practice that is institutionally grounded by revealing the ways institutions of American cultural life are determinants in reading acts, creating literary "traditions" and "canons" while recreating oppressive schemas of "race." And he follows their example by developing a strategy for dismantling those schemas and contesting the acts of cultural imperialism on which they were premised. In order to do so, Reed returns to the first form of African American representation, the slave narrative, and uses that genre to offer a cautionary tale of how minority voices get appropriated at the same time as racial identities get constructed, while offering a historical lesson on how those voices can be recuperated and those texts protected.

Long a critic of what he calls those "'pure race' theorists" who "hold so much sway over our political and cultural life," Reed insists on acknowledging that racial formations are products of historical forces, specific national conditions, and highly concentrated state cultural apparatus. He notes that a set of political ideologues, black and white, were able to use the media to create and market the "concept Black" in the sixties, just as early American nationalists were able to produce "whiteness" as "an American invention" forming the national consciousness in the eighteenth and nineteenth centuries. These "concepts" and "inventions" are reflected in and constructed by the cultural productions of these two nationalists trends. Exploring the ways specific cultural forms create and reinforce schemas of racial difference, Reed attempts to produce a mélange of forms in his own writing to challenge the allegedly exclusive "national" or "racial" identity of those forms and the forms of identity they embody. By his own assessment, *"Flight to Canada* uses European forms, Native American forms, Afro-American forms" to create a "syncretic" text actively denying the idea that there is an inherent racial component in a given literary form.[42] Since cultural forms defined as exclusively or inherently racial become instruments to reproduce racial formations rationalizing the material and social inequities of a racialized state, Reed feels that disrupting the purity of the forms helps demonstrate the poverty of the racial formations they emerge from and support. In his novel, Reed dismantles the racial formation of the Black Nationalists of the sixties, but he does so while also implicitly contesting the racial formation of the early American nation insofar as part of that national identity—the "invention of whiteness"—has to do with issues deeply involved in the literary form Reed is adopting: the slave narrative of the early republic.

Starting with the narrative of Briton Hammon in 1760, the African American slave's textual representation of slavery confronted a threefold set of problems involving production, reception, and mediation. The antebellum slave narrative was the first form of writing in which was inscribed the "primary pre-generic myth for Afro-America"—the wholly interrelated "quest for freedom and literacy." The slave's writing of his or her own narrative exemplified the marriage of these two quests in the production of one text, written by the escaped slave himself or herself. Given that the slave narrative was written in order to promote the antislavery cause, however, these texts had to be concerned with how they would be received. More specifically, the narrative encountered the problem of constructing a readerly "community" more interested in freedom than in literacy, and more concerned with slavery than with the slave. When Frederick Douglass began his career as an abolitionist lecturer, for example, he found he was prohibited from speaking "just the word that seemed to *me* the word to be spoken *by* me." Attempting to be true to himself by articulating his "moral indignation for the perpetrators of slaveholding villainy," he was told to adopt a *"little* of the plantation manner of speech" and curb his learned commentary. "'Let us have the facts,' said the people." As John Collins, the general agent of the Massachusetts Anti-Slavery Society, told Douglass, "Give us the facts . . . [and] we will take care of the philosophy." White abolitionists William Lloyd Garrison and George Foster echoed this advice as they "always wished to pin" Douglass down to his "simple narrative."[43]

Although the audience of the slave narratives did not share the fugitive slaves' "cultural or moral concerns," the fugitive slave narrators nonetheless had to write their narratives in such a way as to "inform and convert" that very audience. Therefore, the slave narrative, like all the "aggregate literature of the Afro-American written tale," had to be concerned with "comprehending the abiding link in America between race and readership" by advancing "appropriately revised models of competent readership." The postbellum device most often employed for this purpose is a framed tale in which a "black storyteller's white listener" is depicted as "socially and morally maturing into competency." The antebellum device for preparing a community of white readers to accept the slave's testimony involved a mediation between the production and reception of the slave's narrative. In the vast majority of slave narratives, the text expressing the slave's literacy and freedom was governed by "other voices which are frequently just as responsible for articulating a narrative's tale and strategy." The primary function of these mediating voices—abolitionists' prefaces, letters, poems, and other textual apparatus—is to "authenticate the former slave's account" in order to promote the "narrative's acceptance as historical evidence."[44] The slave's textual production was mediated by texts that were not of the slave's authoring in order to construct a receptive community that was not of the slave's race.

What links the problems of production, mediation, and reception is the question of the slave's presence or absence. The slave wished to write himself or herself into presence by demonstrating in a literate form the path he or she took toward freedom. The mediating abolitionist and the receptive community of white readers, on the other hand, wished to read the black slave as an essentially *absent* being. From the beginning of black autobiography in America, the regnant presupposition was that "a black narrator needs a white reader to complete his text, to build a hierarchy of abstract significance on the mere matter of his facts, to supply a presence where there was only 'Negro,' only dark absence." In the crucial years between 1810 and 1840, slave narrators experimented with rhetorical strategies that would allow them to manipulate that presupposition to their advantage. One technique was to construct a narrative that would produce what we can call the "appropriating" reader. As William Andrews points out, some slave narrators used a "mode of auto-biographical discourse that subtly reoriented a reader's response" so that, in effect, the narrator "authorized" the reader's "appropriation" of the narrative. This "authorized appropriation" was meant to destroy the white reader's "distanced perspective" and establish in its place a desire for the reader to engage in the world of the slave in an interested way. "Appropriation" in this sense "occasions a dispossession of the [reader's] ego and a discovery of a new self that emerges from the understanding of the text."

An "appropriating" reader, then, is a reader whose engagement with the text is a pretext to that reader's transformation from a disinterested or partially interested reader into a political agent. Ideally, the reader should have walked away from the slave narrative spiritually transformed and willing to act on behalf of the abolitionist cause. What the abolitionist editors discovered, as we saw in the example of Douglass and the abolitionists, was that the story that was most effectively going to be appropriated by its white readers was the story highlighting the institution of slavery by subordinating the slave subject. In other words, the slave narrative that would be most successful for the abolitionist cause was the narrative in which "the blackness of the writer and his experience have been valorized as a 'natural' absence." To a large extent, the slave narratives published between about 1830 and 1860 seemed to contain just such an absence and were certainly read as if they did. As James Olney noted, the "central focus" of "nearly all" those slave narratives "is slavery, an institution and an external reality, rather than a particular and individual life as it is known internally and subjectively." This strategy of denying the subject's presence in the slave narrative worked to "make the slave narrator an eyewitness, not an I-witness." As might be expected, then, an "appropriating" reader, no matter how amiable a construct this kind of "appropriation" might seem, was nonetheless going to appropriate the story of the fugitive slave. The result of that appropriation was the production of the narrator's absence.[45]

Reed takes up the issue of the black subject's "absence" in *Flight to Canada* in quite interesting ways, most startlingly by having the first-person narrator simply disappear after about eleven pages of the novel. Partly an act of literary parody and an exemplary performance of HooDoo practice (points I will discuss presently), Reed's strategic silencing of the first-person narrator is also a critique of how slave narratives required the absence of the African American voice. It is thus a testament to the ways texts are participants in the creation and mobilization of racial formations—in this case, a formation premised on the "absence" of blackness and the presumed "universality" of whiteness. This hegemonic racial formation was contested in the late sixties when the

Black Power movement valorized "blackness" as a way of addressing the historical denigration of people and things African. By emphasizing "racial difference," by celebrating blackness as something not supplemental or deviant from an assumed norm, Black Power advocates demonstrated how "racial indifference" translated into the presumption of "whiteness"—for many, a neutral category with no history. While Reed did not favor this strategy, because he felt "any discussion about pure race is absurd," he nonetheless saw the value in celebrating the "concept Black" as a strategic intervention into the American "invention of whiteness."⁴⁶

Reed represents this shift in racial formation in *Flight to Canada* in the debates Raven has with his Native American girlfriend Quaw Quaw Tralaralara over the concept of "race." Quaw Quaw persistently maintains that "People are people." "What does race have to do with it?" (150). She complains that Raven is "too ethnic" and should be "more universal." He responds by pointing out that material, concrete conditions define consciousness of identity. "How can I be universal with a steel collar around my neck and my hands cuffed all the time and my feet bound? I can't be universal, gagged" (95–96). When Quaw Quaw is mistaken for a Japanese person by the border police at the Canada-U.S. border, Raven mocks her universalism. "Whenever someone confuses you with some other race, why don't you tell them you don't care about race and that you don't have time to fool with such subjects as race; and that you don't identify with any group" (165). Raven's point is not that racial definitions matter in any existential way, but rather that they matter as state-supported strategies for defining inequities in opportunity and treatment, for deciding at the literal borders of a nation who should occupy the figurative borders of the nation's social and cultural life because they are African American, or Native American, or otherwise othered by being ascribed a "race." As Reed shows, race matters because it is a schema that exemplifies and historically possesses resonant power. Pirate Jack, an exemplary "white man in a white man's country," accurately notes that those who hold and would maintain their power do so by defining racial identity. "The difference between a savage and a civilized man is determined by who has the power" (149).

This power is exercised in the state apparatus not only at the physical borders of the nation, but also in the institutions that define cultural production, particularly literature and especially in terms of "form" and "tradition." For instance, whereas Harriet Beecher Stowe produces a work that introduced the "American novel" to Europe, the black authors whose work she "borrows" get accused of writing merely "autobiography," a form of writing requiring no imagination and particularly suitable to people of African descent because they are "literal-minded, as Mr. Jefferson said" (8, 63). These schemes of classifying and defining categories of knowledge are not whimsical but institutionalized. As Raven tells Quaw Quaw, white institutions of higher education will get "your Indian and my Slave on microfilm and in sociology books" because the so-called African American and Native American experiences constitute the "exotic of the new feudalism" (96). These classifactory schemas affect lives—Quaw Quaw's brother is buried alive in a "sealed-off section of the Metropolitan Museum" (123)—as well as writing. When Stowe sets out to put together "an anthology of slave poetry," her work will no doubt be placed in the library in the appropriate place for poetry; but when slaves themselves publish *The Anthology of Ten Slaves,* their work gets housed in the "anthropology section of the library" (173, 63). The cultural apparatus of this society—libraries, publishers, museums, universities—constitute the machinery of the racialized state; and not only does writing have its accepted forms and genres and disciplines, but these forms, genres, and disciplines are part of the mechanism for defining racial identity.

By showing how writing is a primary site of racialization in the state's cultural apparatus, Reed is able not only to contest definitions of writing premised on "universalist" notions—that is, the idea that people have equal access to the state's resources—but also to demonstrate the specific forms of appropriation that produce and support that inequality. Jean-Paul Sartre provides us with an example of a universalist definition of writing. To write, notes Sartre, is "both to disclose the world and to offer it as a task to the generosity of the reader. It is to have recourse to the consciousness of others in order to make one's self be recognized as *essential* to the totality of being." Sartre can make this claim because he presupposes an act of writing premised on a contract of equality in which racial inequity is not an issue, and therefore reciprocity not an impossibility. According to Sartre, "the one who writes recognizes, by the very fact that he takes the trouble to write, the freedom of his readers; and since the one who reads, by the mere fact of his opening the book, recognizes the freedom of the writer, the work of art, from whichever side you approach it, is an act of confidence in the freedom of men."[47] As we have seen, however, writing for the fugitive slave does not work this way. The reader does not recognize the freedom (or even the presence) of the slave narrator, since the genre itself denies that possibility. Writing in the condition of unfreedom operates along quite different lines and assumes a rather different dynamic, since it is always a terrain of contestation between master texts and slave narratives.

Douglass provides us with a definition of writing more attentive to the ways material and social inequalities affect the would-be writer's "quest for freedom and literacy." Following a series of cunning acts in which he fooled the young boys in the neighbourhood into giving him "lessons in writing," Douglass finally succeeds in "learning how to write" by "writing in the spaces left in Master Thomas's copy-book, copying what he had written." Rather than emerging as a writer confident in the "freedom of men," the fugitive slave has to write on the margins of a master's text, imitating the master's hand, until, at the end of the slave narrative, he is able to "subscribe" himself and conclude his own "little book." Writing, in the slave narrative, is a process of undoing the master's text by rewriting its contents in the margins, while producing one's own identity in an act of revisionist imitation fraught with contradictions. Abdul JanMohamed has noted that the "most crucial aspect of resisting hegemony consists in struggling against its attempt to form one's subjectivity, for it is through the construction of the minority subject that the dominant culture can elicit the individual's help in his / her oppression."[48] And, we may add, it is through that oppression and the construction of the minority subject that the dominant culture recreates the hegemonic schemas of racial difference.

Writing in the condition of unfreedom, then, involves the slave's creating an enabling subject position against the racialist national hegemonic discourses. "Writing is strange" under these conditions, as Raven notes, because the slave narrative becomes the site of both identity formation and co-optation (8). The co-optation can take two forms: outright appropriation and ascription of influence. While writing is where the slave like Josiah Henson creates himself, constructs the "thing that is himself," it is also the site where dominant writers like Harriet Beecher Stowe appropriate that self, "borrowing" it and reconstructing it in a master text (8). In contemporary African American writing, co-optation takes on the form of a critical discourse that persistently assumes and ascribes white influence on black authors. Reed himself was subject to this kind of treatment, as he was relentlessly treated as someone who had "furtively pilfer[ed]" from "white masters," William Burroughs in particular. In *Flight to Canada,* Raven fears that white critics will not notice his indebtedness to black authors, such as William Wells Brown, but will instead "give [him] some kind of white master" (121).[49] In either case, whether a white author "borrows" a black-authored story or a white author is assumed to have influenced a black author, master texts supplant slave narratives. In both cases, the "dark absence" of the black writer leads to the appropriation of her or his narrative. Reed diagnoses and disrupts this disturbing dynamic in his Neo-slave narrative.

He shows how minority authors are presumed absent and slave narratives are vulnerable to appropriation because they are "tracked"—that is, their texts are subject to the "traditions" and "values" governing the field of cultural production, which of course embodies the nation's material and social inequities. Reed's answer is to produce a slave narrative that enacts its own liberatory ideals by "untracking" itself through an act of parody (dismantling mainstream tradition) and an act of defiance (challenging hegemonic values). In order to resist the appropriative tendencies of the mainstream literary establishment, Reed employs a "literary style" based on "Hoodoo culture," about which "white literary culture knew little." He claims that his use of "Neo-Hoodooism was an act of literary defiance"[50] allowing him to develop a form of writing that (1) promoted a cultural identity premised on neither the presumed absence nor the exaggerated racial presence of the black author, (2) offered protection to the text since it was no longer bound to the traditions and values supporting the slave narrative–master text dynamic, and (3) opened up new reading strategies for texts that had previously been appropriated.[51]

Reed begins by offering us a text that is "tracked."[52] Although Raven is able to escape slavery, his written work endangers his freedom because it allows his dyslexic master Swille to "track" him down (13).[53] His slave narrative, a poem recounting the details of his escape, contains a "trace" that betrays his presence, allowing Swille to send out the "NEBRASKA TRACERS, INC." to find and return Raven to his Virginia plantation (52, 62). In other words, the poem acts as an informant against its author's intentions because it contains a surplus meaning that leaves it "tracked."[54] When his poem gives him away, Raven wonders: "Did that make the poem a squealer? A tattler?" The poem, Raven realizes, is both his "creation, but in a sense, Swille's bloodhound" also (85). Reed develops the significance of this ambivalence by noting that, on the one hand, Raven's poem "'Flight to Canada' . . . tracked him down" while, on the other, "'Flight to Canada' was responsible for getting him to Canada" (88–89). Reed manages to capture the ambivalent senses of writing as dangerous and as liberating—as something that aids Raven in his escape from the Swille plantation and something that also endangers Raven because he is part of the "trace" of the text and the text is therefore able to "track" him down. Part of what Reed is doing in representing a text that is both a means to freedom and an endangering of that freedom is paying tribute to those antebellum slave narratives that had earlier recorded this same dilemma.

James Pennington noted at the beginning of his slave narrative that it is important for any human being to have a sense of "family history"—a situation in which a son (in his case) can "appeal to the history of his family in vindication of his character." Although Pennington attempted to write himself a family history in the form of *The Fugitive Blacksmith,* he found at the end that he could not make full disclosure of his "family history" since doing so would deleteriously affect precisely those people making up his "family." Near the close of his narrative, he noted that while he had "many other deeply interesting particulars touching our family history," he was unable to disclose them for fear of harming "those members who are yet south of Mason and Dixon's line." Likewise, while Douglass deeply regretted the necessity that impelled him "to suppress any thing of importance connected with [his] experience in slavery," he thought he had to forgo the pleasure of giving his readers "an accurate statement of all the facts pertaining to [his] most fortunate escape" in order not to close "the slightest avenue by which a brother slave might clear himself of the chains and fetters of slavery." Henry "Box" Brown, whose escape in a box mailed through the U.S. postal system was actually not the first attempt made by a slave to be delivered of the peculiar institution in this way, said that he had imagined various other schemes before settling on this one. He chose not to reveal those schemes or plans, because "some unfortunate slaves may thereby be prevented from availing themselves of these methods of escape."[55]

By showing how a text is tracked, Reed is establishing the primary and integral function of the "trace" in acts of fugitive slave writing, textuality, and self-representation—showing how, in the condition of unfreedom, writing is not an "act in the confidence of the freedom of men" but rather a tremulous entry into a terrain fraught with social and cultural inequities. On that terrain, according to the traditions and values of that field of cultural production, slave writings and stories remain "tracked" and subject to theft by unscrupulous white masters-authors. That, according to Reed, is precisely what happened to Josiah Henson. In commenting on Stowe's alleged plagiarism-theft of Henson's slave narrative, Raven states: "It was short, but it was his. It was all he had. His story. A man's story is his gris-gris, you know. Taking his story is like taking his gris-gris. The thing that is himself" (8).[56] Raven's story or "writings" are subject to the same kind of treatment. We are told his "poems were 'readings' for him from his inner self, which knew more about his future than he did. While others had their tarot cards, their ouija boards, their I-Ching, their cowrie shells, he had his 'writings'" (88). Ironically, those stories and "writings" are liable to being stolen insofar as they are treated as "possessions."[57] What Raven discovers is that he cannot control his story so long as it remains only *his* story. A personal story must become an expression of collective identity and a representation of communal experience in order not to be appropriated. Having shown that the danger to Raven will persist so long as he treats his story as an individual possession in a "tracked" text, Reed goes on to demonstrate how Raven "untracks" his text by employing a form of writing that will not betray his identity, one less susceptible to appropriation.

Reed delineates the interrelated two-part process of "untracking" the text. First, he uses parody as a means of dismantling the hegemonic tradition that sanctions acts of appropriation and promotes the critical discourse ascribing white influence on black authors. Second, he employs the principles of Hoodoo to promote an African American subjectivity and form of writing that protect the text from appropriation. Parody, then, is the deconstructive aspect, Hoodoo the productive, of Reed's form of resistant writing practice. For Reed, parody constitutes a literary strategy with the potential to disrupt the conventions and traditions of mainstream literary history. "When the parody is better than the original a mutation occurs which renders the original obsolete. Reed's Law."[58] "Reed's Law" is a counterintuitive statement of how intertextual relations are established and how they can operate. It demands that we see the relationship between a parodic text and its "host" text in new ways, that we redefine what we can mean when we say that one text "influenced" another, or one author is another's "master." In more specific terms, Reed offers us an imaginative new way of rethinking the relationship between master texts and slave narratives.

Theorizing the art of resistant parody as a critical intervention into the field of cultural production, Reed helps us appreciate the complexities of his syncretic, multiform text and the terrain on which it is waging battle against cultural imperialism. Reed uses a form of intertextual literary intervention to contest those works of art that constitute acts of cultural appropriation and also to challenge the academic and social institutions sanctioning those acts. Like the Black Power intellectuals in the Clarke collection, Reed shows how cultural productions emerge from specific historiographical traditions, and, he, like them, attempts to "subvert history from within" by showing that the historical representations are based on the absence of the testimony of slaves while the fictional works are based on appropriation of the voices of slaves.[59]

Reed's critique of those who have ignored or abused slave narratives is complicated, though, because the formal properties of *Flight to Canada* are so complex. Obviously, the main target of Reed's parodic impetus is Stowe's *Uncle Tom's Cabin.* Reading the novel as a parody of only *Uncle Tom's Cabin,* some critics have argued that in "*Flight to Canada,* Reed parodies the classical historical novel, inviting the reader to flout the very generic contract he has invoked." What we have to consider, however, is that Reed is also casting his novel into the *form* of a slave narrative, that Reed gives us nothing less than a thorough "revision of the form of the earliest popular Afro-American writing, the fugitive slave narrative." The novel begins with the fugitive slave Raven's three-page poem called "Flight to Canada" (3–5). The prose narrative begins with Raven's four-and-a-half-page first-person meditation on his own poem and on the crime Stowe committed against Henson when she "borrowed" his story. Abruptly, Raven's first-person voice falls silent and the rest of the narrative is offered through a third-person omniscient narrator who tells us that Raven has been commissioned to write Uncle Robin's story (11). In other words, *Flight to Canada* takes on the formal properties and assumes both the first-person and third-person voices of the fugitive slave narrative and the classical historical novel.[60]

Reed's parodic strategy implies that the "original" that would be rendered "obsolete" if his parody is successful is not only Stowe's classical historical novel, but also the slave narrative itself, which is, after all, the form in which he begins writing his novel. Revising the strategy of the writers in the Clarke collection, Reed is also mak-

ing a point about the institutional determinants of "first readings." Reed applies
"Reed's Law" both to the master texts that appropriate slave narratives and to the appropriated narratives themselves—in the one case to *savage* the appropriating master text, in the other to *salvage* the appropriated slave narrative. We can say, then,
that Reed produces a slave narrative that is itself a resistant reading of a master text.
While parodying Stowe's novel by recasting some of her characters and rewriting
some of her scenes in order to redress her "theft" of Henson's autobiography and
render her book obsolete, Reed also inhabits and revises the formal properties of
slave narratives such as Henson's in order to establish a new space between Henson's
text and its historically established intertext, Stowe's novel, thereby also rendering
the intertextual relationship between those two books obsolete. He offers a parody
of slave narratives *as they were read* as a way of reconstructing potential readings of
slave narratives *as they can be read.* Since *Uncle Tom's Cabin* is not original but
nonetheless acts as a mediating force that governs the reading of original slave narratives written by people like Henson, a parody that renders *Uncle Tom's Cabin* obsolete simultaneously opens up the possibility for fresh readings of those co-opted
slave narratives. In other words, what Reed is rendering obsolete are readers' reading
patterns and expectations. That, we can say, is the corollary to "Reed's Law." What he
is establishing is nothing less than a reading strategy that is not based on appropriation. And he is doing so by returning to the form of writing which, in African American literature, provided both the first form of black representation and resistance
and the first literary instance of white appropriation of black texts and voices.

At the same time that he is deploying parody as a way of dismantling mainstream literary tradition, Reed employs what he calls "HooDoo writing" to demonstrate a culture-specific way of constructing black subjectivity and protecting black-
authored texts (10). Premised on the religious practice of Voudon, Reed's version of
HooDoo allows him to develop a model for the performance of African American
identity that does not answer the presumed absence of black authors with an exaggerated or hyperracialized presence, since that strategy would play into precisely the
kind of rugged individualism and "pure race" thinking Reed eschews. Instead,
HooDoo provides Reed with a method for constructing a more flexible, less essentialized racial subjectivity, premised on Vodoun's most basic "belief that the African
'gods,' or loas, are present in the Americas and often use men and women as their
mediums."[61]

As well as having a religious purpose, spirit possession in Voudon also has bear-
ings on a more strictly political issue—the question of whether any kind of transcendence is an act of resistance against or acquiescence to an intolerable material condition, since possession can be interpreted as either "recognition and acceptance of
dependency toward the spirit world" or "protest against inferior status and dependency toward the wider society." Like Michel Saturnin Laguerre, Reed believes that
being possessed "is a political act inasmuch as it is a symbolic reaction against a dependent societal status." There is another feature of possession, however; and that
has to do with how possession acts to produce a sensibility of the possessed person's
belonging to and being identified with the *sociéte* of Voudon believers. In other
words, spirit possession has an oppositional substance and style because it prob-
lematizes rather than asserts individual identity. Because the spirits in Voudon are al-

ways "functions of rather exigent . . . socio-political situations," we must imagine a terrain "where laws of identity and contradiction no longer work" in the ways a "Western Atonist" would imagine them working.[62]

What possession in Voudon does, then, is produce two interrelated effects. First of all, the possessed person loses the sense of a reified and stable "selfhood." The relationship between the loa and the person possessed by the loa is one of contingency. As Maya Deren writes in her classic study of Haitian Vodoun, when the loa "enters reality it not only acts upon that reality but is, of necessity, defined, shaped and modified by it." The subjective experience is modified by becoming part of the divine experience. Likewise, the fact that the divine principle is altered by being manifest in human forms means that the sense of identity bound with being possessed becomes radically problematized: "The very notion of what constitutes a person or identity is indelibly tied to the loa, whose lineaments are in turn dependent on the contingent and human." Therefore, although possession can be understood as a "transitory period of exalted and exclusive obsession with a principle," possession also entails that the possessed person assume a "quality of selflessness, discipline and even of depersonalization. The performer becomes as if anonymous." Selfhood is eschewed as "the source of all virtuosity . . . whose pride is the pleasure of unique achievement." Such aspects of selfhood as volition are subsumed in the state of possession. "The person mounted," writes Zora Neale Hurston, "does nothing of his own accord." Indeed, in the state of possession, when the "spirits have entered his head," they must have already "driven his own consciousness out." Possession by a loa, therefore, "soothes all the diversity of singular fears, personal losses, and private anxieties" because there is actually no "self" in the possessed person since "the self must leave if the loa is to enter."

This loss of self is not the same as Protestant self-abnegation, because it is not a prelude to the individual's becoming one with God in an act of private salvation; rather, loa possession is the act of a god's possessing an individual primarily for the "reassurance and instruction of the community" since the "affairs of the loa are the affairs of the sociéte." This is the second effect of possession in Voudon. The possessed person's loss of a sense of distinction between self and other leads to a renewed sense of collective identity. The possessed person "becomes aware of his interdependence with the members of the society and the mutuality of their destinies." The subjective self is possessed by a "loa [which] contains both subject and object" for the benefit of the collective community.[63] In other words, possession provides people practicing Voudon with the process and benefits of intersubjectivity: the means by which individual identity is problematized so that individual experience intersects with collective experience, becomes validated as part of the community enterprise, and is then translated back into the transcendental principles governing the subject and the community. Loss of self in loa possession, then, involves intersubjectivity in terms of both persons and communities.

Reed's HooDoo clearly involves the same practice—spirit possession—and is aimed toward the same end—intersubjectivity—as Voudon. In particular, he notes, it is "Afro-American writers [who] still summon the loas." In *Flight to Canada,* after meditating on the idea that "writing is strange," Raven establishes the conditions for what he calls his "HooDoo writing" (8, 10): HooDoo writing is akin to possession by a loa in that it puts him "in contact with those fleeting moments which prove the existence of the soul," because writing provides him with the capacity for becoming less solipsistic and more attuned to the benefits of selfless possession. It also provides Reed with a means of connecting his experience to a collective experience. HooDoo writing permits the possessed person to be intimately at one with others in his or her community. "HooDoo artists," he concludes, "serve the community as 'soothsayers, exorcisers, organizers of public entertainment, and choirmasters.'" The ultimate purpose of Reed's HooDoo aesthetic enterprise, I am arguing, is to reproduce the conditions essential to Vodoun—a form of possession premised on the principle that the individual subject must lose his or her self in order to merge with the loa. What Raven calls "HooDoo writing" is a result of spirit possession, and *Flight to Canada* is an enactment or performance of that Voudon principle. Whereas "most Afro-American writers" are HooDoo artists "in principle," Reed is, just as he says of David Henderson, "a HooDoo poet in substance as well."[64]

Writing, as we recall, had been dangerous to Raven because his text was "tracked." Not only had slavery still pervaded his social and interpersonal relationships, but his writing itself continued to threaten his freedom. Slavery residually affected his psychic and social life, and his writing was ambivalent because he treated his writing as a material "possession." His writing had to become less his material possession and more the product of a spiritual possession. Ironically, the way to control one's own narrative in *Flight to Canada* is to allow the writing to possess oneself instead of having oneself possess the writing. Once Raven learns to think of his writing as a loa, he is able to understand how best to remove the dangerous "track" from his narrative. Only then can "writing" become "his HooDoo. Others had their way of HooDoo, but his was his writing. It fascinated him, it possessed him; his typewriter was his drum he danced to" (88–89). Once writing possesses the writer, the story becomes no longer dangerous to him or her—but only to whoever would attempt to steal it. "When you take a man's story," notes Raven, "a story that doesn't belong to you, that story will get you" (9).

In being possessed by writing, Raven not only produces a narrative endangering whoever attempts to co-opt it, but he also creates the conditions for healing those victimized by the experience of slavery. According to Reed, "HooDoo writing" is essential to that act of collective healing necessary for slavery to end its influence on the behavior of its survivors. The primary example of that writing and healing is in the two main characters in the novel—Raven and Uncle Robin. We are told that Raven "had never gotten along with Uncle Robin in slavery, but away from slavery they were the best of friends" (13). They become so amicable after slavery because Raven and Robin then build their relationship on the basic tenets of HooDoo writing. In other words, Raven learns to write in the manner of HooDoo and thereby changes the relationships among the slaves on what used to be Swille's plantation. Before he engaged in "HooDoo writing," Raven was unable to write in a way that was solely positive—even when writing against the institution of slavery as when he rewrote Swille's receipts so as to destroy the records of his ownership of slaves, or when he wrote out passes or freedom papers for the other fugitives, or even when he wrote his own slave narrative-poem. Only when he starts to employ "HooDoo writing" is he able to write in a positive way.

Here, now, we can turn to Reed's play with the form of the Neo-slave narrative. Having shown us that slaves *perform* their racialized roles (especially when they are pretending to be docile), and that slaves are inspired by the gods when they engage in resistance, Reed shows us that the way for slaves to avoid having their texts appropriated or their racial identities entirely subject to the hegemonic racial formation is for slaves to produce narratives that are just as performative as their lives. What Reed has Raven do is produce a slave narrative that enacts the Vodoun practice of spirit possession. Consider the strategic beginning of the novel. The book opens with Raven's signed poem, "Flight to Canada" (3–5). Then for the first four and a half pages, we have Raven's first-person narration-meditation on the mysteries of history, the dangers of stealing someone else's story, and the principles of "HooDoo writing" (7–11). After an abrupt shift to third-person narration in the middle of the first chapter, we are informed that Raven has been commissioned to write "Uncle Robin's story" (11). Thereafter, the narrative becomes what Raven alternately calls "my story" and "Robin's story" (14).[65] In these first eleven pages, we find Raven referring to the process by which stories become merged so that the writing is no longer about the self or the other, but about the intersubjective relations between the two. Not only does Reed break with the traditional form of biographical or autobiographical writing as the story of an individual by having both forms operate in the same text, but he also gives that multiply voiced text the agency of divine possession.

What Raven calls "my story" and what the narrator calls "Robin's story" are in effect the same story because it is Raven who is also the possessed narrator. Indeed, what Reed is attempting to do in a literary text is not simply describe but truly to enact what Joan Dayan calls "the *crise de loa*—that moment when the god inhabits the head of his or her servitor."[66] The last thought Raven has in his interior monologue is: "Harriet saying that God wrote *Uncle Tom's Cabin*. Which God? Some gods will mount any horse" (11). Immediately thereafter, the narrative is related through a third-person narrator. In other words, the writing possesses Raven—"Do the lords still talk? Do the lords still walk? Are they writing this book?" (10)—and thereby produces the conditions for an intimate intersubjective connection between Raven and Robin, which, in turn, protects the text from appropriation. By producing a text that is spiritually possessed—Robin had told him to "put witchery on the word" so that "to lay hands on the story would be lethal to the thief" (13, 11)—Raven produces a text that is safe from being materially possessed and frees his body from the danger of being literally repossessed. As a way of showing how performance underwrites racial roles, Reed produces a narrative that is itself performative, a text that frustrates not only the slave narrative form, but more important, the masters themselves, who lack the intellectual resources to track such a slave because they lack the imagination to read such a narrative. Just prior to his possession, Raven argues that the gods conceal themselves "to spite the mean-minded, who are too unimaginative to recognize the new forms" the gods have given themselves (9). One of those forms in which the gods perform occurs in a Neo-slave narrative based on what Raven calls his "HooDoo writing."[67]

Latent in Raven's writing, then, is a magic that allows him to represent himself and other slaves in a different way—a way that would not permit the text to "track" down its author or its subject precisely because, as HooDoo writing stipulates, the text has no single subject. Having been possessed by writing, Raven is able to embark on an autobiographical act not based solely on the representation of self but necessarily based on the imbrication of self and other. HooDoo writing literally frees the subject from an enslaving concept of solipsistic individuality. By offering us a narrative structured as a form of spirit possession and thereby producing intersubjective relations between the slave subjects of the narrative, Reed is also making a point about his own "originals," arguing that slave narratives need not be read as statements of radical *subjectivity* in order for a revisionist reader to answer their having been previously read as expressions of their narrators' *absence*. Instead, we need to read the classic slave narratives in a way that enables us to attend to the strategies fugitive slave narrators used in writing their texts so that those texts were going neither to deny the presence of their subjects nor to endanger the paths to freedom of their brethren.

I suggested earlier that Olney is largely correct in noting that "slavery"—and not the former slave—was primarily the subject of representation in most slave narratives published after a foundational abolitionist press was established in America. However, there are exceptions and narratives that disrupt the conventional form of the abolitionist narratives. They are the kinds of slave narratives reclaiming the stories of their author's lives and the life of the author's community. These slave narratives situate themselves as narratives authorizing the "appropriating" reader's reading at the same time as they subtly construct what we can call an "appropriate community" of other readers, readers whose claim to authority is their having shared with the author the experience of slavery. In these particular narratives, I think we find the fullest manipulation of and resistance to the presupposition that "a black narrator needs a white reader to complete his text." As Andrews points out, in the 1840s there emerged in some slave narratives a "sense of an individual authorial personality, the sound of a distinctive authorizing voice." These slave narrators made a claim to authority by announcing "that truth to the self takes priority over what the white reader may think is either probable or politic to introduce into discourse." In this way, the slave narrator claimed "allegiance to the self rather than to the other, the reader."[68] By noting the distinction between self and other—instead of eliding it *as a way of surrendering the self*—these narrators were able to refashion a healing relationship between the self and another community of readers, a different set of others.

The most important slave narrative to exemplify this claim is Douglass's 1845 *Narrative*. Early on, Douglass makes the claim to his reader that his story is resolutely his and that the reader is not invited to appropriate it: "I prefer to be true to myself, even at the hazard of incurring the ridicule of others, rather than to be false, and incur my own abhorrence." Having made the distinction between self and other in order to make the claim of being true to himself, Douglass is then able to claim the authority that comes from experience. Throughout his narrative, Douglass informs the reader of the reader's limitations. Rather than inviting the reader to join him in rejoicing at the feeling of empowerment he enjoyed after defeating Covey in their fight, Douglass informs the reader that this sense of empowerment will be comprehensible to only a select few: "He only can understand the deep satisfaction which I experienced, who has himself repelled by force the bloody arm of slavery." Likewise, rather than assuring the reader that he or she knows what it is to feel distrust, Douglass insists on informing the reader that "to understand it, one must needs experi-ence it, or imagine himself in similar circumstances." But to "imagine" what a fugi-tive slave feels, Douglass adds, is possible only to one who has "experienced" the life of a "fugitive slave in a strange land": "then, and not till then, will he fully appreciate the hardships of, and know how to sympathize with, the toil-worn and whip-scarred fugitive slave." By insisting on the authority of experience, Douglass vali-dates another community of readers as participants in his story. Ironically, the com-munity of what Douglass calls "the society of my fellow-slaves" turns out to be based on relations that appear not too strictly founded on firm distinctions between self and other. Writing about the slave community, Douglass notes that "[w]e were linked and interlinked with each other. . . . We never moved separately. We were one."[69] His story, Douglass suggests, is their story; their story is his story.

Authors of slave narratives after Douglass follow his example in making a "de-clarative act of defining autobiographical truth as one's inalienable private posses-sion." Pennington, for instance, finding himself accosted by a group of captors dur-ing the course of his escape, decides to lie about his background because he decides that the "facts in this case are my private property" which would have been ill used by those to whom they were honestly disclosed: "Knowing the fatal use these men would make of *my* truth, I at once concluded that they had no more right to it than a highwayman has to a traveller's purse." Also like Douglass, these narrators use their claim to their own experience and their own truth to construct a community of appropriate readers. Near the close of his narrative, Pennington performs two sig-nificant acts toward that end. He writes a letter to the members of his family who are still in bondage in order to tell his mother that his story and hers are intimately con-nected: "Thy agonies are by a genuine son-like sympathy mine; I will, I must, I do share daily in those agonies of thine." He also writes a letter to his former master telling him that although Pennington was "bred, born, and raised in your family," he cannot call him a "father in Israel" or a "brother in Christ" because "mockery is a sin."[70] In other words, having claimed his story as his "private property," Penning-ton declares that it is to be shared with one family—the "dearly beloved in bonds"—but not with another, falsely called "family" of readers.

Slave narrators such as Douglass and Pennington repudiated the premise of an "absent" slave subject by writing themselves more resolutely as agents who can and do manipulate discourses. What is worth noting is that the fugitive slave narrator proclaims that his or her story is never just his or her story at the same time as the narrator notes that not all "others" are equally invited to be equal sharers in this story. Employing different discursive means of self-representation—open proclama-tion or covert silence about a personal and private truth—slave narrators maintain that while the story they will tell deals, as Olney puts it, with slavery as an "institu-tion and an external reality" and not with an "individual life as it is known internally and subjectively," they also insist that the story they tell is not theirs alone. We can say that Pennington, Douglass, and other slave narrators offer an individual life as it is known intersubjectively, as it is revealed to a community of readers as part of a collective experience.

That is also what Reed does in *Flight to Canada*. He offers us a text that is both tracked and untracked, in danger of being appropriated until it is addressed to an appropriate *sociéte* of readers. Parodying major texts of mainstream literary history, casting a HooDoo spell on Western notions of the ontic status of self and other, challenging the hegemonic racial formation of the state and the cultural apparatus used to support that formation, Reed follows the example of the Black Power intellectuals in the Clarke collection by recuperating an original slave narrative from its historical appropriation and showing that "readings" are not neutral and innocent, but are acts prompted and directed by institutional imperatives, by the majoritarian society's need to conceptualize its racial other in particular ways (absence or deviance). Like his predecessors in the Clarke collection, Reed shows how the values and traditions of the hegemonic field of cultural production build and rely on readerly expectations that inexorably lead to misreadings of these early texts of African American subjectivity. The difference is that Reed's resistant rereading recuperates not only the text but the very form of the slave narrative. Indeed, what Raven says of his poem "Flight to Canada"—that is it is "more of a reading than a writing" (7)—is assuredly true of *Flight to Canada*, the first of the Neo-slave narratives mobilized by the new discourse on slavery.

5

Meditations on Story

Sherley Anne Williams's Dessa Rose

The first Neo-slave narrative appeared in the mid-seventies, a period of wide-spread but critical nostalgia about the sixties, when former activists and their adversaries reassessed the political achievements of the decade in light of the declining economic strength of the United States, the "benign neglect" of the Nixon administration to African American life, and the rising tide of neoconservative politics. The next three Neo-slave narratives, however, appeared in the eighties, a period of far more polarized responses to the sixties, when former radicals and liberals felt that the enthusiasm and energy of the sixties seemed "far away and unreal" and yet the sole remaining "hope of our society" in a period of reactionary retrenchment, while conservatives and neoconservatives demonized the "adversary culture" of what they called that "destructive generation." When Reagan's Republicans came to power in the wake of the sixties, largely by employing a political rhetoric appealing to those "middle Americans" alienated by the cultural and social developments associated with the sixties, they began dismantling the remnants of the Great Society "entitlement" programs, themselves last-gasp efforts of a declining New Deal Order. In particular, the so-called "Reagan revolution" attacked Title VII of the 1964 Civil Rights Act (the "affirmative action" that became "reverse discrimination" in neoconservative political rhetoric) and rendered irrelevant those agencies designed to protect newly won civil rights by appointing black conservatives to head them (Clarence Pendleton for the U.S. Commission on Civil Rights, Clarence Thomas for the Equal Opportunity Employment Commission).[1]

It was within this political and intellectual climate that the largest body of literature on the sixties emerged, much of it "written in defiance of Reaganism or in anticipation of its demise," some of it "prompted by the political conservatism of the Reagan era." The majority of historians (many of them former activists in the movement) produced notable appreciative studies to mark the twentieth anniversary of each important event in the civil rights movement. Beginning with William Chafe's 1980 history of the 1960 sit-in movement, scholars commemorated the sixties in a series of monographs and conferences that culminated in 1987 and 1988 with the convergence of studies respectively marking the twenty-fifth anniversary of the Port Huron Statement and Students for a Democratic Society and the twentieth anniversary of 1968 as the watershed year of the movement. There were notable voices of dissent, however, coming primarily from those sixties activists who had adopted conservative and neoconservative politics in the eighties. Gathering together in the fall of 1987 to discuss the "sixties" and in the spring of 1990 to discuss "race in America," a group of former radicals met in a mood of "obdurate anti-nostalgia" to "look back in anger , or at least contentiousness, at the 1960s." At what they called these "Second Thoughts Conferences," they certainly did not come to praise but rather to condemn the decade of their youthful exuberance and the nation's promise. In the eighties, then, the sixties came to represent not simply "a mother lode of nostalgia suitable for commercial exploitation," but either an "inspirational model of social change" or the "explanation for many of the nation's current woes."[2]

Feeling the effects of both the charged political rhetoric and the concrete economic realities of the Reagan revolution, black intellectuals began to assess African American gains and losses since the sixties: a 400 percent increase in the black middle class, a devastating rise in the black underclass, and a steady decline in the median income and quality of life for the majority of African Americans. These factors, coupled with the erosion of social support service programs and the courts' assault on affirmative action, produced what came increasingly to be called "the *post*–civil rights era of the Eighties." The economic fissuring of the "black community" led to or revealed the political and intellectual diversity in black America. Left-liberal black intellectuals questioned how the aspirations and legal achievements of the sixties had been betrayed, while black conservatives and neoconservatives turned on those achievements, especially affirmative action. Black liberals and leftists generally saw through the Republican strategies of co-opting the rhetoric of the early sixties in declaring, as did Pendleton, that America was or could be imagined to be a "color blind society that has opportunities for all and guarantees success for none." Living in a society neither color-blind nor offering opportunities for all, but one that nonetheless did produce the conditions for economic success for some African Americans, black liberals and radicals saw the evil intent in promoting the "racial equality syndrome" in a nation where resources and rewards were unequally distributed. Black neoconservatives, on the other hand, defended the Republican rhetoric by appealing to simple-minded pop psychology ("black Americans are today more oppressed by doubt than by racism"), by advocating a muscular individualism (respect would be won for the race through "the outstanding achievements of individual black persons"), by emphasizing cultural and ignoring historical factors ("*no* policy can apply to history"), and by demanding of their leftist compeers "sixties-style proof for eighties-style racism." For both black leftists and conservatives, though, the sixties represented the moment defining their contemporary politics, whether, with Lerone Bennett, they believed it to be "one of the great decades of the century" or, with Glenn Loury, they condemned the "nihilism and moral relativism of '60s countercultural thinking" as the most notorious and "detrimental legacy of that infamous decade."[3]

Effects of the sixties and widely evident in the eighties, the changes in black demographics and black intellectual alignments are important to our study because these changes affected the contours and subject matter of post civil rights black fiction in general and the Neo-slave narratives of the eighties in particular. The growth of the black middle class had an overall positive effect on black cultural production. The significant presence of members of the black middle class as literary agents, editors, and reviewers signaled the demise of the "old black talent / white management pattern," altering the institutional structures within which African American cultural workers produce their art. Moreover, the rise of a black reading public associated with the growing black middle class fueled a virtual renaissance of the black novel, whose authors no longer felt constrained to address themselves to a predominantly white readership but instead expressed the "desires and anxieties" of the new black middle class "freely and from the inside." Second, the divided political affiliations of that black middle class has given black novels in general, and Neo-slave narratives especially, a new salience, as these works of fiction represent and contribute to the political dialogue of the post–civil rights era.[4] Somewhat like the African American novels of the 1890s and early 1900s, which had representative characters debate the relative merits of the political visions of Booker T. Washington and W. E. B. DuBois, the novels of the 1980s raise the topics at issue in black intellectual circles ranging from interracial romance to affirmative action. Nonetheless, while the Neo-slave narratives of the eighties are aimed at a black readership and address the social issues important to and political divisions within the black intelligentsia, they are also very much concerned with the long-standing issues of social and economic inequities between blacks and whites in American society and culture.

The Neo-slave narratives of the eighties, then, remain resolutely concerned with the dynamic that animated the Neo-slave narrative from its origins in the sixties. Moreover, both Sherley Anne Williams and Charles Johnson, the authors of the Neo-slave narratives of the eighties, write novels deeply immersed in the sixties, not only because the form in which they are writing (and the debates in which they are therefore engaging) originated in that decade but also because both were involved in sixties cultural politics and both began writing their Neo-slave narratives in the sixties. That neither could find a publisher willing to take a chance on their novels until the eighties led them to explore how the institutions in the field of cultural production operated to produce and reproduce racial schemas, how the political apparatus create conditions for cultural appropriation and delimit options for certain kinds of liberating racial identity. Like Reed, both Williams and Johnson produce Neo-slave narratives mobilized by the discourses on slavery created and contested in the sixties, contribute to the cultural politics and institutions of their own time, and raise again the question of what kind of black subjectivity is possible in the post–civil rights era.

In *Dessa Rose* (1986), Williams produces a meditation on the interrelated ways power inhabits the field of cultural production and the terrain of personal life. Primarily interested in how socially liberating narratives are filtered and contained through state apparatus, Williams writes a novel in which she produces her own culturally empowered filters while exposing the precise ways the unequal power relations created by the institutional structures of a society are imbricated in the daily lives of its citizens. Williams begins by diagnosing the processes through which institutions like the publishing industry and the popular media control and categorize the cultural production of minority peoples. She exposes the ways these institutional arrangements create conditions for cultural appropriation, using as her example the case of William Styron's *Confessions of Nat Turner,* which, she notes, was "greeted with wild applause by white critics who know nothing of the history of experience which Styron sought to portray." Finally, she demonstrates how these institutional arrangements and appropriative tendencies operate in the unreflective attitudes and unwitting actions of individuals, the daily acts of white people who recreate racial categories by subtly appropriating the "stories" of black people. At each point in her examination of the levels of oppression in society, Williams displays the acts of resistance exercised by those people whose lives and narratives are at stake. Arguing strenuously that the movements of the sixties helped change the dynamics of the literary world by changing the social relations in the nonliterary world, Williams exposes the power relations in literary institutions, considers the significance of individual writers' acts of appropriation, and demonstrates the pliability of race by dwelling on the performativity of racial roles, especially racial roles inherited from slavery (Sambo and the slave rebel, whose modern counterparts are the "Integrationist Negro" and the "Black Nationalist").[5]

Creating strategic culture-specific filters as a kind of performative prophylactic for her own narrative—using fantasies of slave love as "a prism" through which tales of slave suffering "must be read," using accounts of slave cultural activity, like corn-husking, to mark the continuity of cultural life from slavery to freedom—Williams undertakes the dual but imbricated tasks of demonstrating that racial roles are performed and developing a narrative form that contests and prevents the appropriative acts of would-be literary masters. She dismantles both the master narratives that define and reify racial categories and the master texts that appropriate and colonize enraced voices. Williams does this by showing us how a written text attempts to circumscribe racial identity, how that written text inhabits and draws from oral forms of narrative (especially narratives about kinship), and finally, how a radical and performed oral formation disrupts and eventually subsumes that written text. In the end, Williams exposes what she calls the "hypocrisy of the literary tradition" and its institutional supports, demonstrates the ideological ramifications of this "literary tradition" in the daily recreation of race, and represents the process by which the historically oppressed recuperate their own narratives, telling "the story of how the dispossessed become possessed of their own history."[6]

Williams on the Black Power Sixties

More explicitly than the other authors discussed in this study, Williams produces a Neo-slave narrative that situates itself in an extended dialogue with the prototype of the Neo-slave narrative form, Styron's *Confessions of Nat Turner.* We saw that in *Flight to Canada* Reed had made scattered allusions to the debate over Styron's *Confessions,* while also choosing as his subject an analogous case of an earlier white author's attempt to master a slave's narrative. We will see in the chapters following this one that Johnson also situates his two Neo-slave narratives in an intertextual relationship with Styron's novel through more elusive means: in *Oxherding Tale,* by metafiction-ally theorizing that the slave narrative form contains properties of enduring significance that residually affect later deployments of the form, and demonstrating this by creating an allusive signifying chain from *Uncle Tom's Cabin* to *Flight to Canada;* and in *Middle Passage,* by symbolically reversing Styron's act of appropriation in his depiction of an ex-slave in the act of reappropriating a master text and transforming it into a slave narrative.

In *Dessa Rose,* Williams makes an explicit connection between her novel and the prototype of the Neo-slave narrative. Urged by her publisher and editor to describe the circumstances motivating her to write the novel, she produced an "Author's Note" in which she refers to being "outraged by a certain, critically acclaimed novel" that had "travestied the as-told-to-memoir of slave revolt leader Nat Turner." As both reviewers and critics have noted, Williams then goes on to parody Styron's *Confessions of Nat Turner* in the section of the novel entitled "The Darky" (pp. 9–72) by having the white Adam Nehemiah play the role of Thomas Gray to Dessa Rose's Nat Turner. Nehemiah interviews Dessa while she is in jail just as Styron had Gray interview Turner; Nehemiah's motive is to write a tract advising masters how to prevent slave revolts, just as Gray had attempted to write a document that contained the Turner rebellion and defused public fear over slave rebelliousness by diagnosing the roots of the rebellion in the slave revolt leader's lust for a white mistress.[7] That section of the novel is a rewritten version of a short story Williams had originally entitled "Meditations on History" (parodying the term Styron employed in his "Author's Note" to describe the kind of fiction he was writing: "less an 'historical novel' in conventional terms than a meditation on history").[8]

Williams situates her novel so closely to Styron's partly because she started writing her "Meditations on History" in the late sixties, when, she says, "many, many black intellectuals were still incensed about Styron's portrayal of Nat Turner." She recalls that she was writing her story at the same time that John Henrik Clarke's *William Styron's Nat Turner: Ten Black Writers Respond* appeared. Yet she also insists that "Styron's influence" on *Dessa Rose* was "pretty much confined to the original short story."[9] Her novel was not meant to be a thorough revision of Styron's text, nor did she attempt to establish a consistent formal intertextual relationship with Styron's *Confessions.* While his novel might have outraged her, it did not ultimately condition the terms of her own work. Rather, she wrote a novel that directs our attention to the disparity in access to power between those who write master texts and those who produce slave narratives, that attempts to come to terms with the historiography of American chattel slavery, and finally, that articulates its own vision of the Black Power politics that had surrounded the emergence of the form in which she is writing. In other words, she wrote a Neo-slave narrative that established a discontinuous intertextual relationship with the social and historical epoch of its formal origins. In this way, she produced a work that not only shares the formal properties of *Flight to Canada* and *Oxherding Tale,* Neo-slave narratives published before hers, but also, like them, presents itself as a strategic intervention into the field of cultural production.

Like the other authors treated in this study, Williams had an ambivalent attitude toward the Black Power and the Black Arts movements. We saw that Reed broke off his affiliations with Black Power in the late sixties, mocked the movement in the early seventies, arrived at a sort of tentative *rapprochement* in the mid-seventies, before becoming much more appreciative of the achievements of the Black Power movement in American society in the eighties. We will also see that Johnson, who had attempted to write fiction in the prescribed form of the Black Aesthetic in the late sixties, tended to oscillate between an abiding respect for the accomplishments of Black Power cultural nationalists and an almost equally abiding difficulty with the rigid principles of the Black Aesthetic. While Williams shares this ambivalence with Reed and Johnson, though to a lesser degree, she also seems to have had an unswerving respect for the principles for which Black Power stood. This was the case from her earliest contact with Black Power advocates in the late sixties to her most recent reflections in the nineties. Williams noted that her "disenchantment with the exponents of Black Power began in 1967" when she encountered some Black Power advocates at Howard University who disparaged her writing because it was insufficiently like Richard Wright's. She would later lament what she calls these "strictures of the black consciousness movement," believing that they were both unproductive and conducive to a counter-revolutionary schism that alienated the majority of black people and caused the wholesale dismissal of some crucially important African American expressive forms. Like Reed and Johnson, Williams found herself put out by the programmatic and formulaic naturalism endorsed by some Black Arts advocates; and like Reed especially, she found herself puzzled and frustrated by a movement that would consciously condemn past generations and disparage historical cultural formations that Black Nationalists deemed "unheroic" or "counterrevolutionary."[10]

Yet Williams's disenchantment with certain Black Power advocates did not diminish her respect for Black Power principles and the general concepts of the Black Aesthetic. The critical book she published in 1972, *Give Birth to Brightness: A Thematic Study in Neo-Black Literature,* was certainly informed by the Black Arts movement and it heartily endorsed the basic ideas of the Black Aesthetic. And whatever misgivings she may have had about the misdirected enthusiasm of those Black Power advocates who had unfairly criticized her writing in 1967, she was herself by 1972 fully committed to discovering "the relationship between revolutionary consciousness and Black writing." Nor did her regained faith in Black Power wane when it became fashionable to have "second thoughts" about the sixties. Throughout the eighties, she remained "more firmly now than then, a proponent of Black consciousness, of 'The Black Aesthetic,'" and she wrote Black Power poems about Malcolm X and sixties' campus movements against the Vietnam War. In the midst of a neoconservative backlash against the sixties and the movements it spawned, she remained convinced that Black Power and the Black Aesthetic movements and feminism were "far more egalitarian" than the predominant humanist modes of inquiry, and that these movements had given African Americans an invaluable form of self-discovery, opening up "new means of exploring ourselves that were not there before" and offering "not only the possibility of changing one's *reading* of the world, but of changing the world itself."[11]

While the Black Power movement did produce the means for African Americans to develop a new, healthier cultural identity and propose a set of principles for altering American society, it accomplished these revolutionary goals largely by creating a program for "changing one's *reading* of the world," in this case, the world of the antebellum South, which it did by provoking historians to develop a new discourse on slavery based on different historical methods, founded on previously ignored resources, and demonstrating a more progressive political impetus. Williams recalls that as a child growing up in the forties and fifties, she had read history with the dismaying knowledge that "there was no place in the American past I could go and be free" (x). She found her childhood imagination "stopped" when it "came up against the institution of slavery," primarily because the histories of slavery she was reading were either insulting versions of the plantation romance or the facile efforts of consensus historians. By the time she came of age, she diagnosed the flaw in these histories and found that the "histories of slavery available during the late sixties and early seventies"—that is, the transitional works not fully influenced by the Black Power–inspired discourse on slavery—"were of little help" to her because "they focussed on issues that could be traced through archival material in which the slave's voice was largely missing, his or her person treated as mute commodity." Whether these works "concluded that the Negro under slavery was necessarily a sambo or quietly heroic, they all seem to issue from a mindset that saw the Negro as a pawn of History, rather than as someone capable of influencing developments."[12]

She found Styron's novel flawed, as did other Black Power intellectuals, primarily because he reproduced that historical record instead of seeking to discover how slave revolt leaders "have come down to Black people in legends, in historical and fictional accounts of their deeds, as men of great nobility and physical prowess." By the time she was writing her novel, she could draw on that new discourse on slavery, formed in the late sixties, based on a respect for African American slave culture, invoking the testimony of fugitive and former slaves, and treating the subjects of history as agents in their own lives and communities. These developments, as Williams eloquently testifies, were the products of the "Black Power movement [that] provided the pride and perspective necessary to pierce the myths and lies that have grown up around the antebellum period as a result of Southern propaganda and filled us also with the authority to tell it as we felt it."[13]

Inspired by the Black Power movement, her thinking mobilized by the new discourse on slavery produced by that movement, Williams makes the connection between her historical fiction and the Black Power politics it embodies by prefacing her short story with an epigraph from Angela Davis, to whom to the story is dedicated. "We, the black women of today, must accept the fully weight of a legacy wrought by our mothers in chains . . . as heirs to a tradition of supreme perseverance and heroic resistance, we must hasten to take our place wherever our people are forging towards freedom." Inspired by this vision of the connectedness of the slave past to the politicized present, Williams bases her novel on two incidents, which she discovered in Davis's groundbreaking black feminist and materialist exploration of slave women's experiences "Reflections on the Black Woman's Role in the Community of Slaves" and in Herbert Aptheker's *American Negro Slave Revolts.* Using the work of two Marxist historians—both of whom argued for the widespread existence of slave resistance, and both of whom also dealt with the acts of resistance performed by slave women—Williams implicitly criticizes those historians who had denied the extent of slave resistance and negated the role of African American women in the slave community. In her novel, Williams explores the conditions and motives for slave rebelliousness, particularly the acts of resistance of several heroic slave women. She also writes movingly about the existence of communal and romantic connections within the slave community. Scholars like Davis and Aptheker taught her that "slavery eliminated neither heroism nor love; it provided occasions for their expressions." The "Davis article" in particular "marked a turning point in [her] efforts to apprehend" what she calls "that other history" (x).[14]

That "other history," the history of courageous resistance and love and the expressive cultural practices of the slave community, deeply informs Williams's novel. A large part of what motivates Williams in her revisionist fiction is a desire to recover the hidden or misperceived history that representations like Styron's had misserved, of "saying to Styron 'See what you missed. You went for the easy thing—the stereotyped thing. This is the real story that you missed.'" Williams wished not only to resuscitate the stories of the historically oppressed, though; she also wished to represent the process by which they themselves recuperated their stories of their past. In *Dessa Rose,* she brilliantly succeeds in performing that task by offering us a Neo-slave narrative divided into two major sections, the first dealing with how cultural institutions and antagonistic individuals misserve those in pursuit of one's own story and the second with how apparently benign and sympathetic individuals can also hinder the process of recovery.[15] At the heart of her critique of political inequities, then, is an indictment of the social effects of domination, especially the appropriative acts that occur both in the cultural apparatus of a racialized state and in the daily actions of individuals residing in that state.

The Racialized State of Writing: Subjects of Resistance

Discussing the "communicative interactions" among the black population of St. Vincent, Roger Abrahams concluded that the "given" in these interactions is that the "individual presence residing in the voice assumes . . . that a sense of community exists." Williams argues that since literature is also about "community and dialogue," about how voices in communication construct a sense of community, then "theories or ways of reading ought actively to promote the enlargement of both" a sense of community and dialogue.[16] Following her own prescription, Williams proposes in *Dessa Rose* two conflicting "theories or ways of reading" leading to either dialogue and community or to dissonance and chaos. Reading, in this sense, is more than the perusing of texts; it is equally the ability to engage with people or to control them. There is a form of reading in which two individuals come to a mutual understanding of each other; this is reading as dialogue and is based on a desire for genuine community. There is also a form of reading in which an individual attempts to master another and recreate the prevailing schemes of domination prevailing in the state. This is the reading strategy employed by Nehemiah in the first section of the novel. As Dessa says at the end of the novel: "I never will forget Nemi trying to read me" (260). Nehemiah ("Nemi") attempts to master Dessa in his reading of her character and his writing of her history, part of which he plans to use to produce a full-length book entitled *The Roots of Rebellion in the Slave Population and Some Means of Eradicating Them* (16). Reading here is an act of control, having nothing to do with community or dialogue but only with assuming mastery over others and producing documents that help the state maintain that mastery.

Williams presents Nehemiah as a representative of that form of hegemony that attempts to reenslave Dessa by inscribing her within a "discourse that suppresses her voice."[17] The first section of *Dessa Rose* is essentially concerned with showing us the battle between Nehemiah and Dessa, fundamentally the battle between Nehemiah's literacy attempting to master Dessa's body and self and Dessa's orality attempting to establish a community beyond the confines of imprisonment. By having Nehemiah write out Dessa's character and her role in the revolt on the coffle, Williams demonstrates how African Americans have been "betrayed" by and "remain at the mercy of literature and writing" (ix). In the character of Dessa, though, Williams also shows how African Americans "survived by word of mouth" (ix). As a literal example of this kind of surviving by orality, Williams has Dessa talk with Nehemiah as if their conversation were a "game," and shows her "playing on words" with him, using misleading words that eventually lead him on a false search for fugitive slaves, thereby helping her effect her escape (58–59). Likewise, Dessa communicates with those who rescue her and help her escape by singing in a call-and-response rhythm from her jail cell. Unlike writing, which isolates and alienates its subject, Williams implies that oral performance is a form of authentic dialogue that actively promotes inter-subjectivity. When Dessa sings, "her voice blended with" others' in "communion" (63). At the end of the first section, Dessa defies Nehemiah's attempt to read her, and Williams dismisses his theory of reading as detrimental to the potentials for dialogue and the formation of community.

In the first part of the novel, then, Williams deals with what Robert Stepto noted to be the "primary generic myth for Afro-America"—the interrelated "quest for freedom and literacy"—by representing in this particular instance what Stepto terms "the culture's distrust of literacy." In this cultural drama, the written word represents the processes used by racist white American institutions to proscribe and prescribe African American subjectivity. In the nineteenth-century slave narratives, writing represents primarily racist institutions against which the slave gains his or her subjectivity by assuming control over his or her "voice." In the classic slave narratives of the late eighteenth century, this process of discovering the black voice operated through what Henry Louis Gates calls the "trope of the talking book," whose modern counterpart in contemporary African American writing is the "speakerly text," a text privileging "the representation of the speaking black voice." In the first part of *Dessa Rose,* Williams represents the process by which Dessa struggles against Nehemiah's hegemonic writing and frees her voice; in other words, she represents the process by which Dessa uses her voice to gain her actual and representational liberation from the prescriptive pen of Nehemiah's written record.[18]

In representing Dessa's struggle to resist Nehemiah's power and to find her own voice, this first section also speaks to Williams's own struggles and travails as an author, her own search for a suitable formal structure within which to represent her story, and her subtle critique of the mediating institutions which create a literary field that enacts the power struggles of the society within which it is placed. Elizabeth Ammons has shown us how American women writers of the turn of the century represented their creative female characters in the act of struggling toward and searching for a formal means through which to intervene in their societies, exhibiting "an interest in radical experimentation with narrative form" most suitable for addressing a "network of recurrent, complicated themes which, though constantly shifting and even at times conflicting, finally interlock in their shared focus on issues of power."[19] In *Dessa Rose*, Williams also experiments with narrative form in her attempt to revise the Neo-slave narrative; in particular, she experiments with formal devices that challenge the assumptions behind Styron's artistic choices about the structure of his novel. Likewise, as we expect of contemporary Neo-slave narratives, *Dessa Rose* is very much about issues of power. These issues also turn out to be about Williams's own multiple acts of resisting the proscriptive categories of the publishing industry in the racialized state of America.

This first section, as was noted above, was originally a short story begun in 1968 and both thematically and titularly a response to Styron's *Confessions of Nat Turner*. Although Williams tried "for several years to find a journal willing to publish 'Meditations on History,'" she was unsuccessful because the editors at the one black journal to which she sent it were too swamped with submissions and the editors at "white journals denied that there was a 'historical precedent' for Nehemiah's character." From her attempted entry into the fiction marketplace, Williams learned that the field of cultural production contained the same inequities as the social terrain of the United States. She found this out even more poignantly when she finally entered into that marketplace. Preparing *Dessa Rose* for publication in 1985, she resisted her editor's suggestion that she include a statement declaring that the novel was not based on what her editor called a "historical incident." Her editors "seemed scared to death readers wouldn't know where fact ended and fiction began." The editors obviously missed the point of her novel, since it was precisely her point that historical constructs were fictional to the extent that they achieved their coherence by acts of exclusion and that fictional renditions could illuminate largely unexplored areas of the past. Reluctantly, and somewhat resentfully, she relented and wrote what we have as the "Author's Note" prefacing the novel. Recently Williams revealed that she "wrote the 'Author's Statement' that opens *Dessa Rose* under protest."[20]

Williams was especially piqued because she knew that other writers were not subject to this kind of editorial harassment. She notes that "white boys won prizes" for creating fictions that were obvious reconstructions of the past, and this "sudden concern for 'historical accuracy'" struck her as a way of telling her that she was not one of the white boys. Six years after her novel was published, Williams continues to believe "that I wouldn't have been asked to write a disclaimer 'separating fact from fiction,' as my editorial guarantors put it, had I been white." What struck Williams was not so much the fact that there existed inequities in the field of cultural production, since she obviously knew that from her earlier experiences, but rather that this inequity assumed a form that precisely replicated the earliest confrontation between master texts and slave narratives. The word "guarantors" which Williams uses to describe her editors is Stepto's term for those white men and women who wrote "master texts" in the form of prefatory letters attesting to the authenticity of the antebellum slave narratives they introduced.[21] Ironically, Williams's Neo-slave narrative was being treated like an antebellum slave narrative, her authority questioned the same way fugitive slaves' had been. Given what we now know about Williams's relationship with her editors and publishers, it would be worth returning to the novel and examining anew the dynamic of the first section. The three subsections of that section—the "Author's Note," the "Prologue," and "The Darky"—are about how Williams, like Dessa, resists the constraints put on her own voice while also revealing the institutional source of those constraints.

Williams attached the "Author's Note" to the front of the novel "rather than tucking it away in the back" primarily so that "Dessa would have the last word" in the book. Unlike Styron's *Confessions,* in which Styron gave the last words to William Drewry and the Bible, Williams wished for us to leave her novel with Dessa's mediated though unhindered voice resonating in our minds. In putting her "Author's Note" in the front of her book, though, Williams has also structured her novel along the same lines as Styron's, who likewise prefaced his novel with an "Author's Note." In fact, Williams seems to be directly responding to Styron in several ways in her "Author's Note." Whereas in his note Styron insisted on the singularity of his subject and its historical documentation—the "only effective, sustained revolt," "the single significant contemporary document"—Williams insists on duality. *"Dessa Rose* is based on two historical incidents"; and her documentation comes from two historians (ix–x). Whereas Styron claimed a place for his imagination in those "areas where there is little knowledge," he nonetheless granted authority to "history," claiming that his novel remains "within the bounds of what meager enlightenment history has left us about the institution of slavery." Williams situates herself differently in relation to "history." She says that as a child she used to love reading history until a friend told her that "there was no place in the American past I could go and be free" (ix–x). She learns later that there is "that other history," unappreciated in the historical profession, a history showing just how "meager" an enlightenment "history has left us." While Styron claimed to be true to the *"known* facts" and called his novel a "meditation on history," Williams, at the insistence of her editors, noted that her novel is "fiction." Even while the characters and the terrain through which they travel are "based on fact," they remain nonetheless her "invention" (x). She does add, in a sentence that demonstrates her resistance to the editorial fiat regarding the utter separability of fact and fiction, that "what is here is as true as if I myself had lived it" (x). With this subtle declaration, Williams makes an important point about "truth" value in a society in which the lived experiences of people of African descent get discounted in the compilation of official records. In such a society, there is nothing singular except the oppression exercised to deny the duality (the multiplicity) of the American experience.[22]

Whereas Styron began his novel with a four-page passage from Gray's *Confessions,* including Gray's signature and the authenticating statement and signatures of the six members of the court that tried Nat Turner, Williams begins her novel with a "Prologue" that offers us a brief portrait of the ardent and moving love between Kaine and Dessa (1–5). Williams notes that she began with a rendition of "one of Dessa's recurring fantasies about her life with Kaine" so that this representation would act "as a prism through which the rest of the story must be read." The authenticating device here is Dessa's own fantasy, her own reminiscence about her first husband, which is also a testament to the domestic and romantic lives of American slaves. Although written in the third person, the narration is clearly from Dessa's perspective and the free indirect discourse suggests it is also largely in her voice (1, 2). So, too, the section entitled "The Darky" begins with a paragraph in Dessa's voice before we discover that this voice is contained in Nehemiah's diary (9). Even so, Williams took pains to show that Dessa's voice was never fully contained by Nehemiah's pen. Of the various revisions Williams made to the original short story, this is probably the most important one. In "Meditations on History," Williams had started the section after the prologue with a diary entry written in the voice of Nehemiah; the first time we get any substantial representation of Dessa's voice is in the fifth diary entry. In the novel, however, Williams "subsumed" Nehemiah's voice within a third-person omniscient narrator, claiming in an interview that she "didn't want to give him that much importance or that much control."[23]

Williams's other notable revisions between the short story and the novel, aside from changing the date of the events from 1829 to 1847, also suggest that she is expanding her focus on the sources of power in society.[24] Described in the short story as a writer with no institutional affiliation, the Nehemiah of *Dessa Rose* is a functionary of larger sectional and national interests operative in the field of cultural production. Whereas his first book, *The Complete Guide for Competent Masters in Dealing with Slaves and Other Dependents,* is his own idea (25), the "idea for this book about the origins of uprisings among slaves had come from Nehemiah's publisher, Browning Norton" (17). Indeed, when Nehemiah proves reluctant to write another book about slavery so soon after completing the *Guide,* "Norton had pressed" him to take on the task (18–19). "A book on slave uprisings, touching as it must upon the secret fears of non-slave holder and slave holder alike, should be an immediate success," and "would establish Nehemiah as an important southern author" (19). Nehemiah was not successful in his initial attempt to be a writer without institutional affiliation, printing "at his own expense a collection of his sketches that he sold, with indifferent success, through subscription" (18). As an artist outside the economic structures of the established publishing market, Nehemiah had failed. As a writer within the mainstream publishing industry, he is on his way to producing a "magnum opus" and becoming "an important southern writer." What we have in *Dessa Rose* that we do not in "Meditations on History," then, is not simply a critique of an individual racist writer inadequately equipped to handle the task of writing a story about African American life, but rather an indictment of the cultural apparatus that markets artistic productions according to the governing interest of the hegemonic class, and an institutional system producing categories that recreate governing values ("important") and reproduce literary traditions ("southern"). What we have, in other words, is an indictment of the cultural apparatus that creates both masters and master texts. This is not to say Nehemiah is beyond reproach for his role within the field of cultural production; he is not. Like Reed's Harriet Beecher Stowe, who calls Uncle Robin from the "offices of Jewett Publishers in Boston" to get him to sell her his story, Nehemiah is not merely an effect of the system but an operative agent within it.[25]

In the person of Nehemiah, Williams not only parodies Styron (and Thomas Gray) but she also alludes to both mythical and historical figures who produced master texts. Nehemiah's full name is apt since it alludes to two biblical functions: "Adam (namer) Nehemiah (chronicler)." He fails in both these tasks, since he misnames Dessa, referring to her as either the "darky" or "Odessa," and proves unable to name Kaine—phonetically pronounced like the name of Adam's own son—because he does not listen carefully to Dessa (35). He likewise fails to produce a chronicle, since he is unable to get the story he is after; his chronicle at the end of the novel consists of scattered pages either blank or filled with illegible scribbling (255). Dessa gets her revenge by calling him "Nemi," designating him as "nobody" and "her nemesis," and by having her son write down her orally delivered tale and read it back to her (260). That chronicle, and not his, is the one we get. Nehemiah, we might say, is a failure of biblical proportions.[26] Williams also uses Nehemiah to allude to a historical figure who wrote a particularly noxious master text.

Adam Nehemiah is a reversed version of Nehemiah Adams, the author of *A South-Side View of Slavery* (1854), who, like the fictional Nehemiah, is a northerner traveling through and falling in love with the South. After a three-month sojourn through the South, Reverend Adams wrote an ambiguously proslavery tract in which he recoiled in horror at the destructive features of slavery, mostly the domestic slave trade and the slave auction itself, but found himself entirely comfortable with what he saw as the ameliorating effects of slavery. He concludes his tract by stating his belief that the imposition of the "yoke" of physical slavery on peoples of African descent far outweighs the far heavier bondage of spiritual infidelity. His evidence came from an interview with a slave whom he asked "whether he would like to be free." Looking at the white man asking him this question, the laboring slave responded slowly and deliberately: "I want to be free from my sins; them's all my burden; and if I can get that, the balance of the rest may go from me."[27] Believing that the slave wished to be freed from only his sins, Adams did not consider that the slave's comment about "the balance of the rest" is a direct comment on those whose sins included enslaving others, nor did he read the slave's comment as a statement on how his freedom from sin should lead to his physical freedom.

In her reflections on northern writers' incompetence in decoding slave testimony, Harriet Jacobs mocks those "doctors of divinity" who travel south, feigning hatred of slavery, only to be cozened by the aristrocatic practices of slaveholders. So inclined to believe the masters, these northern travelers inquire of the slave "if they want to be free" and are satisfied with the slave's coerced response: "O, no, massa." Such religious leaders go home and "publish a 'South-Side View of Slavery,'" and complain of the "exaggerations of abolitionists." Jacobs's point is that master texts are produced not necessarily by determined proslavery ideologues, but by those who do not take the time to consider that slaves are not free sources of information about their condition, that slaves "dared not tell" about the horrors of the institution because to do so would endanger their lives and their kin. As Frederick Douglass pointed out, slaves claimed to be contented with slavery because masters would often send spies among them "to ascertain their views and feelings in regard to their condition." Believing rightly that "a still tongue makes a wise head," the slaves chose to "suppress the truth rather than take the consequences of telling it."[28]

Williams makes the same points about Nehemiah as does Jacobs about his historical counterpart. Like others who attempted to record and contain the voices of slaves, Nehemiah is insufficiently attentive to the conditions within which he is gathering his information. Williams stated that what appealed to her about this kind of situation in which a person "was trying to act as an amanuensis for somebody over whom they really have quite a bit of control in professing to tell their stories" is that it lent itself to showing the strategies by which slaves managed to tell their own "true story" while the amanuensis remained "ignorant of what was being said."[29] The first section of *Dessa Rose* enacts just that kind of situation, by showing Nehemiah's ineptitude at listening and his lack of control over the story he is trying to tell. Given his previous experience at compiling a documentary study of slavemasters' writings on slave management, Nehemiah proves adept at reading masters' texts (18). Precisely because of this skill, though, Nehemiah proves equally inept at listening to slaves' narratives. When Dessa speaks, he becomes puzzled at the "unfamiliar idiom" and loses track of the "tale in the welter of names" Dessa recites in her narration. Fascinated though uncomprehending, Nehemiah would sit rapt, "forgetting to write" down what Dessa told him. His document, then, is not an accurate reflection of Dessa's story, but rather a "deciphered" and "reconstructed" version written down "as though he remembered it word for word" (10).

Nehemiah is also not in control of this interview. When he asks Dessa a question, he never gets a straightforward answer. She answers him "in a random manner, a loquacious, roundabout fashion," if, that is, she answers at all (16). Like Nat Turner, Dessa does not respond to the interviewer's questions directly, because she (like Turner) uses the occasion to create the story of her life. This act is in many ways as revolutionary as her action on the slave coffle uprising. As William Andrews points out, the slave of "antebellum southern myth and propaganda is and must always be a constant, constitutionally averse and impervious to change, for the sake of himself, his white folks, and the southern ideal of civilization." Nat Turner destroyed that myth, first, by organizing and leading a revolt against his enslavers, and, second, by creating for himself a life history, thereby making Thomas Gray's *Confessions* the "first significant chronology of an African American life in southern literature." Although Gray asks Turner only for a "'history of the motives' that led to his uprising," Turner responds by "making a history of *himself*." So, too, although Nehemiah attempts "to discover and analyze the motivating factors which culminated in this outrage against the public safety," he receives from Dessa only what he calls "this darky's story" (16). Dessa, meanwhile, uses the opportunity of this interview to create for herself a life history, and to record herself in history, thereby disrupting the misconception of a static African American mythic stereotype and disturbing the processes of what Williams elsewhere calls "the discourse of History itself." Nehemiah's "misreadings of control and power in his contacts with Dessa" allow Dessa to create her own story and construct her own subjectivity.[30]

For instance, she recalls Kaine telling her that white people do not "piss champagne," that their "bowels move the same way ours do; [and] they shit stank just as bad." At first, she is "shocked and a little frightened to hear him talk under white folks' clothes like that." After some reflection, though, she realizes that this initial shock was necessary for her to think more deeply on his point and begin to realize that "white people, except for their skin color, were no different from her, from him—from any of the people" (44). Dessa achieves this matured reflection only when she generates her story through her uneasy and discontinuous dialogue with Nehemiah. In conversation with Nehemiah, Dessa felt "she saw the past as she talked, not as she had lived it but as she had come to understand it" (56). Her conversation provides her with a transformative understanding of her past, a kind of knowledge that not only changes in retrospect but also creates the conditions for her to change herself and her circumstances. In the course of these dialogues, she learns to see white people not only as biological beings, but also as social forces in her life. "Caught in her own flow, she listened and continued, *seeing as she spoke* the power of Master as absolute and evil" (55, my emphasis). It is in retrospect, then, that she understands what forces conditioned her life and, more important, she appreciates the simplest meaning of the act of violence she committed against the representative of those forces.

Writing about slavery, Williams notes that there is an alienation in black culture manifesting itself in a curious duality, appearing at times as a "seeming docility" and at others in brief episodes of "flaring violence."[31] Dessa, for instance, had not been notably resistant when she was a slave on the plantation; she was frightened by every unorthodox gesture Kaine made, constantly fearing he would be sold away. Having lost several siblings to the domestic slave trade, Dessa maintained a low profile on the plantation; whatever acts of daily resistance she performed were too subtle to be noticed. Yet, when called upon, Dessa was able to effect physical violence against her master and mistress before killing a man on the coffle during the uprising. Again, in conversation with Nehemiah she is able to understand the will she exercised in those acts. "I kill white mens," she tells Nehemiah, "I kill white mens cause the same reason Masa kill Kaine. Cause I can" (13). Power, she thinks, is a raw property; it exists for whoever would act on it, for whoever would perform acts of violence against enemies. At this point in the narrative, at the end of the first section, she believes that access to power requires acting on her innermost will. So long as she is willing to suffer bodily pain or death, she can as freely exercise her will on the world as can her master. Later, she will refine this insight with a fuller understanding of the economic and social institutions channeling the circulation of power; she will then understand, as did the Black Power advocates, that violence often takes on institutional forms and needs to be contested in those forms rather than through random though justifiable acts of violence.

Those institutions, she will also learn, create the conditions for property and define some humans as the property of others. Like the Black Power advocates, Williams deals with two senses of property. As property, Dessa commits acts toward her liberation; once liberated, she participates in actions intended to diminish the system that had previously enslaved her by participating in a scheme in which the itinerant group sell slaves who escape and rejoin them. Although she performs murder in the first and a form of fraud in the second of these activities, she does so because she rightly believes that the entire social system based on slavery makes impossible the practice of obedience to constitutional law. Property, as Williams writes, "cannot, of course, commit any crimes." It is the second sense of property that plays a more prominent role in this first section, though. As in the other Neo-slave narratives, the property at issue is the "story" of the individual, which in this case Nehemiah attempts to appropriate and Dessa attempts to express and yet protect, to articulate and yet keep invulnerable. For Nehemiah, Dessa's story is purely a functional property he requires for his own work. When she falls ill, he prays that "this darky don't die before I get my book!" (27). For Dessa, though, her story is a personal property she requires to sustain herself and to transform her condition and it is also a countervailing force against the kind of representation Nehemiah would perpetuate. It is what Williams, quoting Sterling Brown's description of slave narratives, calls a "literary weapon," a means of disrupting the historical chronicles that portray slavery without consulting this kind of testimony and also a means of contesting fictional misrepresentations in master texts.[32]

In the first section of the novel, Williams reflects on the triad of topics surrounding the formal origins of the Neo-slave narrative by having Dessa generate a prototypical Black Power sense of identity by learning not to fear white people, develop a basic model for understanding her acts of violence against an oppressive force by stating the simple proposition of will-to-power ("cause I can"), and begin to empower herself through a transformative understanding of her history and an appreciation that her story is her cultural property. In the second section of the novel, Williams reflects on this triad of topics through a different filter while Dessa lives under different conditions. Dessa says that she "began another part of [her] education" and discovers a different identity once she is beyond slavery. "I was someone I knowed and didn't know, living in a world I hadn't even knowed was out there" (214). She learns about the connection between the systemic violence that defines people of African descent and the sanctioned violence defining black and white women in American society (220). Dessa will also learn to manipulate the discourse of property that had earlier commodified her, using the language of commerce to ensure her freedom (243). More to the point, though, Dessa also learns how to disrupt an appropriated narrative intended to commodify her. Williams accomplishes all of this while also signaling her own acts of resistance, attesting to her own firm belief in Black Power, her own exploration of those institutional forces that made her entry into the field of cultural production difficult, and her own thorough revision of the master text assuming the form of a Neo-slave narrative.

Talking Friends: Subject of Relation

If the first part of *Dessa Rose* is about the tension between an oppressive literacy and an emancipatory orality, then we can say the second part of Williams's novel is also about "the struggle for discursive power," in which "the fictions take the form of quests for voice, for authority over the narration itself."[33] In this scenario, precisely as in the dramatic encounter between literacy and orality, the struggle is between one form of representation that has historically been used to generate and transmit African American culture and another employed to traduce and control that culture. The difference between this struggle and the confrontation between literacy and orality is that the conflict here is waged within the same medium, and the hegemonic presence is an antagonistic person or an oppressive community whose intent is to control the individual's narrative. In the second section of *Dessa Rose,* Williams presents us with two less clearly opposed theories of reading than in the first section, and she represents a much more complicated but also more informative confrontation between them, in order to show us how intimate relations are refracted enactments of larger social formations.

After Dessa escapes, she gives birth and ends up at Sutton Glen, the plantation owned by Ruth Elizabeth Sutton (née Carson, and known familiarly as Miz Rufel).

In the course of their developing friendship, each learns to revise and expand her theory of how to "read" people as people. As she watches Rufel nurse her baby, Dessa finds herself disoriented from the terms of her world as it had hitherto existed for her: "It went against everything she had been taught to think about white women" (123). Likewise, Rufel finds that her conversations with Dessa force her to alter the ways she too had been taught to think about African American women in terms of her own existence. Taking us into "the world that black and white women shared in the antebellum South," Williams raises questions about the historical and present possibilities for interracial coalitions.[34]

Slaveholding women held on to the metaphor "my family, white and black" as a way of capturing an "important, if elusive, vision of an organic community." It was an ideal that was more than elusive, though; it was delusive. White mistresses attempted to suggest that not only were they "sisters" with their enslaved siblings, but they were "abolitionists in their hearts and hot ones too," as Mary Chesnut Boykin wrote in her diary. There is, however, far too much evidence to the contrary. Historians have noted that "patterns of mistress-initiated violence toward black women suggest that such acts were just as often spontaneous outbursts of rage as they were deliberate measures to reform behavior." When chastising their slaves, "white women devised barbaric forms of punishment that resulted in the mutilation or permanent scarring of their female servants." The slavemistress was equally violent with her pen. After reading scores of diaries and private papers of slaveholders, one historian sadly concludes that "the racism of the women was generally uglier and more meanly expressed than that of the men."[35] The antebellum South was a world whose history renders it virtually incapable of sustaining any romantic ideals about positive and healthy relations, including those between black slave women and white slaveholding women.

It was, nonetheless, a world providing rare and fleeting instances of friendships between black and white women—friendships that might well have taken the metaphor of a communal, interracial "family" as a serious tenet instead of a mutual self-delusion. If we attend to Williams's own construction of her scene of inspiration—her description of what stories and events inspired her to write the novel she wrote—we find that her initial desire was to represent the meeting of two historical women who might well have formed a genuine friendship. Having read in Angela Davis's article an account of a slave woman who "helped to lead an uprising on a coffle" in 1829 in Kentucky, Williams tracked Davis to her source, Aptheker's *American Negro Slave Revolts,* and discovered there a story about a "white woman living on an isolated farm" in North Carolina who was reported to have "given sanctuary to runaway slaves" in 1830. Thinking it "sad" that "these two women never met" (ix), Williams, by "signifyin(g)" on history, that is, recreating a historical episode so that it can be revised and rendered differently, creates a fiction in which they do meet.[36]

Most of the critics writing on *Dessa Rose* emphasize the positive features of the relationship between Dessa and Rufel, seeing in the novel a "depiction of a black and white female friendship that withstands the stress of confronting both the psychological and the historical wounds, that accords each woman the dignity—and sometimes the humor—of her own experience and perspective." Reading the novel as an attempt to "break" the "grammar of racism," Elizabeth Meese, for instance, argues that "Williams (un)writes the plantation novel, separating the white woman from white racism (the socioeconomics of the planter class) and the white academic and literary discourses of slavery," creating instead "a romance of race, a u-topic fiction of hope and a 'happy ending.'" A few feminist and womanist critics have discerned a less utopic relationship between the two women, noting that while the two women do "increasingly learn from and respect each other," Rufel is still "full of contradictions," somewhat bothersome as an antebellum "closet Negrophile," and ultimately "not attuned to her complicity in the system of slavery."[37]

The critics who argue for the so-called "happy ending" use the scene at the end of the novel to make their point. Having spent a few months at Sutton Glen, forming a tentative and yet volatile relationship, Dessa and Rufel decide with the others to set out on a trip during which they sell slaves who then escape to be resold further down South. They raise a large amount of money in this scheme, half of which is strapped to Dessa in a money belt under her dress. In their penultimate destination, Arcopolis, just after Rufel and Dessa have a fight, Nehemiah spots Dessa on the street and has her arrested. Rufel arrives in the jail and hears from Nehemiah a fabulation in which Dessa is a hypersexualized and murderous slave who has slept with and attempted to murder her master (250). The story strikes a chord in Rufel's mind, since, according to Dessa, this was "what she'd thought about me at first, what she thought about all of us" (251). Whatever she may believe, Rufel nonetheless defends Dessa and requests that the sheriff release her. Dessa takes no chances on "friendship"; she makes a motion to Rufel informing her that she is wearing the money belt. "Whatever she thought about me, whatever Nemi knowed on her, that money was real" (252). Rufel then presses her point more forcefully, after which the sherriff calls in a slave woman to examine Dessa to see if she has the scars Nehemiah claims. When Aunt Chole arrives, Dessa looks into her milky, perhaps blind eyes, gives her a "quarter coin," passes the examination, and goes free (254). According to Meese's reading of this scene, "Dessa is saved by Ruth and Aunt Chole."[38] This is an inaccurate description, at best, and seems to me to elide the numerous acts by which Dessa saves herself by acting toward and paying for her freedom. When Dessa concludes her tale by noting that she hopes the children "never have to pay what it cost us to own ourselfs," she obviously means the expense of spirit (260); but the fact that she could not trust Rufel or Chole to act on entirely disinterested motives suggests that part of that payment was material. Whatever basis there is for the friendship between Rufel and Dessa—and it is a friendship more in the remembrance than in the experience—it is important to note that Dessa cannot completely trust Rufel without referring to Rufel's own material interests. Recalling that Rufel had already attempted to commodify her through narrative means, Dessa's final act reminds us of the connection between story and property.

It is instructive to note the differences between Dessa's actions toward Rufel and toward Chole, for the two forms of payment she makes to each woman are not similarly motivated, nor are they communicated in the same way. In signaling to Rufel that she has the money on her body, Dessa performs an extravagant set of gestures: "'Mistress.' She turn her head. I patted that money belt under my dress. I looked at her and down at the hand patting my waist. . . . 'Mistress.' I looked at her and I looked at Nemi. . . . She looked at him" (252). She has to perform in an exaggerated manner because she must *contest* what Rufel might already believe about her. Rufel has brought with her a preconception of Dessa (and of other African American women) that Nehemiah's stories buttress; the only way Dessa can save herself is to challenge those stories by appealing to Rufel's own material interests. In her payment to Chole, though, Dessa is more subtle because she does not have to contest a narrative that has already determined her subjectivity. She whispers to Chole that she "was scarred as a girl child" and that she is "much ashamed of them scars" (253–54). Herself a slave woman, Chole knows the codes through which Dessa is informing her of her life's story. Chole does not even bother to feel the scarred place on Dessa's body, stopping Dessa as she prepares to lift her skirt (254). Dessa's story requires no visual proof; Chole is inclined to believe it because she has a framework for understanding the travails of a slave woman's life, and, more important, because of her own experiences she has an inclination to believe what others tell her about their experiences. Rufel does not; and Dessa knows she does not because she has herself experienced Rufel's imperiousness.

While Rufel and Dessa do grow closer as they walk down the street after this scene, and Rufel grows even more significant in Dessa's stories to her children and grandchildren, there remains between them a less than perfect friendship, because the society in which they live creates a disequilibrium in their personal lives based on their unequal access to power in their social roles. "Negro can't live in peace under protection of law, got to have some white person to stand for us," notes Dessa. "And who can you friend with, love with like that?" (259). This is Dessa's belated response to Rufel's earlier plea: "I'm talking friends" (239). The kind of social inequity Dessa describes creates deviant relationships between individuals who are differently categorized in the society not only because it forces them to assume relations of dependency rather than interdependency, but also, and more important, because the hegemony of white supremacy operates through forceful and not easily resisted ideological means by circulating and reinforcing mythic stereotypes which white people like Rufel unconsciously use when organizing their responses to people of African descent. In Rufel's case, we find this mind-set exemplified in her capacity for denying her own race privilege and in her self-delusion about the familial basis of plantation slavery, which manifest themselves in her tendency to create appropriative narratives. In this, her relations with Dessa are akin to and a structural continuation of those of Nehemiah's with Dessa.

In their relations, Nehemiah attempted to make Dessa's life history a kind of empty signifier—a series of events culminating in a random act of slave rebellion which could be understood in isolation and then easily prevented in the future. When Dessa asks Nehemiah the reason he is writing about her, he replies: "I write what I do in the hope of helping others to be happy in the life that has been sent them to live" (41) As he declaims the orotund sentence to himself and glows in the warmth of self-satisfaction, Dessa questions how it is that her life, so oppressive in the living, can be the referent for that particular kind of message. "'You think,' she asked looking up at the white man, 'you think what I say now going to help peoples be happy in the life they sent? If that be true,' she said as he opened his mouth to speak, "why I not be happy when I live it'" (47)? Her life can represent so radically different a message to its readers than it does to its bearer not only because it is re-

constructed within the medium of writing, but primarily because of the appropriative gesture preceding the media transmission. *Before* he writes down Dessa's story,
Nehemiah transforms it by mishearing and misconstruing it (10). What is crucially
important to note is that Nehemiah's original act of appropriation is not in the
recording of Dessa's tale, but in his willfull imaginary "reconstruction" of it. It is not
his pen that prevents him from producing a nonappropriative representation but his
will-to-power, not the medium so much as the motive.

In the second section of the novel, Dessa encounters another kind of control
and a different motive for asserting that control; yet she nonetheless encounters precisely the same appropriative gesture. Rufel is not a writer; nor, for that matter, is she
altogether intent on controlling Dessa's life for any explicitly racist agenda such as
Nehemiah's. While Nehemiah represents a form of politically motivated control
when he uses Dessa's life story to write a tract on the prevention of slave revolts,
Rufel represents the ways the politically motivated forms of control inhabit the "personal." Rufel would control Dessa's story—the narrative of her past adventures and
social relations—just as firmly as would Nehemiah; but unlike Nehemiah, whose
desire to control Dessa's narrative is motivated by his desire to regulate the economic
transfers of society, Rufel would control Dessa's story because it is the only meaningful way she knows of forming relationships with persons of African descent. In other
words, whereas Nehemiah appropriates Dessa's story in order to incorporate it into a
text containing an agenda for sustaining the present political program, Rufel appropriates Dessa's story because it is the only way she knows how to form social connections with African Americans within that political program. For her, making a
slave woman part of her "family" means taking the slave woman's story and imbri-
cating it into her family's narrative.[39]

Williams represents the confrontation between Dessa and Rufel in terms of
what we may call a "subject of relation." The "subject" in this case is truly an absence
in the novel—she is Dorcas, Rufel's slave "Mammy." She is an absence because she
does not exist as a character in the present action of the novel, having passed away a
few weeks before the action takes place. She exists only as a mental presence in
Rufel's mind. She is, then, a "relation" in two interrelated ways. She is a "subject of
relation" because she is putatively related to Rufel under the terms of that delusive
model of "my family, white and black," and she is also "subject to relation" in that
she exists only as a product of Rufel's narrative imagination. Her subjectivity and her
subjection are issues dependent on a model of kin relations, the model in which she
is called "Mammy," and on Rufel's capacity for narrative relation, a capacity through
which her slavemistress narrates her as a "mammy." At one point in the story, Rufel
talks to herself about how she constructs her familial sense in her imagination:
"There you go again, she told herself angrily, expecting all darkies to be like Mammy.
Like family, a voice wailed silently within her" (135). The meeting with Dessa provides Rufel with a sense of how a simile of "family" is an oppressive structure under
the conditions of plantation culture. The figure of the "Mammy," then, and a
"mammy" who is a virtual absence in the action of the novel, provides Williams with
a way of exploring the meeting of two women working toward a definition of how to
read other people in the hope of achieving meaningful dialogue and managing a
sense of supportive community.

Demonstrating the forms of delusion operative in a slave system nominally structured along familial terms, Williams exposes the irreducible paradox where the "slave is given an important role within a family's domestic economy but stands outside the delicate dynamics of kinship psychology." Williams explores this paradox and the fissures it creates in the psyches of those who fail to understand the power differential that negates illusory family bonds, while negotiating the tension between the two major forms of fictive kin ties—"adoptive" and "quasi-filial" kinship—in order to demonstrate their differences and to suggest something about their shared ideas of oppression. The difference between the two fictive kinship systems is that in "adoptive" kinship the slave is welcomed into the slave community with the intent of "genuine assimilation" and is given "all the claims, privileges, powers, and obligations of the status he or she has been ascribed," while in "quasi-filial" kinship the slave is welcomed only nominally and the "language of kinship" is used as a means of expressing, at the same time as it hides, "an authority relation between master and slave."[40] While Williams shows that in the end Rufel's relationship with Dorcas was modeled on "adoptive kinship," she takes pains to demonstrate the destructive processes at work in generating and maintaining that sense of adoption.

Rufel's desire to appropriate "Mammy" Dorcas's story takes on two interrelated strategies. First, she attempts to reconstruct Dorcas's voice so that it echoes her own, and second, she wishes to restructure the most significant events in Dorcas's life so that the whole life becomes supplemental to her own. Rufel's relationship with Dorcas is revealed exclusively through Rufel's memories of her recently deceased slave. Within the subjective memory of her slaveholder, as we might expect, the figure of Dorcas takes on qualities of superhuman patience and maternal love. Yet, Rufel's remembering function seems invested with some degree of dialogic capacity, for she feels compelled to represent even the most subversive and resistant of Dorcas's actions and words.

For instance, as she is reflecting on Dessa's age, Rufel begins to think how no slave ever knows his or her exact age or birthday. Even Dorcas has no better way of determining her birthday than by vague seasonal signifiers—"planting time" or "picking time." Because "Mammy hadn't known how old she was or even her own birthdate," Rufel took it upon herself arbitrarily to choose "Valentine's Day as Mammy's birthday" (92). In choosing what day will represent Dorcas's birth, Rufel affirms her control over the narration of Dorcas's life; it is she, Rufel the slaveholder, who can establish the dates and raw data of Dorcas's history. What Rufel does in giving Dorcas an arbitrary birthday confirms the slaveholding system, since she requires her slave to structure her life according to the terms chosen for her by her mistress. Dorcas, however, was resistant to the forms of control Rufel attempted to impose on her. Dorcas "had refused to accept a date—'This way I don't have to age, see,' she had joked, 'I just gets a little older'" (92). Recalling this instance of her "mammy's" subtle insubordination, Rufel finds herself pained by the "wound of that memory." The memory is painful partly because Dorcas has so recently passed away; but it is also painful because Rufel is forced to confront an image of Dorcas as something other than her alter ego. Rufel thinks of Dorcas as an extension of herself and is troubled when she recalls that Dorcas often held an opinion contrary to her own. When that happens, Rufel employs the second strategy in her appropriation of Dorcas's life story—she reconstructs her slave's voice.

For instance, after Ada, a fugitive slave living on Rufel's plantation, tells the story of how her cruel and lecherous master had "lusted with her and then planned the seduction of Ada's daughter, Annabelle," Rufel finds herself offended at "Ada's story" (93). The first thing she does in attempting to feed her indignation is to reconstruct the story itself. "'No white man would do that,' she'd insisted" (94). When she then tries to get Dorcas to support her subversion of Ada's story, Dorcas responds with some heat: "'Miz Rufel,' Mammy had said sharply. 'You keep a lady tongue in your mouth . . . men can do things a *lady* can't even guess at.'" Dorcas's emphasis on "lady" is worth attending to. By telling Rufel to keep a "lady tongue" in her mouth, Dorcas is telling her not to pretend to be able to speak for a slave woman. A "lady tongue," Dorcas implies, cannot say what a *"lady* can't even guess at." Rufel responds insolently by noting that "Everyone know men like em half white and whiter." "'Miz Rufel,' Mammy had snapped, 'Lawd know it must be some way for high yeller to git like that!'" Having silenced Rufel, Dorcas appears to have had the final word in this exchange. Moreover, that final word testifies to a history of slaveholding abuse and oppression. By pointing out to Rufel that there is a reason for and a history to the spectrum of colors in black America, namely masters' rape of enslaved women, Dorcas insists on looking historically at an individual slave's story of sexual abuse.

However, because Dorcas exists in this relation relative to Rufel's representational whimsy, she cannot have the final word. In much the same way as she is able to appoint her slave's birthdate, Rufel is also able to reconstruct her slave's voice, and, failing that, to reconstruct her slave's motives for speaking. Recalling the scene with Ada, Rufel decides that "Mammy had probably not believed Ada's story herself" but did not wish to "antagonize Ada" for fear that Ada would leave and not help Rufel (95). Rufel takes what had apparently been Dorcas's words and intent and reconstructs them so that they now replicate her own sentiments. Indeed, as Rufel reconstructs what she wants to be Dorcas's true meaning, it turns out that Dorcas probably foresaw "her own death" and was "trying to secure the help Rufel would need" afterwards. By the time she is finished with the reconstructed memory of her slave's birth, thoughts, and beliefs, Rufel has truly made Dorcas's life story the supplement to her own. Dorcas lived at Rufel's behest (symbolized by Rufel's assigning her a birthdate) and died with Rufel's best interests occupying her final thoughts. Such is Rufel's narrative imagination regarding her slaves; she owns them and she owns their stories.

As she has done with Dorcas, Rufel first attempts to structure Dessa's life story through her own desires. Finding the story she hears from the fugitives on the plantation unacceptable, Rufel concludes that "there was more to the girl's story than the darkies were telling" (99). Rufel deals with Dessa's "story" the same way she had dealt with Ada's. Her immediate assumption is that the narrative she receives from the "darkies" cannot possibly be complete or accurate, since completion is the prerogative of a white voice, accuracy the product of a white imagination. That is Rufel's method of controlling the lives of those around her. Although Rufel does not own the bodies of the fugitive slaves who work on her plantation, she maintains remarkable control over their narratives. She even sends her son to the slave quarters because "the darkies talked before him as they would not with her," and through the information he provides she is able to keep "track of the comings and goings in the

Quarters" (100). Rufel's control also works in another way. She attempts to make her slaves part of the fabric of her life by talking them into it, literally.

Dorcas had become Rufel's slave through an economic exchange. She is made Rufel's "Mammy" through a narrative imbrication. Although Dorcas is Rufel's "weddin gif"—an owned chattel—she becomes part of her family by being knit into it just as Rufel knits her other memories "into the commonplace fabric" of her life (112). We have seen how Rufel imbricates Dorcas into her (Rufel's) mental life by reconstructing Dorcas's voice so that it expresses what Rufel wishes it to express no matter what it actually says. The obverse side of that "relation"—based on familial ties (kin relation) and narrative interpellation (relations of histories)—involves constructing Dorcas as a willing auditor to those narratives. Dorcas becomes both the subject of Rufel's narratives and subject to them. There is an informative ambiguity to the sentence describing what Rufel misses most about the deceased Dorcas: "Mammy died. Rufel could not get used to that fact. Nothing in the days and weeks since Mammy's death had filled the silence where her voice used to live" (118). Whose voice, we wonder? Mammy's or Rufel's? We might think the voice belonged to Mammy—she is departed, so is her voice—but given that Rufel reconstructs Dorcas's voice to suit her purposes and temperament, the sentence might well be describing how Rufel's voice has no place to live since Dorcas's death. After failing to imbricate another slave woman into her narrative, "as she used to do with Mammy," Rufel has to confront a disturbing truth that the community she imagined is now, and might always have been, a delusion (102).

It is not only Rufel's prerogative to keep track of the lives of the black folk living on her plantation; it appears her special desire to have her voice live in some slave woman's presence. Dessa, however, is unwilling to make even the simplest gestures of courtesy when Rufel starts to tell her narratives about her relationship to Dorcas. Unlike the battle between Dessa and Nehemiah, which was premised on a contest of media (writing or orality) based on the meaning of slave resistance and slave life, the battle between Dessa and Rufel is premised on a contest of narratives (whose story is it and who gets to tell it) based on symbolic words.[41] The key word upon which they construct their conflicting narratives is "Mammy"—a signifier both women feel entitled to use to describe their relationships to an earlier presence and a preceding generation.[42] The relationship between the two women reaches a crisis when Dessa resists Rufel's narrative about Dorcas and challenges her use of the term "Mammy" (124–25). At stake in the competing narratives is the symbolic signifier around which each of the women constructs a narrative of her own life. The confrontation between Dessa and Rufel leaves each of them in a state of crisis. Their divergent responses to that crisis informs us of the difference in their ways of thinking about dialogue and community. Going into a trancelike state, Dessa recollects her family— "Remembering the names now the way mammy used to tell them, lest they forget, she would say; lest her poor, lost children die to living memory as they had to her in the world" (126)—in order to establish her connection to her mother. Meanwhile, Rufel suffers a crisis of identity, feeling more poignantly what had intermittently troubled her before: that Dorcas might not have willingly loved her, that Dorcas's disagreements with her might have been manifestations of the hatred a slave can feel for a master.

Dessa is able to return to her memory and feel connected to her mother because she grants her mother's voice a living presence in her mind. In fact, Dessa's present memory of her family members' names follows the contours her mother had already established; she calls them out to herself "the way mammy used to tell them" to her. Rufel, on the other hand, cannot return to her memory easily because she can find only her own voice there. Here, we learn, is the cost of reconstructing others' voices in our minds; eventually, our own voices are the only ones inhabiting our mental life. To employ Mikhail Bakhtin's useful term, we can say that Rufel's mind takes on the qualities of a "monological steadfastness." She denies the dialogue of voices in her imagination and thereby loses the opportunity for communal connection. She needs to develop a dialogical attitude toward the language of others, an attitude based on communicative norms in which the discourse of our mental lives "is half ours and half-someone else's."[43] Rather than treating Dorcas as an alter ego, rather than reconstructing Dorcas's voice so that it resembles her own, Rufel must allow Dorcas's voice the play of its own pitch; she can do that only when she begins to think of Dorcas as an autonomous person, not "an extension of herself" (157). That, however, cannot happen so long as Rufel thinks of Dorcas as her slave. Dorcas's voice cannot reside in Rufel's mental life until Rufel learns to recognize the living presence of someone other than herself.

Rufel's way of thinking about Dorcas is part of the legacy of her family. She thinks of Dorcas as a maternal figure because that is how her family taught her to palliate the harshness of a slave–master relationship. When the Carson family purchased Dorcas for $1,100, they immediately "called her Mammy because Mrs. Carson thought the title made her seem as if she had been with the family for a long time" (130). Taking away Dorcas's history and name in an act of intentional amnesia, Mrs. Carson teaches her daughter how others become incorporated into the Carson family history through a shared delusion. At first, Rufel surrenders to the self-delusion of the fictive kinship ties. She wants, desperately, to know that Dorcas "loved her. It was Rufel Mammy loved" (130). The confrontation with Dessa, however, forces Rufel to consider how the fictive ties on which she had based her most intimate bonding relationship are "fictive" in the worst possible sense—they are delusions. The best response Rufel can manage to Dessa's challenge is that she (Rufel) was "like" Dorcas's child. The slave system allowed Rufel this delusion by using familial terms to name a master-slave relationship. What the crisis with Dessa forces Rufel to understand is that the relation between slaves and masters—in a system of either adoptive or quasi-filial kinship—is never premised on love freely given. What Rufel goes through in her struggles with Dessa is akin to what Eugene Genovese called the "terrible moment of truth" in the South, when the "slaveholders' understanding of themselves and their world suffered a severe shock during and immediately after the war, when 'their black families' appeared in a new light." Expecting filial "obedience internalized as duty, respect, and love" from their former slaves, the slaveholders were traumatized to discover, like Rufel, that the fiction was over.[44]

Unlike the slaveholders who respond to their epochal crisis by creating Black Codes in law and the Confederate romance in imagination, Rufel goes through a process of revision which gives her the opportunity to appreciate better what life in slavery entails, forcing her to reconsider the familial terms with which she was taught to mask that social relationship, and also teaching her how not to think of other peoples' stories as either untrue or subject to her whimsical and self-centered interpretation of their value. Rufel's already unstable imagination becomes even more febrile after the crisis, and she finds herself confronting an image of "Mammy" that is no longer a replication of her own thoughts, but a "stranger" instead (136). For her to refamiliarize herself with her "Mammy," Rufel must learn to listen to those who have lived the same life and experienced the same social condition as had Dorcas, and to appreciate the depth and integrity of their stories.

No longer eager to "talk about herself" to a slave in order to create a bond between the slave and herself, Rufel learns "to listen" to the stories told her by former slaves (157–58). In learning to listen with attention and empathy, she begins to resist the "history of white women who are unable to hear black women's words" and thus gains the "ability to allow the Other to be sufficient unto itself and also a part of the self's life."[45] Rufel no longer tries to talk through Dessa, but engages in the kind of dialogue necessary to refiguring the terms of community. When Rufel learns that Dessa's mistress abuses her "Cause she can," Rufel is forced to hear "the ring of utter truth in the statement" and recognizes her own deep complicity in the slave system (149). She learns that as a slavemistress she had absolute power over Dorcas, and that absolute power, even when not exercised to its absolute limits, is always a condition in which human relationships are inevitably corrupted. Rufel realizes that what she and her family have done to Dorcas—taken her name, her history, her body, her birthday, her voice—was done because they could. It is only after Rufel genuinely listens to the stories of other slaves and undergoes a traumatic discovery of the powers she wielded over Dorcas that she can begin to renegotiate the terms of their relationship.

By listening to the fugitive slaves, by giving them the space to tell her things and teach her how others live in the world, Rufel gains the capacity to tell anew Dorcas's story in a less hegemonic way. Since "telling grows out of listening," Rufel learns to create her narrative of Dorcas in a new and fundamentally different way. Williams is not arguing that Rufel lacks the power or should be denied the place to tell Dorcas's story; she is saying that Rufel has choices about the kind of narrative she will construct, whether it is an appropriative one premised on ignorance or an informed one emerging out of an authentic effort to listen to the chorus of stories attesting to the communally shared life of African American peoples. Like the narrator in James Alan McPherson's wonderful short story "Elbow Room," Rufel comes to understand and proclaim: "It was from the beginning not my story. I lack the insight to narrate its complexities. But it may still be told." Rufel, that is, unlike Stowe in Reed's *Flight to Canada,* unlike Nehemiah in her own novel (or Styron in the historical case on which she is reflecting), discovers in time that "When you take . . . a story that doesn't belong to you, that story will get you."[46] She must now discover the means by which she can tell a story that she now realizes doesn't belong to her.

The issue at the heart of Rufel's revisionist story of Dorcas is the tense kind of love that could have existed between slaveholder and slave. Realizing that her own desire is "to believe that Mammy had loved her not only fully, but freely as well," Rufel is nonetheless also forced to acknowledge that she had been "personally responsible for Mammy's pain" (147). When she begins to retell the story of Dorcas,

Rufel stops romanticizing Dorcas's personality and grants it an ambivalence, an open-endedness, she had earlier been unwilling to ascribe to Dorcas. Thinking about how "hateful and spiteful" Dessa had been to her, Rufel thinks that "even if Mammy herself had been spiteful, bitter, secretly rebellious, Mammy, through caring and concern, had made Rufel hers, had lain claim to her affections. Rufel knew this as love" (158). Rufel does two important things here. First, she rephrases the terms of love so that it is Dorcas whose agency is important. Dorcas, we are told, "had made Rufel hers." By granting Dorcas the agency to possess Rufel in love, Rufel might be deluding herself—but there is, I think, sincerity in her sentiment. One measure of that sincerity is the second thing Rufel does here. She allows Dessa's character to help her recreate Dorcas's personality so that it is multifaceted and not simply a romanticized extension of her own. She realizes that Dorcas, like Dessa, was a slave; and she understands that the only way she can reform her understanding of what sentiments Dorcas may have felt as a slave or what thoughts might have gone through her mind is by granting someone who has experienced what Dorcas had experienced the authority to speak for that station. As the fugitive slave Mary Prince says in claiming precisely that authority: "I have been a slave myself—I know what slaves feel—I can tell by myself what other slaves feel, and by what they have told me."[47] Rufel learns to listen to fugitive slaves as a way of understanding her deceased one.

The telling moment in Rufel's process of deromanticizing her tales of Dorcas comes when she talks directly to Dessa and addresses the misunderstanding that initiated her crisis: "'that other day, we wasn't talking about the same person. Your mammy birthed you, and mines, mines just helped to raise me. But she loved me,' she couldn't help adding, 'she loved me, just like yours loved you.'" Dessa responds: "'I know that, Mis'ess,' she sighed. 'I know that,' she said without anger or regret'" (167). Rufel needs Dessa's voice to confirm what she intuits about Dorcas's sentiments. It is an interesting reversal of the values with which she had begun her relationship with Dessa, the same set of values she had used to maintain her relationship with Dorcas for eleven years. Seeing Dessa's scarred body, she realizes that there is indeed a "deeper story" behind Dessa's "tale"; and, moreover, she is right to sense that it is a story "not entirely unrelated to her concern for Mammy" (151). It is clear, though, that Dessa's reply is undeniably ambiguous. After all, she does not declare she "knows" that Dorcas loved Rufel; she could well have been commenting on only the first of Rufel's observations—that they were not talking about the same person—instead of also agreeing with Rufel's other claim that Dorcas did indeed love Rufel. It is possible, even likely, that Dessa was commenting on both observations, but the ambiguity in her reply is part of Williams's consummate artistry in concluding her representation of Rufel's reconstruction of her "Mammy."

In the end, Dessa provides Rufel with both the crisis and the terms of reconciliation. For Rufel to restructure her mental narrative of her relationship with Dorcas, she has to incorporate Dessa into her life. Because Dessa has lived life in the same condition as Dorcas, she can provide Rufel with a voice that Rufel can install into her mental representations of Dorcas. Dessa's voice serves Rufel's memory, in the state of psychic crisis, by forcing Rufel to hear again what Dorcas may actually have been saying in her covert way. In the end, though, Rufel is not fully free of her wonted skepticism about the testimony of African Americans. In a state where black lives and black life stories are commodities for white consumption, Rufel cannot transcend those material conditions or remain aloof from the supporting ideological constructions that define and maintain the social inequities between black and white Americans. Even though she feels physically empathetic to Dessa's sufferings, Rufel nonetheless doubts their very existence (144). She has learned to control the lives and stories of her slaves to such an extent that she cannot believe what slaves tell her without seeking visual proof. As Dessa says in a moment of profound insight into the ways black lives are commodified: "Miz Lady had to *see* the goods before she would buy the story" (205). Rufel's desire for controlling the black Others in her life becomes somewhat less urgent, as is demonstrated by her willingness to address Dessa directly instead of constructing her narrative from various scraps of information she gathers, but it is by no means dissipated, as is evidenced by her susceptibility to the ideological stereotypes circulating through the narratives of people like Nehemiah.

The Militant Mammy: Performing Racial Identity, Forming Literary Voice

The ambiguity in the exchange between Rufel and Dessa should not be downplayed; Dessa's final word on Dorcas is hardly definitive. Melissa Walker's belief that "Dessa's response, 'I know that, Mis'ess,' settles the matter for good" seems premature and grants Dessa an authority she neither claims nor possesses.[48] However, what should also not be glossed over is the fact that the final word is Dessa's. Dessa, let us recall, has not only not spent enough time with Rufel and Dorcas to be able to determine whether or not they shared a love. *She has never met Dorcas.* Yet hers is the final word on the relationship between Dorcas and Rufel, and an apparently ambiguous final word at that. And that ambiguity and deferral of authority mark one of Williams's most significant contributions to the reconstruction of the mythology of the "Mammy." Williams uses the figure of "Mammy" not only to define the contested terrain between Dessa and Rufel, but also to make her most concerted commentary on the discourse of slavery mobilizing her Neo-slave narrative by: (1) undoing the strategies through which the historiography of slavery created the docile "Mammy" as the female equivalent to "Sambo"; (2) offering a particularly trenchant reading of Styron's representation of a docile female slave; and (3) leveling a critique at one of the tendencies of Black Power that she found disturbing. The revision of "Mammy," then, allows Williams to comment on the social movement and the historiographical debate surrounding Styron's *Confessions of Nat Turner,* while also permitting her to render her final critique of the novel itself, and, finally, developing the trope that demonstrates the deep relationship between the performance of racial roles and the form of the Neo-slave narrative she is writing.

In a comment on the American historiographical tradition, Williams noted that the major function of what she calls "Lion's history"—that is, the simple revisionist history that would retell the major events of a nation's narrative through the perspective of the conquered peoples instead of the victorious ones—is "to balance the representation of the character of institutional oppression rather than to change the discourse of History itself."[49] Changing the "discourse of History itself" requires a more concentrated exploration of the major tenets of historiography. Using the figure of "Mammy" for the task, Williams examines the deep discourses that create the representations of African Americans in the American historical profession.

The "Mammy legend" can be traced to the proslavery writings of thirty or so years prior to the Civil War, precisely the time proslavery ideologues are creating the "Sambo" stereotype. Constructed to personify "the ideal slave, and the ideal woman," the "Mammy" emerged at the nexus between the ideology of benign planter paternalism and the cult of domesticity, and therefore represented the "centerpiece in the antebellum Southerner's perception of the perfectly organized society." Projected as a woman who "suckled and reared white masters," the "Mammy" image "displaced sexuality into nurture and transformed potential hostility into sustenance and love." In other words, the combination of the cult of true womanhood and proslavery ideologies was meant to create a stereotype, disguising or mystifying objective social relations, and creating an ahistorical structure, what Patricia Hill Collins calls a "controlling image" defining and objectifying African American women, which serves as part of a "generalized ideology of domination."[50]

Representing a critical point in the emergent romance of the Confederacy, the "Mammy" also acts as a perfect gauge for the historiography of the antebellum South. In the early years of the professionalization of American history, as historians simultaneously created a national historical profession and contributed to the "great task of national reconciliation, healing the wounds of the Civil War and Reconstruction" by creating a "nationalist and racist historiographical consensus," the "Mammy" figure was celebrated in the southern plantation romance tradition of historians such as Ulrich Phillips and novelists like Margaret Mitchell. In response to this nostalgic tradition in American historiography, African American intellectuals created a countermythologizing discourse exemplified in Charlotte Hawkins Brown's 1919 critique of the treatment of those ex-slave women "left destitute in old age" by their white former owners and in W. E. B. Du Bois's 1924 strategy of translating the "Mammy" from an idealized mother figure into an equally idealized martyr figure, "one of the most pitiful of the world's Christs," little more than "an embodied Sorrow, an anomaly crucified on the cross of her own neglected children for the sake of the children of masters who bought and sold her as they bought and sold cattle." This struggle over the figure of the "Mammy" was epitomized in 1923 in the African American community's vigorous dissent to the Daughers of the Confederacy's attempt to get Congress to set aside a site in Washington for the erection of a statue in tribute to "Mammy."[51]

Despite these early battles over historical representations, the myth of the "Mammy" dominated historical portraits until the early seventies. Even after "Sambo" had been rendered suspect, "Mammy" remained relatively unreconstructed. As late as 1974, historians noted that "no figure stands out so prominently in the moonlight-and-magnolias legend of the Old South" as does "Mammy." Historians working within the new discourse on slavery began to undo that image by reading antebellum slave narratives in which the "Mammy" is represented not as a devoted, self-abnegating maternal figure but rather as someone "cunning, prone to poisoning her master, and not at all content with her lot."[52] Cultural workers realized that an effective response to the "moonlight-and-magnolias legend" was not a countermyth, though that is a nec-

essary stage in the dismantling of a stereotype, but rather a more historicized examination of the intellectual and political conditions within which the stereotype began
to assume authority.

Williams performs this kind of archaeology by highlighting the imaginative
structures used to develop and transmit the myth of the "Mammy." Williams shows
how "Mammy" figures are recreations of romantic memories and memorials that
have to be disrupted and destroyed in order for any revisionist historical reconstruction to be performed. The "Mammy" Rufel remembers before Dessa's intervention is
not a human but an icon, not a person with a will and a story of her very own but a
figure as frozen in time and space as the statue of "Mammy" the Daughters of the
Confederacy wanted to erect. Like the docile male slave of "antebellum southern
myth and propaganda," the "Mammy" must "always be a constant, constitutionally
averse and impervious to change, for the sake of [her]self, [her] white folks, and the
southern ideal of civilization."

Dessa's intervention does for Dorcas what Dessa earlier did for herself in conversation with Nehemiah, and what Nat Turner did for himself in conversation with
Thomas Gray: she creates for her a narrative that destroys the static quality required
to sustain her as a stereotype. Rufel is forced to acknowledge that Dorcas had a past,
a life, a story Rufel does not know and can never know because she had been so engaged with the activity of narrating Dorcas into her life that she did not bother to listen to Dorcas's own narratives. Dessa hints at this hidden story by providing Rufel
with clues about the life of a slave. There is a danger involved in doing this, however. While Dessa's providing Dorcas with a narrative does disrupt Rufel's tendency
to think of her as a stable icon, it nonetheless leaves that narrative itself in danger of
appropriation. For that reason, it is important that Dessa complete the intervention
into Rufel's mythic imagination by taking on the functions and title of "Mammy" and
thereby showing Rufel that it is a performative role, not a stable and enduring entity
but a guise under which there exists as resentful and resistant a slave as there were
under all other guises and masks slaves have been forced to adopt (213).

While demonstrating that the role is a performance, Williams nonetheless also
respects the irreducible ambiguity of the silent and deferred "Mammy," the "most
elusive" and the most "enigmatic" of slaves.[53] It is crucial to note that there is only
one person who lives and dies a slave in *Dessa Rose*—and that is Dorcas. The rest are
all either fugitive ex-slaves—Dessa, Harker, Nathan, Cully, Ada, and Annabelle—or
freed at the end, as Uncle Joel and Dante are when Rufel goes to "Philly-me-York—
some city didn't allow no slaves" (259). It is worth noting, then, that Williams places
only one voice beyond the realm of freedom and, coincidentally, represents only that
voice as always a reconstruction of someone else's imagining. Perhaps Williams's
most stunning accomplishment is her implicit representation of the proper respect
due the enigma and the ambiguity of the slave's voice. The fact that Williams ensures
that we never directly hear Dorcas's voice or immediately encounter her words except through others' representations suggests something about the limitations on
our ability to hear the slave voice.

Williams employs two interrelated strategies to represent what Du Bois calls the
"voice of exile" with which "the slave spoke to the world."[54] First, she defers the representation so that Dorcas's voice always appears as the recreative supplement of

Rufel's narrative imagination. Second, she insists that the only humane way to recreate that voice is to supplement it by placing it amid a chorus of voices of people who have lived the same life and experienced the same condition as Dorcas. By allowing Dessa to aid in the recovery of Dorcas's story, Rufel shows us how historians should proceed in reconstructing the portrayal of slavery by consulting those who experienced it. The voices and testimonies and stories of slaves, she suggests, would disrupt the static and romanticized image of the institution and produce in its stead a more dynamic and satisfactory rendering of the heroism, the love, and the suffering in what Williams calls "that other history" which challenges the "discourse of History itself."

Those intellectuals unwilling to challenge dominant historical discourses inevitably produce cultural works that replicate rather than resist controlling stereotypical images and the technologies of domination they represent. Again, using "Mammy" as the concept around which she organizes her critique of those intellectuals, Williams returns to Styron's *Confessions* in the second section of her novel. Whereas her critique of Styron in the first section focused on the appropriative gesture of an amanuensis unwilling to hear the deeper story behind the guise of a recalcitrant slave, her critique in the second is on his inability to appreciate the acts of resistance performed by slave women. Having shown that racial roles are fluid and contingent, Williams offers us a portrait of a "Mammy" figure who is creative in her intellectual habits, imaginative in her domestic economy, and ultimately resistant in her dealings with her mistress. We learn, for instance, that Dorcas possessed an astute managerial mind. After Rufel's husband failed to return to Sutton Glen, Dorcas took over the business of caring for the plantation, inaugurating a new plantation system, rotating the crops to prevent depletion of the soil, and changing the plantation's main crop from cotton to more immediately usable cultures. More important than her work of organizing the plantation's crop schedule was Dorcas's insight that a new labor regime was in order. Instead of employing slave labor, Dorcas inaugurated a free labor system based on sharecropping principles, which proved considerably more successful (161). Even Rufel had to admit that the free fugitives "seemed to work with a better will than darkies on the place had ever done" (116). Dorcas effectively ran the plantation and managed to command assent from Rufel, who found herself relying completely on "Mammy's judgment" (117). Dorcas was able to act on her own initiative because Rufel's husband was away from the plantation; she was therefore able to doff one persona of domestic caretaker and assume another as plantation manager. In doing so, she demonstrated the fluidity of her character, the multifaceted aspects of her subjectivity, while also subtly showing Rufel that the persona a slave adopts is largely a response to institutional and material conditions.

This lesson that slaves' racial roles are performed is reinforced when Dessa accepts the role of a "Mammy" during the trip South and succeeds in caring for both Rufel and her baby Clara (213). If Dessa, the so-called "devil woman," could act out the part of "Mammy," could Dorcas not also have felt the murderous rage Dessa attests to feeling, the "flash that'd nelly-bout killed Master and almost strangled Mistress, that rode [her] in the fight on the coffle" (199)? By demonstrating the performative nature of the slave's subjectivity, Williams contests Rufel's tendency to think in static terms and, by allusion, offers her critique of Styron's inability to think of slaves as anything but docile. We saw how Styron represents the male slave as an "unspeakable bootlicking Sambo." All the male slaves, with the exception of Harker, Will, and Turner, are described as "hopelessly docile." And even these three are suspect, since Harker reverts to docility in jail after the rebellion, Will is described as an unreflecting murderous automaton, and Turner is cast as an ineffective and ambiguously motivated leader. We also saw how Styron represents practically the only slave woman in the novel, Lou-Ann Turner, as an unequivocally docile slave who responds with pleasure to her rape. Obviously troubling and disgusting in itself, this representation also belies what history has recorded about Nat Turner's actual mother, Nancy Turner. According to the oral tradition on which William Drewry based his account, Nancy Turner was far from docile. A native of Africa, she had to be tied down to prevent her from murdering her newborn baby son. Styron ascribes this act to Nat's grandmother instead in order to detach Turner from the traditions of African and African American resistance. In a statement that again belies Nat Turner's own statement in Gray's *Confessions*, Styron has his Turner say, "I never laid eyes on my grandmother." When he states "there is a left-over savage part of me that feels very close to my grandmother," we are meant to assume that his acts of resistance are indebted to some kind of atavistic gene rather than to the social communication he had with his grandmother and his parents.[55] Lou-Ann Turner, meanwhile, must have inherited the docility gene.

Williams challenges Styron's representation by offering us the character of Linda, a slave purchased and added to the coffle in Montgomery. Every night since she was added to the coffle, one of the white guards would thrash off "into the underbrush" and rape Linda. Each night, the slaves on the coffle are made wretched by their inability to respond to Linda's "pleas and pitiful whimperings." One night, the pleas and whimperings are replaced with silence, then a "dull thud, startlingly loud in the stillness." As the slaves watch, Linda appears in the clearing, "her dress torn and gaping, the bloody rock still clutched in her manacled hands" (60). Her act of murdering her would-be rapist initiates the coffle uprising. The uprising, then, is a result of the actions of two women, Dessa and Linda. Resistance, Williams suggests, is not solely a male prerogative; and rape, she insists, is never a form of violence that can be mistaken for pleasure. The representation of Linda suggests the possible subjectivities any and all the slave women in this novel can occupy. Let me be clear: Williams is not arguing that slave women have choices in the sense of options they are free to will or acccept. She is arguing that the subject positions they occupy are responses to material conditions, which are not necessarily as immanent as they seem from the view of slavemasters and slavemistresses. That is precisely what Williams demonstrates by showing us a continuum of the subject positions a slave woman may occupy: Dessa can be rebel or "Mammy" just as Dorcas can be "Mammy" or plantation manager. Resistance is not genetic, as it appears to be in Styron, but a product of a resourceful education within a community. It is worth noting that when Dessa is at her lowest ebb and meditates on suicide, it is the lesson of her "Mamma Hattie" that comes to mind as she considers swallowing her tongue the way "the first women had done" (62). Resistance emerges from a set of social conditions and it has a tradition.

Having seen how Williams disrupts the discourse of History and disturbs Styron's meditations on history, we can now finally turn to Williams's use of "Mammy" as a way of delineating her critique of Black Power and generating a trope of expressive cultural production representing her take on the relationship between the formal properties of her novel and the racial formation she is contesting. Although Williams held an almost constant respect for Black Power from the late sixties to the present, she did have a concern about one particular principle (other than her concern with the rigidity of an aesthetic program valorizing only social realism). Like Reed, Williams was concerned that Black Power advocates tended to think of themselves as the first rebellious generation; likewise, she was dismayed by those Black Power advocates who repudiated or dismissed earlier African American rebels who adopted less revolutionary means than the sixties generation. She especially praised Ernest Gaines for creating Miss Jane Pittman as a character who represented "the past and the present, [and] the struggle for the future." The "past" in *The Autobiography of Miss Jane Pittman* "is a living force which struggles to make the spirit of past events manifest in the still oppressive present."[56] Black Power advocates who would eschew elder rebels like Miss Jane failed to recognize the social conditions limiting earlier generations from adopting more demonstrative stances of resistance. We saw that Reed asked similar questions and posed as his metaphor for the generational problem in Black Power the misunderstood "Uncle Tom," a figure who represented an underappreciated revolutionary tradition.

The female equivalent of "Uncle Tom," of course, is "Mammy." In her novel *Kindred,* Octavia Butler dealt with the same generational problem. Having traveled back from 1976 to a slave plantation in nineteenth-century Maryland, the narrator Dana feels disdain for the slave Sarah who chooses to do "the safe thing." She considers Sarah "the kind of woman who might have been called 'mammy' in some other household. She was the kind of woman who would be held in contempt during the militant nineteen sixties. The house-nigger, the handkerchief-head, the female Uncle Tom." Dana revises her opinion after she herself finds the life of a slave almost unbearable; Sarah, she recognizes belatedly, is a heroic woman whose achievements should be celebrated in even the most "militant" decades. As Butler herself noted in an interview, the character who had been called "mammy" had "her own forms of resistance" which those Black Power advocates not inclined to respect the revolutionary actions of earlier generations needed to appreciate. *Kindred* "was a kind of reaction to some of the things going on during the sixties when people were feeling ashamed of, or more strongly, angry with their parents for not having improved things faster." Her plot device of taking "a person from today and send[ing] that person back to slavery" was ingenious because it allowed the militant Dana to recognize the strength and resilience of those women whose unearned titles ("Mammy") became a term of contempt in the sixties.[57]

Just as Reed salvaged "Uncle Tom" in the character of Uncle Robin, so does Williams salvage "Mammy" in the character of Dorcas. Her aim was to emphasize that Black Power should not be premised on a rupture with the past, nor should it establish its revolutionary credentials by dismissing those people in the past whose lives and forms of resistance appear at odds with contemporary social movements. For that reason, she chose the term "Neo-Black," not only because it described the impetus of the present "Black revolution" but also because the term "suggests continuity with the past and a reinterpretation of it instead of an abrupt break or sharp veering off into something entirely different from what has gone before." She claims that she never understood "how these brothers could so calmly propose the death of so much family, so many friends. How could one work for a black revolution in which so many casualties were black," she asked?[58] Williams challenges this kind of thinking by producing an archaeology of "Mammy," demonstrating both how the figure is a caricature based on the planter class's desires and a racial role as performative as that of the militant revolutionary.

Instead, Williams proposed a communal dialogue with the past based on a form of expressive culture that some Black Power advocates found as suspect as the figures of "Uncle Tom" and "Mammy"—the blues. Williams points out that she began "to delve into the blues as an act of quiet rebellion against the cultural nationalists who proclaimed the blues counterrevolutionary because they were 'morose' songs that reminded people of 'slavery times.'" For Williams, these songs provided her with access to the past, with what might have been the sole means of engaging in a nonhegemonic dialogue with "slavery times." Frederick Douglass, for instance, insisted that the only means through which one could understand slavery and the condition of the slave was to listen to the slave songs: "the mere hearing of these songs would do more to impress some minds with the horrible character of slavery, than the reading of whole volumes of philosophy on the subject could do." "In these songs," echoed Du Bois, "the slave spoke to the world." Because Rufel cannot experience slavery and thereby understand Dorcas's words, she learns to listen to the voices of the fugitive slaves on her plantation. In them she hears the blues chorus that provides her with a means of more generously recreating Dorcas's enigmatic voice. The blues, as Williams says, is "about dialogue" and therefore a form of communication in which there is "a very close and personal relationship among singer, song, and the group tradition on which all depended for the act of creation, and which the act of creation affirms and extends." The blues provides the conditions for understanding those ancestral voices recreated with every song—and whose recreation allows the singer and the audience to constitute and reconstitute their own selves. Moreover, the very ethic of the blues is premised on its ability to negotiate the enigmatic: "the blues deals with a world where the inability to solve a problem does not necessarily mean that one can, or ought to, transcend it. The internal strategy of the blues is action, rather than contemplation."[59]

In the end, Williams posits the "blues" as her theory of "reading" as a way of making possible both dialogue and community. In a novel she had wished to call "Dessa's Song," Williams represents the ways several voices contribute to the "collective blues dialogue," and she demonstrates how communal narratives about the absent ancestors are wrought of that dialogue.[60] Rufel listens to the voices of those fugitive slaves whose stories she had earlier tried to control in order to give herself the space and capacity to recreate Dorcas's voice. By listening to the "collective blues dialogue," instead of attempting to reconstruct the individual voices or control the various stories, Rufel permits herself to *participate* in the community to which Dorcas also belonged. She is not the only one to benefit from that dialogue, though. Dessa also gains a form of communication by which she can reconstitute the selfhood Nehemiah threatened. In conversation with Nehemiah, Dessa had felt "she saw the past as she talked, not as she had lived it but as she had come to understand it" (56). Her understanding of her past, in that case however, was mediated through Nehemiah's "reconstruction." Just as Dorcas had been subjected to Rufel's narrations of her own life, so was Dessa subject to the questions Nehemiah directed at her. We have to remember that Nehemiah had recorded Dessa's life to signify something entirely foreign to its lived experience. The figure of Dorcas provides Dessa with the dialogic space and a theory of reading countereffective to the ones Dessa had internalized when subject to Nehemiah's relations. By being made a corporate part of a collective voice, Dessa regains her past "as she had lived it," or at least she regains a sense of the past with an understanding no longer so oppressively mediated by Nehemiah's reconstructions. We should recall that whatever ambiguity Dessa's final words on Dorcas's relationship with Rufel contain, those words are also a testament to her own, intimate knowledge: "I know that, Mis'ess," she sighed. "I know that."

In a large measure, then, "Mammy" represents the making of *Dessa Rose* as a Neo-slave narrative through its focus on performance as subversion (of racial roles), performance as communion (in the blues chorus), and performance as recuperation (in the salvaging of Dorcas's story). At the same time as she shows that racial roles are performed in certain material conditions, Williams simultaneously demonstrates that different kinds of texts (written documents sanctioned by the cultural apparatus of the racialized state and oral family narratives produced within and mobilized by the racial formation of that state) appropriate the voices and life stories of African American peoples. To counteract both the "public" and "private" texts that recreate oppressive racial formations which in turn promote acts of cultural appropriation, Williams produces a performative text that, like Reed's, formally establishes itself as a defiant challenge to those appropriating master texts. Williams achieves this end by showing us the incremental stages in Dessa's assumption of voice. In each of the first two parts of the novel, Dessa challenges the representational strategies of those master texts that would possess her story or reify racial roles.

Dessa challenges Rufel's personal memory in the same way she had resisted Nehemiah's political document: by placing her life, her story, and her fluid performances of diverse racial roles as a subversive supplement to the master texts of the hegemonic racial formation. Nehemiah's written text cannot contain or appropriate Dessa's story. Rufel's imagination can no longer subscribe to the hegemonic racial formations that texts like Nehemiah's produce and mobilize. Meanwhile, by subversively inhabiting Nehemiah's written text and supplanting Rufel's personal memory, Dessa is incrementally assuming a voice that not only resists and revises master texts, but also claims itself as a resplendently clear and inviolate production not subject to the kind of appropriation and commodification to which her body had been subject. In the first section, Dessa engaged in an oral performance which not only gained her physical freedom but exorbitantly exceeded the attempt Nehemiah made to control her in his sanctioned text. In the second section, Dessa continued to develop her voice in such a way as not only to resist those who would dominate her personally but also to challenge the hegemonic racial formation that dominated all peoples of African descent. Her oral performances here salvage the life stories of those whose voices were rendered silent in order to render them static, in particular, "Mammy" Dorcas.

As a sign of an unacceptable absence, Dorcas provides Dessa with an opportunity to recreate her past life, and therefore she represents a key figure in Dessa's assumption of voice at the end of the novel.[61] "I hopes I live for my people like they do for me," Dessa intones at the end, at the same time as she asserts that *"this the childrens have heard from our own lips"* (260). By the final section of the novel, Dessa becomes the narrator; and in the epilogue, we learn that hers has been the governing voice in the novel as a whole, subverting Nehemiah's public writing and Rufel's personal memories. Formally, a novel that had begun as a written representation of a master text ends as an oral performance of a slave's narrative. Moreover, it is an oral performance that appropriates—or better, creatively and resistantly subsumes—those political and private acts through which racial roles are reified. Like Reed, Williams teaches us to read resistantly, to look for the submerged voices in master texts, to examine the cultural apparatus that create hegemonic literary traditions, and to recuperate the performative acts that trace the fault lines of any oppressive racial formation.

6

Serving the Form,
Conserving the Order

Charles Johnson's Oxherding Tale

In order to demonstrate how race is a proscriptive political construct created and recreated in daily life, both *Flight to Canada* and *Dessa Rose* explore the performative aspect of a given social role and challenge those who hold simplistic notions of authenticity. Ishmael Reed and Sherley Anne Williams complicate representations of black social subjects by showing how racial identities, even those held to be most inauthentic historically and most dangerous for contemporary racial politics (the "Uncle Tom" and the "Mammy"), are based on intricate performances within perilous social conditions. Like Reed and Williams, Charles Johnson also demonstrates the ways the machinery of an oppressive society operates to delimit options and opportunities by producing prohibitive intellectual formations on race. Unlike them, though, Johnson explores not only how those intellectual formations define racial *roles* but also how they create proscriptive concepts of racial *subjectivity* itself. Whereas the Neo-slave narratives that focus on the performance of racial roles examine how certain discourses constitute strategies for defining authenticity, those focusing on the performance of racial subjectivity explore the processes through which race itself is reinscribed in daily actions, superstructural activities, and infrastructural developments.

In almost all his fiction, and in much of his critical writing, Johnson has articulated and worked out his concerns with the problematics of race and personal identity. He claims not to believe in "the existence of the ego," and "race" he considers an "illusion, a manifestation of *Maya.*" Conceiving "identity" itself as a "theoretical concept," he nonetheless believes that it is deeply implicated in the politics of racial inequity in American society. Johnson notes that "black subjectivity" is produced through the "intentionality" of white agency which ascribes to black subjectivity the "contents that white consciousness itself fears to contain or confront." Agreeing with Frantz Fanon that "not only must the black man be black; he must be black in relation to the white man," Johnson writes that "it is from whites that the intention, the 'meaning' of the black body comes." Under that particularly oppressive, dominating gaze, the African American subject becomes what Johnson calls "black-as-body."

This perception of "black-as-body" not only operates in the consciousness of the perceiver, but also enters the self-conception of the perceived, who derives the "meaning" of black subjectivity from the "white Other" and remains "still susceptible to whatever meanings the white gaze assigns to it." Although Johnson here offers no compelling answers to this dilemma—he admits there are none—he does elsewhere suggest that the most salutary means of encompassing the dilemma is to historicize the search for identity—to realize that asking "Who am I?" is the same as asking "By what social forces have I been shaped?"—because identity is so much a product of social and institutional forces that one cannot understand it outside of the historical social forces that produce it.[1]

Only a few characters in Johnson's fictional world possess or demonstrate the capacity for appreciating and accepting this knowledge of the structures governing their behavior. But their ability to understand and accept this knowledge is more than a gauge of the characters' growth; it is, in fact, a determinant in the formal properties of a given literary work, since Johnson defines "form" according to the characters' ability to accede to this kind of knowledge. He defines the "fable" or the "parable," for instance, as a form of representation in which the protagonist is unable to see the mysterious "laws" underpinning the operation of the world, "the ways things work beneath the level of mere appearances." His novels of slavery, on the other hand, usually contain "a moment of awareness, an epiphany if you like, a place where the character is smashed into a larger vision under the pressure of events," able to grow from ignorance to wisdom, from nonbeing to being, in the process.[2] A character's knowledge, then, or self-consciousness of the social forces operating to create his or her identity, is both a barometer of the degree of enlightenment the character achieves and a means of appreciating the author's attitude toward the literary form employed. The form Johnson adopts and transforms in his exploration of the play of race and personal identity is the first-person Neo-slave narrative.

Yet, the narrators of Johnson's two Neo-slave narratives do not receive the same quality of epiphany or achieve the same depth of vision. In *Oxherding Tale,* Andrew Hawkins gains crucial knowledge about the social forces impinging on personal identity when he encounters the brutal machinery that generates the social order of a slave society. His knowledge remains partial, though, because he continues to deny those forms of violence that subscribe "white" identity. Andrew proves himself either incapable or unwilling to explore more deeply the social and historical forces determining his identity. Once he passes into the white world, he chooses to believe in that mythic individualism of what Johnson elsewhere calls the "lonely Leibnizean monad." In this way, then, *Oxherding Tale* is partly a fable or a parable, since Andrew is not fully aware of "the ways things work beneath the level of mere appearances." In *Middle Passage,* though, Johnson presents us with a narrator who succeeds in exploring the world of appearances more rigorously and achieving a more complete epiphany. Rutherford Calhoun is more successful because he undertakes a more ambitious task: examining and then exposing the capitalist structures operative in the social definition of personal identity. As he sets out to create or discover the "'I' that I was," he is forced to recognize that the reason "the (black) self was the greatest of all fictions" has a great deal to do with the "invisible economic realm . . . behind the sensuous" realm directing the actions and limiting the kinds of social identities and relationships possible between human beings.[3]

The difference between these two characters' explorations of the significance of racial identity is demonstrated most conclusively in the two distinct forms the Neo-slave narratives adopt; and their formal differences, I would suggest, reflect the mobilizations of different racial formations in the two historical moments of their composition. Published in 1990, *Middle Passage* was written in the mid- to late eighties, when Johnson believed the "optimistic vision . . . black people had all through the civil-rights years" was deteriorating "because of the Reagan years." Reflecting Johnson's sensibility that the 1990s was likely to be "the most race-conscious decade we've had this century," *Middle Passage* is an exploration of how the construction of race is deeply implicated in the economic order. *Oxherding Tale,* on the other hand, was originally conceived in the "turbulent late 1960s," when Johnson sought and found "clarity and consolation" from the "anger and violence" of the time in Buddhist writings, including "the 'Ten Oxherding Pictures' of twelfth-century Zen artist Kakuan Shien." Johnson wrote the first version of the novel in the summer of 1970, completed the first draft in the summer of 1975, and wrote the final version between 1975 and 1982.[4] Although published in 1982, *Oxherding Tale* is very much involved in the issues of race raised during the sixties and seventies, the Black Power moment when it was first conceived and written. As we might expect, then, *Middle Passage* asks questions about the meaning of race in Reagan's America at a time race was being debated through the rhetoric of the conservative backlash to affirmative action, whereas *Oxherding Tale* asks questions about the viability of cultural nationalist theories and Black Power rhetorics of black social identity.

Johnson himself believes *Oxherding Tale* the more complex of his two Neo-slave narratives; he refers to it as his "platform book," meaning that everything else he "attempted to do would in one way or another be based upon and refer to it." It is certainly the more complex book in the sense that in it Johnson works out more agonistically the questions he raises in each of his Neo-slave narratives. What did the sixties and the legacy of black cultural nationalism mean for African American cultural life? How could he locate his representation of slavery in terms of the ongoing debate between the hegemonic and emergent discourses on slavery and the social topics of violence, property, and identity raised in that shifting dialogue? In what ways could he use the form of the Neo-slave narrative to talk about contemporary political issues, especially those conventionally defined as "racial" issues? How, in other words, could he deploy the form of the "slave narrative, one of the oldest literary forms indigenous to the American experience," in order to make "the seminal work of the past" address "issues relevant to this age"? In answering these questions, Johnson adopts what he theorizes as a phenomenological position in order to challenge what he considers facile and ideological notions about identity, race, and racial identity. Having a keen sensitivity to the ways a literary form not only is capable of addressing contemporary issues but also is "history-laden," that is, indelibly marked with the signature and thematic concerns of its originators and his predecessors, Johnson uses the Neo-slave narrative form to intervene in those sixties debates about racial identity and the politics of cultural representation.[5]

Charles Johnson on the Black Power Sixties

Unlike Reed or Williams, Johnson is unable to be romantically or even critically nostalgic about the Black Arts and the Black Power movements, because he believes that the black cultural nationalism of the sixties still informs and deforms the contemporary African American field of cultural production in the eighties and nineties. Although I shouldn't like to stress the point too much, for it is accurate only to a degree, Johnson's animus against the sixties is similar to that motivating the participants in the Second Thoughts conferences. Like them, ruing his earlier participation in the sixties movements, especially the Black Arts movement, which he felt restricted his artistic creativity, he assiduously seeks out and laments any ideological continuity—what they term the "Sixties-within-the-Eighties" phenomenon—in contemporary American culture. In his explorations of contemporary African American writers, for example, he discerns residues of the sixties in recent black fiction either to diagnose it (Reed's recent fiction constitutes "a particular spin on cultural nationalism") or to dismiss it (Toni Morrison's *Beloved* is the "penultimate or final fruit of the Black Arts Movement"). ("People killing their kids to save them from slavery?" he querulously asks. "Come on, we're still talking the sixties here").[6]

Also like the former radicals who formed the Second Thoughts contingent, Johnson views the sixties as a seamless monolith with variations on a limited set of themes. The "dominant themes in black arts and letters" in the "weird, self-flagellating days of the 1960s," he writes, "were paranoia and genocide." These fictions both were supported by and helped in turn to support new historical works "such as those of Stanley M. Elkins and Eugene Genovese [that] drove home the sense that black history was, and might always be, a slaughter-house—a form of being characterized by stasis, denial, humiliation, dehumanization, and 'relative being.'" Because he is determined to find continuity rather than diversity of intellection in the decade, Johnson is able glibly and inaccurately to lump together Elkins and Genovese as if both were saying the same thing, and as if both were saying what black intellectuals of the sixties were saying. As we saw in chapters 2 and 3, not only were Elkins and Genovese saying radically different things about American chattel slavery, but neither was in favor of or agreement with the Black Power intellectuals. In any case, we can take Johnson's point that there is an intimate connection between historiographical writing and cultural production; and by the late eighties, he was suggesting, historical writing had given us an entirely different portrait of slavery, not based on slaves' "humiliation, dehumanization, and 'relative being,'" but rather emphasizing the slave community, slave culture, and slave religion, and giving renewed attention to the revolutionary acts of individual slaves as well as the daily resistance of collectivities of plantation slaves. Yet the cultural production emerging from the late eighties, such as *Beloved,* was apparently still entangled in the sixties, according to Johnson.[7]

Unlike Reed and Williams, then, Johnson has remained consistently critical of what he does acknowledge to be the important cultural movements of the sixties. There are certainly times when Johnson sounds appreciative of "contemporary Cultural Nationalist writers," such as his 1988 comment that no "one should doubt, not ever, the contribution of these men and women. Or their value. The truth, which is hardly said enough, is that black writing of the 1980s stands on the shoulders of the confrontationalist fiction of the Angry School. Without it, we could not stand at all." Yet both before and after 1988, Johnson was critical of the Black Arts movement in ways that suggest his enduring uneasiness with the cultural wing of the Black Power movement. In 1980, Johnson had castigated the current production of African American writers who represented what he called "the Black world-qua-sewer," a "Black world without freedom, grimy with sexual humiliation, shame, where human contact is a variation on Hegelian Master-Slave bondage, and escape is possible only through death and deeper levels of self-betrayal," a static worldview he traces to the artistic trends "codified and institutionalized in the 1960s and 1970s." In 1993, Johnson reiterated his critique of the Black Arts movement, which he claimed imposed limitations on creative and intellectual freedom because it was "ideological," even though it was not a homogenous ensemble of ideas, or a "coherent, consistent or complete" body of thought.[8]

Employing "ideology" in a Marxist rather than an Althusserian sense—that is, as a false consciousness rather than a hegemonic and inescapable form of being recruited into the workings of capitalism—Johnson believes the Black Arts movement of the sixties was ideological, and the residue "more or less alive today as a quasi-philosophical position" remains so, because it did not and continues not to interrogate and problematize essential questions of the political construction of "race," the vexing issue of "identity," or the complicated nature of "experience." Believing that instead of freeing up the artist to imagine a world differently organized, the Black Arts movement forced the artist to hew to the vision of the world he or she was given in accord with the political mandate of the Black Power movement, Johnson examines the aesthetic, philosophical, and cultural questions raised by Black Power intellectuals. What role did art play in the creation of a new social order, and what function should an aesthetics serve in promoting that kind of art? What strategically was most effective in the transformation of that social order—an "identity politics" emphasizing "differences" along the fault lines of race or a "commonality politics" emphasizing the shared or "universal" qualities among persons and groups? What relationship did or could exist between the cultural productions of a minority group and the economic apparatus of a majoritarian culture—one of shared and reciprocal respect or one of appropriation? The primary issues for the Black Arts movement, then, and those with which Johnson took issue, fell into what we may call the politics of representation, the politics of identity, and the politics of culture. After seeing how Johnson intervenes in each of these specific debates, we may examine the phenomenological position he adopts to transcend the ideology of identity politics.[9]

Troubled by the way Black Power intellectuals theorized art as "part of the revolutionary machinery of change," Johnson found "enormous problems with the apparently deathless idea that art must be 'useful,' especially useful to some passing social or political trend." He held up Maulana Karenga as an example of someone in the sixties who created a theory of art as "agitprop and Kitsch." Johnson is equally troubled by the contemporary form of identity politics which holds that "literature should be used as a means of African-American empowerment," that fiction could help black people "maintain connection with a heritage, an ethnic identity that might be lost or appropriated by mainstream culture," or that writers could "use literature as a means of counteracting oppression and historical conditions." Calling

these claims for black literature "simplistic," Johnson presses for more specific definitions of "appropriation" and examples of "empowerment." "How does [Morrison's]
Jazz counteract oppression and historical conditions? How does any literature do
that?" he asks. "Is *The Great Gatsby* about empowering white people, is that what
that's doing?"[10] Johnson's refusal to acknowledge that there is a difference between
representations of a white empowered majority and the representations of a disempowered ethnic minority, that *Jazz* and *The Great Gatsby* are indicative of a differential in power in the field of cultural production, is particularly troubling because he
is not acting on the knowledge he has exhibited elsewhere about how cultural representations affect the daily lives of people who belong to ethnic minorities, of how in
the United States in particular there is both an appropriation of African American
culture and a concomitant demonization of African American peoples.

Johnson is here working with a curious notion of how literature can be used for
ethnic empowerment, how it can counteract oppression and can respond to historical conditions, how, in a word, a novel can be political.[11] He does admit that some
literature can be considered explicitly political. He mentions only one work—*Uncle
Tom's Cabin*—and suggests that it is a novel that had a "huge impact" during the abolitionist movement. "There are direct connections—this led to that in the public
sphere." The present claims for African American literature, he argues, cannot show
those direct connections. "[C]laims are being made here for literature that have not
been demonstrated at all." He responds to one of those claims more specifically.
When "someone makes the claim that what we've done is empowered a certain class
of people by giving a representation of them on the page, I'm not sure what that
means." He will grudgingly grant that it is important to have such representations,
but he doesn't see much in it. At an earlier time, but still after he was finished with
his Black Arts movement days, he did see something in it. His 1982 short story
"Popper's Disease" is about a black physician called on to diagnose an extraterrestrial
forced to leave the planet because he or she is "different" and therefore condemned.
Henry Popper, the physician and narrator, sees how he is especially fit for this diagnosis since he, like other people of African descent, can attest to the "primordial
feeling of *thrownness* that every Negro experiences when hurled into a society that simultaneously supports and . . . annihilates him, because he can find reflections of
himself nowhere in it." Those "reflections" or "representations" are psychically healing because they are also culturally empowering; without them, the ethnic minority
feels "annihilated."[12]

Popper is able to diagnose the alien because he knows about alienation from his
diagnoses of American popular culture, which in turn he is able to critique because
he has developed a sense of collective identity as an African American person who
does not find a "reflection" of black cultural lifestyles in "mainstream" representations. In other words, Popper is able to see how representations of ethnic identity
and heritage can be empowering, because he is able to see the ways representations
premised on the absence of "ethnicity" are disempowering. What those mainstream
representations attempt to do is propose that their intellectual content is "universal"
despite the differences in the material realities of the lives represented and the lives
lived by those who are not part of that mainstream. The issue in the contemporary
and sixties debate, then, was "universality," and the revolution Karenga spoke of

when he noted that the "real function of art is to make revolution" is partly, at least, a revolution against an intellectual tradition that was not merely "passing" but was rather the legacy of the Enlightenment, and that had long-term deleterious effects on the social and political lives of peoples of color. For Black Power intellectuals, art was a means of resisting the "white racism" infecting "all the vital areas of national life," and a way of challenging the idea that "blackness" signified "absence" ("zero and negative image-myths"), by contesting one of the basic premises of Enlighten-ment thought: what one Black Power intellectual called "the simple-minded, fascist, pseudo-Europeanized mandate of 'universality.'"[13]

For Johnson, who proudly claims to "stump endlessly for the importance of 'universality' in black fiction," the Black Power critique of universality is part of the political program for black nationalist separatism jarring with what he identifies as his own "integrationist position." He feels that the kind of critical talk employed by Black Aesthetic advocates and their contemporary filiations leads to a politically mischievous divisiveness. By arguing that there are "two aesthetics," one white and one black, these theorists create distinct value systems premised on uniformly un-derstood cultural imperatives. Johnson believes that those "so-called differences be-tween the white and black aesthetic do not make a great deal of sense," both because there are not two sets of uniformly understood cultural imperatives and because the emphasis on "difference" is untrue to national history and unproductive for future race relations. Black people, he argues, are "intertwined with every event in Ameri-can history," and the impetus to separate traditions endangers that historical legacy. Moreover, he believes that since "the things that separate us make up one percent of who we are, [and] that ninety-nine percent of our lives are similar," it is disingenu-ous if not mathematically wrongheaded to dwell on what some would make unalter-able differences. For these reasons, then, he speaks of "the Black Arts Movement as an ideology."[14]

It was precisely the point of Black Power advocates, though, that the concept of "universality" was no more and no less ideological than was the concept of "differ-ence." While not going so far as Althusser, who defines "ideology" as a force "om-nipresent, trans-historical and therefore immutable in form throughout the extent of history," the Black Power intellectuals do make the point that what the West has cre-ated in its assumptions about "universality" is ideological, just as the necessary re-sponse to them in the form of the Black Power critique may be said to be ideologi-cal. In other words, they contest the notion—basic to intellectual hegemons—that only the critique is ideological. Black Power intellectuals stated that they "would like to see the idea of 'universal' laid to rest" because it was at best premature and in re-ality operated prejudicially. If a given form or aesthetic constituted only a "Western way of seeing things," then, logically it was "not 'universal.'" Moreover, the concept of universality was historically constructed by valorizing one Western set of impera-tives and denigrating numerous non-Western aesthetic and social values. As Addi-son Gayle noted, the "belief in the superiority and dominance of the cultural arti-facts of men of white ancestry over those of people of different skin color" is a basic premise and result of "White Nationalism." Black Nationalists challenged the effects of this history by dismantling the hegemonic terms used to sacralize it and reevalu-ating the insulting terms used to protect it. Estranged from the "dominant culture," they claim, the black artist cannot in any meaningful sense be "successful" or "good" in terms of "white critical evaluations." "In our movement toward the future, 'ineptitude' and 'unfitness' will be an aspect of what we do. These are the words of the established order—the middle-class value judgments. We must turn these values in on themselves. Turn them inside out and make ineptitude and unfitness desirable, even mandatory."[15]

Theirs, then, is a self-conscious critique of a hegemonic intellectual system. The emphasis on "difference," the belief that "Black culture implies, indeed engenders, for the black artist another order, another way of looking at things," is necessary because the system is hegemonic and the belief in false "universality" pervasive. Of course, assertions of "difference," like statements of specific social locations as self-evident and epistemologically privileged, may guard against "certain presumptions of universality" but they also often rely on what Michael Awkward elegantly calls the "psychic protections of essentialism." We may and indeed should in the late-nineties eschew uncomplicated claims of undifferentiated differences and expose "protectionist critical maneuvers," but we also need to understand the strategic force of those claims and manuevers in the mid-sixties. Moreover, we should also appreciate how those Black Power intellectuals situated their sense of "difference" within significant historical frameworks, primarily by showing the institutional structures that presuppose and abet the creation of the "universal." By demonstrating that the dominant cultural imperatives, variously called "Western" or "European" or "white," are partial, contingent, and products of an interested social class, Black Power intellectuals challenge the heart of what James Stewart calls "white Western aesthetics"—the idea of separating art from society. Indeed, according to Black Power intellectuals, the "core of the Black Aesthetic ideology" is that the field of cultural production is deeply within and intricately related to the field of power. Some future concept of "universality" will be the product of a genuinely multicultural aesthetic, which in turn can come about only in an entirely reconstructed social order. Before "beauty can be seen, felt, heard, and appreciated by a majority of the earth's people," writes Gayle, "a new world must be brought into being"; and the new world will be brought into being, Black Power intellectuals suggest, by the insurgent acts of artists who challenge the present order.[16]

Because they insisted that aesthetics is a realm within the social order, and not transcendent, that, indeed, the division between "ethics and aesthetics in Western society is symptomatic of a dying culture," Black Power intellectuals were also wholly aware of the function of "cultural dominance" and the evidence of "cultural imperialism" in the field of cultural production. In other words, because they conceived of artistic production and consumption as social relations, and, in the United States, as social relations premised on the same quality of gross inequities that marked the field of power, the Black Power intellectuals were vigilantly aware of any gestures toward and acts of cultural appropriation. The debate over Styron's *Confessions of Nat Turner* was only the most spectacular of what was a persistent problematic. For Johnson, though, this insistent seeking out of the literary and cultural crimes of white artists was troubling because it was premised on beliefs he deems notoriously ill conceived: assertions of pregiven social identities, notions of cultural purity, and claims of cultural artifacts both as transparent reflections of racial experience and as property. Situated in the nineties, he challenges contemporary intellectuals to develop a "definition of how something is appropriated by something else and what that means."[17]

Johnson's demand for clarity is understandable, especially given the complexities of the issue of appropriation, involving as it does questions of what we mean by "identity," "culture," and "property," how we conceive of individual and collective experiences, subjectivities, and perspectives, and where we situate the field of cultural production in the contemporary social order and in historical framework. Given these complexities, we can offer a tentative definition as follows: something gets appropriated by something else when a productive or expressive form or practice, let's say jazz or blues or agricultural methods for growing rice, develops within one disempowered cultural group but gets used by and enriches only or mostly another empowered cultural group. The distinction between cultural groups has to do most emphatically with each group's relationship to power, controlling the means of material production and controlling the means of mental production. When, as is the case in the United States, the cultural groups have historically been defined through racial terms, while simultaneously defining and recreating the very concept of race, the cultural groups become socially defined by those racial terms. It will not do for us simply to believe that, once the perceived reality behind those terms gets disproved (as race has been disproved biologically), the now false consciousness will not continue to live in the public sphere, to have very real social effects, and to continue to structure the relationships within and among cultural groups. One of the marks of that relationship between an empowered and a disempowered cultural group is that the empowered group is able to take possession of those material products, physical labors, and cultural forms and practices developed within the disempowered group. Once that something is "appropriated," it no longer functions to enrich materially or to empower socially those within whose cultural group that something developed. That, I take it, is a "definition" of how something is appropriated.

It is far more difficult to answer the second part of Johnson's question, regarding the "meaning" of appropriation. In a highly cogent discussion of the range of contemporary attitudes toward appropriation, Awkward has noted that, depending on one's identity politics or "politics of location," one may believe either that "cultural forms should be utilized by people from every conceivable location who take an interest in them" or, as August Wilson argues, the "cultural experiences of identifiable groups" should "remain the property and possession of the people who develop them."[18] For those who believe that cultural production ought to exist in a sphere separate from the sphere involving political and economic issues, their answer would be that "appropriation" is only another name for multicultural sharing or artistic freedom. For those who believe that cultural production is intimately related to the economic and political spheres, who are unwilling to grant art an exclusive realm unaffected by and not affecting social relations, but who hold rather that artistic representation is an exercise and form of power, "appropriation" is the name given to those acts and strategies whereby the dominant cultural group takes possession of and enriches itself from the use of those cultural forms and practices developed within a disempowered cultural group.

Even as he calls for more specific definitions of appropriation, Johnson can be said to be fairly sympathetic to the Black Power premise that literature and language are pervasively ideological systems and contain presuppositions radically inimical to women and people of color. He describes what he calls "Caliban's dilemma" as the problem of "contemporary black and feminist writers" who discover that every attempt to express an "experience" is couched in a "compromise between the one and the many, African and European, the present and the past," and for Johnson the past—"the experience, the sight (broad or blind) of others formed into word"—is a "tissue of interpretations," most of which are "male-chauvinist and bigoted." The art of writing for those who discover that the history of language and fiction is *"not* sympathetic with their sense of things" becomes an art of writing against a tradition— indeed, of contesting the "antithetical vision and perspectives" of those "predecessors" who "despoiled words."[19]

At the same time as he diagnoses "Caliban's dilemma," though, Johnson remains suspicious of the concept of cultural appropriation, because he believes that it is his birthright as a writer and citizen of the world to inherit all cultural practices and all cultural productions. Asked in an interview about the "emphasis on parody and intertextuality" in his fiction, the "sense of creative theft or borrowing" in his works, Johnson responds by noting that he reads a range of materials on a given subject in order, first, to gain complete knowledge about the concrete realities about which he's writing and, second, to familiarize himself with the "literary universe" of the subject, to understand the "disclosures, the meanings that other writers for two thousand years have had for this particular phenomenon." Having done research to gain an understanding of the material reality of his subject and to get a sense of the symbolic reality of its treatment by previous writers, he does not feel that the terms "borrowing" or "theft" or "intertextuality" adequately describe his motives or his acts, because "all knowledge, all disclosure, all revelation from the past, from our predecessors, black, white, and otherwise, is our inheritance," his to claim in order to "understand what others have brought to the rendering and disclosure of the subject" so that he can engage in dialogue with them by developing and altering the subject and the form in which he is writing.[20]

I also suspect Johnson resists confronting the issue of cultural appropriation partly because he wants very much for there to be a homogeneously applicable aesthetic standard. This desire is particularly evident in his critical comments on multiculturalism. He says that when it comes to the very fundamental issue of believing that people ought to be exposed to a series of cultures other than the ones into which they are born, the advocates for multiculturalism are "absolutely right." Unfortunately, he also disengages the question of multiculturalism from the question of power. Arguing that race is a false concept, he criticizes the multiculturalists for using an "outmoded notion of race" and thereby producing problematic categories. He says he would not read fiction by a given author simply because that author is Asian American, or Native American, or African American. "I want to read finely articulated thought, by whoever it is, anywhere on the planet, any culture," he says. "But it has to be something that meets the standards I bring to all literature, which means it has to disclose, reveal, and it needs to be worked over a lot in terms of revision and polishing." What he does not say, and presumably would not admit, is that those "standards" every reader inherits from his or her culture are already going to prejudice the reader from appreciating works produced according to other cultural standards.

In this specific case, we can see that Johnson's respect for disclosure and revelation already forecloses the possibility of his appreciating works not based on a contract in which the author holds in abeyance and then produces information for the reader—works, for instance, in which there is no closure, no finality, no sense that there is "authority" in the sense we readily assume in the Western tradition. So, too, his respect for works that are products of but do not demonstrate revision, works that are polished, valorizes works that hide or deny their spontaneity and is prejudiced against those produced according to standards in which incompleteness is not a mark of incompetence, those, perhaps, that are joyously unfinished as a testament to the author's or culture's attitudes toward "work" itself. Likewise, it is difficult for a member of one culture to tell what in a work of another culture is "polished" or evidently the product of plenty of "revision," since the standards for "polishedness" differ in different cultures. The very terms the West has used to discuss works produced in Asia and Africa are already permeated with the sense that Third World art is "raw" and "primitive" (both terms suggesting that they are unready for consumption or incomplete according to the dictates of civilization). The values, in other words, are culture-specific, the product of an educational system, both formal and informal. This fact does not mean either that these values are uniformly or universally held by everyone in the culture or that they are the only values anyone in that culture can hold, but it does mean that they are products of a hegemony, which can be contested but also subsumes the majority of efforts to resist it.

It is clear from the foregoing discussion that there is a crucial and informative tension in Johnson's thinking about the operation of power in social relations. While recognizing that in a racially bifurcated and unequal society "black subjectivity" is subject to the power of what he calls the "white gaze" and "white consciousness," he nonetheless also wants to hide whatever social forces created the aesthetic standards in which he believes, to deny the power that structures the field of cultural production in ways reflecting the material inequities of that society. While recognizing the source of "Caliban's dilemma," he is unwilling to question Prospero's power. On the one hand, for example, he appreciates that personal identity is primarily a product of the political powers and institutions of a given state; he proposes that because the "personality, those special aspects" one believes "individual and subjective and unique," has its "origin" in the "public sphere," the way to self-knowledge is to ask: "By what social forces have I been shaped?" On the other hand, though, Johnson also wishes to assert that individuals are responsible for their own identities and are not entirely bound to the social forces shaping them; he argues, for instance, that "no student can hold the elementary school, high school, and university he attends responsible for his intellectual life. The only person responsible for someone's intellectual life is that person." In some ways, that informative tension between respecting the social forces that form identities and believing in an autonomous self responsible for its formation is precisely the result of Johnson's situation as a cultural worker living out the "Sixties-within-the-Eighties" phenomenon, torn between an intellectual moment that revealed the perdurable but malleable social forces that locally and globally institutionalized racial, economic, and gendered oppressions (one thinks of Paul Potter's "We must name that system") and an intellectual moment emphasizing neoconservative preferences for "the bourgeois ethos" with its virtue of "self-reliance" and the valorization of "individual rights" over "group rights" (one thinks of Nathan Glazer's "group identities are respected as private and individual choices").[21] For our purposes, that tension in Johnson is significant because he works out that ambivalence about the sources of identity in his fiction.

Johnson also works it out in his philosophical musings on European phenomenology, which is important to him—he calls it his "first philosophy"—because it allows him to restructure that sixties debate over "identity" ("difference" / "universality") in terms of a philosophy of "intersubjectivity," and to respond to the challenge of the Black Arts movement by theorizing an aesthetic that partially accounts for the unequal relations within the field of cultural production. Following the lead of Edmund Husserl's phenomenological project, Johnson is concerned with understanding a subject's "experience" and the constitution of intersubjective relations, with interrogating the connections between a subject's experience and a community within which experience is made possible and then validated. For Husserl, part of the transition from a "pure phenomenology" to a "phenomenology of reason" involves seeing the relation between "an essentially possible individual consciousness" and "a possible community-consciousness." This "community-consciousness" is composed of a "plurality of personal centres of consciousness and streams of consciousness enjoying mutual intercourse." It is only within such a community that any "experience" can be "given and identified intersubjectively." Once an experience is so identified, we have a significant alteration in the relations between the individual subject and the community, and *within* the individual subject itself. The "experiencing subject" must become part of an "intersubjective community," a transcendent community of the spirit, so that what is critically called "subjective experience" gives way to what Husserl calls "objectivities of higher order."[22]

Using phenomenology to intervene in the debate over "difference" and "universality," Johnson argues for what he calls the "enduring truth that if we go deeply enough into a relative perspective, black or white, male or female, we encounter the transcendence of relativism." Arguing against a pluralist conception of the world, Johnson strenuously maintains that "we share, all of us, the same cultural Lifeworld," and to "think of this world properly is to find that all our perspectives take us directly to a common situation, a common history in which all meanings evolve." Johnson's interesting phrase, "transcendence of relativism," then, carries with it a plurality of meanings. Not only does it articulate a form of transcendence in which intersubjective relations are made possible, in which "relativism" is a condition of being open to others and their ideas; but it also suggests that this transcendence is part of an overall project in which "relativism" will be transcended, in which "intersubjective experience" will supersede what, since Kant, has been criticized as being merely "subjective experience."[23]

In his fiction, Johnson created the trope I have elsewhere called the "phenomenology of the Allmuseri" to embody this philosophical mode. A fictitious culture from West Africa populating each of Johnson's narratives of slavery, the Allmuseri eschew the "world of multiplicity, of *me* versus *thee,*" and believe in a form of intersubjectivity so basic that the "failure to experience the unity of Being everywhere was the Allmuseri vision of Hell." According to Allmuseri phenomenology, the ideal of intersubjectivity includes the condition of the individual's being "unpositioned" in the world, of each person's having a relationship with the tribal community so integral that the individual is rendered "invisible" in the "presence of others." This is a form of intersubjectivity—the sharing of the "same cultural Lifeworld," a "common situation, a common history"—premised on the "transcendence of relativism." Even as it theorizes such a radically postindividualistic mode of being, though, Allmuseri phenomenology nonetheless espouses a somewhat severe form of self-responsibility. The soul, we are told, is "an alchemical cauldron where material events were fashioned from the raw stuff of feelings and ideas," and experience, therefore, is not an entity that goes into a person but is rather that quality that comes "out" of a person who "outpictures" the world from deep within her or his own heart.[24] The phenomenology of the Allmuseri, then, perfectly reflects that tension in Johnson's thought between the demands of a collective, intersubjective sensibility and the demands of an excessive, rugged individualism.

In addition to allowing him to intervene in the debate over "identity" from a universalist standpoint based on the imperatives of intersubjectivity, Johnson's phenomenology serves him well in formulating his considered response to the "ideology" of the Black Power sixties. Arguing that not "everything is ideology," not "every idea that we have, every ensemble of beliefs, must necessarily be ideology," Johnson asseverates that philosophy in general and phenomenology in particular are modes of inquiry free from ideological constraint. Johnson argues that Black Power was ideological because it relied on the premises of identity politics. Even as they claimed "the importance of the black *self*" and "what they called the 'black experience,'" Black Power intellectuals did not "define the self they spoke about" or give a "systematic clarification" of "what we mean by 'experience' as such." Phenomenology, on the other hand, skeptically examines the logical presuppositions of identity itself, refusing to "build up an architecture of propositions" but rather going back and trying "to eke out an understanding of what we think we already know," assuming a perpetually "interrogative mode toward the world." Black Power intellectuals queried Western cultural norms by demonstrating their historical contingency and their political saliency in the creation and maintenance of a racist social order. Instead of exploring how social relations effect epistemological conditions, how power affects perspectives, Johnson, following the lead of European phenomenology, argues that undoing "this heavily conditioned seeing, this calcification of perception," requires the artist to undertake an act of philosophical self-critique, what Husserl calls "a sort of *radical, skeptical epoché* which places in question all [the philosopher's] hitherto existing convictions, which forbids in advance any judgemental use of them." For Johnson, the "phenomenological *epoché,* or 'bracketing' of all presuppositions," allows the artist to "seize a fresh, original vision" instead of being constrained by an ideological one.[25]

Likewise, Johnson maintains that the solution to "Caliban's dilemma" is not to accept reified American racial categories but to rethink the relationship between literature and life, between sign systems and referents, to realize that the problem of "recording" the "black experience" is a problem about the nature of "experience" at the same time as it is a problem about the nature of "recording." African American history "must be seen as an ensemble of experiences and documents difficult to read, indeed, as an experience capable of inexhaustible readings." Experience, he contends, is not the given or the presupposed in any act of representation, but rather a constituted product of that representational act. Writing "doesn't so much record an experience—or even imitate or represent it—as it *creates* that experience." Once we appreciate the productive nature of representation, we are better able to deal with the dangers of living with language and literature "despoiled" by those who came before. Recognizing that acts of intertextuality are not simple or servile but rather constitutive and contestatory, and accepting that "language is not—nor has it ever been—a neutral medium for expressing things," we can use to our benefit the fact that "intersubjectivity and cross-cultural experience are already embodied in the most microscopic datum of speech." Writing is liberating, then, because the writer is not without agency and subject to what Maurice Merleau-Ponty refers to as the "trespass" of the "other upon me" but is also a contributor to the dialogue and therefore able to exert "oneself upon the other."[26]

Phenomenology provides Johnson with an intellectual system for encompassing those sixties debates about identity politics and the politics of letters, raising anew and reconfiguring the topics of appropriation and the problematic condition of a minority writer's having to express his or her identity by using language and forms stained by the previous writers who developed them. More specifically, in his fiction, particularly in his Neo-slave narratives, "the phenomenology of the Allmuseri" functions as a trope, like Reed's NeoHooDoo and Williams's blues, representing specifically "Africanist" forms for creating intersubjective connections and dismantling previous modes of reading that are oppressive and appropriative.[27] Like Reed and Williams, then, Johnson takes up the original form of African American autobiography and political representation, the slave narrative, and makes it both a site for historical recovery and a space for intervening in the cultural debates of the post–civil rights era.

Making a Way out of Many Ways:
The Form and Subject of *Oxherding Tale*

For Johnson, the development of a sensibility both multicultural (drawing on the "revitalizing influences of cross-cultural fertilization") and phenomenological (offering artists an "ever-expanding community" premised on the "curious, social, intersubjective side of art") depends on the artist's capacity for engaging in "technical virtuosity" and deploying "formal variations" in his or her literary work. A text resplendently postmodern in not respecting formal specificity, *Oxherding Tale* exemplifies this belief as it dissolves generic boundaries distinguishing forms of writing as different as "nonfiction, autobiography, the eighteenth-century English novel, the slave narrative, and the Zen parable." As important as are the diversity of forms Johnson experiments with in the novel, it is nonetheless clear that the two major forms he adopts are the slave narrative and the Zen parable. Johnson himself describes *Oxherding Tale* as a "metaphysical slave narrative" or, more specifically, a "modern, comic, philosophical slave narrative—a kind of dramatization of the famous 'Ten Oxherding Pictures' of Zen artist Kakuan-Shien."[28] The tension between these two forms and their impetus—the slave narrative describing material flight toward physical liberation, the Zen parable philosophical search for spiritual enlightenment—is homologous to the tension we've seen in Johnson's thinking about the relationship of power to aesthetics, of social forces to the processes of identity formation, and it perfectly suits the subject of *Oxherding Tale*: Andrew Hawkins's search for physical, intellectual, perceptual, and social liberty.

Toward the end of *Oxherding Tale,* Peggy Undercliff tries to explain her ambivalent feelings about her wedding day to her husband, the narrator Andrew, using as her example the tension between art and power. Asking whether one can "still love and believe in something when it's so beautiful it blinds you, and you *know* you can't have it," she wonders whether this inability or incapacity to have what is beautiful is a species of denial wrought of a subject's living under oppressive social conditions. "You start feeling that goodness and beauty are for other people," she notes. "For men, if you're a woman. Whites, if you're nonwhite." In explanation, she offers an anecdote about a mutual friend of theirs, Evelyn Pomeroy, a writer whose first novel received some critical acclaim (leading to a divorce and a lawsuit from those who weren't so appreciative of the *roman à clef*) and whose second novel is still in progress thirty years later. Having met the author of and read Harriet Beecher Stowe's *Uncle Tom's Cabin,* Evelyn decided that she loved both book and author. Although constitutionally a "romantic writer," she decides she must follow Stowe's example and write "protest fiction." After writing "a hundred pages of a protest novel," Evelyn "discovered that she hated Stowe's book. She found faults, first with her novel, then turned on the Novel itself." Acting on that discovery, she begins writing a "parody of *Uncle Tom's Cabin,* a clever, sneering lampoon that was, after the first few laughs, *ugly*—ugly and spiteful because it burlesqued something it couldn't be, and all because Evelyn *did* love Harriet Beecher Stowe." It took Evelyn years to admit to her feelings because it would have been "tantamount to confessing that she was *beneath* the beauty of fiction."[29]

Johnson's anecdote about the intellectual machinations of a frustrated writer who attempts to write in a proscriptive form unsuited to her talents is particularly resonant because it not only reads like his own miniature *roman à clef*—he had written "protest fiction" before he rejected the "protest novel" for "esthetic reasons" as being not his "province"—but also because it imaginatively creates a chain of allusions marking the pervasive intertextuality in African American literary history. As an allusion to Richard Wright, who in *Native Son* had written the classic parody of *Uncle Tom's Cabin,* which, according to James Baldwin, another critic and uneasy practitioner of protest fiction, read less like a parody and more like a "continuation, a complement of that monstrous legend it was written to destroy," Johnson's comment tells us about the perdurable significance of literary form. As an allusion to Ishmael Reed's *Flight to Canada,* the most recent parody of *Uncle Tom's Cabin,* and the only one genuinely clever and funny, Johnson's comment suggests something about the potential for and the danger of taking a given literary form and transforming it into a "vehicle for the exploration of the most deep-plowing contemporary questions."[30]

Since practitioners of protest fiction necessarily generate their works out of earlier writings in the same form, invoking that original form either servilely to replicate or creatively to transform it, Johnson's point is that there is neither innocence nor autonomy in the historical field of cultural production, because artists "begin their lifelong odyssey in art with expression or experience *interpreted* by others," and their work is therefore the product of engagement and "struggle with the forms which others have imposed on life." Literary form, then, is not an empty "vehicle for the transmission of information about an extrinsic referent," but a history-laden "apparatus for the production of meaning." There is a dynamic interplay in which form gives shape to and is shaped by the materials of narrative. Johnson suggests that like the student of Asian martial arts who performs a "kata, or prearranged set of fighting moves," the writer who works within the "galaxy of forms we inherit" must "honor the form." Honor, however, is not an act of simple replication, since servile imitation resembles nothing so much as a parody of the form.[31] Rather, honoring the form requires "moving the form forward" through the writer's "own interpretation of possibilities made real by this historical moment," revising the form so that it expresses the social conditions of its reproduction and articulates the energetic dynamic of its cultural moment.[32] The question of form is clearly at the heart of Johnson's aesthetics, the idea through which he attempts to resolve "Caliban's dilemma," the issue around which he organizes his meditations on the relationship of art to politics, of social forces to individual responsibility.

There are two self-referential or metafictional chapters in *Oxherding Tale,* one about the *"form* of this Narrative" (118) and the other about the philosophical presuppositions of "first-person viewpoint" (152). In these chapters—Johnson calls them "intermissions" and "essayist chapters"—it is difficult to say whether or not the narrator is still Andrew Hawkins, who narrates the other eleven chapters of the narrative. I suspect that the narrator in these two chapters is not Andrew. Not only does the narrator refer to Andrew in the abstract or in the third person in these two chapters, something Andrew doesn't do in the other chapters, but he also refers to events that would happen when Andrew is approximately 100 years old (there is also one footnote elsewhere referring to events occurring when Andrew would be about 102 [110]).[33] The question of whether or not there is an additional narrator in the novel might seem trivial, were it not indeed one of the primary issues raised by *Flight to Canada,* the previous Neo-slave narrative Johnson is intertextually revising, and were it not also a question deeply involved with Johnson's examination of the "subject" of "individuality."

Elsewhere, Johnson states that he does not "believe in the existence of the ego," calling it a "theoretical construct." If there is such a thing as "identity," he notes, it is neither "fixed" nor "static," but rather a "process." Citing both Hume and Buddhist traditions to make his point that the "self" is an illusion, he argues that identity, "if it is anything at all, is several things, a tissue of very often contradictory things." Given his beliefs about the illusory nature of the individual self, it seems reasonable to infer that there are several narrators in *Oxherding Tale,* even when Andrew appears to be the only narrator. To a large extent, such an inference would not go against the grain of Johnson's novel, nor do injustice to its narrators. As Johnson notes, "Andrew Hawkins's identity in *Oxherding Tale* is that of a free-floating creative force." Whatever subjective element it may possess, Andrew's narrative impetus is ultimately an attempt at radical "intersubjectivity."[34] This sense of a discontinuous identity both describes the philosophical movement in his narrative—from ignorance and nonbeing to wisdom and being—and suggests something of the aesthetic imperative involved in Johnson's use of the slave narrative as a form.

Commenting on the "history-ladenness" of literary form, the narrator points out that no "form . . . *loses* its ancestry," because the historical "meanings" of earlier deployments "accumulate in layers of tissue as the form evolves" (119). The modern writer can delve into the hidden secrets beneath the form of this narrative and understand better the relationship between the history of form *and* the form of history, if that modern writer is willing to "dig, dig, dig—call it spadework" (119). The slave narrative, then, is not a simple paradigmatic form, beginning with "I was born" in the South and ending with literacy and freedom in the North. It is a form that has sedimented meanings inscribed into the structures themselves, possessing a "long pedigree that makes philosophical play with the form less outrageous than you might think" (118). The form, in other words, is not an empty vehicle, but a repository of evolving historical significance that affects and is affected by the uses to which it is put by subsequent writers. Like Reed before him and Williams after him, Johnson creates a Neo-slave narrative in which there is a deep play between literary form and individual subjectivity. Unlike Reed and Williams, though, both of whom use intersubjective narrators as a means of protecting the text from cultural appropriation, Johnson uses intersubjective narrators as a means of opening up the text to "universal" appreciation.

The first "intermission," "On the Nature of Slave Narratives," appears just after Andrew and Reb the Coffinmaker escape enslavement and are about to unpack in Spartanburg. Defining the three forms of slave narratives—the interviews conducted with former slaves in the 1930s by the Works Project Administration (the WPA narratives), the fraudulent slave narratives commissioned by northern abolitionists as propaganda, and the authentic slave narratives written by escaped slaves—the narrator acknowledges that the narrative has so far been "worrying" the "formal conventions" of the "Negro Slave Narrative" (118). The narrator then compares the authentic slave narrative to the early American Puritan Narrative, arguing that both forms are the offspring of the original narrative confessions of "the first philosophical black writer: Saint Augustine," since all share the movement from a state of "ignorance to wisdom, nonbeing to being" (119). As the narrator puts it, "the Slave Narrative proper whistles and hums with this history." History is not something that exists as recorded, since the devices for recording it already possess an immanent history which necessarily transforms the materials. In other words, the life of a slave in the form of a slave narrative exists as part of a much larger project, the discovery of which requires what the narrator calls "archaeological work." Moreover, this archaeological work would provide ample evidence for Johnson's strongly integrationist position. Because the quest for freedom structures both the African American slave narrative and the earliest European, African, and American autobiographies, because the form of writing in which these quests are inscribed is part of a long tradition created from the complexly intertwined cultural histories of Europe, America, and Africa, Johnson's point implicitly is that the quest, form, and tradition are common to various cultures; one might say they are "universals." The slave narrative form, then, is not exclusively a part of the "black experience," another entity Johnson has "worried," but rather one of the many shared properties in the human struggle to find meaning in life and history.

Having complicated "form" and "history" in the first intermission, the narrator complicates "subjectivity" in the second. In the eleventh chapter, entitled "The Manumission of First-Person Viewpoint," the narrator notes that "the Subject of the Slave Narrative" is not someone who "interprets the world" but rather someone "who *is* that world" (153). The subject of the slave narrative, in other words, is writing (process, not product), and, for Johnson, "writing doesn't so much record an experience—or even intimate or represent it—as it *creates* that experience."[35] What Johnson is striving to do in this second intermission is provide a rationale for how intimate first-person narration is truly a form of "universality." He begins by defining what is possibly the "only invariant feature" of the slave narrative: "first-person viewpoint" (152). What the reader most values in first-person narration is precisely the *"limitations* imposed upon the narrator-perceiver," who is denied access into other characters' thoughts. What "we lack in authority," he notes, "we gain in immediacy." But because the "subject" necessary for a first-person narration is a philosophical fiction ("He is, in fact, nobody; is anonymous"), the limitations fall away and the narrator becomes "transcendental." No longer a subjectivity but "an opening through which the world is delivered," the narrator assumes a voice that Johnson calls "first-person . . . universal" (153). As a "universal" entity, the first-person narrator becomes a respository vehicle in almost the same way as a literary "form." "The Self, this perceiving Subject who puffs on and on, is, for all purposes, a palimpsest, interwoven with everything—literally everything—that can be thought or felt." Like literary form, the subject also has sedimented layers of meaning and resists stasis in favor of accretion. This "subject," then, is "forever *outside* itself in others," drawing its life from everything it is not (generally called "others") at precisely the instant that it makes possible the appearance of those others (152).

In his philosophical explorations of form, writing, and subjectivity, then, Johnson challenges and indeed almost undermines the presuppositions governing the writing of the other Neo-slave narratives. Reed and Williams believe that the slave narrative was a form of writing peculiar to the African American experience, subject to theft or unlawful borrowing by European Americans, particularly because the "black subject" had historically been rendered "absent" through appropriative misrepresentations. They therefore resist those acts of appropriation by developing models of intersubjectivity in which their narrators creatively play with their "absence," their "invisibility," in order to liberate their representations. Johnson argues against the very idea of "appropriation" by noting that the form of the slave narrative is part of world culture in its use of the quest motif and its deployment of the "first-person . . . universal" viewpoint, and that all "subjects" of writing are "absent" because the practice of writing requires such. In his aesthetic, a specifically "racial" form becomes "multicultural," a uniquely social condition is revealed to be philosophical, and a literary crime is instead described as a process of artistic cross-fertilization.

Nonetheless, as we might expect of a novelist who has exhibited persistent tensions in his work, who treads on the borders of a conservative and an oppositional aesthetic, *Oxherding Tale* is not only an articulation and a manifestation but also a critique of those beliefs. In delineating Andrew's search for physical and intellectual liberty, Johnson shows us the promises and the problems of not asserting "racial"

identity, of not insisting on the primacy of the social, of denying appropriative behavior. At the same time that he represents Andrew's desire to claim responsibility
for an autonomous and transcendent self, Johnson inscribes a critique of that model
of identity formation. As we also might expect of an intellectual so deeply aware of
the residual influence of forms, *Oxherding Tale* is built largely on the structural
equivalent of literary form for human experience—what Johnson, following Buddhist tradition, calls a "Way." Ways are to lived experience what forms are to literary
content. Like literary forms, Ways are also repositories of past experiences and wis-
doms, not singular and empty structures awaiting subjective experience to complete
them, but living, changing forms that likewise "whistle and hum with the history" of
their sedimented meanings and render meaningful the lives they inhabit and the
lives inhabiting them.

One of the material objects helping Andrew understand the lesson of multiform
Ways is the sculpture Reb makes of him. Andrew describes the work as he handles it:

> The replica was finished, but only the first side bore my likeness: a face of feathery
> lines, which felt—beneath my fingers—smooth-grained. Unstained. The second
> portrayed someone else, the knife marks deeper gouges in wood that gave the por-
> traiture a splintered feel, its expression a worldly blend of ecstasy and pain, sickness
> and satiation. The third side was stranger still: a Master who had made his fortune
> long ago; aging, he would be on the Village Board, the Chamber of Commerce—a
> Whig in political matters, perhaps a church father. The fourth side was blank. The
> back, I supposed as I drifted off mercifully to sleep, was where one mounted this
> odd figurine. (77)

Ways are not predeterminations of the paths lives are destined to take—a Way is not
a Calvinist structure—but rather are potentialities lives may assume, depending on
the depth to which one excavates and the identities one sheds and assumes. Like literary forms, Ways can be "worried" and allow for philosophical play. The blank
fourth side of the sculpture, cast after all by an Allmuseri (this "four dimensional
culture"), represents the potential identities at the back of all assumed identities. In a
novel that has on its title page the "Taoist symbol for a man traveling on the Way,"
Johnson has inscribed the multiple complexities and possibilities of "Ways" of
"being human, the parameters, the infinite, individual variations onto which our
lives open."[36]

A Way, then, is not a predetermined structure for living or a constraint or limi-
tation on possibilities. Nor, finally, is it possible to exist either with one Way, what
Andrew in an echo of Frank Sinatra mistakenly calls "*my* Way" (77), or, on the other
hand, without a Way at all. Andrew gives us an exemplary meditation on how his
individualist sentiments are disturbed at discovering the necessity of Ways. Like
Peggy, finding the occasion of the union of bodies and souls a fit time to reflect on
structures of life and representation, Andrew spends his wedding day considering
his situation as a fugitive slave who is passing for white and about to marry the
daughter of Spartanburg's town doctor. He celebrates the fact that his life "was a
patchwork of lies," his "personality whipstitched from a dozen sources" (139).
Given the multiple richness of his personality, he finds himself offended at the
monoform ceremony for the wedding. Marriage in such a prepackaged ceremony in
which individuals were interchangeable left him less developed as a person. Indeed,

in the course of the spectacle he feels a "new, subtle, loss of identity." "We were *fed*, I thought, into a form that flattened our humanity. My liberal-humanist hackles rose. Better we should create our *own* ceremony!" (139). He then casts his eye on Beatrice Jackson, a 78-year-old woman playing the organ, and sees clearly, "with the simplicity of a child," that "every molecule of the old woman, every wrinkle, every cell and ancient desire wrecked or realized in her 78 years, gave the abstract form flesh, glorified this woman—all of us; all through a ceremony that suspended Time" (139–40). Just as ceremonies attest to and commune with the past by using the same ritual forms as those used by ancestors from time immemorial, so do Ways provide personalities with intersubjective means of expression. Following his realization of the significance of ceremonies, Andrew views the wedding in a different light: "We stood, I felt, translated, lifted a few feet off the ground, exchanging replies in old, old voices in a different tongue we borrowed from our better selves—the people we were intended to be—in some parallel world, where the absences of this life were presences, the failures here triumphs there, a realm of changeless meaning for which the only portal was surrender" (140). This wisdom Andrew acquires quite late in the narrative.

We need to return to his earliest lessons in order to see how he reached the knowledge that permitted him to make a Way out of many Ways. Andrew's quest for a Way begins with his realization of his social status. He recalls the day a candidate for the job of becoming his teacher looked at him and asked his slave owner, Jonathan Polkinghorne: "Is he yours?" Jonathan responded by glancing at Andrew, wagging his head, and saying, "No. . . . What I mean to say is that Andrew is my property and that his value will increase with proper training" (12). Here, for the first time, Andrew learns how ownership destroys the potential of any relationship. Upon discovering how corrupt the term "yours" becomes once it signifies ownership, Andrew begins to think anew about his status: "And what was I thinking? What did I feel? Try as I might, I could not have told you what my body rested on, or what was under my feet—the hallway had the feel of pasteboard and papier-mâché. A new train of thoughts were made to live in my mind" (12). Those new thoughts center on how to escape "the sausage-tight skin of slavery" and to become what the age called a "self-made man." "My argument was: Whatever my origin, I would be wholly responsible for the shape I gave myself in the future, for shirting myself handsomely with a new life" (17). Realizing he was "property"—his clothing, knowledge, language all "second-hand, made by, and perhaps for, other men," his identity a "living lie" and a virtual absence in a society in which clothing, knowledge, and language make the man—Andrew responds to his propertylessness ("I owned nothing") with a sense of what Cornel West calls "rugged and ragged individualism," attempting to transcend both "origins" and institutional forces in the creation of an inhabitable subject position.[37]

Setting out to find material manifestations of individuals who attempt to be "wholly responsible" for the shapes of the lives they lead, Andrew is exposed to and discerns the flaws and pitfalls in the "Ways" of his teacher, Ezekiel William Sykes-Withers; his lover, Flo Hatfield; and his father, George Hawkins. Although they teach him different and often contradictory lessons—from Ezekiel he learns asceticism, from Flo unchecked sensuality, from George racial chauvinism—their

"Ways" are all fundamentally flawed because they depend on a divisive and appropriative attitude toward others. Consider, for instance, Ezekiel's lesson on manhood.
Arguing that "women are, in a strange sense, more essential to Being" than are men
because the universe failed to give men a "function," Ezekiel holds that all *"male
works"* will perish in history—"history, a male concept of time, will vanish, too"—
while "the culture of women goes on, the rhythms of birth and destruction, the Way
of absorption, passivity, cycle and epicycle" (30–31). In order for Ezekiel to teach
Andrew about manhood as an essentialized and existential state, he has to divide the
world in gendered terms and appropriate the category of "Woman."

Flo's Way of sexual fulfillment also depends on division and appropriation. A
protofeminist when she complains about a society which stipulates that "a woman is
nothing without a man" (59), Flo is also cannibalistic insofar as each of her reflections on black men is couched in terms of appetite. She "feeds" on her slave lover's
anxieties (39), looks at her slaves "like a woman comparing chunks of pork at Public Market" (41), or as if one of them were "a six-foot chicken quiche" (42). Equating
sex with physical consumption —"Eating a good piece of meat is like making love"
(42)—she ponders aloud in the presence of Andrew: "I wonder what you'd taste
like" (45), getting her answer when she licks Andrew and discovers he tastes "milky"
(53). This image of ingestion is crucial to understanding Flo, for what Andrew
learns from Flo is that making love can be used as a way of incorporating others
within oneself. At one point in their sexual relationship, Andrew asks Flo, "What do
you feel when you touch me?" She responds, "Me. . . . I feel my own pulse, My
own sensations." "That's all you feel?" "Yes" (53). The "education of the senses," it
turns out, is an education in a form of appropriation, of denying the other (in this
case, the sexual partner) any existence save as a part of the self. In this appropriative
act, Flo does nothing less than deny the "very concept of experience" to understand
which "one must begin to identify with the other."[38]

The Way of racial chauvinism is likewise premised on division and appropriation. George tells his son that everything Andrew does either "pushes the Race forward, or pulls us back." "If you fail, everything we been fightin' for fails with you"
(21). This sort of obligation is the obverse side of what Edward Bland calls "pre-
individualistic thinking." Johnson has argued that the social constraints wrought
from pre-individualistic thinking and imposed by the community on its own members are destructive and prohibit genuine creativity.[39] In the novel, he shows how
George's lesson carries with it a necessary corollary. Because he sees everything the
individual does as either raising or lowering the race's ideals ("*If* you succeed . . .
If you fail"), George himself lives a "life that could only be called conditional" (102).
Moreover, to determine the world in these conditional terms, George has to view the
world in alienating, binary terms, simplifying a "world so overrich in sense it out-
stripped him" (142). In the end, George finds himself wholly alienated from everything: "this warped and twisted profile of the black (male) spirit, where every other
bondsman—everything not oneself—was perceived as an enemy" (50).

At the end of his time in slavery, then, Andrew has been exposed to several false
notions of identity premised on discovering essentialized gender and racial roles and
on acting in an appropriative way. Each of the notions is false because they all share
what Johnson calls "a rigid, essentialist notion of the self," and they therefore pro-

hibit genuine intersubjectivity. Recognizing that such reductions of the complexity of existence are untenable, Andrew must dismiss George's "racial dualism," Ezekiel's gendered essentialism, and Flo's appropriative sexuality, rejecting all intellectual schemes based on marked divisions between male and female, whites and blacks, self and other. As he proceeds toward an intersubjective sensibility, though, Andrew is tempted to use each of his teacher's ideas. At one point, he muses on how "Being" was a "vast feminine body," and he theorizes that *"men* were unessential " because they "fell back on thought in the absence of feeling, [and] created history because [they] could not live Being's timeless cycles" (55). At another point, he meets a man who had engaged in sex with Flo and finds himself drawn to this man as a friend, exemplifying how the bonding of men takes the form of sexual commerce in women.[40] As Andrew notes of his new friendship, it was based on the kind of relationship "only shared by men who have slept in the same places" (96). In other words, Andrew acts on what he learned from Flo: to discount the being of others (make people into "places") in the service of selfish love. None of these models of selfhood can teach Andrew to be a social being because each creates an appropriative self; they would at best teach him to reduce "everything not oneself" to the role of cosmic or consumable others, of Woman as "Being" or woman as "place." What Andrew needs in order to contest these lessons is a phenomenology that brackets the presuppositions of gender and race and selfhood and therefore allows him to achieve a genuine intersubjectivity.

That phenomenology in this novel, as in all his narratives of slavery, comes from the Allmuseri character in *Oxherding Tale,* Reb the Coffinmaker. Drawing on the Allmuseri phenomenology he has inherited and embodies in his own life experiences, Reb the Coffinmaker teaches Andrew about true interdependence, about an authentic form of intersubjectivity that does not rely on Ezekiel's gender essentializing, George's racial divisiveness, or Flo's appropriative attitude toward others. Reb teaches Andrew to place in suspicion all pronouns of selfishness and to distrust all designations of racial distinction (36). Andrew also learns that Reb "hated personal pronouns." In fact, the "Allmuseri had no words for *I, you, mine, yours.* They had, consequently, no experience of these things, either, only proper names that were variations on the Absolute" (97). Recognizing that identity is formed not in the Absolute but in a social order, which is itself established on a historical terrain marked by material and political inequities, the phenomenology of the Allmuseri also develops a scheme of identity formation that accounts for the unequal distribution of power. "If you got no power," notes Reb, "you have to think like people who *do* so you kin make y'self over into what they want" (62). To make oneself over into what the powerful want appears to be another aspect of pre-individualistic thinking, but, as Reb makes clear, it is really but a subversive way of unpositioning oneself in the world, part of a strategy of joining the "shared hallucination" of social life as an equal, as a subject. Learning this lesson, Andrew comes to recognize how the African American subject is "the finest student of the White World, the one pupil in the classroom who watches himself watching the others, absorbing the habits and body language of his teachers, his fellow students" (128). This is the education of Allmuseri phenomenology—the empowering of the individual who surrenders to Being instead of dwelling on the divisions and becomes absorbed in its diverse unity through acts of understanding and sympathy, not appropriation.

Turning the Allmuseri phenomenology on its head, Bannon the Soulcatcher exemplifies the dangers of not "bracketing" philosophical presuppositions about identity and experience. Bannon lives by the idea of empowering himself by absorbing the habits and existential traits of others. As he explains to Andrew, "You *become* a Negro by lettin' yoself see what he sees, feel what he feels, want what he wants" (115). After intellectually absorbing his prey's modalities of experiencing the world, Bannon easily manages to capture his victims, who are then physically absorbed into his body. But what Bannon does once he is able to assume this state of sublime sympathy is murder; and murdering, he tells Andrew, is his "nature." "Ah knows mah nature. It ain't an *easy* thing to accept yo nature, the nature you born with" (111). In other words, while he has the capacity for utterly denying his own selfhood in order to see, feel, and want what others see, feel, and want, Bannon still holds to an intractable sense of an innate and essential personality structure. Because he does so, Bannon represents the corruption of Allmuseri phenomenology, the form of surrender not to the Absolute but to a facsimile of the Absolute. He represents what happens when one understands only half of Reb's philosophy—making oneself over into what the powerful want *without* unpositioning oneself. His, then, is an extreme form of appropriation.

At the end of the novel, it turns out that Bannon is able to appropriate George Hawkins, whom he murders because George was bound to the world by "fifty-'leven pockets of death in him," possessing "li'l pools of corruption that kept him so miserable" he simply desired death (174). Bannon is unable to appropriate Reb, though, because Reb desired nothing, "wasn't *positioned* nowhere," and therefore "didn't have no place inside him"—nothing "dead or static" like a negative image of the self—for Bannon to settle (174). In the last scene, Andrew accedes to the lesson of Allmuseri phenomenology. As Bannon takes off his shirt in order to show him how George has become part of the topography of his body (as did everything Bannon murdered), Andrew finds the truth about intersubjective relations, "the profound mystery of the One and the Many" (176). He learns, with a Wordsworthian flair, that the relation between them is reversible in the terms of Western chronology and history: "I was my father's father, he my child." And he learns, in the end, that "all is conserved; all." The lessons on which Andrew concludes are numerous, although they can be summed up by saying that he learns to surrender to the world of Being, to be unpositioned in the way that, in this novel, only Reb was unpositioned. Andrew must cease to see distinctions of gender, of race, and, ultimately, of self and other. The intersubjective identity that becomes possible after such a complete surrender to the Whole would apparently be as rewarding as it is complex.

Andrew, however, does not reach that position because he is not able to transcend the perceptual apparatus forcing him to see the world in starkly gendered terms and apparently compelling him to see himself in startlingly individualist terms. What is troubling about the conclusions Andrew reaches is that they contradict the social positions he has adopted. More specifically, Andrew clings to two lessons that do not cohere with the beliefs he claims. First, he continues to believe to the end that the world is an essentialized feminine realm: the "woman I had sought in so many before . . . was, as Ezekiel hinted, Being, and she, bountiful without end, was so extravagantly plentiful the everyday mind closed to this explosion, this efflorescence of sense, sight frosted over, and we . . . became unworthy of her, having squandered to a thousand forms of bondage the only station, that of man, from which she might truly be served" (172). This way of seeing Being, though, *"seeing distinctions,"* leaves him capable of imagining but not fully inhabiting a worldview in which he is no longer bound to a way of seeing the world in terms of division, as he is doing here (male person / female Being).[41]

Here also the second problem arises. Andrew does not surrender to Being, cannot in fact, because he still fervently retains a sense of autonomous selfhood this novel critiques, particularly in its rendition of the Allmuseri phenomenology. Andrew concludes the novel with the same sense of rugged individuality with which he had begun (vowing to be "wholly responsible for the shape I gave myself in the future"). He considers his father's life a failure because George did not learn just this lesson. Believing "all that was necessary to break this spell of hatred, this self-inflicted segregation from the Whole, was to acknowledge, once and for all, that what he allowed to be determinant for his life depended on himself and no one else," Andrew criticizes his slave father because he *"chose* misery" and *"needed* to rekindle racial horrors, revive old pains, review disappointments like a sick man fingering his sores" (142).[42] He rejects in George, then, what he calls "the *need* to be an Untouchable." The argument Andrew is making that one is wholly responsible for determining which social forces will impinge on one's life, or that those social forces will be meaningless because one has made the choice not to dwell on them, is not only foolishly dangerous, but, more to the point here, also quite at odds with what Johnson has been presenting as a phenomenological position. To believe that the determination of one's life "depended on himself and no one else" is the same thing in fact as believing in a "self-inflicted segregation from the Whole."

Andrew continues to express his sense of autonomous individuality in even more striking terms later in the novel. Responding to the fact that Peggy does not respond with any sort of racist gestures when she discovers that he has been passing (although it is not clear that Peggy actually discovers he is passing), Andrew decides that his whole life was misguided. "I had prepared myself for oppression by preliving episodes of disappointment, obstacles, and violent death; I felt a shade disappointed that everyone in the White World wasn't out to get me. (The truth, brothers, is that it was pretty vain to think oneself that important: *hubris,* thinking I, one fragile thread, made that much difference in the fabric of things.)" He calls this set of beliefs a "self-induced racial paranoia as an excuse for being irresponsible" (162). Again, Andrew thinks of himself as an individual in a situation that clearly calls for analysis of collective behaviors. What forced Andrew to prepare for oppression was the reality of oppression—in his case, being enslaved; in the analogous contemporary case, the systemic racism pervasive in American society. The truth is that the other brothers (and sisters) are not victims of "racial paranoia"; they are victims of racial oppression, which is not about "one fragile thread" in the fabric of American society, but rather forms the warp and woof of the whole cloth.

Andrew, then, would appear incapable of surrendering to Being so long as he retains so strong a sense of rugged individualism and so exaggerated a sense of self-responsibility, the basis of which involves his resolute denial of social forces. This denial of the institutional powers exercised over his life and his father's and his mother's is most poignantly felt when he defines slavery as a perceptual rather than a social condition. As he notes, "I was returned to slavery; I have never escaped it—it was a way of seeing, my inheritance from George Hawkins: *seeing distinctions*" (172). Slavery is not a way of seeing; it is a way of having one's physical and mental labor appropriated, a way of having one's children categorized as property, a way of having one's social condition defined as chattel, a way of being wholly under the command of another, a way of having body and soul daily stolen. These are the "ways" of slavery, and Andrew makes a serious error in reducing the social relation to a philosophical condition. Slavery becomes a way of seeing because of the material conditions in which slaves live, material conditions that need to be changed before the perceptual apparatus can be transcended. These are things Andrew does acknowledge because he has been exposed to them (a point I will discuss in the final section), but he has not fully accepted them. At the very end of the novel he is groping his way toward accepting them, but his is finally, like the Invisible Man's, an incomplete striving, albeit one with a strong promise for future political activity. Intersubjective relations based on "shared meaning, a shared vision" require more selfless participants, subjects able to challenge the polarization of gender and to dismantle the conventional gendering of Being as feminine, subjects, finally, capable of understanding the social conditions behind others' experiences. Without that kind of understanding, the subject will continue to perceive women as "Woman" and continue to conceive of others in an appropriative and ultimately uncomprehending manner.

In *Oxherding Tale*, then, Johnson posits and partially works out the tensions in his own thinking about the relationship of form to content, the issues of appropriation and universalism, and the question of identity as either a product of social forces in the public sphere or an atomistic and largely autonomous entity. Part of Johnson's achievement is to promote the "curious, social, intersubjective side of art" and describe the immense benefits obtaining for us if we act on this desire to inhabit fictional worlds that challenge our parochialism. "I think that's what fiction ought to be about," he notes, "getting beneath those sedimented meanings, all the calcified, rigid perceptions of the object." Using the slave narrative, a form he calls the "ancestral roots of black fiction," Johnson is able to show us how the sedimentations in certain forms have prevented us from seeing what he insists is a beauty all people can appreciate. Even so, his emphasis on universalism, partially premised on the eschewing of history and the denial of the social forces at work in creating inequities in the distribution of power among ethnic groups, is also tempered by his awareness of the institutional powers operative in American society. Like Reed and Williams, he knows full well that what he calls the fiction of "Americans who happen to be black" is also fiction produced and published "against stupendous odds in a white-dominated marketplace." His own experience showed him the difficulties of publishing his novel at a time when the work of African American writers "was systematically downplayed and ignored in commercial, New York publishing."[43] In *Oxherding Tale*, he represents that tension in his thinking, between appreciating the immense powers of the state apparatus and believing in a rugged individualism and austere responsibility of self, by having Andrew pursue one penultimate Way, a Way that prohibits him from acknowledging precisely those social forces that define his assumed racial identity. I will now turn to the final literary form *Oxherding Tale* honors—the novel of passing. It is here, I think, where we can most clearly define in what ways Johnson is situating his Neo-slave narrative in a discontinuous intertextual relationship with that contemporary cultural conversation regarding the representation of slavery in the first person.

Passing Politics: The Way of White Folks

It is worth recalling that Johnson began writing *Oxherding Tale* shortly after the heated debate over Styron's *Confessions of Nat Turner.* His novel, like Sherley Anne Williams's, is a reflection on the sixties not only because those years constitute the moment of origin for its formal prototype but also because his novel was originally conceived during and remains residually a product of those years. So, when he notes that "no form . . . *loses* its ancestry" because it accumulates "meanings" in "layers of tissue" that affect later deployments of that form, Johnson is referring not only to the slave narrative but also to the Neo-slave narrative (119). Given the social context in which he started writing and his awareness of the residual influence of form, it is not surprising to see Johnson taking on the Black Aesthetic issues of appropriation and universality. And, given his belief that "honoring the form" requires raising what he calls "issues relevant to this age," it is apt that he meditates on the triad of social issues involved in the discourses of slavery in the sixties: violence, property, and identity. Like Reed and Williams, Johnson is aware of how the intersection of professional American historiography and the Black Power movement created the contemporary discourse on slavery, and, like them, he inscribes into his novel a critique of the historiographical work on slavery and an exploration of the tenets of Black Power politics.[44]

It is also important to recall that Johnson wrote the bulk of *Oxherding Tale* around the time *Flight to Canada* was published, and, in many ways, as the allusion to writers who parody *Uncle Tom's Cabin* suggests, he situates his Neo-slave narrative in an intertextual dialogue with Reed's. The two novels share some common ground. Like Reed, Johnson had no interest in repeating the paradigmatic story of the black slave protagonist in the field struggling valiantly against his master. While Reed gave us trickster house slaves rebelling against a hedonistic masochist, Johnson's hero is a mulatto living "right on the dividing line between the races" whose "evil male slave owner" was not "another version of Simon Legree" but rather a "woman of bottomless desires."[45] As well, both writers are irreverently humorous in their parodies of slave narrative conventions. Just as Reed had the chicken-stealing slave become a successful entrepreneur, so does Johnson grotesquely exaggerate the *topos* of a slave who learns to read as the first act of striving toward liberty by having his slave narrator learn to read in about six languages under the tutelage of one of the world's experts in ancient, Oriental, and Germanic tongues. Frederick Douglass may have struggled with the *Columbian Orator,* but Andrew Hawkins smoothly makes his way through Xenophon, Plato, Schopenhauer, Hegel, Lao Tzu, and Chaun Tzu (12–13). Both Reed and Johnson also reconfigure the formal properties of the narrative, defying the basic movement of the slave narrative from the slave South to the free North by having the fugitive narrators remain in or return to the South. Finally, and most important, both are intent on "liberating the first-person viewpoint," which Reed accomplishes by showing us a narrator in the state of spiritual possession who achieves an intersubjective relation with another subject of the narrative, and Johnson by showing us a narrator in the state of transcendent dissolution of ego striving to achieve an intersubjective relation with the world ("all is conserved; all").

There, though, the similarities end and their differences emerge. The differences in their respective representations stem primarily from their different stands on the politics of art, which in turn issue from their perspectives on the Black Power sixties. While noting that Reed does not "fully agree with all the black nationalists," Johnson still argues that Reed's most important beliefs are filiations of Black Nationalist ones and his "ideas on art present a highly personalized twist on the Black Aesthetic and cultural nationalism." Like the sixties' cultural nationalists, Reed "rejects the idea of white liberals (he sees it as their idea) that black writing must be 'universal,' an idea he calls Atonist." As we saw above, Johnson rejects the idea that African American writing should be anything but universal, which it can aspire to be by having black writers adopt all possible forms and explore all potential Ways. Whereas Johnson wishes ideally to adhere to a single aesthetic standard—"great writers are sexless, raceless, and have no historical moment circumscribing their imagination and curiosity"—Reed insistently focuses on the specific ways social inequities originating in the sphere of material production also inhabit the realm of cultural production.[46] For Reed, since those inequities exist and therefore define the relations between and among ethnic groups, disempowered cultural groups are still liable to have their cultural forms and productions appropriated. Therefore, Reed casts his novel as a slave narrative in order to make several key points about the appropriation of the lives and cultural productions of people of African descent, while Johnson casts his novel as a slave narrative in order to excavate from that form of writing its sedimented meaning for all peoples and in order to achieve what he calls the slave narrative's "first-person . . . universal" viewpoint.

Those differences appear most dramatically in the ways each artist takes up the issues of violence, property, and identity. In *Flight to Canada,* Reed ultimately establishes a dialectic between violence and spirituality, between private property and communal institutions, while salvaging the "authenticity" in the racial identity of the house slave. Exploring and then dismissing the potential resistance embodied in violence and property, Johnson instead exposes the dialectic between power and identity and exemplifies a form of resistance in which, assuming what he calls a phenomenological posture of "standing in an interrogative mode toward the world," he questions the basis of racial subjectivity by demonstrating the insidious processes and operations through which the state apparatus create and reify racial identities.

Like Reed, who concluded his novel by asking whether Nat Turner or Uncle Tom acted on wiser principles, Johnson ends his novel by examining this same choice between violent revolutionary action and property ownership. Whereas Reed used symbolic characters to explore the tensions in Black Power politics (Nat Turner and Uncle Tom), Johnson uses the idea of generations to demonstrate the evolution and growth from one politics to another. At the end of the novel, the propertied Andrew Hawkins considers the futility of his father's life and death. Although George Hawkins is not the only revolutionary character in the novel, he is the one most closely aligned with Black Power advocates. George shares a philosophy associated with the Nation of Islam under the Honorable Elijah Muhammad, including a theology regarding the creation of the "white race" that received its widest exposure through Malcolm X. White people, according to George, are "Devils, or, worse, derived in some way he couldn't explain from Africans, who were a practical, down-to-earth people" (24). A "black nationalist" forever "suffering from the pains caused by racial dualism," George dies by the violence he espouses.[47]

As theory, the violence George dreams of inflicting is rendered ridiculous. When Mattie hears George utter his prayer, "Oh Lord, kill all the whitefolks and leave all the nigguhs," and slaps him on the back of his head, George yelps: "Lord! Don't you know a white man from a nigguh" (142)? As active force, the violence George does inflict is described in starkly medical and unromantic terms. During a slave uprising on Cripplegate, George strikes Jonathan Polkinghorne a "particularly vicious crack to the skull," pushing the "clivus and anterior edge of the occipital bone" permanently against the "upper anterior surface of the medulla oblongata" (158). Whereas the act of revolutionary violence in *Flight to Canada* was effective insofar as it went unpunished and led to Robin's assuming the property of his former master, the act of physical violence in *Oxherding Tale* destroys only the slave community, whose members are dispersed by sale after the uprising. As for George, he ends up dead and in "West Hell," suffering "the reward all black revolutionaries feared: an eternity of waiting tables" (174–75). George the "black revolutionary" not only dies (like Nat Turner "dead and gone"), but ends up in a menial position in Hell; even the afterlife of revolutionaries doesn't look good. Believing them divisive in just the way Black Power was divisive, Johnson dismisses George's act of revolutionary violence and his black nationalist principles.[48] Unlike Reed, then, Johnson does not establish a dialectic between violence and spirituality. The revolutionary attempts on the capitalist structures in this novel are not predicated on an act of physical violence.[49]

Having rejected the revolutionary violence represented by his father, Andrew considers the question of private property. Like Uncle Robin in *Flight to Canada,* Andrew concludes the narrative by pointing out that property ownership is not at all disagreeable to him, that in fact it could well be that his "dharma, such as it was, was that of the householder" (147). By achieving this stage of domestic comfort (predicated on the ownership of property), Andrew finally manages to adapt entirely to his persona—that of white William Harris. When he first invented the false history he would ascribe to William, he imagined that his parents would be "landowners" (109). He imagined this partly because that background would allow him to traffick among a certain class, but mostly because he had just witnessed the luxuriance of property ownership from the vantage of a hungry, dispossessed fugitive slave. In the course of escaping slavery, Andrew watches with envy a family going about their business in a blur of "warm, dumb domesticity" (107). As the father brings in a pail of fresh milk for the children to drink while they eat their freshly baked biscuits, he spills some of the milk in an "accident so suggestive of casual abundance and unconscious prosperity, of surplus and generosity" that it provokes Andrew to reflect on his miserable station. "I cannot now, with pen or tongue, make you feel the wretchedness and envy that descended upon me, the fugitive, as I watched this white family dine." Recognizing and now questioning the reason philosophers dismissed such a life of domesticity as "beneath" their sensitivity, Andrew considers anew the "quiet, dull, heroic life of the property holder" (107). Watching the ease with which this family inhabits their world, Andrew realizes that he can never *"fake that kind of belongingness, that blithe, numbed belief that the world is an extension of my sitting room"* (109). His success in his household in Spartanburg suggests that he may not have to fake it, since it is apparently his "dharma," his "Way." But again, as with Robin in *Flight to Canada,* Andrew's apparent satisfaction with being proper-tied belies the deeper meanings in his final stance toward the world. For one thing, "householder" is not a title simply of the property owner. In this novel, the only other person called a "householder" is Karl Marx (84).⁵⁰ Moreover, Andrew learns that the phenomenological means of owning property requires him to lose whatever will-to-power motivates his desire to accumulate things.

More important, however, Andrew recognizes that property ownership is in-stated and maintained through a system of violence. He learns this lesson in two sep-arate incidents. First, as he watches the white family in the cabin, he discovers the foundation of that "warm, dumb domesticity" in the Old South. Four white men—nightriders or patrollers—ride by and ask the "property holder" to help them on their hunt for two runaway slaves. Finding a satisfactory answer to his question—"Are they worth looking for?"—he sets out, armed with a "44-caliber percussion plains rifle" (108). Underwriting the "domesticity" and the "property" of this family are the com-mercial gains earned through the policing of slaves. Just as Andrew learns the lesson that the domesticity of the property holder he momentarily admires is based on the re-pressive policing methods for maintaining the slave system, so does he later learn that the property he himself owns does not free him from his social obligations when he witnesses firsthand the machinery for the commercial transaction of slaves. He enters a slave auction and loathes himself for passing—which is, after all, what allows him to fake that "belongingness" and to be a householder. "To see persecution to others and to be powerless to end it," he notes, "to be by accident *above* it—was, I saw, the same as consent" (151). At the auction, he purchases his childhood love, Minty McKay, and takes her back to his cabin. On the doorstep, she calls him "Andrew." Hearing Minty "speaking the name I was called in the quarters . . . gave me a nature that broke my mastery over the cabin forever" (159). His dharma, it turns out, is not that of the householder, if being a householder requires him to assume "mastery" over property. Andrew is recalled to the social condition he had escaped and is forced to confront the political violence that maintains the social order and ratifies the exchange of property (real and human).

It is vitally important to note that Andrew manages to *forget* the political vio-lence that underwrites property ownership and the domesticity superimposed on it at precisely the same time that he is reconfiguring his identity, transforming himself from a fugitive slave to a white husband. He manages to deny or not to mention the "44-caliber percussion plains rifle" used to hunt human beings who are defined as property in order to produce a form of wealth that can purchase other real property as he simultaneously denies the political violence that defines social categories like "black" and "white." In the domestic sphere, Andrew is not only able to forget these things; he *must* forget them. At one point in the course of an evening's conversation with his wife, he criticizes Peggy for "thinking *essences* again. Giving nouns the value of existence. People endure. Not names. There are no 'Negroes.' Or 'women'" (146). What Andrew seems to be proposing here is a quite useful argument that challenges an essentialism positing that things are what they are naturally or inherently, replacing it with a theory that things become what they are according to their specific situation within a set of concrete social relations. In other words, "Negroes" and "women" become what they are ("Negroes" and "women") because of the social system in which "whiteness" and "maleness" assume dominance.

Yet what is precisely missing in this insight—and what was not missing when Andrew thought on these subjects when he was a fugitive slave—is the element of political force. Just before he set out to escape from Flo Hatfield's plantation, he came to the realization that social determinants are what made "blacks" and "women" what they are. "Again and again, and yet again," he muses, "the New World said to blacks and women, 'You are nothing.' It had the best of arguments to back this up: nightriders" (75–76). Here, when he is a fugitive, Andrew shows his understanding of the institutional forces at work in the oppression of black men, black women, and white women, and, concomitantly, at the reproduction of white maleness. The oppression works not only by reinforcing ideologies ("You are nothing") but also by backing up the ideological state apparatus with repressive state apparatus: nightriders. Violence, Andrew understands, becomes a means of containment and an act ritually performed toward defining the differences between social classes. Andrew realizes that all these factors are determinants in social identity, yet, as we saw above, when he finally comes to sum up his sense of moral action, he decides that an individual is responsible for denying the effects of those very determinants.

The main and practically inescapable reason Andrew denies those forces in his later meditations is that he has to—and he has to because he is *passing*. Here it is necessary to recall that this Neo-slave narrative, like Reed's *Flight to Canada*, is a mixed-genre piece of fiction. Whereas Reed toyed with mixing the slave narrative and the classical historical novel (among other things), Johnson divides his novel into a slave narrative and a novel of passing.[51] The first half of the book, "House and Field," is about the basic division in the slave community; the second, "The White World," about the basic division in antebellum American society. When Andrew exists in the first, he not only is able to recognize the social forces defining and limiting his life, but is effortlessly able to define the exact location where those forces converge between ideological propaganda and physical policing. He knows not only that nightriders armed with rifles are the forces of violence supporting the ideological superstructure, but also that the system of patrolling and policing slaves is itself part of the larger system that supports property holding and domesticity. As a black slave, as property, Andrew was able to see the range of imperatives and cultural violence necessary to maintaining that social order which defines him as property. As a white property holder, though, he limits his vision and denies or underplays those forces in order to give himself the illusion that the social order in which he is implicated does not depend on those imperatives and that violence.

Andrew's necessary amnesia regarding the forces at work in the social order he can comfortably inhabit tells us something about the social order itself, and the process by which social class formation originated historically and operates in recreating itself daily. Explaining the history of race relations, Oliver Cox has argued that the "concept 'white man'" became a significant social definition only after the legal distribution of power among the colonizing nations of the early modern world, around 1493–1494. First, Pope Alexander VI's bull of demarcation, issued on May 3, 1493, and then its revision by the Treaty of Tordesillas, signed on June 7, 1494, "put all the heathen peoples and their resources—that is to say, especially the colored peoples of the world—at the disposal of Spain and Portugal." What marks the beginning of modern race relations, then, is "a practical exploitative relationship with its socio-attitudinal facilitation"—in other words, force and ideology. Force and ideology also reproduce the terms of those race relations. The "ultimate purpose of all theories of white superiority," writes Cox, "is not a demonstration that whites are in fact superior to all other human beings but rather to insist that whites must be supreme. It involves primarily a power rather than a social-status relationship."[52]

Barbara Fields has more recently argued along the same lines about the creation and recreation of "race" in the United States. Race is not a set of physical attributes, not an element of biology, not even an idea. It is an "ideology," which Fields defines as "the descriptive vocabulary of day-to-day existence, through which people make rough sense of the social reality that they live and create from day to day." Ideology is "the interpretation in thought of the social relations through which [people] constantly create and re-create their collective being." Ideologies "do their job when they help insiders make sense of the things they do and see—ritually, repetitively—on a daily basis." What ideologies have to do in order to create and re-create a society of gross inequities is allow those who benefit from the inequities to define themselves against those who suffer them; and, more to the point, these ideologies succeed most thoroughly when they allow the beneficiaries to deny whatever violent forces historically formed and currently maintain those social relations. As Ernest Renan noted, the "creation of a nation" and the maintenance of "nationality" itself require "forgetting" those "deeds of violence which took place at the origin of all political formations."[53] Likewise, the hegemony of the "concept 'white man'" requires amnesia as well as force.

In *Oxherding Tale,* Johnson shows us the process through which a previously disempowered individual can be recruited into precisely that hegemony and re-create just that ideology. While those moments in which he is shown the rawness of the system in its workings cause him to think anew about his commitment to property ownership and to meditate more closely on the implied consent of assuming a social identity in which he is above oppression, he nonetheless remains propertied and passing for white at the end of the novel. Johnson shows us how Andrew is interpellated into the ideology of property and domesticity in the course of assuming a white identity. *In order to pass,* Andrew is forced to negate or elide those violent social forces he had earlier discovered in the workings of an exploitative society. Underlying what Johnson is saying about Andrew's denials and his amnesia is that "passing" is what one does when one accedes to the present social order, when one does not contest it by assuming a questioning posture about the dictates of what appears to be a natural identity. Andrew's intuition at the slave auction is right: "consent" in the oppression of others is not a matter of active effort, but a matter of historical accident that gets recreated daily. One "passes" if one does not actively contest the privileges that place one "above" the violent forces that oppress those others. And "passing" in this political scenario is an act not of renouncing one's race, but of accepting the ideologies through which race is recreated. According to the social logic of Johnson's novel, then, *whites* pass when they accede to the oppressive social order by forgetting the forms of cultural violence operative in defining and degrading others. Andrew passes not so much when he denies his father and his race, or when he adopts a false history of the Harris family, but rather when he forgets the forms of violence that had earlier defined his social condition. He becomes white when he forgets how whiteness gets made.[54]

In order to pass for white, then, Andrew has to forget what he had earlier, and correctly, called the "best of arguments," that is, the social forces that defined "Blacks" and "women" as addressed absences ("nothing") at the same time as they defined the "New World" as a white male speaking subject: "the New World said to blacks and women. . . ." By showing us the process and politics of passing, Johnson brilliantly illuminates the seductiveness of precisely those ideas that buttress an unjust social order—most specifically, the idea of an autonomous individuality freed from social forces. Since such an individuality might well be the deepest desire of a slave whose racial identity is thoroughly formed by being subject to immiserating social forces, Johnson is able to articulate the troubling options for racial subjectivity in a society whose terrain is bipolar, where conjunctural identity is inaccessible and unrecognized. In *Oxherding Tale,* then, Johnson plays with the form of the novel (as a slave narrative and a novel of passing) as a way of commenting on the racial formation of a social order that creates racially bifurcated identities premised on either oppression or amnesia.

There are hints in *Oxherding Tale* of an emergent resistance to that social order, modes of undoing historical amnesia and contesting racial oppression. At the end of the novel, we are told that Andrew, Peggy, and their daughter Anna "turned to the business of rebuilding . . . the world" (176). We are not told what they will do toward that end, but we are fairly certain that it will not be based on an accumulation of property or involve acts of political violence, since they examined the possibilities of revolutionary violence (in the guise of George) and property ownership and found both wanting. Instead, according to the tenets of this novel, they must assume a more phenomenological position, adopting an interrogative stance to inquire into the history of the social order buttressing their identities and to fashion themselves as more intersubjective beings.

One way they could rebuild the world would be to reconstruct a more critical history of its economic bases. Johnson suggestively alludes to this strategy by naming the first chapter of the "The White World" section "Middle Passage." Ironically inverting the movement of enslavement since it describes Andrew and Reb's "flight from slavery" in the term used to describe the "archetypal journey into slavery," the title of this chapter also suggests that the "middle passage" is to a large extent the historical event that created the "white world." The economic gains from the transatlantic slave trade provided necessary material substance for the republic and transplanted the population, which, in the course of six decades of legal statutes and slave codes, would allow European indentured servants to define themselves as "whites" in the republic. Psychically, socially, and materially, the "White World" in the New World defined itself through both the violent physical force and the ideological force it exerted on those against whom it defined itself; then it had to negate the role of these violences in that class formation. In *Middle Passage,* his second Neo-slave narrative, Johnson would explore this history more thoroughly, exposing the economic structures of social identity in America.[55]

Another strategy would be for Andrew to inhabit more fully the phenomenology of the Allmuseri, especially the Allmuseri dialectic between revolutionary violence and private property, a dialectic that, rudimentary in *Oxherding Tale,* assumes a more prominent place in *Middle Passage.* The only one able to dispossess himself to the extent that his soul develops beyond captivity, Reb unpositions and liberates himself by inhabiting a "Way of strength and spiritual heroism" (77). That "Way" also contains its own philosophy of property and of revolutionary action. By the implicit tenets of this novel, Reb becomes a revolutionary to the degree that he becomes unpositioned in the material world and manages to make his possession of property a means of further unpositioning himself. Being unpositioned, Reb does not leave "residues" of himself on his property. "He was not in the shed. Not in his work. Not truly in the thickness of the world-web" (75). Indeed, Reb is so removed from the desire to accumulate that he even "treated whatever he had as someone else's property, with the care and attention that another's property deserved" (76). Because he learns to defuse the desire that precedes the acquisition of property, since he treats whatever he possesses as if it were to be returned to another possessor, owning property becomes a way of always acting on one's respect for others, even when those others are not implicated directly. Unlike Ezekiel, who was "subversive" in the "sabre-rattling style of Western activists," Reb is subversive "in a much softer and more devastating Old World way that made Harper's Ferry look foolish." What makes Reb's Way so subversive is that it manages to dispossess of potency those who are property owners without actually effecting any violence on their property. "Torching a master's house, Mau-Mauing his property, was fine" for slaves because they "hated being propertyless," which was "exactly a correlate to the emptiness of the ego" (75). In order to fight this "massive assault on the ego," those who are disempowered (blacks and women) "*inverted* the values of whites (or men)—anything to avoid self-obliteration" (76). These inversions, however, become nothing more than exact replications of the desires that had motivated "whites (or men)" to dominate and accumulate property in the first place. The destruction of property bespoke the desire for owning it; inversion did not alter the system of private property itself. Instead of destroying the property or inverting the values of the master class upholding the sanctity of property, Reb "embraced" and "absorbed" self-obliteration (76).

In the world of *Oxherding Tale,* in which the main battle is between "Samsara (the world of appearance)" and "Nirvana (the world to be attained)," Reb's strategy is both the most promising and the one most completely endorsed (92). In this novel, the world of appearance is superseded by the world of spiritual resolve and conservation. In the final chapter, entitled "Moksha" (meaning "enlightenment" or "liberation"), Andrew begins to digest the lessons Reb taught him when he realizes that "all is conserved, all." The vision at the end of *Oxherding Tale* is premised on a world in which the struggle for freedom is won. As Andrew notes, ascribing the thought to Marx, what gave purpose to life, the "thing that, once the furor over freedom died down, made real freedom intelligible," was "Something to serve" (91). Undoubtedly, seeing beyond the struggle is one way of imagining the social order in whose name the struggle is fought. It might even be said to have been the major form of political activism of the early civil rights movement, what Todd Gitlin describes as the "definitive movement style" of the sixties. This style was illustrated most brilliantly by the four African American students who inaugurated the sixties social movements with their Woolworth's lunch counter sit-in in Greensboro, North Carolina. These students did not pronounce that segregation ought to stop, but instead acted as if segregation no longer existed. "They did not petition the authorities, who, in any case, would have paid no heed; in strict Gandhian fashion, they asserted that they had a right to sit at the counter by sitting at it."[56] In this Neo-slave narrative, Johnson seems to endorse this pragmatic mode of changing the world by acting as if one lived in an already changed world. In his next Neo-slave narrative, Johnson endorses a different strategy for "rebuilding . . . the world." There, too, he presents a battle between a world of appearance and a world to be attained, but the emphasis is on the operation of systems less spiritual and more material.

7

Revising the Form,
Misserving the Order

Charles Johnson's Middle Passage

If *Oxherding Tale,* Charles Johnson's "platform book," is a meditation on the sixties, then *Middle Passage,* building on that platform, can be said to be his meditation on the "Sixties-within-the-Eighties." Having explored in his first Neo-slave narrative the ways race is recreated institutionally and then experienced personally, Johnson turns to an examination of how race is structured in the economic sphere. As we saw in the introduction to chapter 5, black intellectuals in the eighties became more aware of the ways national economic policies were creating and accentuating class divisions within the "black community," an entity that was itself becoming less homogenous in fact and a conceptual category more suspect in black public discourse. At the same time, American intellectuals began more rigorously to focus on "race" as a contingent political construct that acquired meaning only through specific sociohistorical forces. Not a transhistorical biological category but rather a social concept recreated in institutional and personal life, race "yet lives because it is part and parcel of the *means* of living." While certain historical factors and cultural practices had more than a residual effect on the present construction of racial meanings—for instance, the late eighties saw a new and thorough inquiry into how nineteenth-century blackface minstrelsy structured black and white identity—race was understood to be recreated primarily in political struggles situated in the crucible of economic affairs.[1]

Affirmative action became one of the primary sites of that political struggle, maybe *the* primary site. Connected with its moment of emergence in 1964, affirmative action was not only a national policy but for neoconservatives a policy marking the detrimental legacy of the sixties. For many, as Lerone Bennett noted, the "massive attacks on the sixties takes the form of antiaffirmative action." Indeed, those gathered at the Second Thoughts conferences spent a good deal of time condemning what they called "the affirmative racism of liberal social engineers." Responding antagonistically to the emergence of what they called "ethnic group interest" in the seventies, neoconservatives belatedly realized and some hypocritically espoused the values of American individualism and a "color-blind society." Unlike those more progressive thinkers who espoused a different kind of color-blind polity based on more revolutionary social programs—to "abolish the white race by any means necessary," as the journal *Race Traitor* put it in its manifesto—American neoconservatives wished rather to quell the insurgence of those social groups (particularly ethnic and racial groups) that had been empowered by the sixties movements and given new (and relatively limited) opportunities through affirmative action channels. For some white neoconservatives, the fact that race was a politically constructed category served as fodder for the attack on affirmative action. In their argument, since black racial identity was created in conditions of discrimination and fostered through acts of racism (a point black progressive thinkers made), and since discrimination and racism were no longer forces in the eighties (a point opinion polls of whites showed), then race itself had become a redundant category to use when addressing socioeconomic inequities.[2]

While black conservatives and neoconservatives supported this syllogism by arguing that cultural differences and psychic ambivalence rather than racism were the causal factors in the continuing disparity between black and white socioeconomic success, black leftists affirmed the reality, the "persistence," and the "permanence" of racism as a "central ideological underpinning of American society," counseling the need for African Americans to develop and maintain a strategic and sophisticated form of black political consciousness until such time as racism no longer played "a consensus-building hegemonic role" in the nation. In other words, black leftists saw no benefit in eliminating race as a prelude to eliminating racism, especially since white racial identity was wholly unproblematized in the course of the debate over affirmative action. Only in the eighties did there emerge a significant body of literature tracing the ways white racial identity had been historically formed and politically sustained in the United States, showing the "historically specific ways in which 'Whiteness' is a politically constructed category parasitic on 'Blackness.'"[3] The debate in the eighties, then, was between those neoconservatives who argued that race was no longer a viable social category for political legislation and those who argued against ahistorical and unreflective thinking about race in contemporary America. Revolving around the issue of affirmative action, the debate focused on those who advocated the principle for neutrally based justice or fairness for individuals and those who discerned the reality of unequal distributions of economic resources and group histories of differential access to power.

Supportive of affirmative action and keenly aware that it was justifiable because blacks and whites have "different historical background[s]," Johnson was nonetheless troubled in trying to reconcile these beliefs with his wish for equitable, universally applicable values and principles of justice and his conviction that race was after all "an illusion."[4] We saw earlier how this ambivalence played itself out in *Oxherding Tale*, where Andrew Hawkins goes from being a black slave acutely aware of the institutional forces creating differentially empowered identities to becoming a passing white property owner necessarily forgetful of the history and ongoing power of those institutional forces. The major institutional sites in *Oxherding Tale*—where Andrew was forced to recognize his status as a black and then his complicity as a white in a slaveholding polity—were the domestic slave trade and the informal order for policing slaves, the first a space for economic transfers and the second a system for regulating the property transferred. In *Middle Passage,* Johnson focuses on rather larger, more global institutional sites as he situates his exploration of racial formation in terms of a longer, more transnational historical framework.

This change in focus is marked in the altered impetus and form of his second Neo-slave narrative. Like *Oxherding Tale, Middle Passage* also disrupts, exaggerates, and refigures some of the notable conventions of the antebellum slave narrative. In *Middle Passage,* however, Johnson tends less to "worry" or play with the conventions of the slave narrative, as he had done in *Oxherding Tale,* and more to reconstruct and resituate the slave narrative form into a larger, more historically resonant context. For instance, not only does Johnson rewrite the basic movement of the fugitive slave narrative in having the manumitted slave go from the North (Illinois) to the South (New Orleans), but he in fact has him continue on to West Africa, thereby both reversing the conventional course of the passage to freedom for fugitive slaves and also recreating the transnational course of enslavement in the Atlantic world system. This move and others like it throughout the novel strike me as less an attempt to parody the *topoi* of the slave narrative and more an effort to create in his novel an analytical framework through which to explicate the historical and economic *origins* of the enterprise in slaving and slavery. In other words, he here performs that "archaeological work" he had theorized in *Oxherding Tale* of digging until "the form surrenders its diverse secrets." But in *Middle Passage,* the "secret" is not that the slave narrative is part of world culture and related to the Puritan or the confessional narrative in being about the ethical movement "from slavery (sin) to freedom (salvation)," but rather that slave narratives, properly excavated, contain information about the specificity of slavery and the primacy of the economic sphere.[5] This shift in focus and form, it seems to me, constitutes a response to the political discourses and the racial formation of the eighties, as Johnson shows himself to be less concerned with issues of epistemology, how perception shapes thought, how Black Power ideas on racial subjectivity and experience were philosophically flawed, and more concerned with issues of politics, how economic conditions shape possible actions, how the nation's conservative agenda was creating new forms of race and racialism.

Treating race as a "highly contested representation of relations of power between social categories by which individuals are identified and identify themselves," Johnson turns his focus in *Middle Passage* to the economic relations undergirding the identities of slaves and masters.[6] As the narrator of *Middle Passage,* Rutherford Calhoun has three careers, each forming part of his determined effort to create the person he "could rightly call Rutherford Calhoun," or to discover, as he puts it, the "'I' that I was."[7] After he is manumitted by his master in southern Illinois, he becomes a thief—a career, he informs us, he had learned as a slave, and a career that is part of his striving to generate a philosophy of experience. In one way, *Middle Passage* is a story about the conversion of Rutherford from a self-proclaimed "petty thief" and "social parasite" into the chief accuser of the illegal slave traders of New Orleans (2, 200–3). He is transformed from someone who lives outside one set of laws into someone who comes to live within another set of laws. We cannot say that Rutherford undergoes a radical transformation from thief to law-abiding citizen, for two reasons. First, he was never as "petty" a thief as he professes to be because his career as a thief coincides with, and is supported by, an interesting philosophy of revolution and class warfare. Second, he does not simply begin obeying the law after his middle passage. Having discovered the economic and social conditions underwriting large-scale crime—namely, slavery and the slave trade—Rutherford partially reforms his philosophy about stealing property, but he also discovers that blackmail is an effective strategy toward ending the slave trade. In his second career, Rutherford becomes a lover. In many ways, none of them conventional, *Middle Passage* is a love story. The novel begins with Rutherford running off "to sea" in order to avoid a shotgun wedding with Isadora Bailey, and it concludes with Rutherford and Isadora in an "embrace that would outlast the Atlantic's bone-chilling cold" (1, 209). Part of Rutherford's "middle passage," then, is learning to commit himself to his beloved—once he realizes Isadora is just that. Finally, *Middle Passage* is a story about Rutherford as writer, and about writing as a means of subscribing oneself in the act of undermining the economic trade in slavery. In each of his three careers, Rutherford works to create an identity for himself and to criticize the capitalist economic system. In other words, stealing, loving, and writing are ways for Rutherford to determine how "the (black) self was the greatest of all fictions" as well as to maintain a revolutionary attitude toward what he comes to see as the "invisible economic realm . . . behind the sensuous one" directing the actions and limiting the kinds of relationships possible between humans (171, 149).

In this novel, then, just as he had done in his brilliant and tellingly entitled short story "Exchange Value," Johnson explores the ways any person may resist the socioeconomic order of capitalism before it threatens to determine and define all his or her social relationships. While I am not going so far as to say that Johnson is a novelist with some sort of vaguely Marxist agenda, a politics he did embrace in the early seventies, I am saying that one crucial aspect of *Middle Passage* is his representation of individuals who recognize the manner in which the economic order of slavery determines their social relationships and act both to subvert the economic order and to organize the possibility for conceiving of a collective sense of selfhood.[8] Let us also recall that one of the characters in *Oxherding Tale* was Karl Marx, whose visit to the Cripplegate plantation in South Carolina was part of the turning point of the novel (I will discuss this event presently). Like both "Exchange Value" and *Oxherding Tale,* but even more so, Johnson's *Middle Passage* represents that aspect of his work constituting his criticism of that order Fredric Jameson calls "late capitalism." More specifically, *Middle Passage* is Johnson's most complete exploration of the unique relationship obtaining among law, love, and writing as issues affecting the assertion of personal identity for the American slave; for finally, what all parts of Rutherford's three careers—as lover, thief, and writer—have in common is that each happens to be a way for the slave to define self as "person" and defy the master's definition of him or her as "property." For Rutherford, theft is a way of reconfiguring the relationship between self and inanimate Other, love a way of establishing a new relationship between self and animate Other, and writing a way of situating self as an agent in the social order. We can begin our examination of Johnson's play of the congeries of ideas about slave identity by first seeing in what ways love and theft constitute strategies for slave identity formation.

Middle Passages of Desire: Love and Theft

The property that slaves stole most often was food, primarily because they were underfed. As one Virginia slaveholder confessed, "the very best remedy for hog stealing" is to give slaves "plenty of pork to eat." In certain recorded cases, though, slaves stole not only as a way of supplementing their meager diets, but equally as a way of defying the identity the master class would impose on them. A Jamaican slave responded to the charge of stealing sugar from his master by insisting that since "sugar belongs to massa, and myself belongs to massa, it all de same ting." He certainly cannot be called a thief, the slave insists, since he is simply amalgamating two pieces of property belonging to the same owner. The slave informs his interviewer that while he has "taken" the sugar, he has not "stolen" it because only persons can steal. Property cannot be liable to the charge of stealing property. After being caught stealing some of his master's property, Tom, a slave in Alabama in 1855, is reported to have said: "When I tuk the turkey and eat it, it got to be part of me." And "me," he implicitly accuses his master, is property just as the turkey had been. Slaves throughout the New World used the same argument Brazilian slaves typically made: "What I take from my master being for my own use, who am his slave or property . . . he loses nothing by its transfer." Meanwhile, what is implicit in the background of each of these reports is the point former slave Josephine Howard of Texas insightfully makes: "Dey [slaveholders] allus done tell us it am wrong to lie and steal, but why did white folks steal my mammy and her mammy? . . . Dat de sinfulles' stealin' dey is." "Dey talks a heap 'bout de niggers stealin,'" former slave Shang Harris of Georgia agrees, but nobody mentions "de fust stealin' done" in "Afriky, when de white folks stole de niggers." What one historian has playfully called the "slaves' deplorable failure to appreciate the sanctity of private property" was part of the slaves' efforts to gain self-awareness of their social status and to counter the means by which they were historically and currently oppressed, engaging in their task of theft as a strategy for "realizing a larger measure of self-respect" within a classic "oppressor-oppressed situation."9

Moreover, these slaves had a wider scope of self-awareness and social status than their individual households or plantations; they were identifying themselves within national histories. As Josephine Howard's and Shang Harris's statements suggest, the act of theft was a matter of the slaves' defining their relationship to the whole of American history and the social order based on the profits of the slave trade. Frederick Douglass's ruminations on this issue, as on so many others, is exemplary. Having moved from the household of Hugh Auld, where food was plentiful, to the household of stingy Thomas Auld, where food was scarce, Douglass realizes that he would have to steal from his master if he was to avoid starving. Troubled by his conscience at the thought of stealing, he finds after much reflection that "there was no other way to do, and that after all there was no wrong in it." He develops three reasons in justification. First, he argues that what he steals is still retained as the property of his master. "Considering that my labor and person were the property of Master Thomas," Douglass was doing no more than "simply appropriating what was my own to the use of my master, since the health and strength derived from such food were exerted in his service." Second, he sees this personal relationship in terms of American history, since slaveholders are "only a band of successful robbers" who traveled to Africa "for the purpose of stealing and reducing my people to slavery." Third, he positions his personal and historical situation in terms of a broadly conceived American social order. Having to justify stealing from neighboring plantations not owned by his master, Douglass formulates a social logic of the ways the entire social order is implicated in specific acts of slaveholding. He determines that he is "not only the slave of Master Thomas, but . . . the slave of society at large," since all the economic and police forces have "bound" themselves "in form and in fact to assist Master Thomas in robbing me of my rightful liberty." Therefore, he concludes, "whatever rights I have against Master Thomas I have equally against those confederated with him in robbing me of my liberty. As society has marked me out as privileged plunder, on the principle of self-preservation, I am justified in plundering in turn. Since each slave belongs to all, all must therefore belong to each."[10]

Like Douglass, Rutherford Calhoun has a formidable philosophical argument to justify his stealing and a strong sense of how the machinery of the state is implicated in a slave economy. A self-confessed "petty thief" and "social parasite," Rutherford begins his slave narrative by describing how he reneges on his debts to the Creole gangster Phillippe "Papa" Zeringue and steals passage on Captain Ebenezer Falcon's *Republic* (2). Although he claims a political motivation for his attacks on other people's property, Rutherford's primary interest is neither politics nor material goods but rather a form of phenomenology. Ever since he can remember, he possessed an unfathomable desire to accumulate experiences: "I hungered—literally *hungered*—for life in all its shades and hues: I was hooked on sensation, you might say, a lecher for perception and the nerve-knocking thrill, like a shot of opium, of new 'experiences'" (3). He admires Falcon because he is like him in enjoying "any experience that disrupted the fragile, artificial pattern of life on land" (33). Experience for Rutherford, though, is more than a sensation (mental, sensual, or physical) or an affect (emotional or sensible); it is a property, "a commodity, a *thing* we could cram into ourselves" (38). Believing himself "too refined to crave gross, physical things," Rutherford "heaped and hived 'experiences' instead," his fundamental desire being "to steal things others were 'experiencing'" (162).

Rutherford's career as a thief and his philosophy of stealing as a way of accumulating experience began when he was a slave. Like the slaves who stole out of hunger, Rutherford notes that he "never had enough of anything." The abject poverty of enslavement is something that creates a series of crises in the daily life of the slave: "If you have never been hungry, you cannot know the *either/or* agony created by a single sorghum biscuit—either your brother gets it or you do. And if you *do* eat it, you know in your bones you have stolen the food straight from his mouth, there being so little for either of you." What he calls "the daily, debilitating side of poverty," the "perpetual scarcity that, at every turn, makes the simplest act a moral dilemma," leads Rutherford to conclude that stealing is his cultural inheritance: "was I not, as a Negro in the New World, *born* to be a thief? Or, put less harshly, inheritor of two millennia of things I had not myself made" (47)? The sentiment Rutherford is articulating and Johnson signifying on here—a sentiment Rutherford will repudiate once he learns more about the Allmuseri culture—is that of the early James Baldwin, whose trip to Europe taught him that the cathedral at Chartres (one of those monuments making up "two millennia of things") says something to those whose ancestors built it that it can never say to him. Even though Baldwin does maintain that the cathedral can say things to him that it cannot say to the native villagers, he nonetheless concludes his survey of Chartres by noting that the African American "arrived at his identity by virtue of the absoluteness of his estrangement from his past."[11] Unlike Baldwin, Rutherford responds to his sense of estrangement from the "two millenia of things" by intuiting that theft is the way for the slave to define selfhood.

As a slave, Rutherford is made to feel "as if everything of value lay outside me. Beyond." Like all slaves who are forced to perceive the alignment between property and power, Rutherford is made to see that because value resides in private property, his value as a slave also resides beyond what he considers to be his "self." Toni Morrison offers us a similar scene of discovery when Paul D "hears the men talking and for the first time learns his worth. He had always known, or believed he did, his value—as a hand, a laborer who could make profit on a farm—but now he discovers his worth, which is to say he learns his price. The dollar value of his weight, his strength, his heart, his brain, his penis, and his future." Douglass noted that nothing made him more aware of the "brutalizing effects of slavery" than seeing the slaves "all ranked together at the valuation."[12] Rutherford suffers a state of anxiety similar to Paul D's and an anger similar to Douglass's upon learning that value is not an innate or inherent quality but something "Beyond" the slave self. Feeling alienated because he does not possess a coherent and valuable sense of self, Rutherford becomes a thief of others' things and experiences.

Although, it is sometimes a "nervous habit," and a "way to shake off stress and occupy [his] hands" (103), stealing is more often a political act Rutherford uses to impose his sense of order on a world that has excluded him, a political act somewhere between socialist activism and existential transmogrification. After entering a victim's room, he begins to feel a "change" come over him: "a familiar, sensual tingle that came whenever I broke into someone's home, as if I were slipping inside another's soul." "Theft, if the truth be told, was the closest thing I knew to transcendence" (46). Stealing is not simply a way for Rutherford to avail himself of material acquisitions. It is rather a way for him to feel in a heightened and vengeful way what the ideology of slavery had wished him to feel—that his value is "Beyond" himself. Stealing makes him feel beyond himself; he has so far transcended himself that he is capable of enjoying a state of intersubjectivity—a state in which he is able to enter another person's psyche in the most intimate way imaginable. We begin to see, also, how Rutherford's philosophical explanation of theft is akin to love as it is usually conceived. Stealing gives him a feeling of being all atingle, a sense of being outside himself, and a capacity for imagining himself "slipping inside another's soul." These, I think, could adequately describe the typical emotions of romantic love—at least in one of its forms and in one of its stages.

Even more than a way of transcending the limits flesh is heir to, theft is an act he thinks "broke the power of the propertied class" (47). This "pleased" him because it compensated, to a degree, for the pain he had suffered as a slave when he was forced to entertain a Kierkegaardian anxiety of knowing that every morsel he ate was a morsel "stolen" from his brother's mouth, and of knowing that his own value as property lay beyond his inherent self. When he breaks into a victim's room, he often leaves "signatures of defiance"—something like defecating on the satin pillows or writing a message on the wall. The message he was known to write in the past— "I can enter your life whenever I wish"—is meant to inform the victim that private property does not and cannot protect the individual from violation. Insofar as people place their sense of self-worth in the value of the material things they own, or as long as they value their experiences *through* their material possessions, Rutherford realizes that they will always remain potential victims to his brand of anarchic activity. Rutherford breaks the power of the propertied class both by taking their property and by devaluing their own systems of evaluating themselves in terms of that property. Consider the way Rutherford describes the process by which he steals things: "I drifted from object to object at first, just touching things with sweat-tipped fingers as a way to taint and take hold of them—to loose them from their owner" (48). He does not simply remove the item as if it were the material property he was interested in possessing, or even its eventual monetary value. He takes his time to ensure that he takes from the item its essence, its *owned-ness* (we might say). People think (and say) that having something of theirs stolen feels like a "violation" of self. What we mean, I suppose, is that the things we own become extensions of ourselves, and having them stolen feels like a violation of some part of our very sense of selfhood. "Violation," of course, is the term most often used in popular representations of those who are recovering from having their property stolen. What is meant is that some inviolate sense of self has been trespassed. For this ex-slave, whose body and soul have been stolen, and who had imposed on him a definition of value that prohibited his conceiving of selfhood at all, no revenge can possibly be sweeter than violating the property, the property owners, and the system of value they use to define themselves.

Rutherford's career as a thief, then, supplies him with both things he believes life as a slave has denied him—a sense of self-worth and a sense of ownership. He believes that stealing things others own gives him material property and that, in turn, stealing what others value gives him the experiences those people associate with their property. In this way Rutherford fulfills his desire to steal other people's experiences. Eventually Rutherford will realize that he is mistaken in both his suppositions. He discovers he is wrong to think he can steal other people's experiences, because experience is a process and not an entity, as he learns after encountering the Allmuseri, the African tribe whose members are captured and being shipped in the *Republic*. Moreover, he discovers that stealing other people's private property is not a way of breaking the propertied class or a way of radically undermining an economic order based on private property. That lesson too comes from the Allmuseri, who are here anticipating an idea of Marx's.

The Allmuseri belong to a culture that disdains private property and is ambivalent regarding the concept of private experience. The Allmuseri disliked "property," "seldom fought," and "could not steal." In fact, "they fell *sick,* it was said, if they wronged anyone" (78). Their "notion of 'experience'" is more complex than their ethics, though, because they seem simultaneously to believe in both a radical individualism and a radical collectivism. On the one hand, believing that "each man out-pictured his world from deep within his own heart," they "held each man utterly responsible for his own happiness or sorrow, for the emptiness of his world or its abundance, even for his dreams and his entire way of seeing" (164). On the other hand, though, the Allmuseri "were as close-knit as cells in the body," their "[t]ribal behavior so ritualized, seasoned, and spiced by the palm oil, [and] the presence of others [that] it virtually rendered the single performer invisible—or, put another way, blended them into an action so common the one and many were as indistinguishable as ocean and wave" (58, 166). Given this peculiar physically based ethics and psychically based phenomenology, it makes sense for the Allmuseri to believe that "no leaf fell, no word was uttered or deed executed that did not echo eternally throughout the universe" (140). The Allmuseri principle of principles, it would appear, is that what is within (psyche) alters what is without (world) in an ever-expanding set of causes and effects. In other words, each act, which is after all an externalizing of some mysterious inner quality, has a consequence that involves an increasingly larger group of people. Because each person's actions have such radical significance for those beyond him or her, the Allmuseri find themselves connected to one another in a way that mocks Western notions of autonomous being.

Having been exposed to Allmuseri philosophy, Rutherford must reevaluate his own beliefs about theft as a way of establishing connectedness with those he would rob. Stealing does not provide him with some lacking inner set of "experiences" because, according to the Allmuseri, "experience" is something already and only inherent. He *cannot* steal experiences, because they are not material or capable of being possessed; and he *need not* steal experiences to supplement his own psyche, because he has a stock of experiences within him awaiting expression. In other words, the Allmuseri provide answers to the questions Rutherford earlier posed to himself: "was I not, as a Negro in the New World, *born* to be a thief? Or, put less harshly, inheritor of two millennia of things I had not myself made?" He is not born to be a thief, say the Allmuseri, because those "things" constituting two millennia of so-called Western culture are not only his inheritance; they are very much the products of the labor and creativity of his ancestors. So, too, because every action has an expanding set of consequences that not only affect the actor but also alter the condition of the universe, stealing, he begins to understand, is something that carries with it more pervasive ethical consequences than he had imagined. When the Allmuseri rebel and capture the *Republic,* they are forced to murder some of the crew. These acts of what many would consider legitimate self-defense are "seeds" in the Allmuseri universe—seeds that "would flower into other deeds—good and evil—in no time at all. For a people with their values, murder violated (even mutilated) the murderer so badly that it might well take them a billion billion rebirths to again climb the chain and achieve human form" (140). So closely attuned are the Allmuseri to their universe that every act leaves them altered as much as it does the environment. What Rutherford learns is that stealing is wrong not because it hurts the person whose property is taken—an issue of little importance—but because it adversely affects the thief and those who are important to the thief. It might seem that the upshot of the Allmuseri belief is the same as of other conventional ethical schemes meant to protect the property of those whose historical thefts are "on the scale that transforms crime into politics," as Edmund Morgan mordantly puts it.[13] It might seem, in the end, that the Allmuseri belief, like the commandment and the Constitution, effectively ensures that those who own property are not liable to lose it to those who don't own any.

That similarity is deceptive, however. For one thing, Rutherford's belief that his

theft "broke the power of the propertied class" is a delusion. The power of the propertied class does not depend simply on property. It depends on a general belief that
relations between human beings are "relations between *private property owners.*"
Within that general belief—that "private property is man's personal, *distinguishing*
and hence essential existence," theft belongs on the same continuum as other forms
of exchange. As Marx notes, "the felt need for a thing is the most obvious, irrefutable
proof that the thing is part of *my* essence, that its being is for me and that its *property*
is the property, the particular quality peculiar to my essence." These are sentiments a
thief may hold as much as an owner. So even though Rutherford attempts to steal
the essence of the things he lifts from people's homes, he nonetheless only confirms
the system of beliefs whose power he thinks he is "breaking." Any two participants
in a contest over any piece of private property in the end only "confirm private property." A thief, even a thief with Rutherford's political acumen, does exactly the same
thing. The thief, it would appear, is the logical corollary to the owner within the
general belief of private property. As Marx succinctly puts it, "each of us really *does*
act out the role in which the other casts him."[14] The course of political action
Rutherford eventually takes is surprising, but no more surprising than the source
Johnson uses to support that course of action.

The course of action turns out to be "love," and the theorist of such a political
course is Marx himself. In order to see "what love's got to do with it"—to rephrase
Tina Turner's immortal words—when "it" is concerted political action toward changing the foundation of economic conditions in society, we have to turn our attention
to the time Marx makes an appearance in *Oxherding Tale.* At pretty well the nadir of
his career, banished from Belgium to Cologne and finally to London, where, in exile,
he found himself hassled by police and bill collectors and treated with utter indifference by bourgeois publishers, Marx in 1850 makes a trip to visit Andrew Hawkins's
teacher, Ezekiel Sykes-Withers in South Carolina. In a discussion with Ezekiel about
the "Self's ontogenesis" and the emptiness of the "Transcendental Ego," Marx argues
that "to exist is to exist *through* an Other," since when "two subjects come together,
they realize in their reciprocal intersubjective life a common world." Marx concludes
that the "universal name for this final, ontological achievement, this libertation—
Occidental or Oriental—in vhich each subject finds another essential is *love.*" Initially dismissing Marx's statement as foolishness, thinking it impossible that any social or existential good could come out of that "stark, simple experience of which
philosophers never (or seldom) spoke: *love,*" Ezekiel eventually discovers that no
matter how he approaches the problem, he has to conclude that "Spirit *was* love,
and the triumph of the Spirit exiled in World was in our age, or any age, to embrace
things in their *haeceittias,* their thisness, to perceive—mad as this seemed—Matter
as holy."[15]

The Marx who visits Cripplegate plantation in Johnson's novel (we can call him
the fictional Marx) expresses ideas we might not readily ascribe to the other Marx—
the one who did not visit the plantation (we can call him Marx). But Marx did write
about the ideas Johnson has the fictional Marx articulate. We recall that Marx concluded his examination of how private property was upheld in cases of contested
property by noting that "each of us really *does* act out the role in which the other
casts him." Much of the debate between Johnson's fictional Marx and Ezekiel is con-

cerned with examining the meaning of what relations obtain for a self existing through an Other. Returning to the early Marx's examination of James Mill's economics, we discover that when Marx is explicating the ways private property is confirmed, he is simultaneously defining the permutations of *desire* within the state of capitalist production. In that state, desire takes on the character that Rutherford is desperately trying to shed—the character of indenture. Within a system in which each individual produces something in order to acquire what others are producing—that is, the stage of surplus production—desire, notes Marx, is not the agent directing one toward an object, but the object itself. A dialogue between two producers examining their relationship to each other would go as follows: "Your own object is merely the *sensuous husk,* the *hidden form* of my object. For its production *signifies expressly:* the *acquisition* of my object. Thus you have really become a *means,* an *instrument* of your object even for yourself; your desire is its slave and you have performed menial tasks so that the object need never again become the fulfillment of your desire. If our mutual servitude to the object really appears at the beginning of the development as the relation of *dominance* and *slavery,* this is no more than the *brutal* and *frank* expression of our essential relationship."[16] Not only does Marx here replicate the master-slave dialectic of Hegel—without yet turning it on its head—but he also describes the way desire becomes enslaved to the object of production. That is how things are, Marx sadly intones, when human relations are relations between private properties.

If, though, we "produced as human beings" rather than as acquisitive automatons, then the dialogue would take on an entirely different form and the relationship between people would acquire an entirely different character. "In my *production* I would have objectified the *specific character* of my *individuality* and for that reason I would both have enjoyed the *expression* of my own individual *life* during my activity and also, in contemplating the object, I would experience an individual pleasure, I would experience my personality as an *objective sensuously perceptible* power *beyond all shadow of doubt."* Moreover, in "your use or enjoyment of my product I would have the *immediate* satisfaction and knowledge that in my labour I had gratified a *human* need, i.e. that I had objectified *human nature* and hence had procured an object corresponding to the needs of another *human being."* Therefore, because "I would have acted for you as the *mediator* between you and the species, . . . I would be acknowledged by you as the complement of your own being, as an essential part of yourself. I would thus know myself to be confirmed both in your thoughts and your love."[17] In the end, what Marx prophesies here, which sounds remarkably similar to what Johnson's fictional Marx says, is something like the end of "desire" and the beginning of "love" (desire signifying the alienation and absence of the object, love its presence).[18] It appears, then, that both the fictional Marx who visited Cripplegate plantation in Johnson's novel and the real Marx offer "love" as part of the means of achieving an ideal state of human actualization based on communal production and not premised on the exploitation of labor and concomitant accumulation of surplus value. It is a lesson Rutherford will come to appreciate.

Just before the *Republic* capsizes, Rutherford comes to the realization that theft, within the order and epistemology of capital, does not challenge that order because it leaves intact the issue of "desire"—as Marx had put it, "your desire" is the "slave" of the "object." Rutherford had conducted himself as a thief by acting on precisely that sense of desire created by his intimation that he was divided from things—from "two millennia of things," in fact. The means by which Rutherford will answer that desire, and thereby challenge the order of the propertied class in a more radical way, is the one Marx noted in the previous novel: love. "Love" seems hardly a solution to many problems, especially those dealing with a need to reform the economic infrastructure of a given society, if by "love" we mean something like romance or even charity. In these senses there is little love can do. But love as James Baldwin defines it—"not merely in the personal sense of being made happy but in the tough and universal sense of quest and daring and growth," in the social sense of recognizing that to "encounter oneself is to encounter the other: and this is love"—provides a more promising understanding of how love is politically transformative, producing the potential for reconstructing the social fabric by organizing a renewed attitude toward selfhood and a renewed understanding of freedom.[19]

On the plantation, love, like the act of theft, becomes a way for slaves to assert their capacities as "persons" against their enslavers' definitions of them as "property." There is a danger involved, though, for when love is used as part of a strategy of self-definition where "self" is legally proscribed and "definition" is the prerogative of those in power, then love, as we traditionally understand it, undergoes a radical transformation. In *Oxherding Tale,* Johnson notes that the "view from the quarters changes the character of everything, even love—especially love." Numerous slaves testify to the wisdom of Johnson's observation. When ex-slave, Civil War hero, and eventual member of the House of Representatives Robert Smalls was asked in an interview conducted for the American Freedmen's Inquiry Commission in 1863 whether "colored men fall in love very often," he answered: "No, sir; I think not." Ex-slave Harry McMillan noted that in "secesh times there was not much marrying for love." "Colored people," echoed Jane Johnson, an ex-slave from South Carolina, "don't pay no 'tention to what white folks call love." For good reason, as Harriet Jacobs points out, slaves avoided those personal relationships that left them vulnerable. "Why does the slave ever love?" asks Jacobs. "Why allow the tendrils of the heart to twine around objects which may at any moment be wrenched away by the hand of violence?" Proscribed in slavery, then, love became for many former slaves both a symbol and a reward of freedom, an acknowledgment that the "secesh times" were over or behind them. Both Frederick Douglass, who married Anna Murray "immediately" after his "successful flight" out of slavery, and the countless former slaves who institutionally solemnized their vows during Reconstruction understood, with Sethe in Morrison's *Beloved,* that "to get to a place where you could love anything you chose—not to need permission for desire—well now, *that* was freedom."[20]

Rutherford, too, learns that love is both a danger in slavery and a marker of freedom. At the beginning of his narrative, he thinks of love as a dangerous property: "people fell in love as they might fall into a hole" (7). In the course of the middle passage, though, he learns that love is not always a danger, nor something he can willfully avoid. Robert Hayden, in his description of the middle passage, called it a "Voyage through death, / voyage whose chartings are unlove."[21] Rutherford describes another voyage, with different chartings, because during his voyage he has become responsible for another person's life. He has adopted and assumed the care of one of the young Allmuseri girls, Baleka, whose mother was swept overboard during the passage. His newfound sense of responsibility for another person makes him aware of the limits of living parasitically off other people and creates in him an understanding of how other people's existence align them to one's own. As he says later, "[w]henever Baleka is out of my sight I am worried. If she bruises herself, *I* feel bruised" (195). He is alert, now, to how another person's being is a matter of emotional and indeed psychosomatic importance to one's own psychic health.

Rutherford's middle passage, then, takes him from a career of petty theft to a profession of profound love. Love offers Rutherford something stealing could not: a sense of intimate connection not based on a presumed absence. When he was a thief, he attempted to come into contact with things in their immediate presence, slipping into someone's room as if he were "slipping inside another's soul." Theft, Rutherford had maintained, "was the closest thing I knew to transcendence"—a feeling of being capable of feeling another's sensibilities, a feeling (we might say) of love. But he never achieved that sense of connection to another as he does with Baleka. So long as he acted on his desires, thereby ensuring that things remained absent from him, he could not be a lover; once he learns to love, things and people become present to him. This point is brought forcefully home in his description of his final reconciliation with Isadora. Thinking that sex is what would interest anyone who has had a lengthy sojourn at sea, Isadora becomes sexually aggressive with Rutherford (as she had not been earlier). Rutherford, however, finds himself less interested in sex than in love. He finds his "memories of the Middle Passage" coming back and "reducing the velocity" of his "desire, its violence." His "longing for feverish love-making" is replaced with "a vast stillness that felt remarkably full, a feeling that, just now, I wanted our futures blended, not our limbs, our histories perfectly twined for all time, not our flesh." "Desire," he realizes, "was too much of a wound, a rip of insufficiency and incompleteness that kept us, despite our proximity, constantly apart, like metals of an identical charge" (208). Love, Rutherford finally learns, is neither a hole to fear falling in nor a means of possessing or dominating persons or things. Just like *Beloved,* where Paul D puts "his story next to" Sethe's to symbolize their reconciliation with the haunting past and the exorcism of the plantation culture that had so deformed each's sense of loving, Rutherford's wish to put his story astride Isadora's symbolizes the conclusion of his middle passage and his understanding of its significance. The "voyage," he notes, "had irreversibly changed my seeing . . . and transformed the world into a fleeting shadow play I felt no need to possess or dominate, only appreciate in the *ever extended present*" (187, my italics).[22]

The question, then, is what relationship exists between Rutherford's forging love out of desire and his critique of the capitalist system he had set himself to dismantling? In other words, if "love" is something both Johnson's fictional Marx and Marx himself propose as an effect of a new order of production, what role does it play in the emergence of that new order? According to Marx, in the emergence of the new order "love" asserts the properties of the individual against the properties of "money." "Money," writes Marx in his *Economic and Philosophical Manuscripts,* "appears as an *inverting* power in relation to the individual and to those social and other bonds which claim to be *essences* in themselves." Therefore, money effects "the universal inversion of *individualities.*" Because money mediates the relationship between private properties and private property owners, it becomes, as Marx poignantly phrases it, the *"pimp* between need and object." Under those conditions, in fact, money "is for me the *other* person," which means that it supplants love. Love becomes then, for Marx, a form of true exchange, against the form of confused and false exchange represented by money. Because love is a *"particular expression,* corresponding to the object of your will, of your *real individual* life," it becomes a means of "vital expression" untainted by baser means of mediation. Love, in other words, returns the individual to himself or herself; it creates human subjects instead of inverted individualities. Under those conditions of regained subjectivity premised on human relationships which in turn are based on a true social life, Marx notes, "love can be exchanged only for love."[23]

Love, then, is an effect of the transformation in the economic system, and, like all effects that seem desirable because they promise integrity and coherence instead of fragmentation and alienation, it is therefore meant to make the transformation of systems prohibiting them a desirable proposition. Love in *Middle Passage,* like love in Marx's early writing, is not so much a revolutionary force of change as it is an instigator toward change—a proposition of how things could be if the order of production were changed and the mediation of money in human affairs repealed. It is worth noting that the scene in which Rutherford and Isadora entangle their stories and futures—a symbol of true love—follows immediately the scene in which Rutherford rejects the values of "Papa" Zeringue, who believed that "freedom was property. Power was property. Love of race and kin was property" (199). Rutherford learns that freedom, power, and especially "love" are neither "property" themselves nor based on or mediated by property. Freedom, power, and love are rather based on a sharing of rights, values, and life stories.

Life stories, likewise, are not properties of their individual authors. Unlike Diamelo, an Allmuseri who treats his life story of his enslavement "like a possession" (153), Rutherford is aware of how stories are common properties, whose fullest meanings are manifest only when they are shared. The sharing of stories provides space for us to appreciate what another person's life may have to tell us, allowing us "to inhabit the role and real place of others."[24] Rutherford's eventual understanding that stories and experiences can either be hoarded or be shared—be treated as commodities or considered as means of overturning a system of a general belief in commodification—depends finally on Rutherford's third career, the one encompassing both the others: his career as a writer. It is also in this career as writer that Rutherford finds his most potent means of challenging that "invisible economic realm" of capital.

Writing: The Third Life of Rutherford Calhoun

Like love and theft—markers of identity, ways to contest or signify a change in social status—writing for slaves and former slaves represents an urge to establish and define the parameters of selfhood. Slave narratives constitute a search for self-realization, "the finding of one's voice, the reclaiming of language from the mouth of the white other, and the initiation of the arduous process of fitting language to voice instead of the other way around." For some, like William Wells Brown, this arduous process was represented in simple terms. His final reflection on slavery is to address his former master and attest to his new liberty: "I wanted to see Captain Price, and let him learn from my own lips that I was no more chattel, but a man." For others, like Frederick Douglass, the process was a more measured and torturous one. Well after his escape from Maryland, Douglass still felt the vestiges of slavery keeping him from defining himself as free. It took three acts recorded at the end of his *Narrative* for him to feel free. First, he has to gain employment and reappropriate his inalienable right to his labor in order to feel that "I was now my own master." Second, by addressing a white audience at an antislavery convention, he finds his own voice and begins enjoying "a degree of freedom." The final process for Douglass's consummation of liberty is the writing of his slave narrative. Douglass concludes the 1845 volume in the appendix with the following final signature: "solemnly pledging myself anew to the sacred cause,—I subscribe myself, FREDERICK DOUGLASS." Only with a resolute act of self-expression in writing himself against an institution that both proscribed writing and usurped his labor force can Douglass supplement his claims of self-possession and self-mastery and, finally, come to realize his selfhood: "I subscribe myself." His slave narrative, like those of so many other former slaves who intimately experienced the close connection between "freedom and literacy," is a text that demonstrates the "evolution of a liberating subjectivity in the slave's life, up to and including the act of writing autobiography itself."[25]

Rutherford might well have held Douglass as a model for his own act of writing. But, because Rutherford is also pervasively sensitive to the ways social relations are governed by principles established in the economic realm, *Middle Passage* is probably most like James W. C. Pennington's *The Fugitive Blacksmith,* a slave narrative that contains one of the most sustained critiques of what Pennington calls the "chattel principle." Clearly, most slave narrators reveal to us how the slave's awareness of being the property of another was an essential precondition for the slave's decision to flee slavery and to record the process by which he or she reclaimed himself or herself. The slave narratives, particularly those of the middle of the nineteenth century, were testaments to the processes by which a slave realized, as did William Wells Brown for example, that he should be "free, and [able to] call my body my own." Like Brown, who needed to come to the realization that he "was no more a chattel" in order to run away from his master and become "a man," Pennington had to come to the realization that the "sin of slavery lies in the chattel principle, or relation." The "being of slavery, its soul and body," notes Pennington, "lives and moves in the chattel principle, the property principle, the bill of sale principle." Whatever pains the individual slave suffers is but the logical effect of the system: "You cannot constitute slavery without the chattel principle—and with the chattel principle you cannot save it from these results. . . . The system is master." Few fugitive slaves recorded the fullness of understanding that Pennington demonstrates regarding the systemic oppression of slavery and the economic backdrop to that system. Few, therefore, felt so radically the need to reconstruct their lives in their narratives to the extent of feeling, as Pennington did, that "I must begin the world somewhere." Like Douglass, whose marriage ceremony he performed, Pennington found that "subscrib[ing] himself" was at least one way to begin his "world."[26]

Like Douglass and Pennington, and like Andrew Hawkins in *Oxherding Tale,*

Rutherford writes an autobiography in order to assume and construct a subjectivity which frees him from a former identity as a slave. Unlike Andrew, though, Rutherford is less concerned with the philosophical problem of writing as the constitutive act of "a narrator who *is* that world: who is less a reporter than an opening through which the world is delivered," "drawing his life from everything he is not, and at precisely the instant he makes possible their appearance," and more concerned with the politics of the literary form he is employing, more attentive to the ways a document *becomes* a slave narrative.[27] For Rutherford's slave narrative does not begin as his or as an autobiographical narrative, and its most radical critique of the order of capital lies in its description of the process by which it becomes both his and a slave narrative.

In a self-reflective, metafictional scene, Rutherford describes how he wrote the document we are reading immediately after he was rescued from the incomplete middle passage of the *Republic*. Taking on two distinct forms and betraying two different motives, his writing is first used to "free [him] from the voices in [his] head, to pour onto these water-stained pages as much of the pain as [he] could until at the end of each evening, after writing furiously and without direction, [he] at last felt emptied and ready for sleep" (189). After writing himself "out" (we might say), he begins to write himself *into* the log: "as our days aboard the *Juno* wore on, I came to it with a different, stranger compulsion—a need to transcribe and thereby transfigure all we had experienced, and somehow through all this I found a way to make my peace with the recent past by turning it into Word" (189–90). Writing in its second form is a way of transforming both "experience" and "self." By the end of this bout of writing and rewriting the log of the *Republic*, Rutherford has not only transformed and transfigured all that had been experienced; he has also written a substantially different record. And herein lies the political significance of what Rutherford has done and the notable difference between Rutherford's writing in *Middle Passage* and Andrew's in *Oxherding Tale*. The major difference is not just in the theory of writing as way of writing a self *out* and then writing a (transformed) self *in*—which only somewhat differs from the theory of the slave narrator as "forever *outside* itself in others"—but rather in the fact that the "writing in" and "writing out" take place in a document conventionally used to record economic transaction in slaves. Johnson's major achievement is that he plays with the fascinating idea of how one form of writing—the sea log or journal—becomes transfigured into another—the slave narrative.

Although the narrative opens as if it were a ship's log—and indeed, its title is "Journal of a Voyage intended by God's permission in the *Republic,* African from New Orleans to the Windward Coast of Africa" (ix)—it quickly becomes apparent that it is the first-person narrative of a self-declared "newly freed bondman" (1). As the novel proceeds, we learn more about how what started out as an official document recording the passage and cargo of a slave ship became the personal narrative of a former slave. What is important to note about this transformation is that Johnson is representing the ways that the written records of the exchange of capital and private property—and slaves are both—can be altered into something critical of capitalist imperatives by someone who, until recently, had himself been defined as private property and chattel. In writing an autobiographical tract, Rutherford breaks the laws forbidding the education of slaves and offers himself as a human agent capable of self-representation, thereby challenging slavery and its basic laws and ideologies. In rewriting the log of a slave-trading ship, Rutherford also undermines the system of written records, receipts, and other means of legally sanctioning and regulating the economic transaction in slaves, thereby challenging the economic infrastructure of slavery insofar as this infrastructure relies on written records. Writing, therefore, is Rutherford's most effective means of doing what he had set out to do earlier by stealing—to break "the power of the propertied class"—and thereby create the conditions for those who have been defined as "property" to define themselves as "persons."

The political significance of what Rutherford does should not be underemphasized, although it is subtly understated. *Over* the record of a ship transporting slaves from the "Windward Coast of Africa" to New Orleans, Rutherford has written a slave narrative. This idea of writing a slave narrative as a palimpsest on a document otherwise meant to serve an economic order—or, more specifically, of rewriting a document otherwise intended to record the trade and traffick in slaves—is potentially revolutionary. Like Ishmael Reed, whose *Flight to Canada* also describes the wiles of a slave who undertakes the rewriting of documents that subscribe capital and what we may call the order of capital (namely, the transmission of capital between persons and between generations, in a word—contracts and wills), Johnson also explores the ways writing, when it is performed by those who are defined as property, becomes subversive of the very records that validate property ownership. Even more subtly than Reed, though, Johnson demonstrates this point by showing us how an economic document recording financial resources and transfers of property becomes a social document recording personal resourcefulness and human relations.[28]

After we are initially given the title of the document—"Journal of a Voyage intended by God's permission in the *Republic*"—we get no substantial explanation about how this document came to be Rutherford's autobiography until halfway through the novel. There are a few scattered hints about the document such as we might expect from a writer with Johnson's quixotic sensibilities. Rutherford does refer early on to the "log in which I now write" (27), but for the most part he does not explain in any meaningful way how the "log" became his record. We receive that information when the log is transferred from its original writer, Captain Falcon, to its new author, Rutherford. After the crew and cargo of the *Republic* have respectively mutinied and revolted, Falcon asks Rutherford to assume authorship of the log. At first unwilling to do so, claiming that "I'm no writer," Rutherford eventually agrees. "I took the logbook from the ruins. But I promised myself that even though I'd tell the story (I knew he wanted to be remembered), it would be, first and foremost, as I saw it since my escape from New Orleans" (146). Immediately after this transfer of authorship, Falcon tells Rutherford about the economic system regulating the slave trade, about the "invisible economic realm . . . behind the sensuous one" making him and all human agents pawns in a "larger game of property" (149–50). With a new understanding of the ways an economic infrastructure governs the lives of individuals, Rutherford assumes his duties as author of one of the records of that "economic realm." By the time he starts regularly referring to his act of writing, he has come to see the log and his life in an intimate relationship, thinking of it first as his personal confidant ("Now, what I am about to say must go no farther than the pages of this logbook" [175]) and then as part of his own existence as he makes an alignment between "the log of the *Republic*—and my life" (185). The "log of the *Republic*" clearly has assumed the place of the slave narrative in Rutherford's thinking. It has become the document that defines him and his life rather than the document cataloguing the human cargo of the ship.

Because Rutherford writes his autobiography within—and literally within—one of the key documents of the economic order of slavery and the slave trade, he demonstrates how identity is both an issue of one's social relations with other human beings and an issue of one's derived relations within the economic order. Rutherford's writing, and especially the place of his writing, therefore, suggest at least one potential site for the struggle for defining a self against documents that would catalogue that self as property. When we first see a physical writing in the log, it is performed by Captain Falcon, who lists the goods taken from Bangalang: hides, ivory teeth, gold, rice, bullocks, sheep, goats, beeswax, and slaves. This is written in the "rough log" which the Captain will later rewrite to produce a "more polished book for his employers" (64). Because it is a record of the economic transfer in slaves, the log plays an enormously important role not so much for the ship's captain but for the financiers who profit from their investment in the slave trade. One of those financiers is "Papa" Zeringue. When he encounters Zeringue aboard the *Juno,* Rutherford realizes that the document he has used to write his own autobiography is a text that subverts Zeringue's illegal enterprise. He carries "Ebenezer Falcon's logbook" as if it were a weapon, and he uses it as such (197). Zeringue is deeply disturbed at the sight of the document. "Naw, I can't be in that book," he asks. "Can I?" The document, as Rutherford realizes, would be "Exhibit A for any investigation into the loss of the *Republic*" (201). As Zeringue stands "glaring at the logbook," realizing that it contains his downfall and the destruction of his financial empire, Rutherford sees even more clearly that his life and the document are now irreversibly intertwined. When Zeringue inquires whether Rutherford is going to destroy the log, Rutherford responds by saying that he will keep it for "insurance," since he did not wish to fall victim to a plan in which Zeringue would hire a henchman "to have me and the logbook conveniently disappear once we were on shore" (204, 203). By writing it as his autobiography, he makes sure that it resonates as both a testimonial of his life and a piece of testimony against the capitalist enterprise in slaving, the slave trade, and slaveholding.

While writing is clearly the career in which he is able to give his boldest testimony to the evils of capitalism, it is also the one in which Rutherford is in most danger of succumbing to the terms of capitalism, of falling into the same dilemma as had Diamelo by considering his story "a possession" and thereby unwittingly ratifying the order he wishes dismantled. Facing the same hazard as had Raven Quickskill and Dessa Rose, Rutherford too feels the tension between claiming his life experience as a possession, making "the property of my blackness" part of the "struggle to define myself as 'somebody,'" and realizing that even biographical cultural artefacts can become a form of "property that fragments collectivity and dehumanizes" those it would represent.[29] All the narrators of the Neo-slave narratives suffer a crisis of representation in which their lives and texts are vulnerable to being stolen, appropriated, or made commodities, and each comes up with an imaginative way of subverting the social order that sanctions the appropriation and commodification of black lives and black life-stories. Raven merges his story and Robin's in a text premised on an act of spiritual possession, rendering him selfless. Dessa contests the written text of her life by supplanting it in a collectively shared oral performance.

Rutherford draws on the knowledge of each of his careers, as thief and lover, to make his writing more critical of the economic system of private property. As a thief who stole in order to transcend himself and enter into communion with another, Rutherford is keenly aware of the ways experiences can be commodified if they are not shared. Likewise in his career as a lover, he learns that love consists precisely in the ability to share histories. Writing as he does, then, he is able to escape the trap of telling his story as if it were a possession, and rather to tell it as an Allmuseri griot might have done, that is, assuming the pose of a narrator so aware of the "presence of others" that it virtually made "the single performer invisible," so aware of the continuity of human experience that when asked to recite "one item of tribal history" he can answer only "by reeling forth the entire story of his people" (166, 169). In the end, Rutherford finally integrates all three careers. By rewriting the documents of the slave trade, Rutherford finally learns what to steal and how best to steal it. By writing a document about sharing histories, about answering a "desire" that is so "much of a wound, a rip of insufficiency and incompleteness" that it keeps lovers apart by concluding with a story about a love that "felt remarkably full" and presaged an "ever extended present" (187), Rutherford represents love in the same way and for the same reasons as Marx did in his early works. Writing, then, for Rutherford is both an act of theft in its appropriation of capitalist documents and an expression of love in its also being a way of transforming self.

In the end, then, *Middle Passage* is about the middle passage to identity—and the ways theft, love, and writing help one ex-slave achieve a semblance of identity. And, just as *Middle Passage* ends while Rutherford and Isadora embrace on a ship still on the ocean in mid-passage, so does Rutherford learn that ultimately identity was also an incomplete journey, that "identity," as he puts it, "was imagined" (171). The difference between Rutherford's insight here about the imaginative construction of identity and the one Andrew has in *Oxherding Tale* about the inessential nature of identity is that Rutherford inscribes this knowledge within a text that explicitly describes the inner workings of the social forces that create identity and limit imagination. Unlike Andrew, Rutherford uses the form of the slave narrative to demonstrate the play of social forces in the construction of identities. In adding to the *topos* of representing slaves in search of identity a political concern with tracing the ways slave identity and crises of slave identity are related to the "invisible economic realm," and, more generally, of the ways inequities in access to power condition the forms of identities that differently situated subjects are able to imagine, Johnson also alters some of the political emphases he had inscribed in his first Neo-slave narrative.

Appropriate Behavior: Toward Freely Imagined Identities

It is fitting that Johnson chose to emphasize his political concerns with the hidden structures of capitalism over his still-evident philosophical concerns about intersubjective relations in his novel about the middle passage, because that historical expe-

rience marks the essential intersection of economics and identity. With the establishment of the great entrepôts in the delta ports at places like Elimina Castle, La Maison
des Esclaves, and Cape Coast Castle, the transatlantic slave trade created "the first
principal manifestations of modern, mercantile capitalism on the west coast of
Africa," from whose "factories" were transported the "human stock essential to New
World wealth" and capitalist production in this country. From this international capitalist enterprise emerged the "identities" of both black Africans and white Euro-
peans, the former stamped as marketable objects, beings alienated from their humanity and valued as commercial commodities, and the latter as free entrepreneurs
within a free market. In colonial America, the middle passage directly led to the historical creation of "whiteness," as six decades of legal statutes and slave codes in the
early republic (from 1619 to 1680) produced the conditions through which European indentured servants defined themselves as "white."[30] Given that the transatlantic slave trade stands as the moment when Africans are first defined as commodities representing the source of initial profit necessary to the economic system based
on the expropriation of labor-time in the making of other commodities, and as the
event leading to the creation of "whiteness," it is perfectly apt that Rutherford should
develop a dual critique of capitalism and of imagined racial identities in the course
of his own middle passage.

In both *Oxherding Tale* and *Middle Passage,* when Johnson's characters confront
the apparatus of the slave trade—domestic or international—they are forced to see
in its most extravagant form how the whole society is complicit in maintaining the
machinery of slavery, and forced to discern the processes through which that machinery affects the creation and maintenance of racial identities. The difference between Andrew and Rutherford, however, is in how each responds to that insight,
how each develops an identity *after* the crucial moment of discovering the range of
social forces at play in the enslavement of people of African descent. We saw that
Andrew responded somewhat ambivalently, by recognizing his own complicity but
still denying as "determinants" in the formation of identity those massive social
forces that generate the machinery of slavery. Rutherford, on the other hand, responds to the moment of crisis with firmer determination, refiguring his subjectivity
in a less ambivalent way that demonstrates his profound understanding of how the
institutions of society are indeed determinants in identity formation. His meditations on violence, property, and identity, then, are more attuned to the precise and
profound ways structural systems govern social relations.

Rutherford does not forget his own enraged feelings when he encounters the
violence of the machinery of enslavement. His thoughts become "murderous" and
he feels his identity as a person of African descent most poignantly when he encounters the mechanics of the slave trade (66). Unlike the other crew members on the *Republic,* all of whom are white, Rutherford "sees himself, his own blighted history, in
the slaves" they purchase. His murderous rage becomes despair at the possibility of
finding meaning in such a world. How, he wonders, could he go on after this? "How
could I feel whole after seeing it? How could I tell my children of it without placing
a curse on them forever? How could I even dare to *have* children in a world so sense-
less?" (67). One of the ways he makes sense of that world is to write about it in order
to discover the governing economic facts fundamental to that disordered world. And

one of the ways he manages his murderous rage is to threaten the very life of one of the financiers whose investments govern and re-create that disorder. Whereas Andrew eschewed all forms of violence in *Oxherding Tale,* Rutherford suggests that some acts of slave violence constitute potentially valuable forms of resistance, and he threatens to bring Zeringue to justice before the maroon societies of runaway slaves "who periodically raid plantations and . . . *kill* slave owners" (201). In neither novel does Johnson espouse any simplistic political vision in which violence produces a healthier social order, but in Rutherford's final political vision slave resistance, including the act of slaves' murdering slavemasters, is seen as at least a feasible threat within the project on which he is embarked.

In terms of its examination of property, *Middle Passage* is also less like *Oxherding Tale* and more like Johnson's "Exhange Value," a tale about two brothers who come into an inheritance only to find that their relationship suffers from the wealth that now divides them from their previous condition of human sociability. The two brothers in *Middle Passage* are Rutherford and Jackson Calhoun, and the inheritance they stand to gain is that of their master, Peleg Chandler. The difference, though, is that the brothers do not inherit Chandler's wealth, because Jackson, the elder brother, rejects the political economy within which that wealth was accumulated. Instead of accepting the wealth offered him from his master's coffers, Jackson resolves to distribute the wealth in the same way it was accumulated, returning to the laborers the wealth formed through the expropriation of their physical labor. He counsels his master that the "property and profits of this farm should be divided equally among all your servants and hired hands, presently and formerly employed." He reasons that since their "labor helped create it," the "fixed capital" accruing from their labor should be "spread among bondmen throughout the county" (112). Initially disgruntled by his brother's socialist thinking, dismayed with the decision, and disaffected from Jackson because of it, Rutherford, in the course of his middle passage, discovers how capitalist economic structures undergird the ills of the contemporary social order and learns to appreciate anew what his brother's decision means, and what his socialist actions portend. Like Andrew, Rutherford had to encounter the machinery of the slave trade in order to reach a vantage from which he could share his brother's vision and see that he could not have "mastery" over property.

In both novels, then, Johnson's narrators explore the ramifications of violence and private property. In *Oxherding Tale,* Andrew rejects violence and the desire to accumulate wealth in the form of private property. In *Middle Passage,* Rutherford sees some limited value for a form of resistant violence against slaveholders and adopts a socialist politics regarding private property. Likewise, in each case, the narrator follows up the exploration of violence and private property with the conclusion that "identity is imagined." Herein lies the major difference, though. We saw that Andrew's identity as "white" required him to *forget* the social forces which produced "whiteness" and a "white" nation through the degradation and oppression of women and people of color.[31] When Rutherford encounters the machinery of the slave trade, he responds to the knowledge that he is complicit in the business of trafficking in slaves with more vigor, more attention to the potential utility of violence, and more of a sense of the need to misserve the oppressive social order in whatever small

way his act of writing is capable of doing, and his writing is effective primarily insofar as it demonstrates how all identities are imagined, that there is no single controlling identity beyond imagination, some identity without "race" or "ethnicity" or
"gender," some identity like "whiteness" which has been naturalized or rendered
ahistorical and beyond analytical excavation. While Andrew provides a case study in
how empowered subjects forget the processes through which social forces create
identities, Rutherford uses the literary form of the slave narrative to display the mobilization of an oppressive racial formation and thereby demonstrate the play of social forces in the construction of all identities, including "whiteness."

Rutherford establishes a genealogy of whiteness and explores how race is recreated by those who construct their identities in a process that limits the freedom of
others to construct theirs. In the process, Johnson revisits some of his earlier statements on appropriation and universality. The ship's captain, Ebenezer Falcon, is the
representative figure here as he attempts to construct his identity through an appropriative gesture. Falcon tells Rutherford that because he (Falcon) is not among the
financier class, then, "he, at bottom, was no freer than the Africans" who are in the
hold of the ship of which he is captain (147). Either Falcon is lying or he has forgot-
ten a great deal about the social forces that have elevated him to the position of
power he occupies. Rutherford's task is to write a history that does not condone that
act of amnesia or dishonesty but shows the development of Falcon's identity, the
identity of the "white" nation he represents, and the concomitant limitations he and
the nation place on those whose identities are not "white." Early on, Rutherford
makes the link between Falcon, the captain of the *Republic,* and the national imperatives of Manifest Destiny. The "nation was but a few hours old when Ebenezer Falcon was born, its pulpits and work places and pubs buzzing with talk of what the
new social order should be" (49). Not only does his birth coincide with that of the
republic, but his actions replicate those of the nation. We are told that Falcon is "like
the fledgling republic itself" in his sense of imperialism, feeling "expansive, eager to
push back frontiers, even to slide betimes into bullying others and taking, if need
be, what was not offered" (50). This imperialism slides into colonialism, especially
in Falcon's belief that there is an intimate connection between "the manifest destiny
of the United States to Americanize the entire planet" (30) and the maintaining of a
social order that respects a "Western civilization" it constructs and defines against
whatever cultural practices and values did not originate with, or were not fully appropriated by, "American racial Anglo-Saxonism."[32]

When Falcon is dying and dreams of the "last hour of history," his nightmare is
about the decline of "the civilized values and visions of high culture"—a decline pre-
cipitated by an influx of "Mudmen and Jews," the "rise of Aztec religion and voodoo as
credible spiritual practices for some," and the spectacle of "Yellow men buying up half
of America" (144–45). His fear is that "whole generations of white children" will be
"strangers, if not slaves, in their own country" (145). Like other conservatives and
neoconservatives who share this vision of the decline of Western civilization in the
United States, Falcon traces the problem partially to the specter of affirmative action
programs, arguing that the problem with the country is that "everyone's ready to lower
standards of excellence to make up for slavery, or discrimination" (32). Like those
neoconservatives Johnson is rightly mocking here, Falcon works with the assumption

that "standards of excellence" are removed from the contested space of their construction, that they are eternal, enduring, and not constructed to serve and maintain a specific hegemonic practice. Put less abstractly, what Falcon means by "standards of excellence" is precisely those standards historically developed by denying certain cultural practices belonging to peoples who are not participants in the project of American racial Anglo-Saxonism, those "Mudmen," Jewish, Native, African, and Asian peoples whose cultural practices have been either denied or appropriated.

Those "standards," of course, are historically created at the same time and in tandem with the creation of racial categories, especially in that era when the United States was "pushing back frontiers," "bullying others," and "taking what was not offered." In the course of the colonial encounters with Native Americans over land and the production of a set of legal statutes defining the labor status of African Americans, English colonists in the United States created racial categories which they then used to justify their exploitation and destruction of Native land and African bodies by consigning the "owners" of those lands and bodies to "races" of "an inferior, lesser human status." When the English settlers first encountered Native Americans, for example, they developed a rationale for their "bullying" imperialism and a justification for their rapacious desire for the land the Native Americans inhabited. Arguing that the Native peoples were improvident for failing to husband more productively the resources God had provided, the English settlers felt no compunction about taking those resources. As a rationalization of that act of imperialism, and as a result of it, they were able to locate and define what they perceived as racial differences, seeing themselves as "hard-working" and the Native peoples as "idle." From an imperialist imperative arose concepts of labor which then emerged as racial difference. "Work and whiteness joined in the argument for dispossession" as the settlers began to conceive of themselves as "hardworking whites."[33] It was from such encounters, predicated on imbalances in material power and confusion over cultural imperatives, that "standards" were developed and naturalized.

In the case of Falcon's comments about "standards of excellence"—and likewise in the case of those who attempt to repeal affirmative action policies by using the same weak-minded reasoning and rhetoric—what those "standards" do, first and foremost, is create a sense of identity based on exclusionary practices. This identity whose source one attempts to forget is a result of power masquerading itself as something else. Like Andrew in *Oxherding Tale*, Falcon has to forget the social forces that created his identity in order for him to maintain the imperiousness of that identity. He has to forget that he is stealing slaves from West Africa in order to claim that he is no "freer" than them. He has to forget how the colonizing enterprise historically developed his identity as a "white man" by defining a set of behaviors and ascribing them to peoples of color. In order to fear the enslavement of future generations of "white children" in "their own country," Falcon has to forget that he and those future white generations came into possession of this country through a concerted series of murderous exploitations of the original people of color inhabiting this country and plundered the natural resources of this land through the slave labor of people of African descent. In other words, he has to forget the very moment and the very series of imperialist activities through which the term "white" emerged as a meaningful marker of identity.

To some extent, Falcon is right to point out that he is merely a member of the professional–managerial class, a middleman between those financing the ship and the proletariat working it. He sails around the world on an imperialist enterprise collecting "plunder from every culture conceivable" in service to the class financing his enterprise—capital (48–49). Yet Falcon is not simply an actor under the command of others, an "effect" of the system beyond responsibility and judgment for these exploits. He is both beneficiary and agent in them. More important, he realizes that these acts of cultural appropriation are precisely the strategy by which to maintain the social order in which "whiteness" remains hegemonic. Therefore, on his own initiative and for his own gain and place in history, he steals the most remarkable "plunder" and the one representative of all the rest—the God of the Allmuseri. By stealing the very God of a culture, Falcon has performed the ultimate act of cultural appropriation. In doing so, he not only becomes a violating presence in that culture—"Centuries would pass whilst the Allmuseri lived through the consequences of what he had set in motion" (144)—but he also embarks on his own imperialist project: to establish the "personal empire he had dreamed of since the Revolution" (103). For Falcon, but not only Falcon, acts of cultural appropriation provide both the material resources for empire building and the psychic resources for his identity as a "white man."

In giving us this genealogy of whiteness based on a historical ideology ("manifest destiny") and a set of material practices (cultural theft), Johnson not only demonstrates how acts of appropriation develop "standards" at the same time as they create and re-create racial categories, but he also seems to suggest how those historical acts have troubled the concept of "universality." While not going nearly so far as Harold Cruse, who argued that "universality" and the "white standard in art and aesthetics" on which universality is predicated are products of "racial exclusion, racial exploitation, racial segregation and all the manifestations of the ideology of white superiority," Johnson's exploration of how "standards of excellence" are always constructed within and serve specific historical moments and political hegemons does raise questions about the "universality" he had espoused more explicitly in *Oxherding Tale*. After all, in *Middle Passage* Johnson dwells on the *differences* between those who are captains of and stowaways on the *Republic*. Rutherford is a thief of "experiences" because he feels disinherited from Western civilization, Falcon a preserver of that civilization he considers his heritage because he is a thief of people and their cultural experiences. So, too, in the field of cultural production, Falcon writes a master text aimed at justifying human immiseration and validating manifest destiny, while Rutherford produces a slave narrative contesting the economic order within which the enterprise of slaving occurs and challenging the construction of whiteness on which manifest destiny is based. Because they are differently empowered and differently situated in the social order, Rutherford and Falcon employ different representational strategies, one implicitly presupposing the naturalness of white identity and standards, the other explicitly undertaking a historical excavation of all identities and standards. While this difference does not render universality impossible, although certainly problematic, it suggests that any project striving to highlight shared properties among peoples also needs to work through the differences, particularly the differences in power.[34]

When Johnson examines the conditions of power in his second Neo-slave narrative, he very clearly diagnoses both the process by which cultural appropriation works and the operative value it serves to the empowered cultural imperialists who perform such acts. He works into the fabric of his novel a socialist sensibility about property, a tentative regard for the value of the threat of violence against an empowered hegemonic class, and a sense of how identity is imagined and mis-imagined within a capitalist world order. What gives this novel a strength of insight which the earlier did not possess in the same degree is that Johnson examines these factors within the context of systemic power structures. In doing so, in showing us how a capitalist system produces a social order destructive of human sociability, he also revisits and revises some of the political arguments Andrew had made in *Oxherding Tale*. Whereas Andrew maintained a belief in a radical sense of self-responsibility premised on an understanding of autonomous subjective existence, Rutherford recognizes that a capitalist social order produces class stratifications that do not permit for philosophies in which individuals are wholly responsible for which determinants will impinge on their lives. For that reason, his sense of what constitutes personal identity also differs from Andrew's. That does not mean that Johnson is posing a more reified sense of race or identity in *Middle Passage* than he had in *Oxherding Tale*, for he is not.

What he is doing is working with a sense of "difference" that is not in isolation from the social forces that produce race and racial difference. To employ a phrase Teresa Ebert uses, we can say that Johnson is engaging in a "postmodern analytics of difference." Whereas Andrew was unable or unwilling to discern those social forces that permitted him to assume an identity as a "white" man, Rutherford examines how "whiteness" was constructed, explores the forms of violence through which it came into power, and analyzes the acts of cultural appropriation with which it maintains its hegemony. Yet Rutherford is not thereby rendered any less sympathetic to how, as Johnson says elsewhere, identity is a "process" and a "tissue of very often contradictory things." Nor is the political vision Johnson presents in this novel based on the outmoded notions of "race" he has accused some multiculturalists of misusing. In this novel, race is contingent, a product largely of historical forces and the ongoing struggle between dominant and emergent racial formations. The All-museri, for instance, are "less a biological tribe than a clan held together by values" (109). Although Rutherford speculates that his brother Jackson might be from their tribe, he does not consider himself to be. Likewise, not every white person in this novel is bound to suffering the same burden as Falcon. Josiah Squib, the ship's cook, undergoes a transformation so thorough that he is rendered no longer "white" but rather truly multicultural. Rutherford looks at him toward the end of their travels and senses "perfectly balanced crosscurrents of culture in him, each a pool of possibilities from which he was unconsiously drawing, moment by moment, to solve whatever problem was at hand" (176). Josiah's sea change is made possible because he exists in a different set of social relations since the rebellion aboard the *Republic*, a historic event described as a "change not in the roles on ship but a revolution in its very premises" (126). Race, then, is shown to be "an illusion," not an essential given of identity but a manifestation of political arrangements within the social order and intellectual engagements in the public sphere.[35]

In both his Neo-slave narratives, Johnson shows us the ways race "figures into how we give form, in literature and life, to our experience," not because race is the biological determinant of that experience but because it provides what Johnson calls a "structure of perception."[36] In his first Neo-slave narrative, Johnson cast the history of slavery into phenomenological terms, examining how personal experience relates to communal, how intersubjective relations can promote less alienating connections among social agents. Cast into the form of a *bildungsroman* and a novel of passing, *Oxherding Tale* is ultimately about the achievement of a "first-person viewpoint" that is simultaneously "universal." Part of the cost of that achievement was that Andrew had to downplay the structural forces that create the social inequities making "universality" impossible, while at the same time proposing it as desirable. In his second Neo-slave narrative, Johnson looks at history in political terms, examining how personal experience is derived from the economic structures that produce a sense of alienation within and between human beings. Taking a document that begins as a captain's log recording the purchase of slaves, Rutherford inscribes into its fabric his own autobiography and, more briefly, the biography of Ebenezer Falcon. Here we find together the life of a black slave who defines himself by his revolts against being colonized and the life of a white captain of fortune who defines himself by his traffick in black slaves and his imperialist designs. By casting these two lives together, Rutherford manages to frame and produce a history that excavates the history and the prehistory of the economic systems governing social relations and regulating the identities we are permitted to imagine within them. The difference between the two narrators is figured in the difference between the two forms in which they present their autobiographical identities. Andrew writes a narrative of passing and achieves his dubious white identity at the end of *Oxherding Tale* by forgetting the social forces operatively producing the conditions in which others are enslaved and otherwise oppressed. Rutherford writes a narrative critical of capitalism and assumes his affirmed (and yet evolving) identity at the end of *Middle Passage* by describing and critiquing those same social forces. We are shown how Andrew conserves the social order by denying or failing to recall the violent forces subscribing it, while Rutherford misserves the order by comprehending and exposing and contesting them.

8

Conclusion

By the end of the 1980s, a large and distinctive body of writing about American chattel slavery had appeared in the form of both historical representations emphasizing the material conditions in the lives of slaves, the healthy legacy of slave cultures, and the infrapolitics of slave resistance; and in fictional works carefully and painstakingly tracing the courage, love, and anxieties of enslaved men, women, and communities. Taken as a whole, these works constitute critical reassessments of a previous generation's historical explorations of slavery and also exemplary expressions of the "creative practice" Raymond Williams describes as part of the active struggle "at the roots of the mind," confronting "a hegemony in the fibres of the self" by reproducing, embodying, and performing "hitherto excluded and subordinated experiences and relationships" in order to articulate and help form "latent, momentary, and newly possible consciousness." The "artistic impulse to revisit this ineffable, sublime terror" of slavery, to evoke the "conspicuous power of the slave sublime," is a critical and a creative practice, simultaneously showing how racial indenture is an "*internal* component of Western civilization," exposing "capitalism with its clothes off," while at the same time demonstrating the "hidden transcripts" of resistance to be found in those subordinated experiences of enslaved peoples.[1] The body of African American writing about slaves and slavery from the sixties to the nineties has served to mark and mobilize the transition from a previous generation's shame that many black Americans testified to feeling about their slave heritage to the Black Power pride they gained when they recognized the humanity and dignity of their enslaved ancestors. Indeed, a prominent feature of the African American "subaltern public sphere" has been its insistence on wedding the memory of slavery to the emergence of a new black cultural identity constantly reinvented and reconstructed as a "sense of ethnic consciousness and pride in our heritage of resistance against racism," a "cultural and ethnic awareness" collectively constructed over "hundreds of years."[2]

The narratives of slavery participate in an intellectual moment when American social groups have undertaken a concerted effort to reorganize their separate and imbricated pasts, to develop a heightened sensitivity to the individual strands of a multicultural tapestry, and to publish a series of fictions, autobiographies, and testimonies about how that ethnic past constituted a stable but malleable group identity. Texts about "the invention of ethnicity"—texts that represent the processes by and through which individual and collective minority identities are constructed and reconstructed—constitute what one critic calls "productive forces in nation-building enterprises." Given the cultural and social work these texts perform, it is crucial for us to reconsider the function of form. Rather than returning to a facile formalism in which form is considered a product of aesthetic imperatives, we need to consider how "issues of power, political struggle and cultural identity are inscribed within the formal structures of texts," to recognize that form is not extrinsic to historical understanding but rather constitutive of it; because the past is "regenerated within the contemporary forms through which its story is told."[3]

The authors of the Neo-slave narratives were self-consciously aware of the cultural and social importance of form. Ishmael Reed demonstrated how literary forms had their specific political valency in a racialized state; Sherley Anne Williams dwelt at length on the concrete ways literary forms are derived from the state's political relations while inhabiting and shaping forms of personal interaction; Charles Johnson showed how the manipulation of literary form either facilitates or exposes certain kinds of exploitative social identities and economic relationships. They were concerned with the cultural origins of the form in which they wrote, the slave narrative, and equally concerned with the social origins of the contemporary reconfiguration of that form, the Neo-slave narrative—the importance of one as the first expression of the political desires and social identity of people of African descent in the New World and its significance as the contested terrain between abolitionists and fugitive slaves; the importance of the other as the most recent expression of the political aspirations and social subjectivity of African American people after Black Power and its significance as the site of dialogue and debate in the field of cultural production.

They were also conscious of the potential in the Neo-slave narrative form they were adopting, since it was both history-laden (it "whistles and hums with th[e] history" of its origins while it accumulates new meanings "as the form evolves") and present-minded ("moving the form forward" through the writer's "own interpretation of possibilities made real by this historical moment").[4] Since the Neo-slave narratives are fully engaged in a dialogue with both the moment of their formal origin and the moment of their production, the best way to appreciate the deep complexity of their formal innovations, the nuanced subtlety of their cultural allusiveness, and the political import of their representational strategies is to explore how the authors collectively revisit the moment of origin for the Neo-slave narrative in the sixties while also engaging in dialogue with the contemporary politics of the seventies and eighties, attending especially to their interventions in the different intellectual formations on the historical representation of slavery, on issues of cultural appropriation, and on the topic of social identity.

When the Neo-slave narratives appeared in the seventies and eighties, they were mobilized by the discourse on slavery that had emerged in the sixties on the contested terrain between consensus and New Left social history. This discourse had emphasized slave culture and slave community by seeing slaves as "subjects in their own rights rather than simply as objects of white oppression," while producing portraits of a slave personality largely constructed against what Robin Kelley calls the "Cult of True Sambohood." By the mid-eighties, American historians began to challenge the hegemony of this historiographical portrait, noting that while the historians who destroyed the "myth that slaves were depersonalized Samboes" performed "an extremely valuable service," there was still a "real danger" in denying or downplaying "the injury slavery caused its victims." Attending to the "poverty of tragedy in historical writing on Southern slavery," they suggested that it is time "to begin the inevitable process of reevaluating the nature and role of the antebellum slave community" as a means of dismantling the quickly growing countermyth of the "idyllic slave community." Satisfied with neither the one-dimensional portrait of dehumanized slaves nor the antithetical representation of superheroically resistant rebels, historians began to "recreate the tragedy of slavery from the slaves' perspectives." In the age of Reagan, a decade marked by "half-hearted commitment to social justice" amid widespread and systemic immiseration, historians thought they would do well "to have a variety of reenactments of the tragedy of slavery, and not just take the tragedy for granted."[5]

The Neo-slave narratives had anticipated this historical trend by generating stories about both triumph and tribulation, about powerful acts of resistance and equally powerful forces of dehumanization. Rebels like Raven and Robin had to overcome a colonized mentality that could create a Cato the Graffado. Dessa takes flight and creates a community, but her body is scarred and horribly mutilated. Andrew's life of an educated mind and a sexually satisfied body is countered by his father's murder and Minty's grotesque bodily dissolution. In *Middle Passage*, the author who noted that stories of people "killing their kids to save them from slavery" were still rooted in the "sixties" had an Allmuseri woman throw her baby overboard to save it from captivity.[6] The Neo-slave narratives, then, were mobilized by the emergent discourse on slavery, but they were also critical of any tendencies to negate the pain and pervasiveness of slavery.

Likewise, the moment of origin for the Neo-slave narratives had a quite different sensibility about cultural appropriation than did the decades when the novels appeared. Whereas the debate over Styron's *Confessions* had produced a fairly widespread consensus about the definition and meaning of a white author's appropriations of black cultural practices and texts, the eighties began to complicate the relationships between social identities and cultural productions. Multiculturalist models and theories emphasized the blurring of boundaries between mainstream and subcultural traditions, the interdependencies and border crossings of all cultural activities, claiming that "the history of all cultures is the history of cultural borrowing," without necessarily attending with sufficient care to the fact that the history of all cultures is also the history of different social groups' unequal access to power.[7] Again, the Neo-slave narratives' intervention into this debate anticipates the newer intellectual developments, as the authors construct texts that value intercultural sharing and demonstrate the hybridity of both literary forms and social identities while also showing that not all individuals affiliated with specific racial groups are equal sharers in this multicultural feast. While Raven, Dessa, Andrew, and Rutherford actively borrow from cultural practices associated with Europe, North America,

Africa, and Asia, they also realize that there are Yankee Jacks, Adam Nehemiahs, Horace Bannons, and Ebenezer Falcons still profiting from the inequities in access to the cultural apparatus of the states whose tastes they dictate.

It is when the Neo-slave narratives take up the topic of social identity that we best see how fruitfully they negotiate the two historical moments from which they emerge and in which they circulate—the Black Power movement of the late sixties and the neoconservative and right-wing backlash to it in the seventies and eighties—and can appreciate how they criticize both intellectual moments on shared but differently motivated ideas about race and history. Many Black Power advocates eschewed a subject position that accepted the "presence of a multicultural synchronicity in a variety of subjects" and instead actively sought the "psychic protections of essentialism," in this case a black essentialism organized around a sense of absolute racial difference and premised on gestures of inter- and intraracial exclusion. Going so far as to declare people of African descent a "different *species*," Amiri Baraka, for instance, argues that racial difference defines not only emotional responsiveness ("Race is feeling," he writes) but also intellectual processes ("If we *feel* differently, we have different *ideas*"). Black Power advocates not only insisted on that sense of racial solidarity but in fact produced and rearticulated that "new consciousness of Blackness" by repeatedly drawing attention to the "social division within the black populace," attempting to establish a positive black subjectivity "not on any sense of inclusiveness with respect to the black community" but rather by producing a "negative foil" in "intraracial division."[8] At the same time, some Black Power advocates established their program of action often by devaluing, sometimes by dismissing, black political and cultural formations of the past, thereby denying the possibility for configuring the new black subject as a social entity emerging from a specific, complex, and hybrid history.

Just as the Black Power movement had politicized black identity and rearticulated black collective subjectivity, redefining the *"meaning of racial identity,* and consequently of race *itself,* in American society," so did the neoconservative backlash mark a crisis in white identity and represent an attempt to "reassert the very meaning of *whiteness*" that had been "rendered unstable and unclear by the minority challenges of the 1960s." Neoconservative intellectuals performed this feat by denying history—or, better, by affecting a highly selective form of nostalgia about historical forces—and rearticulating white identity through a coded racial discourse. In response to the collective subjectivity of Black Power, neoconservatives argued for a so-called "color-blind society" in which only individuals and not collective subjects suffer discrimination, in which opportunity, and equality, and equality of opportunity are available to all, thereby hiding the structural inequities that in fact define "color" in this society. History was also given short shrift. In his paradigmatic 1975 diatribe against affirmative action, Nathan Glazer complains that because "we *now* attach benefits and penalties to individuals simply on the basis of their race, color, and national origins," we are abandoning the "first principles of a liberal society" (my italics).[9] Born of Nixon's "southern strategy" in the late sixties, consolidated in the international economic and national racial crises of the seventies, and emerging as a dominant political idea in the Reagan-Bush era in the eighties, the neoconservative and right-wing agendas of racialized practice in coded language constitute a hegemonic racial formation in which the inequities of present social relations are suppressed and the long history through which those social relations were created and instated is denied.

The Neo-slave narratives take up the issues raised by both the Black Power movement and the neoconservative backlash. In the topics they raise, the narratives they generate, and especially in the form they adopt, the Neo-slave narratives emphasize the historical legacy of slavery, not in the facile sense that we associate with the Moynihan Report (that slavery directly led to present social conditions), but in the sense of unveiling past and ongoing strategies of racial stratification, by showing how a state's cultural apparatus and political machinery create racial categories in the process of defining the differences between those who appropriate labor and those whose physical and intellectual labor is appropriated. They question that neoconservative "now" by showing us just what the first principles of this particular liberal society were in the course of its formation, at the same time as they define how contemporary practices draw on and rearticulate those first principles of a society founded on slavery. Not only do they challenge the silence and amnesia that historically attended and continues to sustain the belief in "whiteness" as that "unmarked category against which difference is constructed," but they also critique the Black Power idea of an essential black subject created by fiat, sustained by social divisions, and freed of its historical moorings.[10] Whether it is by emphasizing that all racial roles are performed or by revealing the economic and social practices subtending the historical formation of all racial subjectivities, the authors of the Neo-slave narratives firmly reject the essentialism and ahistoricism of Black Power and neoconservative intellectuals, and work to reveal the structural mechanisms that historically created and daily re-create "race" in America.

This, then, is the social logic of the literary form of the Neo-slave narrative. Emerging from a specific social crisis of historical and cultural representation, the novels assuming this form have engaged in dialogue with both their moment of formal origin in the Black Power movement and their moment of production in the post–civil rights era. Involved in a discontinuous intertextual relationship with both the prototype of the Neo-slave narrative form and the social movement out of which that prototype developed, the Neo-slave narratives are themselves also discontinuous in their play with voice and their insistence on intersubjectivity. I have so far noted but not dwelt on the fact that all the Neo-slave narratives are ambiguously first-person narrations. In each case, the author undermines the coherent subject of narration by developing a series of other voices which sometimes supplement and sometimes subvert the voice of the "original" narrator. Raven's voice gives way to a third-person narrator as the story he tells becomes both his and Robin's; Dessa assumes her voice only at the end of the fifth section of a novel that becomes almost as choral as it is oral; Andrew's text is interrupted by metafictional chapters theorizing the processes of the narrative he is writing; and Rutherford's narrative, like his identity, is a patchwork of others' writings, ideas, and lives. The play with voices alerts us to the fact that each of these novelists is developing an intersubjective model for the construction of subjectivity; in each case, the narrating subject is not an autonomous individual but part of a communal, collective whole.[11] This strategy also forms a response to Styron's novel, which had assumed a consistent and untroubled first-person narration. By showing the discontinuity in the subjects of slavery, the three novelists show Styron his inaccuracy and presumption in producing a coherent slave subject. At the same time, they are also responding to the political premise of individualism in Styron's representation of Nat Turner and the cultural politics that underwrote this premise.

In his discussion of the shaping of a canon of American literature from 1960 to 1975, Richard Ohmann has shown that the needs and values of the professional–managerial class permeate the "general form," the "categories of understanding," and the "means of representation" of those American novels that potentially have a chance of being included in some eventual canon. An important "premise of this fiction—nothing new to American literature but particularly salient in this period— is that individual consciousness, not the social or historical field, is the locus of significant happening," and the prominent feature of that individualism is the "pursuit of a unique and personal voice." Indeed, Ohmann concludes that the "premise of individualism" is one of the "root elements of the dominant ideology" in this period. Styron's novel actively presents itself as a novel in pursuit of a "unique and personal voice" as it is generated by a narrator with a keen sense of individualism. Styron noted in an interview that Nat Turner was "one of the few slaves in history who achieved an identity." Styron's Turner certainly revels in that identity, and unquestioningly celebrates the individualism on which it is premised. Not only does he eschew the slave community from which he is alienated and despise any communal activity; but he also self-consciously articulates his absolute individualism: "I shiver feverishly in the glory of self."[12]

The Neo-slave narratives contest this premise of individualism and challenge the singular voice in which it is articulated. Reading with more attention and care than had Styron the slave narratives whose form and conventions they adopt, these novelists dwell more on the communal subject positions of the antebellum slave narrators. With more respect for the engima of the station of those people whose voices they assume, they create imaginative fictions about cultural practices like spiritual possession and blues communion, and philosophical concepts like phenomenological dialogue, in order to represent and endorse forms of intersubjective communication in which rugged and autonomous individualism is rendered suspect and reactionary. The four Neo-slave narratives written in the seventies and eighties produce communal voices that capture the best spirit of the social movements of the sixties while resisting the extreme version of individualism the author of their formal prototype endorsed. It is but one more means by which they contest the dictates of master texts and recall the social origins of contemporary African American subjectivity.

Notes

1. Master Texts and Slave Narratives

1. My use of "Neo-slave narrative" in indebted to Bernard Bell, who invented the term, although my definition of a "Neo-slave narrative" differs from his of a "neoslave narrative." See Bernard W. Bell, *The Afro-American Novel and Its Tradition* (1987; Amherst: U of Massachusetts P, 1989) 289; and Ashraf H. A. Rushdy, "Neo-Slave Narrative," in *The Oxford Companion to African American Literature,* ed. William L. Andrews, Trudier Harris, and Frances Smith Foster (New York: Oxford UP, 1997) 533–35.

2. The thirties saw the first concerted collection of materials pertaining to slavery, the slave experience, and slave resistance. The director of the Carnegie Institution initiated two massive multivolume documentary research projects on slavery: Elizabeth Donnan's *Documents Illustrative of the History of the Slave Trade to America* (1930–1935) and Helen T. Catterall's *Judicial Cases Concerning American Slavery and the Negro* (1926–1937). Between 1927 and 1938, scholars and government employees, first at historically black colleges and then through the Works Project Administration, collected interviews with former slaves. Also, throughout the thirties historians and social activists produced numerous studies of slave rebelliousness. See August Meier and Elliott Rudwick, *Black History and the Historical Profession, 1915–1980* (Urbana: U of Illinois P, 1986) 29–30. On the collection of slave testimony, see Norman R. Yetman, "The Background of the Slave Narrative Collection," *American Quarterly* 19.3 (Fall 1967): 534–53; Paul D. Escott, *Slavery Remembered: A Record of Twentieth-Century Slave Narratives* (Chapel Hill: U of North Carolina P, 1979) 3–17; Jerre Mangione, *The Dream and the Deal: The Federal Writers' Project, 1935–1943* (New York: Avon, 1972) 263–65; and *God Struck Me Dead: Voices of Ex-Slaves,* ed. Clifton H. Johnson (1969; Cleveland: Pilgrim, 1993) vii–xxix. For contemporary studies of slave resistance, see L. D. Reddick, "A New Interpretation for Negro History," *Journal of Negro History* 22.1 (1937): 17–28; Harvey Wish, "American Slave Insurrections Before 1861," *Journal of Negro History* 22.3 (1937): 299–320; Herbert Aptheker, "American Negro Slave Revolts," *Science and Society* 1 (1937): 512–38; Aptheker, "More on American Negro Slave Revolts," *Science and Society* 2 (1938): 386–91; Joseph C. Carroll, *Slave Insurrections in the United States, 1800–1865* (Boston: Chapman and Grimes, 1938); Raymond A. Baur and Alice H. Bauer, "Day to Day Resistance to Slavery," *Journal of Negro History* 27.4 (1942): 388–419; Hollie E. Carter, *Negro Insurrections in American History, 1639–1860* (M.A., Howard University, 1936); Stanley Rappaport, "Slave Struggles for

Freedom," *Crisis* 43 (1936): 264–65, 274, 284–86; Charles A. Dinsmore, "Interesting Sketches of the *Amistad Captives,*" *Yale U Library Gazette* 9 (1935): 51–55; Elizabeth Lawson, "After Nat Turner's Revolt," New York *Daily Worker,* August 21, 1936; Percy Waxman, *The Black Napoleon: The Story of Toussaint Louverture* (New York: Harcourt, Brace, 1931); C. L. R. James, *The Black Jacobins: Toussaint L'Overture and the San Domingo Revolution* (New York: Dial, 1938); and James, *A History of Negro Revolt* (London: Fact Limited, 1938). For a superb study of the historical fiction about slavery to emerge from the 1930s, see Hazel V. Carby, "Ideologies of Black Folk: The Historical Novel of Slavery," in *Slavery and the Literary Imagination,* ed. Deborah E. McDowell and Arnold Rampersad (Baltimore: Johns Hopkins UP, 1989) 125–43.

3. Martin Kilson, "The New Black Intellectuals," in *Legacy of Dissent: 40 Years of Writing from* Dissent *Magazine,* ed. Nicolaus Mills (New York: Simon & Schuster, 1994) 249–58.

4. Charles Johnson, *Oxherding Tale* (New York: Grove, 1982) 119.

5. Peter Collier and David Horowitz, *Destructive Generation: Second Thoughts About the Sixties* (1989; New York: Summit Books, 1990) 15, 243.

6. John Lowe, "An Interview with Ernest Gaines," in *Conversations with Ernest Gaines,* ed. Lowe (Jackson: UP of Mississippi, 1995) 316–17.

7. African American writers working within the New Black Aesthetic in the sixties generally experimented with "new forms" and broke down "demarcations between the genres and modes of expression." See Gloria T. Hull, "Notes on a Marxist Interpretation of Black American Literature," *Black American Literature Forum* 12.4 (1978): 152; Joe Weixlmann, "The Changing Shape(s) of the Contemporary Afro-American Novel," in *Studies in Black American Literature: Volume I: Black American Prose Theory,* ed. Weixlmann and Chester J. Fontenot (Greenwood, FL: Penkevill, 1984) 112, 116; John M. Reilly, "The Reconstruction of Genre as Entry into Conscious History," *Black American Literature Forum* 13.1 (1979): 3–6; Reilly, "History-Making Literature," in *Studies in Black American Literature: Volume II: Belief vs. Theory in Black American Literary Criticism* ed. Weixlmann and Fontenot (Greenwood, FL: Penkevill, 1986) 85–120; Jervis Anderson, "Black Writing: The Other Side," *Dissent* 15 (1968): 236, 238; Keith Byerman, "Remembering History in Contemporary Black Literature and Criticism," *American Literary History* 3.4 (1991): 809–16; Barbara Foley, "History, Fiction, and the Ground Between: The Uses of the Documentary Mode in Black Literature," *PMLA* 95.3 (1980): 389–403; and Foley, *Telling the Truth: The Theory and Practice of Documentary Fiction* (Ithaca, NY: Cornell UP, 1986) 233–64.

8. Michael Omi and Howard Winant, *Racial Formation in the United States from the 1960s to the 1980s* (New York: Routledge, 1986) 2.

9. Fredric Jameson, "Periodizing the 60s," in *The 60s Without Apology,* ed. Sohnya Sayres, Anders Stephanson, Stanley Aronowitz, and Jameson (Minneapolis: U of Minnesota P, 1984) 181, 193. For other discussions of the emergence of minority subjectivity in the sixties, see Michele Wallace, "Reading 1968 and the Great American Whitewash," in *Remaking History,* ed. Barbara Kruger and Phil Mariani (Seattle: Bay Press, 1989) 97–109; and Kobena Mercer, "'1968': Periodizing Politics and Identity," in *Cultural Studies,* ed. Lawrence Grossberg, Cary Nelson, and Paula Treichler (New York: Routledge, 1992) 424–38.

10. Pierre Bourdieu, *The Field of Cultural Production: Essays on Art and Literature,* ed. Randal Johnson (New York: Columbia UP, 1993) 162, 163, 163–64, 43, 141, 184–85, 164.

11. Bourdieu, *The Field of Cultural Production* 180.

12. Bourdieu, *The Field of Cultural Production* 33–4.

13. Bourdieu, *The Field of Cultural Production* 181. Bourdieu, *In Other Words: Essays Towards a Reflexive Sociology,* trans. Matthew Adamson (Stanford: Stanford UP, 1990) 147.

14. Abdul J. JanMohamed, "Humanism and Minority Literature: Toward a Definition of Counter-hegemonic Discourse," *Boundary 2* 12.3–13.1 (1984): 298.

15. Cf. Carby, *Reconstructing Womanhood: The Emergence of the Afro-American Woman*

Novelist (New York: Oxford UP, 1987); and Ann du Cille, *The Coupling Convention: Sex, Text, and Tradition in Black Women's Fiction* (New York: Oxford UP, 1993) 146–47, 148.

16. Carby, "The Canon: Civil War and Reconstruction," *Michigan Quarterly Review* 28 (1989): 42.

17. Annette Kolodny, "The Integrity of Memory: Creating a New Literary History of the United States," *American Literature* 57.2 (1985): 291, 292. Robert Hemenway, "In the American Canon," in *Redefining American Literature History,* ed. A. LaVonne Brown Ruoff and Jerry W. Ward, Jr. (New York: Modern Language Association, 1990) 62. On the funding of conservative scholarship, see Jon Wiener, *Professor, Politics and Pop* (New York: Verso, 1991) 99–103.

18. Hemenway, "In the American Canon" 65–66. Cf. Dean Flower, "Desegregating the Syllabus," *Hudson Review* (1994): 683–84.

19. "Toni Morrison Interviews John Edgar Wideman," *Imprint,* Canadian Broadcast Corporation, February 22, 1992.

20. Morrison, "Memory, Creation, and Writing," *Thought: A Review of Culture and Idea* 59. 235 (1984): 389. Morrison, "Unspeakable Things Unspoken: The Afro-American Presence in American Literature," *Michigan Quarterly Review* 28.1 (1989): 33, 23. Nellie McKay, "An Interview with Toni Morrison," *Contemporary Literature* 24.4 (1983): 426.

21. Morrison, "Unspeakable Things Unspoken" 9, 8, 9.

22. Cf. Catherine A. McKinnon, *Feminism Unmodified: Discourses on Life and Law* (Cambridge, MA: Harvard UP, 1987) 34, 40. On "difference" and power relations in literary production, see Edward W. Said, "An Ideology of Difference," in *"Race," Writing, and Difference,* ed. Henry Louis Gates, Jr. (Chicago: U of Chicago P, 1986) 38–58; Kwame Anthony Appiah, *In My Father's House: Africa in the Philosophy of Culture* (New York: Oxford UP, 1992) 71–72; Raymond Williams, *Politics and Letters: Interviews with "New Left Review"* (London: New Left Books, 1979) 252; and JanMohamed, "Humanism and Minority Literature" 295.

23. Cornel West, *Keeping Faith: Philosophy and Race in America* (New York: Routledge, 1993) 38, 37, 43, 34. Cf. David Bradley, "Foreword" to William Melvin Kelley, *A Different Drummer* (1962; New York: Doubleday, 1989) xviii.

24. Michael Kammen, *Selvages and Biases: The Fabric of History in American Culture* (Ithaca, NY: Cornell UP, 1987) 104. Cedric Robinson, "Capitalism, Slavery, and Bourgeois Historiography," *History Workshop* 23 (1987): 135, 136.

25. Michel Foucault, in *The Archeology of Knowledge,* trans. A. M. Sheridan Smith (London: Tavistock, 1972) 38, 79–87, 97, 107, 162, defines a "discursive formation" as a system of "statements," the constitutive units of discourse, "neither entirely linguistic, nor exclusively material." A statement becomes a statement only when it is "related to a whole adjacent field." A discursive formation is "the principle of dispersion and redistribution, not of formulations, not of sentences, not of propositions, but of statements." The term "discourse can be defined as the group of statements that belong to a single system of formation." Archaeology, then, is intended to "reveal relations between discursive formations and nondiscursive domains (institutions, political events, economic practices and processes). These *rapprochements* are not intended to uncover great cultural continuities, nor to isolate mechanisms of causality," but rather to try to "determine how the rules of formation that govern it . . . may be linked to non-discursive systems," defining the "specific forms of articulation." Cf. Foucault, *Language, Counter-Memory, Practice: Selected Essays and Interviews,* ed. Donald Bouchard, trans. Bouchard and Sherry Simon (Oxford: Basil Blackwell, 1977) 113–38; and Foucault, *The Order of Things: An Archaeology of the Human Sciences* (1966; New York: Random House, 1970).

26. Julia Kristeva, *Desire in Language: A Semiotic Approach to Literature and Art,* ed. Leon S. Roudiez, trans. Thomas Gora, Alice Jardine, and Roudiez (New York: Columbia UP, 1980) 36–37. Cf. Kristeva, *Revolution in Poetic Language,* ed. Roudiez, trans. Margaret Walker (New York: Columbia UP, 1984) 59–61; and Margaret Waller, "An Interview with Julia Kristeva," in

Intertextuality and Contemporary American Fiction, ed. Patrick O'Donnell and Robert Con Davis (Baltimore: Johns Hopkins UP, 1989) 280–83. Cf. John Mowitt, *Text: The Genealogy of an Antidisciplinary Object* (Durham: Duke UP, 1992) 104–16.

27. Jay Clayton and Eric Rothstein, "Figures in the Corpus: Theories of Influence and Intertextuality," in *Influence and Intertextuality in Literary History,* ed. Clayton and Rothstein (Madison: U of Wisconsin P, 1991) 4–5. Mikhail Bakhtin; qtd. in Gary Saul Morson and Caryl Emerson, *Mikhail Bakhtin: Creation of a Prosaics* (Stanford, CA: Stanford UP, 1990) 51. Susan Stanford Friedman, "Weavings: Intertextuality and the (Re)Birth of the Author," in Clayton and Rothstein, *Influence and Intertextuality in Literary History* 152.

28. Gerald Prince, *A Dictionary of Narratology* (Lincoln: U of Nebraska P, 1987) 46. Cf. A. J. Greimas and J. Courtés, *Semiotics and Language: An Analytical Dictionary,* trans. Larry Crist, Daniel Patte, James Lee, Edward McMahon II, Gary Phillips, and Michael Rengstorf (Bloomington: Indiana UP, 1982) 160–161. Both Prince and Greimas and Courtés note that "intertextuality" can mean the relations between a literary text and a social text, but they also admit that the majority of critics have used the term as part of a "refurbished vocabulary" for dressing up in new clothes the old idea of "influence" studies.

Acts of purely literary intertextuality can be as thoroughly constricted as Gérard Genette's model of "palimpsests," in which intertextuality signifies a relationship between an earlier text and a later one which has visible traces of the earlier one demonstrably present in it; or it can be as mildly constricted as David Cowart's model of "literary symbiosis," in which intertextual relations are more fluid and openly interpretive, an "active, palpable, and formalized act of reading"; or as completely open-ended as Michel Riffaterre's model of "intertextual mimesis," which promises to consider the relationship between an author's "ideolect" and the "sociolect" but nonetheless situates that "sociolect" as an intratextual device. See Genette, *Palimpsestes: La littérature au second degré* (Paris: Editions du Seuil, 1982) 8; cf. Prince, *A Dictionary of Narratology* 46; and Linda Hutcheon, "Literary Borrowing . . . and Stealing: Plagiarism, Sources, Influences, and Intertexts," *English Studies in Canada* 12.2 (1986): 232. Cowart, *Literary Symbiosis: The Reconfigured Text in Twentieth-Century Writing* (Athens: U of Georgia P, 1993) 3, 20. Riffaterre, "Intertextual Representation: On Mimesis as Interpretive Discourse," *Critical Inquiry* 11 (1984): 148, 160; cf. Riffaterre's earlier model of intertextuality based entirely on verbal echoes in "All-Purpose Words: The Case of French Buttons," in *Intertextuality: New Perspectives in Criticism* ed. Jeanine Parisier Plottel and Hanna Charney (New York: New York Literary Forum, 1978) 247–55; and his later model based on psychoanalytical hermeneutics in which intertextuality is a kind of a "mimesis of repression" in "The Intertextual Unconscious," *Critical Inquiry* 13 (1987): 371–85. For other discussions of intertextuality, see Eric Rothstein, "Diversity and Change in Literary Histories," in Clayton and Rothstein, *Influence and Intertextuality in Literary History* 114–45; Tilottama Rajan, "Intertextuality and the Subject of Reading / Writing," in Clayton and Rothstein, *Influence and Intertextuality in Literary History* 61–74; Thaïs Morgan, "The Space of Intertextuality," in O'Donnell and Davis, *Intertextuality and Contemporary American Fiction* 239–79; O'Donnell and Davis, "Introduction: Intertext and Contemporary American Fiction," in *Intertextuality and Contemporary American Fiction* ix–xxii; and Jonathan Culler, *The Pursuit of Signs: Semiotics, Literature, Deconstruction* (London: Routledge & Kegan Paul, 1981) 100–18.

29. Harold Bloom, *The Anxiety of Influence: A Theory of Poetry* (New York: Oxford UP, 1973) 5, 8; cf. Bloom *Agon: Towards a Theory of Revisionism* (New York: Oxford UP, 1982). Sandra M. Gilbert and Susan Gubar, *The Madwoman in the Attic: The Woman Writer and the Nineteenth-Century Literary Imagination* (New Haven, CT: Yale UP, 1979) 74, 49. Gates, *The Signifying Monkey: A Theory of African-American Literary Criticism* (New York: Oxford UP, 1988) 256. Deborah E. McDowell, "'The Changing Same': Generational Connections and Black Women Novelists," *New Literary History* 18.2 (1987): 294–95. Michael Awkward, *In-*

spiriting Influences: Tradition, Revision, and Afro-American Women's Novels (New York: Columbia UP, 1989) 8. Cf. Karla F. C. Holloway, *Moorings and Metaphors: Figures of Culture and Gender in Black Women's Literature* (New Brunswick, NJ: Rutgers UP, 1992). For a notable exception to text-dominated practices of intertextuality, see Mae Gwendolyn Henderson, "Speaking in Tongues: Dialogics, Dialectics, and the Black Woman Writer's Literary Tradition," in *Changing Our Own Words: Essays on Criticism, Theory, and Writing by Black Women,* ed. Cheryl A. Wall (New Brunswick, NJ: Rutgers UP, 1989) 16–37.

30. Williams, *Marxism and Literature* (Oxford: Oxford UP, 1977) 138, 187. Jane Tompkins, *Sensational Designs: The Cultural Work of American Fiction, 1790–1860* (New York: Oxford UP, 1985) xi, xvii, xi. Nancy K. Miller, "Changing the Subject: Authorship, Writing, and the Reader," in *Feminist Studies / Critical Studies,* ed. Teresa de Lauretis (Bloomington: Indiana UP, 1986) 111. Hutcheon, "Historiographic Metafiction: Parody and the Intertextuality of History," in O'Donnell and Davis, *Intertextuality and Contemporary American Fiction* 3–32. Gabrielle Forman, "'By the Help of God and a Good Lawyer': Histotextuality and Subversive Revision in Postbellum Narratives of Slavery" (unpublished paper) 5–6; I would like to thank my friend Gabrielle for kindly giving me a manuscript copy of the paper she delivered at Wesleyan University's "Race and the Production of Culture / Culture and the Production of Race" conference on April 15, 1994. Friedman, "Weavings," 159, 162, 166. Hutcheon, "Historiographic Metafiction" 6. William L. Andrews, "Inter(racial)textuality in Nineteenth-Century Southern Narrative," in Clayton and Rothstein, *Influence and Intertextuality in Literary History* 298–317. Aldon L. Nielsen, *Writing Between the Lines: Race and Intertextuality* (Athens: U of Georgia P, 1994) 11–22.

31. W. Jackson Bate, *The Burden of the Past and the English Poet* (1970; London: Chatto & Windus, 1971) 3. Bloom, *The Anxiety of Influence* 5. Hortense Spillers, "Black, White, and in Color, or Learning How to Paint: Toward an Intramural Protocol of Reading," in *New Historical Literary Study: Essays on Reproducing Texts, Representing History,* ed. Jeffrey N. Cox and Larry J. Reynolds (Princeton, NJ: Princeton UP, 1993) 288. Spillers, "Afterword: Cross-Currents, Discontinuities: Black Women's Fiction," in *Conjuring: Black Women, Fiction, and Literary Tradition,* ed. Marjorie Pryse and Spillers (Bloomington: Indiana UP, 1985) 251. Spillers, "Introduction: Who Cuts the Border?: Some Readings on 'America,'" in *Comparative American Identities: Race, Sex, and Nationality in the Modern Text,* ed. Spillers (New York: Routledge, 1991) 15, 25 (n. 29).

32. Raymond A. Sokolov, "Into the Mind of Nat Turner," *Newsweek* (October 16, 1967): 65. William Styron, *The Confessions of Nat Turner* (New York: New American Literary, 1968) cover. Albert E. Stone, *The Return of Nat Turner: History, Literature, and Cultural Politics in Sixties America* (Athens: U of Georgia P, 1992) 3. I am indebted to my retired but no less valued colleague Richard Ohmann's work for reminding us that behind the "seemingly neutral marketplace" of literary production and reception, the cultural apparatus operates in a way that demonstrates its class values and its relationship to broader struggles in the social order. See Ohmann, *Politics of Letters* (Middletown, CT: Wesleyan UP, 1987) 68–69.

33. Eric Lott, *Love and Theft: Blackface Minstrelsy and the American Working Class* (New York: Oxford UP, 1993) 11.

34. Omi and Winant, "On the Theoretical Status of the Concept of Race," in *Race Identity and Representation in Education,* ed. Cameron McCarthy and Warren Crichlow (New York: Routledge, 1993 6, 9. Ian F. Haney López, "The Social Construction of Race," in *Critical Race Theory: The Cutting Edge,* ed. Richard Delgado (Philadelphia: Temple UP, 1995) 193, 194.

35. Thomas F. Gossett, *Race: The History of an Idea in America* (1963; New York: Schocken, 1965) 370–408. Audrey Smedley, *Race in North America: Origins and Evolution of a Worldview* (Boulder, CO: Westview, 1993) 302. Leslie Spier, "Some Central Elements in the Legacy," *American Anthropological Association Memoirs* 61.89 (1959): 147. Smedley, *Race in North America* 278. Ashley Montagu, *Statement on Race* (3rd ed.; London: Oxford UP, 1972) 9.

36. Omi and Winant, *Racial Formation in the United States* 68, 4, 61. David R. Colburn and George E. Pozzetta, "Race, Ethnicity, and the Evolution of Political Legitimacy," in *The Sixties: From Memory to History,* ed. David Farber (Chapel Hill: U of North Carolina P, 1994) 121. For an interesting and sympathetic critique of Omi and Winant's "racial formation," see E. San Juan, Jr., *Racial Formations / Critical Transformations: Articulations of Power in Ethnic and Racial Studies in the United States* (Atlantic Highlands, NJ: Humanities Press, 1992) 50–54. For other historical studies on the social construction of race, see Oliver Cromwell Cox, *Caste, Class, & Race: A Study in Social Dynamics* (1948; New York: Monthly Review, 1959); Barbara Jeanne Fields, "Slavery, Race and Ideology in the United States of America," *New Left Review* 181 (1990): 95–118; David Roediger, *The Wages of Whiteness: Race and the Making of the American Working Class* (New York: Verso, 1991); and Theodore W. Allen, *The Invention of the White Race: Volume One: Racial Oppression and Social Control* (New York: Verso, 1994).

37. Lucius Outlaw, "Toward a Critical Theory of 'Race,'" in *Anatomy of Racism,* ed. David Theo Goldberg (Minneapolis: U of Minnesota P, 1990) 76–77.

38. Mercer, "'1968': Periodizing Politics and Identity" 430. Winthrop D. Jordan, *White Over Black: American Attitudes Toward the Negro, 1550–1812* (1968; New York: Norton, 1977) 584.

39. Colburn and Pozzetta, "Race, Ethnicity, and the Evolution of Political Legitimacy" 126. William E. Cross, Jr., "The Negro-to-Black Conversion Experience," *Black World* 20.9 (1971): 15. Nathan Jones, "The Deep Center of Blackness," *Black World* 23.2 (1973): 16. John Oliver Killens, *Black Man's Burden* (1965; New York: Pocket Books, 1969) 18–19, 49. John Henrik Clarke, "The Meaning of Black History," *Black World* 20.4 (1971): 31.

40. Orlando Patterson, in "Race and Racism: American Dilemmas Revisited," *Salmagundi* 104–5 (Fall 1994–Winter 1995): 114. Morrison, "Introduction: Friday on the Potomac," in *Race-ing Justice, En-Gendering Power: Essays on Anita Hill, Clarence Thomas, and the Construction of Social Reality,* ed. Morrison (New York: Pantheon, 1992) xxx. Charles P. Henry, "Clarence Thomas and the National Black Identity," in *Court of Appeal: The Black Community Speaks Out on the Racial and Sexual Politics of Thomas vs. Hill,* Ed. Robert Chrisman and Robert L. Allen (New York: Ballantine, 1992) 84. Jim Sleeper; in "Race and Racism: American Dilemmas Revisited" 125. Barbara Fields; in "Race and Racism: American Dilemmas Revisited" 34.

41. Michael M. J. Fischer, "Ethnicity and the Post-Modern Arts of Memory," in *Writing Culture: The Poetics and Politics of Ethnography,* ed. James Clifford and George E. Marcus (Berkeley: U of California P, 1986) 194–95.

42. Susan Stewart, *On Longing: Narratives of the Miniature, the Gigantic, the Souvenir, the Collection* (1984; Durham: Duke UP, 1993) 25, 7.

2. Toward 1968

1. Stephen J. Whitfield, *A Death in the Delta: The Story of Emmett Till* (Baltimore: Johns Hopkins UP, 1988) 9, 60–62.

2. John Higham, *Writing American History: Essays on Modern Scholarship* (Bloomington: Indiana UP, 1970) 146. David Brion Davis, "Slavery and the Post-World War II Historians," in *Slavery, Colonialism, and Racism,* ed. Sidney W. Mintz (New York: Norton, 1974) 1. Kenneth Stampp, *The Peculiar Institution: Slavery in the Ante-Bellum South* (1956; New York: Random House, 1989) 86–140. Stanley M. Elkins, *Slavery: A Problem in American Institutional and Intellectual Life* (1959: Chicago: U of Chicago P, 1976). Stampp, *The Peculiar Institution* 2.

3. *The Kerner Report: The 1968 Report of the National Advisory Commission on Civil Disorders* (1968; New York: Pantheon, 1988). Daniel Walker, *Rights in Conflict: The Violent Confrontation of Demonstrators and Police in the Parks and Streets of Chicago During the Week of the Democratic National Convention of 1968* (New York: New American Library, 1968). Hugh Davis

Graham and Ted Robert Gurr, *The History of Violence in America: A Report Submitted to the National Commission on the Causes and Prevention of Violence* (New York: Bantam, 1969). Allen D. Grimshaw, ed., *Racial Violence in the United States* (Chicago: Aldine, 1969). Thomas Rose, ed., *Violence in America: A Historical and Contemporary Reader* (New York: Random House, 1969). Graham and Gurr, *The History of Violence in America* xiv, xxv.

4. John Henrik Clarke, ed., *William Styron's Nat Turner: Ten Black Writers Respond* (Boston: Beacon, 1968).

5. Graham and Gurr, *The History of Violence in America* xxx. Todd Gitlin, *The Sixties: Years of Hope, Days of Rage* (1987; New York: Bantam, 1993) 85. Charles McDew, "Spiritual and Moral Aspects of the Student Nonviolent Struggle in the South," in *The New Student Left: An Anthology,* ed. Mitchell Cohen and Dennis Hale (1966; Boston: Beacon, 1967) 57. Thomas Kahn, "The Political Significance of the Freedom Rides," in Cohen and Hale, *The New Student Left* 68.

6. I have drawn on several historiographical studies of slavery, including: Carl N. Degler, "Why Historians Change Their Minds," *Pacific Historical Review* 44 (1976): 167–84; Peter Kolchin, "American Historians and Antebellum Southern Slavery 1959–1984," in *A Master's Due: Essays in Honor of David Herbert Donald,* ed. William J. Cooper, Jr., Michael F. Holt, and John McCardell (Baton Rouge: Louisiana State UP, 1985) 87–111; August Meier and Elliott Rudwick, *Black History and the Historical Profession, 1915–1980* (Urbana: U of Illinois P, 1986) 239–76; and Colin Palmer, "Changing Interpretations of Slavery Since World War II," in *Contemporary Black Thought: Alternative Analyses in Social and Behavioral Science,* ed. Molefi Kete Asante and Abdulai S. Vandi (Beverly Hills: Sage Publications, 1980) 233–42.

7. Stampp, *The Peculiar Institution* vii. Eugene D. Genovese, *Roll, Jordan, Roll: The World the Slaves Made* (1974; New York: Vintage, 1976) xv. Staughton Lynd, "Rethinking Slavery and Reconstruction," *Journal of Negro History* 50 (1965): 209, 207, 205, 203.

8. Jonathan Weiner, "Radical Historians and the Crisis in American History, 1959–1980," in *Professor, Politics and Pop* (New York: Verso, 1991) 175–216. Meier and Rudwick, *Black History and the Historical Profession* 274. Genovese, "The Influence of the Black Power Movement on Historical Scholarship: Reflections of a White Historian," in *In Red and Black: Marxian Explorations in Southern and Afro-American History* (1971; Knoxville: U of Tennessee P, 1984) 237. Nicholas Lemann, *The Promised Land: The Great Black Migration and How It Changed America* (New York: Random House, 1991) 177. Albert E. Stone, *The Return of Nat Turner: History, Literature, and Cultural Politics in Sixties America* (Athens: U of Georgia P, 1992) 3.

9. Daniel Bell, *The End of Ideology: On the Exhaustion of Political Ideas in the Fifties* (Glencoe, IL: The Free Press, 1960) 297. Gene Wise, *American Historical Explanations: A Strategy for Grounded Inquiry* (Minneapolis: U of Minnesota P, 1980) 84–85. Peter Novick, *That Noble Dream: The "Objectivity Question" and the American Historical Profession* (Cambridge: Cambridge UP, 1988) 332, 334. Richard Hofstadter, *The American Political Tradition and the Men Who Made It* (1948; New York: Random House, 1989) xxxvi. Bernard Bailyn, "Review of Daniel Boorstin's *The Americans,*" *The New Republic* 139 (December 15, 1958): 18.

10. Bell, *The End of Ideology* 297. Wise, *American Historical Explanations* 241. Michael Kraus and Davis D. Joyce, *The Writing of American History* (1953; rev. ed., Norman: U of Oklahoma P, 1985) 311. Novick, *That Noble Dream* 323. Hofstadter, "Communication," *Journal of the History of Ideas* 25 (1954): 328–29.

11. Hofstadter, "Reading the Constitution Anew," *Commentary* 22 (1956): 270–74. Arthur M. Schlesinger Jr., "Richard Hofstadter," in *Pastmasters: Some Essays on American Historians,* ed. Marcus Cunliffe and Robin W. Winks (New York: Harper & Row, 1969) 289–92. Eric Foner, "Introduction" to Hofstadter, *Social Darwinism in American Thought* (1944; Boston: Beacon, 1992) xxii, xxi. Hofstadter, "Preface" to *The American Political Tradition* xxviii. Hofstadter, *The Progressive Historians: Turner, Beard, Parrington* (New York: Alfred A. Knopf, 1968)

452 (n.). Foner, "Introduction" xxi. Lynd, "Rethinking Slavery and Reconstruction" 203. For Hofstadter's politics and intellectual development, see Susan Stout Baker, *Radical Beginnings: Richard Hofstadter and the 1930s* (Westport, CT: Greenwood, 1985) 79–93, 139–44; Christopher Lasch, "Foreword" to Hofstadter, *The American Political Tradition* vii–xxii; Schlesinger, "Richard Hofstadter" 278–315; and Daniel Joseph Singal, "Beyond Consensus: Richard Hofstadter and American Historiography," *American Historical Review* 89.4 (1984): 976–1004.

12. Stanley Elkins and Eric McKitrick, "Richard Hofstadter: A Progress," in *The Hofstadter Aegis: A Memorial,* ed. Elkins and McKitrick (New York: Alfred A. Knopf, 1974) 310. Lynd, "Rethinking Slavery and Reconstruction" 205. Irwin Unger, "The 'New Left' and American History: Some Recent Trends in United States Historiography," *American Historical Review* 72.4 (1967): 1239. Genovese, "The Influence of the Black Power Movement on Historical Scholarship" 237.

13. Higham, *Writing American History* 146: "a bland history in which conflict is muted, in which classic issues of social justice are underplayed, in which the elements of spontaneity, effervescence and violence in American life get little sympathy or attention." Cf. Higham, "The Cult of the 'American Consensus': Homogenizing Our History," *Commentary* 27 (1959): 93–101. Higham, *History: Professional Scholarship in America* (1965; Baltimore: Johns Hopkins UP, 1989) 228. Genovese, "Problems in the Study of Nineteenth-Century American History," *Science and Society* 25.1 (1961): 42, 47.

14. Elkins, *Slavery* 82.

15. "The Question of 'Sambo': A Report of the Ninth Newberry Library Conference on American Studies," *Newberry Library Bulletin* 5.1 (1958): 32. On the media coverage of the early civil rights movement and the New Left in general, see David J. Garrow, *Bearing the Cross: Martin Luther King, Jr., and the Southern Christian Leadership Conference* (1986; New York: Vintage, 1988) 127–28; and Gitlin, *The Whole World Is Watching: Mass Media in the Making and Unmaking of the New Left* (Berkeley: U of California P, 1980).

16. Weiner, "Radical Historians and the Crisis in American History" 175, 192, 200.

17. Nathan Glazer, "The Differences Among Slaves," *Commentary* 29.5 (1960): 454–58. See W. M. Brewer "[Review of Elkins's *Slavery*]," *Journal of Negro History* 45.2 (1960): 134–35; David Donald, "[Review of Elkins's *Slavery*]," *American Historical Review* 65.4 (1960): 921–22; Robert Gordon, "*Slavery* and the Comparative Study of Social Structures," *American Journal of Sociology* 66.2 (1960): 184–86; John Hope Franklin, "Slavery and Personality: A Fresh Look," *Massachusetts Review* 2.1 (1960): 181–83; Sidney W. Mintz, "[Review of Elkins's *Slavery*]," *American Anthropologist* 63.3 (1961): 579–87; Genovese, ""Problems in the Study of Nineteenth-Century American History"; and Robert Durden, "[Review of Elkins's *Slavery*]," *South Atlantic Quarterly* 60.1 (1961): 94–95.

18. Stanley Aronowitz, "When the New Left Was New," in *The 60s Without Apology,* ed. Sohnya Sayres et. al. (Minneapolis: U of Minnesota P, 1984) 22. Freedom summer participants are quoted in Doug McAdam, *Freedom Summer* (New York: Oxford UP, 1988) 3. Aronowitz, "When the New Left Was New" 22. Howard Zinn, *SNCC: The New Abolitionists* (1964; Boston: Beacon, 1965).

For information on the early civil rights movement from 1960 to 1965, I have relied primarily on Anne Braden, "The Southern Freedom Movement in Perspective," *Monthly Review* 17(1965): 1–93; Taylor Branch, *Parting the Waters: America in the King Years 1954–63* (New York: Simon and Schuster, 1988); Claybourne Carson, *In Struggle: SNCC and the Black Awakening of the 1960s* (Cambridge, MA: Harvard UP, 1981); Carson et al., eds., *The Eyes on the Prize Civil Rights Reader: Documents, Speeches, and Firsthand Accounts from the Black Freedom Struggle, 1954–1990* (New York: Penguin, 1991); William H. Chafe, *Civilities and Civil Rights: Greensboro, North Carolina, and the Black Struggle for Freedom* (1980; New York: Oxford UP, 1981); Garrow, *Bearing the Cross;* Debbie Louis, *And We Are Not Saved: A History of the Move-*

ment as People (Garden City, NY: Doubleday, 1970); Manning Marable, *Race, Reform, and Rebellion: The Second Reconstruction in Black America, 1945–1990* (2nd ed., Jackson: U of Mississippi P, 1991); Diane Nash, "Inside the Sit-Ins and Freedom Rides: Testimony of a Southern Student," in *The New Negro*, ed. Matthew Ahmann (Notre Dame, In: Fides Publishers, 1961) 43–60; Fred Powledge, *Free At Last? The Civil Rights Movement and the People Who Made It* (1991; New York: HarperPerrenial, 1992); Howell Raines, *My Soul Is Rested: The Story of the Civil Rights Movement in the Deep South* (1977; New York: Penguin, 1983); Massimo Teodori, ed., *The New Left: A Documentary History* (Indianapolis: Bobbs-Merrill Company, 1969); Pat Waters, *Down to Now: Reflections on the Southern Civil Rights Movement* (1971; Athens: U of Georgia P, 1993); Robert Weisbrot, *Freedom Bound: A History of America's Civil Rights Movement* (1990; New York; Plume, 1991); and Zinn, *SNCC: The New Abolitionists*.

19. Martin Duberman, "The Abolitionists and Psychology," *Journal of Negro History* 47.3 (1962): 190, 183. Also see Merton L. Dillon, "The Abolitionists: A Decade of Historiography, 1959–1969," *Journal of Southern History* 35.4 (1969): 500–22.

20. Publications in 1964–1965 include James M. McPherson, *The Struggle for Equality: Abolitionists and the Negro in the Civil War and Reconstruction* (Princeton, NJ: Princeton UP, 1964); Richard O. Curry, ed., *The Abolitionists: Reformers or Fanatics?*; Martin Duberman, ed., *The Antislavery Vanguard: New Essays on the Abolitionists* (Princeton, NJ: Princeton UP, 1965); and Aileen S. Kraditor, "The Abolitionists Rehabilitated," *Studies on the Left* 5 (1965). The year 1965 also saw the beginnings of the scholarship contesting Elkins's method of comparing North American to Latin American slave systems. See Arnold A. Sio, "Interpretation of Slavery: The Slave Status in the Americas," *Comparative Studies in Society and History* 7 (1964–1965): 289–308.

21. Curry, "Introduction," in *The Abolitionists: Reformers or Fanatics?* 8. Duberman, "Introduction," in *The Antislavery Vanguard* ix. Zinn, "Abolitionists, Freedom-Riders, and the Tactics of Agitation," in Duberman, *The Antislavery Vanguard* 446. A. S. Eisenstadt, "The Perennial Myth—Writing American History Today," *Massachusetts Review* 7 (1966): 773, 757. See also Bertram Wyatt-Brown, "Abolitionism: Its Meaning for Contemporary Reform," *Midwest Quarterly* 8 (1966): 41–55.

22. Wyatt-Brown, "New Leftists and Abolitionists: A Comparison of American Radical Styles," *Wisconsin Magazine of History* 53.4 (1970): 259 (n. 12), 258. Albert Turner; qtd. in Howard N. Meyer, "Overcoming the White Man's History," *Massachusetts Review* 7.3 (1966): 578.

23. Earl E. Thorpe, "Chattel Slavery and Concentration Camps," in *The Debate Over Slavery: Stanley Elkins and His Critics*, ed. Ann J. Lane (Urbana, IL: U of Illinois P, 1971) 40–41 (n. 25).

24. Stokely Carmichael, "Power and Racism," in *The Black Power Revolt: A Collection of Essays*, ed. Floyd B. Barbour (Boston: Porter Sargent Publishers, 1968) 61. Gayle Pemberton, *The Hottest Water in Chicago: On Family, Race, Time, and American Culture* (Boston: Faber and Faber, 1992) 138. Henry Louis Gates, Jr., *Colored People: A Memoir* (New York: Alfred A. Knopf, 1994) 186. For other reports on Watts, see Paul Bullock, *Watts: The Aftermath: An Inside View of the Ghetto by the People of Watts* (New York: Grove, 1969); Kenneth B. Clark, "'The Wonder Is There Have Been So Few Riots,'" in *Black Protest in the Sixties*, ed. August Meier, Elliott Rudwick, and John Bracey, Jr. (New York: Markus Wiener, 1991) 107–15; Robert Conot, *Rivers of Blood, Years of Darkness* (New York: Bantam, 1967); Budd Schulberg, ed., *From the Ashes: Voices of Watts* (New York: New American Library, 1967); and C. Vann Woodward, "After Watts—Where Is the Negro Revolution Headed?" in Meier, Rudwick, and Bracey, *Black Protest in the Sixties* 116–26. For discussions of the social conditions giving birth to Black Power, see Paul Feldman, "How the Cry for 'Black Power' Began," *Dissent* 13.5 (1966): 472–77; Allen J. Matusow, "From Civil Rights to Black Power: The Case of SNCC,

1960–1966," in *Twentieth-Century America: Recent Interpretations,* ed. Barton J. Bernstein and Matusow (San Diego: Harcourt Brace Jovanovich, 1969) 531–36; and Gene Roberts, "The Story of Snick: From 'Freedom High' to Black Power," in Meier, Rudwick, and Bracey, *Black Protest in the Sixties* 139–53.

25. McAdam, *Freedom Summer* 102–5. Raines, *My Soul Is Rested* 28. John Lewis; qtd. in Carson, *In Struggle* 115. Dave Dennis; qtd. in Raines, *My Soul Is Rested* 278.

26. For information on the MFDP and the Atlantic City Democratic Convention, I have relied mostly on Carson, *In Struggle* 111–29; Garrow, *Bearing the Cross* 345–51; Gitlin, *The Sixties* 151–62; Kay Mills, *This Little Light of Mine: The Life of Fannie Lou Hamer* (1993; New York: Dutton Signet, 1994) 105–33; and Anne Romaine, "The Mississippi Freedom Democratic Party Through August, 1964" (M.A.; University of Virginia, 1969). For personal reflections on the Atlantic City convention by SNCC and MFDP members, see Charles M. Sherrod, "Mississippi at Atlantic City," in Carson et al., *The Eyes on the Prize Civil Rights Reader* 186–89; James Forman, *The Making of Black Revolutionaries* (Seattle, WA: Open Hand Publishing, 1985) 386–406; Cleveland Sellers with Robert Terrell, *The River of No Return: The Autobiography of a Black Militant and the Life and Death of SNCC* (1973; Jackson: UP of Mississippi, 1990) 108–10; and Len Holt, *The Summer That Didn't End: The Story of the Mississippi Civil Rights Project of 1964* (1965; New York: Da Capo, 1992) 168–83.

27. Martin Luther King, Jr., *Where Do We Go from Here: Chaos or Community?* (Boston: Beacon, 1967) 34. Carmichael; qtd. in Carson, *In Struggle* 161. King, *Where Do We Go from Here* 34. Lyndon B. Johnson's press conference; qtd. in Garrow, *Protest at Selma: Martin Luther King, Jr., and the Voting Rights Act of 1965* (New Haven, CT: Yale UP, 1978) 101. Johnson, "Address on Voting Rights," in *An American Primer,* ed. Daniel J. Boorstin (Chicago: U of Chicago P, 1966) 946.

28. *The Kerner Report* 109. James W. Button, *Black Violence: Political Impact of the 1960s Riots* (Princeton, NJ: Princeton UP, 1978) 32–33; Button gives the figure of 160 riots.

29. John Churchville; qtd. in Carson, *In Struggle* 195. Duberman, "Black Power in America," *Partisan Review* 35.1 (1968): 40–48; cf. Duberman, "Anarchism Left and Right," *Partisan Review* 33.4 (Fall 1966): 610–16. Richard S. Sterne and Jeane Loftin Rothseiden, "Master–Slave Clashes as Forerunners of Patterns in Modern American Urban Eruptions," *Phylon* 30.3 (1969): 252. Cf. Bruce Payne, "SNCC: An Overview Two Years Later," in Cohen and Hale, *The New Student Left* 86; and Lawrence H. Fuchs, *The American Kaleidoscope: Race, Ethnicity, and the Civil Culture* (Middletown, CT: Wesleyan UP, 1990) 176.

30. George Frederickson and Christopher Lasch, "Resistance to Slavery," in Lane, *The Debate Over Slavery* 229, 230, 228, 237. *The Kerner Report* 113. Lasch, *The Agony of the American Left* (New York: Alfred A. Knopf, 1969) 153. Frederickson and Lasch, "Resistance to Slavery" 226, 229, 244. Cf. Genovese, "Rebelliousness and Docility in the Negro Slave: A Critique of the Elkins Thesis," *Civil War History* 13 (1967): 293–314; and S. E. Anderson, "Revolutionary Black Nationalism and the Pan-African Idea," in *The Black Seventies,* ed. Barbour (Boston: Porter Sargent, 1970) 103.

31. Mary Agnes Lewis, "Slavery and Personality," in Lane *The Debate Over Slavery* 78, 85. Sterling Stuckey, "Through the Prism of Folklore: The Black Ethos in Slavery," in Lane, *The Debate Over Slavery* 245, 246, 266, 268, 251, 267.

32. William Loren Katz, ed., *Five Slave Narratives* (New York: Arno, 1968). Arna Bontemps, ed., *Great Slave Narratives* (Boston: Beacon, 1969). Clifton H. Johnson, ed., *God Struck Me Dead: Voices of Ex-Slaves* (1969; Cleveland: The Pilgrim Press, 1993). Charles H. Nichols, *Many Thousand Gone: The Ex-Slaves' Account of Their Bondage and Freedom* (1963; Bloomington: Indiana UP, 1969). Gilbert Osofsky, ed., *Puttin' On Ole Massa: The Slave Narratives of Henry Bibb, William Wells Brown, and Solomon Northup* (New York: Harper & Row, 1969). Norman R. Yetman, ed., *Voices from Slavery* (New York: Holt, Rinehart and Winston, 1970).

George P. Rawick, ed., *The American Slave: A Composite Autobiography* (Westport, CT: Greenwood, 1972), 19 vols. John W. Blassingame, *The Slave Community: Plantation Life in the Antebellum South* (New York: Oxford UP, 1972). Rawick, *From Sundown to Sunup: The Making of the Black Community* (Westport, CT: Greenwood, 1972).

33. Zinn, *The Politics of History* (1970; Urbana: U of Illinois P, 1990) 41. Herbert Aptheker, "[Review of Zinn's *The Politics of History*]," *Political Affairs* 49 (1970): 57. Ulrich B. Phillips, *Life and Labor in the Old South* (1929; Boston: Little, Brown and Company, 1963) 219.

34. Meier and Rudwick, *Black History and the Historical Profession* 250.

35. Thomas F. Pettigrew, *A Profile of the Negro American* (Princeton, NJ: D. Van Nostrand Company, 1964) 13–14. Charles E. Silberman, *Crisis in Black and White* (New York: Random House, 1964) 75, 77, 84–89. Zinn, *The Southern Mystique* (New York, 1964) 36. Robert Penn Warren, *Who Speaks for the Negro?* (New York: Random House, 1965) 55–59. Ralph Ellison, *Going to the Territory* (New York: Random House, 1986) 100, 287. To get an idea of the popularity of the Elkins thesis and this particular misreading of it, see Robert Coles, in "Notes from the Academy: Transcript of the American Academy Conference on the Negro American—May 14–15, 1965," *Daedalus* 95.1 (1966): 329; and Coles, "'It's the Same, but It's Different,'" *Daedalus* 94.4 (1965): 1125–29.

36. [Daniel Patrick Moynihan], *The Negro Family: The Case for National Action* (Washington, DC: Office of Policy Planning and Research, United States Department of Labor, 1965) [iii], 15–16. For information on the events leading up to the writing of the Moynihan Report, see Lemann, *The Promised Land* 170–81. For information on the reception of the Report, see Lee Rainwater and William L. Yancey, *The Moynihan Report and the Politics of Controversy* (Cambridge, MA: MIT P, 1967); Paula Giddings, *When and Where I Enter: The Impact of Black Women on Race and Sex in America* (1984; New York: Bantam Books, 1985) 328; "Rights Unit Quits White House Parley," *New York Times* May 24, 1966; Carmichael, "Notes and Comments" (SNCC Position Paper); James Farmer, "The Controversial Moynihan Report," *Amsterdam News,* December 18, 1965; and William Ryan, *Blaming the Victim* (1971; New York: Random House, 1976) 63–88.

37. Roy Simón Bryce-Laporte, "The American Slave Plantation and Our Heritage of Communal Deprivation," *American Behavioral Scientist* 12.4 (1969): 2–8. Rawick, "The Historical Roots of Black Liberation," *Radical America* 2 (1968): 2, 3, 8, 9, 13 (n. 2). Cf. Rawick, "The American Negro Movement," *International Socialism* 16 (1964): 24, where Rawick had also argued that the "present Negro movement" of 1964 was related to "the life and the community portrayed in the Slave Narrative Collection." In an article in 1971, Elkins began to exculpate himself from what he called a "misreading" that was enjoying such widespread popularity, arguing that those who believe he "extended the Sambo personality to present-day Negro Americans" have missed his point. Such "an extension would have contradicted my entire argument," he notes. "If one is accounting for dependent personalities in terms of a peculiarly coercive slave system, then it ought to follow that those same personalities would be profoundly affected in the reverse direction by the collapse of that system." Elkins, "Slavery and Ideology," in Lane, *The Debate Over Slavery* 256 (n. 28).

38. Thorpe, "Chattel Slavery and Concentration Camps" 40–41 (n. 25).

39. Vincent Harding, "Black Radicalism: The Road from Montgomery," in *Dissent: Explorations in the History of American Radicalism,* ed. Alfred F. Young (DeKalb: Northern Illinois UP, 1968) 342. For *Time* magazine and the *Saturday Evening Post,* see Carson, *In Struggle* 221–22. Duberman, "Black Power in America" 35. Feldman, "How the Cry for 'Black Power' Began" 472. Cf. Samuel DuBois Cook, "The Tragic Myth of Black Power," *New South* 21.3 (1966): 58–64. Joel D. Aberbach and Jack L. Walker, "The Meanings of Black Power: A Comparison of Black and White Interpretations of a Political Slogan," in *Conflict and Competition: Studies in*

the Recent Black Protest Movement, ed. Bracey, Meier, and Rudwick (Belmont, CA: Wadsworth, 1971) 161–62. For the *Christian Science Monitor,* the *Boston Herald,* and *Newsweek,* see Carson, *In Struggle* 222.

40. For the CORE and NAACP conventions, see "'Black Power' Controversy," in *Civil Rights, 1960–1966,* ed. Lester A. Sobel (New York: Facts on File, Inc., 1967) 374–89. Roy Wilkins; qtd. in *The New York Times* (July 6, 1966) 14; and Wilkins, "Whither 'Black Power'?" *Crisis* 73.7 (Aug.–Sept., 1966): 354. Lyndon Johnson; qtd. in *The New York Times* (July 6, 1966) 18. Hubert H. Humphrey, "Address to the NAACP Convention, July 6, 1966," in Robert L. Scott and Wayne Brockriede, *The Rhetoric of Black Power* (New York: Harper and & Row Publishers, 1969) 65–73. Whitney Young; qtd. in Carson, *In Struggle* 220.

41. *Christian Science Monitor;* qtd. in Scott and Brockriede, *The Rhetoric of Black Power* 81. King, *Where Do We Go from Here* 30. Cf. John Oliver Killens, *'Sippi* (1967; New York: Thunder's Mouth, 1988) 382, showing how the media affected the perceptions of those who immediately connected "this new thing, this violence and Black Power."

42. Julius Lester noted that the "concept of the black man as a nation, which is only being talked about now, will become reality when violence comes. Out of the violence will come the new nation (if the violence is successful) and the new man." Lester, *Look Out Whitey! Black Power's Gon' Get Your Mama!* (New York: Dial, 1968) 140. Cf. Theodore Draper, *The Rediscovery of Black Nationalism* (New York: Viking, 1969) 119–31; and William L. Van Deburg, *New Day in Babylon: The Black Power Movement and American Culture, 1965–1975* (Chicago: U of Chicago P, 1992) 283. There were of course some militants who were what Killens, in *The Cotillion* (New York: Ballantine, 1971) 75, called "violence-for-the-pure-and-lovely-sake-of-violence-worshipers," but they were largely marginal to the Black Power movement.

43. Pat Watters and Reese Cleghorn, *Climbing Jacob's Ladder: The Arrival of Negroes in Southern Politics* (New York: Harcourt, Brace, and World, Inc., 1967) 295. Kenneth Keniston, *Youth and Dissent: The Rise of a New Opposition* (New York: Harcourt, Brace, Jovanovich, 1971) 299. Keniston, *Young Radicals: Notes on Committed Youth* (New York: Harcourt, Brace, and World, 1968) 252, 255, 254, 248.

44. Richard Hofstadter and Michael Wallace, eds., *American Violence: A Documentary History* (New York: Alfred A. Knopf, 1970) v. H. Rap Brown; in Carson, *In Struggle* 253–57.

45. Gitlin, *The Sixties* 349 (n.), 348, 316. For the Weathermen, who were originally called the Third Worlders, see Milton Viorst, *Fire in the Streets: America in the 1960s* (New York: Simon and Schuster, 1979) 467–504; Gitlin, *The Sixties* 385–400; and Harold Jacobs, ed., *Weatherman* (np: Ramparts, 1970). H. Rap Brown; qtd. in Gitlin, *The Sixties* 316. Scott and Brockriede, *The Rhetoric of Black Power* 140. Sterne and Rothseiden, "Master–Slave Clashes" 251, 252.

46. King, *Where Do We Go from Here* 54, 55. Eldridge Cleaver, *Eldridge Cleaver: Post-Prison Writings and Speeches,* ed. Robert Scheer (New York: Random House, 1969) 18–20; cf. Lee Lockwood, *Conversations with Eldridge Cleaver: Algiers* (New York: McGraw-Hill, 1970) 90–91. For book sales of *Wretched of the Earth,* see Van Deburg, *New Day in Babylon* 60–61. Dan Watts; qtd. in Matusow, *The Unraveling of America: A History of Liberalism in the 1960s* (New York: Harper & Row, 1968) 358. For the Atlantic Project and SNCC, see Carson, *In Struggle* 192, 198–99, 235. Jack Minnis; qtd. in Carson, *In Struggle* 235. Bobby Seale, *Seize the Time: The Story of the Black Panther Party and Huey P. Newton* (New York: Random House, 1970) 25–26. Huey Newton; qtd. in Matusow, *The Unraveling of America* 368.

47. Frantz Fanon, *The Wretched of the Earth,* trans. Constance Farrington (1961; New York: Grove, 1968), 94, 40, 43.

48. [Cleaver], "On Violence," in *The Black Panthers Speak,* ed. Philip S. Foner (Philadelphia: J. B. Lippincott, 1970) 19. Chafe, *Civilities and Civil Rights* 201, 202. Byron Rushing, "I Was Born," in Barbour *The Black Power Revolt* 230.

49. Carmichael, "Power and Racism," in Barbour, *The Black Power Revolt* 63–64. Carmichael, "Toward Black Liberation," *Massachusetts Review* 7 (1966): 639. Harold Cruse, *The Crisis of the Negro Intellectual* (1967; New York: Quill, 1984) 360. King, *Where Do We Go from Here* 66.

50. "Statement by the National Committee of Negro Churchmen, July 31, 1966," in *Black Theology: A Documentary History, 1966–1979,* ed. Gayraud S. Wilmore and James H. Cone (Maryknoll, NY: Orbis Books, 1979) 24. Tom Hayden; qtd. in James Miller, *"Democracy Is in the Streets": From Port Huron to the Siege of Chicago* (1987; Cambridge, MA: Harvard UP, 1994) 298. Hayden, *Rebellion in Newark: Official Violence and Ghetto Response* (New York: Random House, 1967). Cleaver; qtd. in Van Deburg, *New Day in Babylon* 152. "Young Lords Party 13 Point Program and Platform," in Foner, *The Black Panthers Speak* 237. Cf. Larry Neal, "And Shine Swam On," in *Black Fire: An Anthology of Afro-American Writing,* ed. LeRoi Jones and Neal (New York: William Morrow, 1968) 647, 656; and Neal, "The Black Arts Movement," in Neal, *Visions of a Liberated Future: Black Arts Movement Writings,* ed. Michael Schwartz (New York: Thunder's Mouth, 1989) 71–72.

51. Kwame Ture and Charles Hamilton, *Black Power: The Politics of Liberation* (1967; New York: Vintage Books, 1992) xvi, 37–38. Van Deburg, *New Day in Babylon* 26. Bayard Rustin, "'Black Power' and Coalition Politics." *Commentary* 42.3 (September 1966): 35, 38.

52. Gates, *Colored People* 186. Carolyn M. Rodgers, "Un Nat'chal Thang—The Whole Truth—US," *Black World* 20.11 (1971): 10. Jean Smith, "I Learned to Feel Black," in Barbour, *The Black Power Revolt* 209, 214, 217, 218. William E. Cross, Jr., "Toward a Psychology of Black Liberation: The Negro-to-Black Conversion Experience," *Black World* 20.9 (1971): 13–27. Cf. Killens, *'Sippi* 385: "Black Power means love of our black selves"; and Killens, in *Negro Digest* 16 (1966): 36: "Black Consciousness . . . teaches us that love, like charity, must begin at home; that is must begin with ourselves, our beautiful black selves."

53. Hamilton; in "Black Power: A Discussion," *Partisan Review* 35.2 (1968): 207. Carmichael, "Toward Black Liberation" 647–48. LeRoi Jones, *Home: Social Essays* (New York: William Morrow, 1966) 135. Harding, "Black Radicalism: The Road from Montgomery" 342. Godfrey Cambridge; qtd. in Van Deburg, *New Day in Babylon* 195. Charles Keil, *Urban Blues* (1966; Chicago: U of Chicago P, 1991) 189. Henry Dumas, "Will the Circle Be Unbroken?" in *Goodbye, Sweetwater: New and Selected Stories,* ed. Eugene Redmond (New York: Thunder's Mouth, 1988) 85–91. For discussions showing how, as Stephen E. Henderson says, the "very concept of black power is informed with Soul," see: Mercer Cook and Henderson, *The Militant Black Writer in Africa and the United States* (Madison: U of Wisconsin P, 1969) 115–27; Lerone Bennett, Jr., *The Negro Mood and Other Essays* (1964; New York: Ballantine, 1965) 89–96; Ulf Hannerz, *Soulside: Inquiries into Ghetto Culture and Community* (New York: Columbia UP, 1969); and Rainwater, ed., *Black Experience: Soul* (New York: Aldine, 1970).

54. Dumas, "Will the Circle Be Unbroken?" 86. Alice Walker, "Nineteen Fifty-Five," in *You Can't Keep a Good Woman Down* (San Diego: Harcourt, Brace, Jovanovich, 1981) 3–20. Jones, *Black Music* (New York: Quill, 1967) 205, 206. Robert Blauner, "Black Culture: Myth or Reality?" in *Americans from Africa: Old Memories, New Moods,* ed. Peter I. Rose (New York: Atherton, 1970) 440.

55. Lester, *Look Out Whitey! Black Power's Gon' Get Your Mama!* 97, 93, 84–85. King, *Where Do We Go from Here* 53, 52, 43, 44.

56. Ture and Hamilton, *Black Power* 66, 172–73. Carmichael, "Power and Racism" 70. "Black Panther Party Platform and Program: What We Want, What We Believe," in Foner, *The Black Panthers Speak* 2.

57. Forman, *The Making of Black Revolutionaries* 543–45. Forman, "Manifesto of the National Black Economic Development Conference," in *Black Protest Thought in the Twentieth Century,* ed. Meier, Rudwick, and Francis L. Broderick (1965; Indianapolis: Bobbs-Merrill, 1971) 540.

58. Marable, *Race, Reform, and Rebellion* 97–98. Cf. Nathan Wright, Jr., *Black Power and Urban Unrest* (New York: Hawthorn Books, 1967). Cruse, *Rebellion or Revolution?* (New York: William Morrow & Company, 1968) 207, 206. *The Kerner Report* 235. Richard Nixon; qtd. in Marable, *Race, Reform, and Rebellion* 98. Forman, *The Making of Black Revolutionaries* 459; cf. Cleaver, "An Open Letter to Stokely Carmichael," in Foner, *The Black Panthers Speak* 105–6. For a discussion of the political drift at the Black Power conferences, see Robert L. Allen, *Black Awakening in Capitalist America* (Trenton, NJ: Africa World, 1990) 157–64.

59. Lasch, *The Agony of the American Left* 133, 134. Cornel West, "The Paradox of the Afro-American Rebellion," in Sayres et al., *The 60s Without Apology* 52. Cf. Hamilton, "Afterword, 1992," in Ture and Hamilton *Black Power* 211.

60. Rawick, "The Historical Roots of Black Liberation" 12 (n. 1). Genovese, "The Influence of the Black Power Movement on Historical Scholarship" 231, 232.

61. Genovese, "The Influence of the Black Power Movement on Historical Scholarship" 238–39.

3. The Discourse Mobilized

1. Sterling Stuckey, "Twilight of Our Past: Reflections on the Origins of Black History," *Amistad 2*, ed. John A. Williams and Charles F. Harris (New York: Random House, 1971) 263, 262. Mercer Cook and Stephen E. Henderson, *The Militant Black Writer in Africa and the United States* (Madison: U of Wisconsin P, 1969) 74–75. Cf. Ossie Davis, "Nat Turner: Hero Reclaimed," *Freedomways* 8 (1968): 230–32. For discussions of the emergent Black Power intelligentsia, see Harold Cruse, *The Crisis of the Negro Intellectual* (1967; New York: Quill, 1984) 544–65; and Martin Kilson, "The New Black Intellectuals," *Dissent* 16 (1969): 304–10.

2. William L. Van Deburg, *New Day in Babylon: The Black Power Movement and American Culture, 1965–1975* (Chicago: U of Chicago P, 1992) 255. Eliot Fremont-Smith, "Nat Turner I: The Controversy," *New York Times* (August 1, 1968): 29; Fremont-Smith, "Nat Turner II: What Myth Will Serve," *New York Times* (August 2, 1968): 31.

3. For a notable example of an abolitionist's use of the sentiment behind the phrase, "the slave's point of view," see Wendell Phillips's prefatory letter to Frederick Douglass's *Narrative of the Life of Frederick Douglass,* ed. Benjamin Quarles (Cambridge, MA: Harvard UP, 1960) 17–21. Mary White Ovington, "Slaves' Reminiscences of Slavery," *The Independent* (May 26, 1910): 1131–36. Ovington, "[Review of Phillips's *American Negro Slavery*]," *Survey* 40 (September 28, 1919): 718. W. E. B. Du Bois, "[Review of Phillips's *American Negro Slavery*]," *American Political Science Review* 12 (1918): 723. Carter G. Woodson, "[Review of Phillips's *American Negro Slavery*]," *Mississippi Valley Historical Review* 5 (1919): 480–82. Lawrence D. Reddick, "A New Interpretation for Negro History," *Journal of Negro History* 22 (1937): 20. B. A. Botkin, "The Slave as His Own Interpreter," *Library of Congress Quarterly Journal of Current Acquisitions* 2 (1944): 37–63. Richard Hofstadter, "U.B. Phillips and the Plantation Legend," *Journal of Negro History* 29 (1944): 124. Charles H. Nichols, "Slave Narratives and the Plantation Legend," *Phylon* 10 (1949): 201–10. Nichols, "Who Read the Slave Narratives?" *Phylon* 20 (1959): 149–62.

4. C. Vann Woodward and R. W. B. Lewis, "Slavery in the First Person: Interview with William Styron," *Yale Alumni Magazine* (1967): 39. Woodward, "Confessions of a Rebel: 1831," *The New Republic* (October 7, 1967): 28. Philip Rahv, "Through the Mists of Jerusalem," *The New York Review of Books* (October 26, 1967): 6.

5. June Meyers, "Spokesmen for the Blacks," *The Nation* (December 4, 1967): 597, 599.

6. Seymour L. Gross and Eileen Bender, "History, Politics and Literature: The Myth of Nat Turner," *American Quarterly* 23 (1971): 488. John White, "The Novelist as Historian: William Styron and American Negro Slavery," *Journal of American Studies* 4 (1969): 235. Mar-

tin Duberman, *The Uncompleted Past* (New York: Random House, 1969) 216, 206, 218, 222. Samuel Coale, *William Styron Revisited* (Boston: Twayne, 1991) 81, 96.

7. Fremont-Smith, "Nat Turner I: The Controversy" 29. Gross and Bender, "History, Politics and Literature" 506. William E. Akin, "Toward an Impressionistic History: Pitfalls and Possibilities in William Styron's Meditation on History," *American Quarterly* 21 (1969): 808. Robert F. Durden, "William Styron and His Black Critics," *South Atlantic Quarterly* 68 (1969): 181, 184. Eugene D. Genovese, "William Styron Before the People's Court," in *In Red and Black: Marxian Explorations in Southern and Afro-American History* (1971; Knoxville: U of Tennessee P, 1984) 200. Douglas Barzelay and Robert Sussman, "William Styron on *The Confessions of Nat Turner: A Yale Lit* Interview," in *Conversations with William Styron,* ed. James L. W. West III (Jackson: UP of Mississippi, 1985) 101, 107, 108.

8. Genovese, "William Styron Before the People's Court" 215. Peter Chew, "Black History, Black Mythology?" *American Heritage* 20 (1969): 6. Cf. Ernest Dunbar, "The Black Studies Thing," in *Black Protest in the Sixties,* ed. August Meier, Elliot Rudwick, and John Bracey, Jr. (New York: Markus Wiener, 1991) 243–61; and Genovese, "Black Studies: Trouble Ahead," in *In Red and Black* 218–29. For a discussion of the *Freedomway* intellectuals, see Cruse, *The Crisis of the Negro Intellectual* 225–52, 305–44.

9. Duberman, *The Uncompleted Past* 217, 218, 221. Genovese, "William Styron Before the People's Court" 202. Cf. Arthur Schlesinger, Jr., "Nationalism and History," *Journal of Negro History* 54 (1969): 28. Gross and Bender, "History, Politics and Literature" 516, 506, 489. Vincent Harding, "You've Taken My Nat and Gone," in *William Styron's Nat Turner: Ten Black Writers Respond,* ed. John Henrik Clarke (Boston: Beacon, 1968) 26. Cook and Henderson, *The Militant Black Writer* 74. Addison Gayle, Jr., "Cultural Hegemony: The Southern White Writer and American Letters," in *Amistad 1,* ed. Williams and Harris (New York: Random House, 1970) 23.

10. Genovese, "William Styron Before the People's Court" 202. Duberman, *The Uncompleted Past* 217, 218, 221.

11. Gross and Bender, "History, Politics and Literature" 492. Duberman, *The Uncompleted Past* 220, 203.

12. Mike Thelwell, "Back with the Wind: Mr. Styron and the Reverend Turner," in Clarke, *William Styron's Nat Turner* 82. Styron, *The Confessions of Nat Turner* (1967; New York: Vintage International Edition, 1992) [xi]. Hereafter all quotations from Styron's novel will be taken from this edition and cited parenthetically in the body of the text. Lerone Bennett, Jr., "Nat's Last White Man," in Clarke, *William Styron's Nat Turner* 4–5 (n. 1). Harding, "You've Taken My Nat and Gone" 24. Thelwell, "Back with the Wind" 87. Cf. William W. Nichols, "Slave Narratives: Dismissed Evidence in the Writing of Southern History," *Phylon* 32 (1971): 407.

13. Genovese, "William Styron Before the People's Court" 210–11. Barzelay and Sussman, "William Styron on *The Confessions of Nat Turner*" 106. Ralph Ellison, William Styron, Robert Penn Warren, C. Vann Woodward, "The Uses of History in Fiction," in West, *Conversations with William Styron* 135. Gross and Bender, "History, Politics and Literature" 513.

14. Anna Mary Wells; in "An Exchange on Nat Turner," *The New York Review of Books* (November 7, 1968): 31. Gross and Bender, "History, Politics and Literature" 513.

15. *Richmond Constitutional Whig,* September 26, 1831; reprinted in *The Southampton Slave Revolt of 1831: A Compilation of Source Materials,* ed. Henry Irving Tragle (Amherst: U of Massachusetts P, 1971) 92. Samuel Warner, *Authentic and Impartial Narrative of the Tragical Scene Which Was Witnessed in Southampton County (Virginia) on Monday the 22nd of August Last* (1831); reprinted in *The Southampton Slave Revolt of 1831* 296. Tragle, "Styron and His Sources," *Massachusetts Review* 11 (1970): 145–46.

16. The reports from the *Richmond Whig* and the *New York Morning Courier and Enquirer* are taken from *Nat Turner,* ed. Eric Foner (Englewood Cliffs, NJ: Prentice-Hall, 1971) 19, 24.

17. Genovese, "William Styron Before the People's Court" 206–16.

18. Stanley Kauffmann, "Styron's Unwritten Novel," *Hudson Review* 20.4 (Winter 1967–1968): 677, 678, 680.

19. Bennett, "Nat's Last White Man" 7, 6 (n. 3).

20. Clarke, "Introduction," in *William Styron's Nat Turner* vii–ix. Loyle Hairston, "William Styron's Nat Turner—Rogue Nigger," in Clarke, *William Styron's Nat Turner* 72; cf. Hairston, "Rescuing Nat Turner from American History," *Freedomways* 8 (1968): 266–68. Thelwell; in "An Exchange on Nat Turner" 34. Also see Herbert Aptheker, "Styron-Turner and Nat Turner: Myth and Reality," *Political Affair* 46 (1967).

21. James Jones and William Styron, "Two Writers Talk It Over," in West, *Conversations with William Styron* 45. Robert Canzoneri and Page Stegner, "An Interview with William Styron," in West, *Conversations with William Styron* 72. Cf. John Thompson, "Rise and Slay!" *Commentary* 44 (1967): 84. Curtis Harnack, "The Quiddities of Detail," *Kenyon Review* 301 (1968): 128, 130.

22. Thomas R. Gray, *The Confessions of Nat Turner, The Leader of the Late Insurrection in Southampton, VA.* (Baltimore, 1831); reprinted in *The Southampton Slave Revolt of 1831* 317. Hereafter all quotations from Gray's *Confessions* will be taken from this edition.

23. Albert Murray, "A Troublesome Property," *The New Leader* 50.24 (December 4, 1967): 19. Cf. Clarke, "Introduction" vii; Genovese, "William Styron Before the People's Court" 212; Harding, "You've Taken My Nat and Gone" 28; Alvin F. Poussaint, "The Confessions of Nat Turner and the Dilemma of William Styron," in Clarke, *William Styron's Nat Turner* 20, 21; Hairston, "William Styron's Nat Turner—Rogue Nigger" 71; Charles V. Hamilton, "Our Nat Turner and William Styron's Creation," in Clarke, *William Styron's Nat Turner* 74, 77; and Lloyd Tom Delaney, "[Review of Styron's *Confessions of Nat Turner*]," *Psychology Today* 1.8 (1968): 12.

24. Bennett, "Nat's Last White Man" 4, 6 (n. 2).

25. Bennett, "Nat's Last White Man" 12. Thelwell, "Back with the Wind" 85. John Oliver Killens, "The Confessions of Willie Styron," in Clarke, *William Styron's Nat Turner* 40–41. Cf. Harnack, "The Quiddities of Detail" 129.

26. Louis D. Rubin, Jr., "William Styron and Human Bondage: *The Confessions of Nat Turner,*" *The Hollins Critic* (1967): 11–12. Marc L. Ratner, "Styron's Rebel," *American Quarterly* 21 (1969): 604. Harnack, "The Quiddities of Detail" 129. Cf. Albert E. Stone, *The Return of Nat Turner: History, Literature, and Cultural Politics in Sixties America* (Athens: U of Georgia P, 1992) 92.

27. Okon E. Uya, "Race, Ideology, and Scholarship in the United States: William Styron's *Nat Turner* and Its Critics," *American Studies International* 15 (1976): 78.

28. Frantz Fanon, *Black Skin, White Masks,* trans. Charles Lam Markmann (1952; New York: Grove, 1967) 165. Lynne Segal, *Slow Motion: Changing Masculinities, Changing Men* (New Brunswick: Rutgers UP, 1990) 201–2. Winthrop D. Jordan, *White Over Black: American Attitudes Toward the Negro, 1550–1812* (1968; New York: Norton, 1977) 151, 152. Peter H. Wood, *Black Majority: Negroes in Colonial South Carolina from 1670 through the Stono Rebellion* (1974; New York: Norton, 1975) 236–37. Jordan, *White Over Black* 152, 153. Wood, *Black Majority* 237. I would like to thank my colleague and friend Susan Hirsch for directing me to Lynne Segal's book; I greatly profited from Susan's reading of this section, her conversation, and her own thoughtful writing on the topic of rape. See Susan F. Hirsch, "Interpreting Media Representations of a 'Night of Madness': Law and Culture in the Construction of Rape Identities," *Law and Social Inquiry* 19 (1994): 1023–56.

29. George Fredrickson, *The Black Image in the White Mind: The Debate on Afro-American Character and Destiny, 1817–1914* (1971; Middletown, CT: Wesleyan UP, 1987) 43, 52–53, 54.

30. Ida B. Wells, *Southern Horrors: Lynch Law in All Its Phases* (New York, 1892); Wells, *A Red Record: Tabulated Statistics and Alleged Causes of Lynchings in the United States* (Chicago, 1895); and Wells, *Mob Rule in New Orleans: Albert Charles and His Fight to the Death* (Chicago, 1900). Hazel V. Carby, "'On the Threshold of Woman's Era': Lynching, Empire, and Sexuality in Black Feminist Theory," *Critical Inquiry* 12 (1985): 268. Angela Y. Davis, *Women, Race and Class* (1981; New York: Random House, 1983) 173. Martha Hodes, "The Sexualization of Reconstruction Politics," *Journal of the History of Sexuality* 3 (1993): 412. Robyn Wiegman, "The Anatomy of Lynching," *Journal of the History of Sexuality* 3 (1993): 459. Paul Hoch; qtd. in Wiegman, "The Anatomy of Lynching" 463. Other discussions of sexuality in post-Reconstruction America that I found particularly useful include: Jacquelyn Dowd Hall, "'The Mind that Burns in Each Body': Women, Rape, and Racial Violence," in *Powers of Desire: The Politics of Sexuality,* ed. Ann Snitow, Christine Stansell, and Sharon Thompson (New York: Monthly Review, 1983) 328–49; Trudier Harris, *Exorcising Blackness: Historical and Literary Lynching and Burning Rituals* (Bloomington: Indiana UP, 1984) 1–28; and Gail Bederman, "Civilization, The Decline of Middle-Class Manliness, and Ida B. Wells's Anti-Lynching Campaign (1892–94)," *Radical History Review* 52 (1992): 5–30.

31. Susan Brownmiller, *Against Our Will: Men, Women, and Rape* (New York: Simon and Schuster, 1975) 14; paraphrased in Sharon Marcus, "Fighting Bodies, Fighting Words: A Theory and Politics of Rape Prevention," in *Feminists Theorize the Political,* ed. Judith Butler and Joan W. Scott (New York: Routledge, 1992) 395. Davis, *Women, Race and Class* 178. Paula Giddings, *When and Where I Enter: The Impact of Black Women on Race and Sex in America* (1984; New York: Bantam, 1985) 310. Cf. Hall, "'The Mind that Burns in Each Body'" 341. Marcus, "Fighting Bodies, Fighting Words" 395, 400. Richard Dyer, *The Matter of Images: Essays on Representations* (London: Routledge, 1993) 113. Segal, *Slow Motion* 181. Cf. Lesley A. Hall, *Hidden Anxieties: Male Sexuality, 1900–1950* (Cambridge: Polity, 1991) 1–14; and Mark Strage, *The Durable Fig Leaf: A Historical, Cultural, Medical, Social, Literary, and Iconographic Account of Man's Relations with His Penis* (New York: William Morrow, 1980) 257–70.

32. Styron, "Overcome," *New York Review of Books* (September 26, 1963): 18. James Baldwin, *No Name in the Street,* in *The Price of the Ticket: Collected Nonfiction, 1948–1985* (New York: St. Martin's, 1985) 481–82. *No Name in the Street* was originally published in 1972; Baldwin was living in the Styrons' guest house for part of the time Styron was writing the *Confessions.*

33. Davis, *Women, Race and Class* 182, 196. Nell Irvin Painter, "Hill, Thomas, and the Use of Racial Stereotype," in *Race-ing Justice, En-gendering Power: Essays on Anita Hill, Clarence Thomas, and the Construction of Social Reality,* ed. Toni Morrison (New York: Pantheon, 1992) 209. Cf. Barbara Bush, *Slave Women in Caribbean Society 1650–1838* (Bloomington: Indiana UP, 1990) 110–18.

34. Will's murder of Mrs. Whitehead is also cast in starkly sexual terms: "the tar-black man and the woman, bone-white, bone-rigid with fear beyond telling, pressed urgently together" (412).

35. Genovese, "William Styron Before the People's Court" 205. Gross and Bender, "History, Politics and Literature" 507. Genovese, "William Styron Before the People's Court" 211. On reports of the absence of rape in the revolt, see *The Constitutional Whig,* in Tragle, *The Southampton Slave Revolt* 51, 52; and William Sidney Drewry, *The Southampton Insurrection* (1900; Murfreesboro, NC: Johnson, 1968) 117. Cf. Roy Arthur Swanson, "William Styron's Clown Show," in *William Styron's The Confessions of Nat Turner: A Critical Handbook,* ed. Melvin J. Friedman and Irving Malin (Belmont, CA: Wadsworth, 1970) 162.

36. Richard Wright, *Native Son* (1940; New York: Harper & Row, 1966) 213–25. The irony is that when Bessie fears Bigger will be accused of raping Mary—which she knows is a crime worse than murder in the society they inhabit—he, for the first time, starts to articulate

what "rape" means for him. For Bigger, rape becomes a disembodied crime: "rape was not what one did to women. Rape was what one felt when one's back was against a wall and one had to strike out, whether one wanted to or not, to keep the pack from killing one. He committed rape every time he looked into a white face" (214). Having articulated a philosophy of rape as a metaphysical and existential response to the world, he then proceeds physically and brutally to rape Bessie, murder her, and dispose of her body (while referring to her constantly as "it").

37. Stone, *The Return of Nat Turner* 59–60. Darwin T. Turner, "[Review of Styron's *Confessions of Nat Turner*]," *Journal of Negro History* 53.2 (1968): 185. Clarke, "Introduction" viii. Thompson, "Rise and Slay!" 83, refers to Turner's "helplessly compliant mother."

38. Stryon; in "Symposium: Violence in Literature," *American Scholar* 37 (1968): 485.

39. Robin Morgan, *The Demon Lover: On the Sexuality of Terrorism* (New York: W. W. Norton, 1989). Catherine A. MacKinnon, "Sex and Violence: A Perspective," in *Feminism Unmodified: Discourses on Life and Law* (Cambridge, MA: Harvard UP, 1987) 92.

40. Harnack, "The Quiddities of Detail" 129.

41. Tragle, *The Southampton Slave Revolt of 1831* 301. Styron; qtd. in Woodward and Lewis, "Slavery in the First Person" 34. Cf. Canzoneri and Stegner, "An Interview with William Styron" 67.

42. William L. Andrews, *To Tell a Free Story: The First Century of Afro-American Autobiography, 1760–1865* (Urbana: U of Illinois P, 1986) 72. Gray, *The Confessions of Nat Turner* 306. Andrews, "Inter(racial)textuality in Nineteenth-Century Southern Narrative," in *Influence and Intertextuality in Literary History,* ed. Jay Clayton and Eric Rothstein (Madison: U of Wisconsin P, 1991) 305. Andrews, *To Tell a Free Story,* 76, 77. Eric J. Sundquist, *To Wake the Nations: Race in the Making of American Literature* (Cambridge, MA: Harvard UP, 1993) 40–41, 43, 48.

43. Gray, *The Confessions of Nat Turner* 305, 317, 303.

44. Thomas R. Dew, "Abolition of Negro Slavery," in *The Ideology of Slavery: Proslavery Thought in the Antebellum South, 1830–1860,* ed. Drew Gilpin Faust (Baton Rouge: Louisiana State UP, 1981) 77, 26, 68, 27, 67, 38, 57, 60, 65, 66, 67. John Hamden Pleasants; in *Nat Turner* 21. For a more thorough study of Dew's pro-slavery thought, see Dickson D. Bruce, Jr., *The Rhetoric of Conservatism: The Virginia Convention of 1829–1830 and the Conservative Tradition in the South* (San Marino, CA: The Huntington Library, 1982) 179–88. Fredrickson notes that "open assertions of *permanent* inferiority [of Black people] were exceedingly rare" prior to the 1830s. Jordan also discovered that the "Sambo image of the slave simply was not reported . . . prior to the 1830's." Fredrickson, *The Black Image in the White Mind* 43, 52–53. Jordan; qtd. in Mina Davis Caulfield, "Slavery and the Origins of Black Culture: Elkins Revisited," in *Americans from Africa: Slavery and Its Aftermath,* ed. Peter I. Rose (New York: Atherton, 1970) 186. Caulfield cites "personal communication" for the Winthrop Jordan observation and alludes to a paper he delivered at the American Historical Association meetings in December 1964 (192, n. 45).

45. Dew, "Abolition of Negro Slavery" 25.

46. James Jones and William Styron, "Two Writers Talk It Over," in West, *Conversations with William Styron* 45. Canzoneri and Stegner, "An Interview with William Styron" 70, 71. George Plimpton, "William Styron: A Shared Ordeal," *The New York Times* (October 8, 1967): 32. Woodward and Lewis, "Slavery in the First Person" 36. Raymond A. Sokolov, "Into the Mind of Nat Turner," *Newsweek* (October 16, 1967): 67. Woodward and Lewis, "Slavery in the First Person" 36. Canzoneri and Stegner, "An Interview with William Styron" 70.

47. Barzelay and Sussman, "William Styron on *The Confessions of Nat Turner*" 100. Ben Forkner and Gilbert Schricke, "An Interview with William Styron," in West, *Conversations with William Styron* 193, 192. Styron, "Afterword to the Vintage Edition: Nat Turner Revisited," in Styron, *The Confessions of Nat Turner* 341.

48. Styron, "Afterword to the Vintage Edition: Nat Turner Revisited" 443, 446. For contemporary and near-contemporary reports of Nat Turner's wife, see *Richmond Constitutional Whig,* September 26, 1831; reprinted in Tragle, *The Southampton Slave Revolt of 1831* 92; Warner, *Authentic and Impartial Narrative of the Tragical Scene Which Was Witnessed in Southampton County* 296; Thomas Wentworth Higginson, *Travellers and Outlaws: Episodes in American History* (Boston, 1889) 280–81; and Tragle, "Styron and His Sources," *Massachusetts Review* 11 (1970): 145–46. For Turner's reasons for hiding his wife's existence from Gray, see Wells; in "An Exchange on 'Nat Turner'" 31; cf. Daniel Panger, *Ol' Prophet Nat* (Winston-Salem: John F. Blair Publishers, 1967) 58. For the information on Styron's copy of Drewry's *The Southampton Insurrection,* see Arthur D. Casciato and James L. W. West III, "William Styron and *The Southampton Insurrection,*" *American Literature* 52 (1981): 569 (n. 9).

49. Styron, "Afterword to the Vintage Edition: Nat Turner Revisited" 444. Canzoneri and Stegner, "An Interview with William Styron" 68, 69, 75.

50. Warner, *Authentic and Impartial Narrative* 287. Bennett, "Nat's Last White Man" 13–14. Gray, The *Confessions of Nat Turner* 313, 312, 313. Tragle, "An Approximate Chronology of the Southampton Slave Revolt," in *The Southampton Slave Revolt of 1831* xv–xviii.

51. Woodward and Lewis, "Slavery in the First Person" 37, 38.

52. Again, I am not denying that in a society such as ours it is almost impossible to make firm distinctions between sexual desire and violence. Cf. MacKinnon, "Sex and Violence" 88; and Marcus, "Fighting Bodies, Fighting Words" 392, 396.

53. Canzoneri and Stegner, "An Interview with William Styron" 69. Woodward and Lewis, "Slavery in the First Person" 38. Plimpton, "William Styron: A Shared Ordeal" 32.

54. Bennett, "Nat's Last White Man" 8. Stanley Elkins, *Slavery: A Problem in American Institutional and Intellectual Life* (1959; Chicago: U of Chicago P, 1976). [Daniel Patrick Moynihan], *The Negro Family: The Case for National Action* (Washington, DC: Office of Policy Planning and Research, 1965).

55. Bennett, "Nat's Last White Man" 9, 11. Gray, *The Confessions of Nat Turner* 306. Harding, "You've Taken My Nat and Gone" 26, 29. Cf. Thelwell, "Back with the Wind" 82–83. George Core, *"The Confessions of Nat Turner* and the Burden of the Past," in *The Achievement of William Styron,* ed. Robert K. Morris and Irving Malin (1975; rev. ed.; Athens: U of Georgia P, 1981) 218.

56. Styron, "Overcome" 18–19.

57. Bennett, "Nat's Last White Man" 7.

58. Ernest Kaiser, "The Failure of William Styron," in Clarke, *William Styron's Nat Turner* 56, 57. Thelwell, "Back with the Wind" 87. Bennett, "Nat's Last White Man" 7.

59. Bennett, "Nat's Last White Man" 16. Hamilton, "Our Nat Turner and William Styron's Creation" 74, 78. Clarke, "Introduction" x. Thelwell, "Back with the Wind" 91. Cf. Killens, "The Confessions of Willie Styron" 44. Gray, *The Confessions of Nat Turner,* in Clarke, *William Styron's Nat Turner* 93–118.

60. Genovese, "William Styron Before the People's Court" 203. James H. Cone, *Black Theology and Black Power* (1969; San Francisco: HarperSanFrancisco, 1989) 131.

61. Stephen B. Oates, "Children of Darkness," *American Heritage* 24 (1973): 42–47, 89–91.

62. Styron's letter; in "Postscripts to History," *American Heritage* 25 (1974): 101. Styron, *This Quiet Dust and Other Writings* (1982; New York: Vintage International, 1993) 6–7.

63. Daniel Panger's novel *Ol' Prophet Nat* is a much-ignored but important representation of Nat Turner which has suffered critical neglect mostly because it was distributed by a small press, John F. Blair Publishers, operating out of Winston Salem, although the novel was reprinted that same year (1967) in a Fawcett Gold Medal Books paperback edition. I have no information about its sales; but there is virtually no body of critical reception of either edition.

64. Foner, *Nat Turner* 141–51, 158–66, 172–74. Tragle, *The Southampton Slave Revolt of 1831* 12–13. F. Roy Johnson, *The Nat Turner Story: History of the South's Most Important Slave Revolt, With New Material Provided by Black Tradition and White Tradition* (Murfreesboro, NC: Johnson, 1970) 179–80. Oates, *The Fires of Jubilee: Nat Turner's Fierce Rebellion* (1975; New York: Harper & Row, 1990) 147–54.

65. Harding, "You've Taken My Nat and Gone" 29. Genovese, "William Styron Before the People's Court" 202. Harding; in "An Exchange on Nat Turner" 35–37.

66. Ellison, Styron, Warren, and Woodward, "The Uses of History in Fiction" 127. Ellison, *Shadow and Act* (New York: Random House, 1964) 148.

67. Thelwell, in "An Exchange on Nat Turner" 34. Thelwell, "Back with the Wind" 87 (n. 2).

68. Cf. Caulfield, "Slavery and the Origins of Black Culture: Elkins Revisited" 171–93. To see how the debate over Styron changed the tenor of the debate over Elkins, compare the writings of three historians who wrote on Elkins before and after the controversy. See Genovese, "Problems in the Study of Nineteenth-Century American History," *Science and Society* 25.1 (1961): 38–53; and Genovese, "The Influence of the Black Power Movement on Historical Scholarship," *Daedalus* 1 (1970): 473–94. See Stuckey, "Through the Prism of Folklore: The Black Ethos in Slavery," *Massachusetts Review* 9 (1968): 417–37; and Stuckey, "Twilight of Our Past" 261–95. See Roy Simón Bryce-Laporte, "The American Slave Plantation and Our Heritage of Communal Deprivation," *American Behavioral Scientist* 12 (1969): 2–8; and Bryce-Laporte, "Slaves as Inmates, Slaves as Men: A Sociological Discussion of Elkins's Thesis," in *The Debate Over Slavery: Stanley Elkins and His Critics,* ed. Ann J. Lane (Urbana: U of Illinois P, 1971) 269–92. To appreciate the extent to which Styron (and Moynihan) assumed a new level of importance in the critique of the Elkins thesis after the debate over Styron, one should also compare Bryce-Laporte's 1971 essay with the original section of his doctoral dissertation from which it is taken. Cf. Bryce-Laporte, "The Conceptualization of the American Slave Plantation as a Total Institution" (Ph.D.: University of California at Los Angeles, 1968) 237–69.

69. Fremont-Smith, "'A Sword Is Sharpened,'" *New York Times* (October 3, 1967): 45. Fremont-Smith, "'The Confessions of Nat Turner'—II," *New York Times* (October 4, 1967): 45. Duberman, *The Uncompleted Past* 214–15.

70. Fremont-Smith, "Nat Turner I: The Controversy" 29. Fremont-Smith, "Nat Turner II: What Myth Will Serve?" 31. Duberman, *The Uncompleted Past* 220, 203, 221, 203. At the end of his review, Duberman remained largely resistant to those very imperatives of New Left social history that critics brought with them to the debate over Styron's novel. He claims to be still "leery of the 'oral tradition' which some of the writers [in the Clarke collection] are reduced to citing." That "oral tradition," of course, not only would become a prominent feature of social history in the seventies and eighties, but would also play a fundamental role in Duberman's own work after the debate. His magnificent biography of Paul Robeson would have been unimaginable without the "oral tradition" on which he there draws with such expertise.

71. For his 1966 position, see Genovese, "The Legacy of Slavery and the Roots of Black Nationalism," *Studies on the Left* 6 (1966): 3–64, which contains the responses by Aptheker, Kofsky, and Woodward, and Genovese's rejoinder. For his 1970 position, see Genovese, "American Slaves and Their History," *New York Review of Books* (December 3, 1970): 34–43; and Genovese, "The Influence of the Black Power Movement on Historical Scholarship," 230–55. Cf. August Meier and Elliott Rudwick, *Black History and the Historical Profession, 1915–1980* (Urbana: U of Illinois P, 1985) 260–62.

72. Sherley Anne Williams, "The Lion's History: The Ghetto Writes B[l]ack," *Soundings* 76.2–3 (1993): 248. Robert A. Gross, "The Black Novelists: 'Our Turn,'" *Newsweek* (June 16, 1969): 94–98. Nathan Irvin Huggins, *Afro-American Studies: A Report to the Ford Foundation* (New York: Ford Foundation, 1985). Cf. Van Deburg, "No Mere Mortals: Black Slaves

and Black Power in American Literature, 1967–80," *South Atlantic Quarterly* 83 (1984): 297–311.

73. Murray, *The Omni-Americans: Some Alternatives to the Folklore of White Supremacy* (New York: Da Capo, 1970) 7.

74. Styron's interview; Braudeau, "Why I Wrote *Sophie's Choice,"* in West, *Conversations with William Styron* 245. Cf. Styron, *This Quiet Dust and Other Writings* 5: "the first novel in the long annals of American publishing to evoke such an immediate, entirely hostile attack." Styron, "Afterword to the Vintage Edition: Nat Turner Revisited" 450. Foner, *Nat Turner* 180.

75. Frederick Karl, *American Fictions: 1940–1980* (New York: Harper & Row, 1983) 340, 343, 344. Richard Gray, *The Literature of Memory: Modern Writers of the American South* (Baltimore: Johns Hopkins UP, 1977) 292, 305.

76. Cf. Victor Bernstein, "Black Power, 1831," *Hadassah Magazine* (1967): 16, 37; Granville Hicks, "Race Riot, 1831," *Saturday Review* 50 (October 7, 1967): 29–31; and Wilfrid Sheed, "The Slave Who Became a Man," *The New York Times* (October 8, 1967): 3.

77. Barzelay and Sussman, "William Styron on *The Confessions of Nat Turner*" 87, 96. Styron, "Afterword to the Vintage Edition" 454, 451.

78. Thelwell, "Back with the Wind" 79. Cf. Clarke, "Introduction" ix. Genovese, "The Influence of the Black Power Movement on Historical Scholarship" 240. Cf. Alice Rewald, "William Styron," in West, *Conversations with William Styron* 82: Styron predicted the "Black Power radicals will hate" this novel.

79. Nancy Armstrong and Leonard Tennenhouse, "Introduction: Representing Violence, or 'How the West Was Won,'" in *The Violence of Representation: Literature and the History of Violence,* ed. Armstrong and Tennenhouse (New York: Routledge, 1989) 8. Teresa de Lauretis, "The Violence of Rhetoric: Considerations on Representation and Gender," in Armstrong and Tennenhouse, *The Violence of Representation* 242; cf. Wini Breines and Linda Gordon, "The New Scholarship on Family Violence," *Signs: A Journal of Women in Culture and Society* 8 (1983): 511. Bennett, "Nat's Last White Man" 11. Cecil M. Brown, "Marse Styron Revisited: Plus a Note on Black Writing," *Negro Digest* 17 (1968): 55.

80. Malcolm X, with Alex Haley, *The Autobiography of Malcolm X* (1965; New York: Ballantine, 1992) 203. Editors, "[Introduction to] T. R. Gray, 'The Confessions, Trial, and Execution of Nat Turner, the Negro Insurrectionary,'" *Negro Digest* 14 (1965): 28. Lester, "The Angry Children of Malcolm X," in *Black Protest Thought in the Twentieth Century,* ed. Meier, Rudwick, and Francis L. Broderick (2nd ed. New York: Macmillan, 1971) 483. Lester, "The Necessity of Violence," in *Revolutionary Notes* (New York: Grove, 1969) 42. Harding, "Where Have All the Lovers Gone?" *New South* 21 (1966): 28, 35. Gayle, "Nat Turner vs. Black Nationalists," *Liberator* 8 (1968): 6. For other references to Nat Turner before Styron, see Killens, *Black Man's Burden* (1965; New York: Pocket Books, 1969) 26; Killens, *'Sippi* (1967; New York: Thunder's Mouth, 1988) 150; Eldridge Cleaver, *Soul on Ice* (New York: McGraw-Hill, 1968) 110, 209; and Williams, *The Man Who Cried I Am* (1967; New York: Thunder's Mouth, 1985) 388.

81. Harding, "You've Taken My Nat and Gone" 26, 32. Cf. Killens, "The Confessions of Willie Styron," 36, 43–44; and Williams, "The Manipulation of History and of Fact" 45, 49.

82. Thelwell, "Back with the Wind" 82.

4. The Possession of Resistance

1. Peter N. Carroll, *It Seemed Like Nothing Happened: America in the 1970s* (1982; New Brunswick: Rutgers UP, 1994) xiii. Peter Clecak, *America's Quest for the Ideal Self: Dissent and Fulfillment in the 60s and 70s* (New York: Oxford UP, 1983) 92–93. Cf. David Deleon, "The American as Anarchist: Social Criticism in the 1960s," *American Quarterly* 25 (1973): 516–37; Andrew Kopkind, "Looking Backward: The Sixties and the Movement," *Ramparts* 11 (1973);

James M. Fendrich, "Activists Ten Years Later: A Test of Generational Unit Continuity," *Journal of Social Issues* 30 (1974): 95–118; and Daniel A. Foss and Ralph Larkin, "From 'The Gates of Elden' to the 'Day of the Locust': An Analysis of the Dissident Youth Movement of the 1960s and Its Heirs of the Early 1970s—The Post-Movement Groups," *Theory and Society* 3 (1976): 45–64.

2. Michael Harrington, *Decade of Decision: The Crisis of the American System* (New York: Simon & Schuster, 1980) 287. Michael Crozier, Samuel P. Huntington, and Joji Watanuki, *The Crisis of Democracy* (New York: New York UP, 1975) 8. Richard G. Braungart and Margaret M. Braungart, "Political Career Patterns of Radical Activists in the 1960s and 1970s: Some Historical Comparisons," *Sociological Focus* 13 (1980): 237–54. R. Weiner and D. Stillman, *Woodstock Consensus: The Nationwide Survey of the Sixties Generation* (New York: Viking, 1979). "Savio, Leader of '64 Student Revolt, Returns to Berkeley a Changed Man," *Washington Post* (December 6, 1970): A4. R. Boeth, "The Return of Mark Rudd," *Newsweek* (September 26, 1977): 34. "Abbie Hoffman Tells of His Life during 20 Months as a Fugitive," *New York Times,* December 7, 1975. For reports on Eldridge Cleaver, see T. D. Allman, "The 'Rebirth' of Eldridge Cleaver," *New York Times Magazine* (January 16, 1977): 10–11, 31–34; and news stories in *New York Times* (November 18, 1975): 37 and *New York Times* (January 4, 1980): 10, cf. Carroll, *It Seemed Like Nothing Happened* 328. Eldridge Cleaver, "The Facists Have Already Decided in Advance to Murder Chairman Bobby Seale in the Electric Chair: A Manifesto," in *The Black Panthers Speak,* ed. Philip S. Foner (1970; New York: De Capo, 1995) 117–19. Edward P. Morgan, *The Sixties Experience: Hard Lessons about Modern America* (Philadelphia: Temple UP, 1991) 288 (n. 8). Cf. Michael Omi and Howard Winant, *Racial Formation in the United States from the 1960s to the 1980s* (New York: Routledge, 1986) 118–31; and Clecak, *America's Quest for the Ideal Self* 76–91.

3. Allman, "The 'Rebirth' of Eldridge Cleaver" 10–11, 31–34. Todd Gitlin, "SDS Around the Campfire," *The Nation,* October 22, 1977. Jack Whelan and Richard Flacks, *Beyond the Barricades: The Sixties Generation Grows Up* (Philadelphia: Temple UP, 1989) 252. Carl Oglesby; in Joan Morrison and Robert K. Morrison, *From Camelot to Kent State: The Sixties Experience in the Words of Those Who Lived It* (New York: Times Books, 1987) 307. Tom Hayden; qtd. in Lauren Kessler, *After All These Years: Sixties Ideals in a Different World* (New York: Thunder's Mouth, 1990) 63.

4. Alice Walker, *Meridian* (1976; New York: Pocket, 1986) 188–89, 24, 33. Morris Dickstein, *Gates of Eden: American Culture in the Sixties* (New York: Basic, 1977) 272, 213, 270.

5. Nathan Hare, "Division and Confusion: What Happened to the Black Movement," *Black World* 25.3 (January 1976): 26. Richard Long, "Renaissance Personality: An Interview with George Schuyler," *Black World* 25 (1976): 75–76. Larry Neal, "And Shine Swam On," in *Black Fire: An Anthology of Afro-American Writing,* ed. LeRoi Jones and Neal (New York: William Morrow, 1968) 653–56. Neal, "The Black Contribution to American Letters, Part II: The Writer as Activist—1960 and After," *The Black American Reference Book,* ed. Mabel M. Smythe (Englewood Cliffs, NJ: Prentice-Hall, 1976) 783–84. Cf. Abby Arthur Johnson and Ronald Johnson, "Charting a New Course: African American Literary Politics since 1976," in *The Black Columbiad: Defining Moments in African American Literature and Culture,* ed. Werner Sollors and Maria Diedrich (Cambridge, MA: Harvard UP, 1994) 369–81.

6. Ismael Reed, *Shrovetide in Old New Orleans* (1978; New York: Atheneum, 1989) 5, 17, 70, 72. Reed, *Mumbo Jumbo* (1972; New York: Atheneum, 1988) 98. For the Umbra Poets Workshop, see Lorenzo Thomas, "The Shadow World: New York's Umbra Workshop & Origins of the Black Arts Movement," *Callaloo* 1 (1978): 53–72; Thomas, "Alea's Children: The Avant-Garde on the Lower East Side, 1960–1970," *African American Review* 27 (1993): 573–78; and Calvin Hernton, "Umbra: A Personal Recounting," *African American Review* 27 (1993): 579–84. For a discussion of Reed's representation of Black Power in *The Last Days of*

Louisiana Red, see Norman Harris, *Connecting Times: The Sixties in Afro-American Fiction* (Jackson: UP of Mississippi, 1988) 166–86; cf. Houston Baker, "[Review of] *The Last Days of Louisiana Red,*" *Black World* 24 (1975): 51–52, 89. For a discussion of *Flight to Canada* as a commentary on the sixties, see Harris, "The Gods Must Be Angry: *Flight to Canada* as Political History," *Modern Fiction Studies* 34 (1988): 111–23.

It should be noted that Reed was playfully parodic of the Black Power movement from his earliest prose fiction. In his first novel, *Free-Lance Pallbearers,* completed in August 1966, he parodied the Black Power press by having *Poison Dart,* "the magazine of black liberation," concern itself with issues such as the proper way for black writers to "glare at Charlie" and part their hair as "grave issues" for the liberation movement (*The Free-Lance Pallbearers: An Irreverent Novel* [1967; New York: Atheneum, 1988] 106–7). He also parodied the Umbra group by having one of the poets belonging to an "artistic community" say "mothafuka in public by night, but by day . . . stacking milk bottles in the closet instead of taking them back to the store for two cents deposit" as a way of "out-maneuvering whitey" (98). There is, nonetheless, a discernible difference between this playful parody and the kind of critique we find in *Yellow Back Radio Broke-Down,* completed in June 1968, where Reed criticizes the aesthestic narrowness of the Black Arts movement in Loop Garoo's debates with Bo Schmo and the neosocial realist gang (*Yellow Back Radio Broke-Down* [1969; New York: Atheneum, 1988] 34–36), or *The Last Days of Louisiana Red,* completed in December 1973, where Reed dismisses the "sixties" as a time when Moochers "roam[ed] the world, unchecked, hustling like [they] never hustled before" (*The Last Days of Louisiana Red* [1974; New York: Atheneum, 1989] 118).

7. Gaga [Mark S. Johnson], "Interview with Ishmael Reed," in *Conversations with Ishmael Reed,* ed. Bruce Dick and Amritjit Singh (Jackson: U of Mississippi P, 1995) 54. "The Writer as Seer: Ishmael Reed on Ishmael Reed," in Dick and Singh, *Conversations with Ishmael Reed* 71. "Before Columbus Foundation Interview," in Dick and Singh, *Conversations with Ishmael Reed* 161. Stanley Crouch, "Interview with Ishmael Reed," in Dick and Singh, *Conversations with Ishmael Reed* 103, 105. Reed, *Shrovetide in Old New Orleans* 257, 281. Reed, *Airing Dirty Laundry* (Reading, MA: Addison-Wesley, 1993) 201.

8. Reed, *Writin' Is Fightin': Thirty-Seven Years of Boxing on Paper* (New York: Atheneum, 1988) 193. Shamoon Zamir, "An Interview with Ishmael Reed," in Dick and Singh, *Conversations with Ishmael Reed* 277, 280. Reed, *Airing Dirty Laundy* 218. Zamir, "An Interview with Ishmael Reed" 282. Reed, *Writin' Is Fightin'* 5. Reed, *Airing Dirty Laundry* 92. Reed, *Writin' Is Fightin'* 113.

9. Reed, *Airing Dirty Laundry* 93, 103. Reed, *Shrovetide in Old New Orlean* 142, xv. Reed, *Airing Dirty Laundry* 100.

10. Reed, *Shrovetide in Old New Orleans* 41, 257.

11. Reed, *Shrovetide in Old New Orleans* 71. Reed, "The Reactionary Poet," in *New and Collected Poems* (New York: Atheneum, 1989) 158. Reed, "Flight to Canada," in *American Poets in 1976,* ed. William Heyen (Indianapolis: Bobbs-Merrill, 1976) 270, 272. Reed initially conceived of *Flight to Canada* as a science fiction novel; the earliest excerpt from it appeared in *Statements: New Fiction from the Fiction Collective* (New York: George Braziller, 1975) 158–60.

12. Reed, *Shrovetide in Old New Orleans* 71. Reed, "Black Power Poem" in *New and Collected Poems* 19. Reed, *Mumbo Jumbo* 200, 87.

13. Reed, *Flight to Canada* (1976; New York: Atheneum, 1989). Hereafter all quotations from *Flight to Canada* will be taken from this edition and cited parenthetically in the body of the essay.

14. Lerone Bennett, Jr., "Nat's Last White Man," in *William Styron's Nat Turner: Ten Black Writers Respond,* ed. John Henrik Clarke (Boston: Beacon, 1968) 5.

15. William L. Van Deburg, *New Day in Babylon: The Black Power Movement and American Culture, 1965–1975* (Chicago: U of Chicago P, 1992) 266, 267.

16. Wilson Jeremiah Moses, *Black Messiahs and Uncle Toms: Social and Literary Manipulations of a Religious Myth* (1982; University Park: Pennsylvania State UP, 1993) 226, 49–66.

17. Addison Gayle, Jr., *The Black Situation* (New York: Horizon, 1970) 58, 59, 68, 69, 70.

18. Reed, *Shrovetide in Old New Orleans* 210. Ruth Abbott and Ira Simmons, "An Interview with Ishmael Reed," in Dick and Singh, *Conversations with Ishmael Reed* 81–82. Reed, *Shrovetide in Old New Orleans* 104.

19. Abbott and Simmons, "An Interview with Ishmael Reed" 91. Michael Helm, "Ishmael Reed: An Interview," in Dick and Singh, *Conversations with Ishmael Reed* 160, 150. Reed, *Shrovetide in Old New Orleans* 281.

20. Reed, "Flight to Canada" 267. William Styron, *The Confessions of Nat Turner* (1967; New York: Random House, 1992) 111. Reed, *Airing Dirty Laundry* 123, 93, 103, 100.

21. For different readings of the reference to Nat Turner, see Charles de Arman, "The Black Image in the Black Mind; or, *Flight to Canada*," *College Language Association Journal* 33 (1989): 166, 176; and Joe Weixlmann, "Politics, Piracy, and Other Games: Slavery and Liberation in *Flight to Canada*," *MELUS* 6 (1979): 49.

22. Hortense Spillers, "Changing the Letter: The Yokes, the Jokes of Discourse, or, Mrs. Stowe, Mr. Reed," in *Slavery and the Literary Imagination*, ed. Deborah E. McDowell and Arnold Rampersad (Baltimore: Johns Hopkins UP, 1989) 47. Robert Elliot Fox, *Conscientious Sorcerers: The Black Postmodernist Fiction of LeRoi Jones / Amiri Baraka, Ishmael Reed, and Samuel R. Delaney* (Westport, CT: Greenwood, 1987) 69. Henry Louis Gates, Jr., "[Review of Reed's *Flight to Canada*]," *Journal of Negro History* 63 (1978): 80. Weixlmann, "Politics, Piracy, and Other Games" 48. Keith Byerman, *Fingering the Jagged Grain: Tradition and Form in Recent Black Fiction* (Athens: U of Georgia P, 1985) 232.

23. Edgar Allan Poe, *The Fall of the House of Usher*, in *The Collected Tales and Poems of Edgar Allan Poe* (New York: The Modern Library, 1992) 245. Reed, *Writin' Is Fightin'* 137.

24. Josiah Henson, *The Life of Josiah Henson, Formerly a Slave, Now an Inhabitant of Canada, as Narrated by Himself* (Boston, 1849) 42–43. Since the first edition of Henson's autobiography is considerably rarer and more difficult to find than the second and third, I will also cite the parallel texts. Cf. Henson, *Truth Stranger than Fiction. Father Henson's Story of His Own Life* (Boston, 1858) 89–90; and Henson, *An Autobiography of the Rev. Josiah Henson ("Uncle Tom") from 1789 to 1881* (London, Ontario, 1881) 53–54. This first edition of Henson's autobiography is the one to which Reed refers in *Flight to Canada*, but it is most likely not the only one on which he bases his novel. Reed refers to information not contained in the first autobiography but contained in the second and third editions of his autobiographies— for instance the fact that Henson's settlement at Dawn went bankrupt and that Henson "fell in love with wood" (*Flight* 8).

25. Harriet Beecher Stowe, *Uncle Tom's Cabin Or, Life Among the Lowly*, ed. Ann Douglas (New York: Penguin, 1981) 560–61.

26. Reed, *Mumbo Jumbo* 24, 172.

27. Malcolm X, *February 1965: The Final Speeches*, ed. Steve Clark (New York: Pathfinder, 1992) 27; cf. Calvin Hernton, "Dynamite Growing Out of Their Skulls," in Jones and Neal, *Black Fire* 78–104, esp. pp. 91–92; and Q. R. Hand, "[untitled poem]," in Jones and Neal, *Black Fire* 258. Reed, *Shrovetide in Old New Orleans* 143, 142.

28. Van Deburg, *New Day in Babylon* 270–71. Nikki Giovanni, "Concerning One Responsible Negro with Too Much Power," in *Black Feeling, Black Talk, Black Judgment* (1970; New York: Morrow, 1979) 52–53. Giovanni, "The True Import of Present Dialogue, Black vs. Negro (For Peppe, Who Will Ultimately Judge Our Efforts)," in *Black Feeling* 19–20. Van Deburg, *New Day in Babylon* 271. Neal, "The Black Arts Movement," in Neal, *Visions of a Liberated Future: Black Arts Movement Writings*, ed. Michael Schwartz (New York: Thunder's Mouth,

1989) 77, 73. Neal, "Love Song in Middle Passage," in *Visions of a Liberated Future* 213. Cf. Alvin F. Poussaint, "A Negro Psychiatrist Explains the Negro Psyche," in *Black Protest in the Sixties,* ed. August Meier, Elliot Rudwick, and John Bracey, Jr. (New York: Markus Weiner, 1991) 135: "feet-shuffling, scraping and bowing, obsequiousness and Uncle Tomism may actually indicate inner rage and deep hatred." Cf. John Oliver Killens, *Black Man's Burden* (1965; New York: Pocket Books, 1969) 13.

29. Abbott and Simmons, "An Interview with Ishmael Reed" 81–82.

30. John O'Brien, *Interviews with Black Writers* (New York: Liveright, 1973) 179.

31. Eugene D. Genovese, *Roll, Jordan, Roll: The World the Slaves Made* (New York: Random House, 1974) 597–98, 591, 598, 659.

32. Genovese, *Roll, Jordan, Roll* 617. Robert Edgar Conrad, *Children of God's Fire: A Documentary History of Black Slavery in Brazil* (Princeton, NJ: Princeton UP, 1983) 251, 254.

33. A. Leon Higginbotham, *In the Matter of Color: Race and the American Legal Process: The Colonial Period* (New York: Oxford UP, 1978) 179.

34. Samuel A. Cartwright, "Diseases and Peculiarities of the Negro Race," in *The Cause of the South: Selections from De Bow's Review, 1846–1867,* ed. Paul F. Paskoff and Daniel J. Wilson (Baton Rouge: Louisiana State UP, 1982) 42. For more information on Samuel Cartwright's life and ideas, see James Denny Guillory, "The Pro-Slavery Arguments of Dr. Samuel A. Cartwright," *Louisiana History* 9 (1968): 209–27. Cartwright diagnosed two diseases to which slaves were prone: "Drapetomania, or the disease causing Negroes to run away," and "Dysæsthesia Æthiopica, or Hebetude of Mind, and Obtuse Sensibility of Body—A Disease Peculiar to Negroes—Called by Overseers, 'Rascality.'" When Swille discovers that Stray Leechfield, 40S, and Raven Quickskill have absconded, he tells Uncle Robin that these fugitives have "contracted Drapetomania, as that distinguished scientist Dr. Samuel Cartwright described in that book you read to me." Uncle Robin responds by offering Swille the name of the other disease Cartwright diagnosed: "Dysæsthesia Æthipica, Mr. Swille?" "Exactly, Robin," responds Swille, "that disease causing Negroes to run away" (18). Swille is confused between the two distinct diseases because Robin has confused him, giving him the wrong term. This confusion between the two diseases is significant because Swille, like Cartwright, finds it useful to confuse the relationship of medicine to property rights. Immediately after stating his desire to cure the ailing slaves, Swille proclaims he will "never yield a piece of property" (19).

35. John C. Calhoun, "Remarks Made during the Debate on His Resolutions, in Respect to the Right of States and the Abolition of Slavery,—December 27th, 1837, *et. seq.,*" in *The Works of John C. Calhoun,* 6 vol., ed. Richard K. Crallé (New York: D. Appleton, 1853), vol. 3: 180.

36. James W. Button, *Black Violence: Political Impact of the 1960s Riots* (Princeton, NJ: Princeton UP, 1978) 158, 159, 164, 152.

37. Gayle, *The Black Situation* 214, 215, 219, 221. By late 1966, Killens had likewise changed his opinion that Black Power required violence. In an article in the December issue of *Negro Digest* in that year, he maintained, contrary to his previous declarations, that "Black Power is not an advocate of violence. It advocates non-violence, but in depth. It keeps everybody non-violent. It stays the hand of the practitioners of violence." Killens; qtd. in Harold Cruse, *The Crisis of the Negro Intellectual* (1967; New York: Quill, 1984) 561.

38. Cruse, *The Crisis of the Negro Intellectual* 548–49, 86, 466, 505. For Reed's comments on Cruse, see Walt Sheppard, "When State Magicians Fail: An Interview with Ishmael Reed," in Dick and Singh, *Conversations with Ishmael Reed* 7; and Reed, *Airing Dirty Laundry* 8.

39. Reed, *Shrovetide in Old New Orleans* 238, 41. John O'Brien; Dick and Singh, *Conversations with Ishmael Reed* 24. Reed, "Before Columbus Foundation Interview" 175, 177. Abbott and Simmons, "An Interview with Ishmael Reed" 76.

40. For two different readings of what Robin and his wife do with the Swille plantation,

see Sondra A. O'Neale, "Ishmael Reed's Fitful *Flight to Canada:* Liberation for Some, Good Reading for All," *Callaloo* (1978): 176; and Peter Nazareth, "Heading Them Off at the Pass: The Fiction of Ishmael Reed," *Review of Contemporary Fiction* 4 (1984): 213.

41. A firm believer in the liberatory possibilities of democratically controlled small presses, Reed was not only writing about the possibility of intervening in the cultural scene in America, but also actively intervening in that scene. At the same time that he was writing *Flight to Canada* in 1976, Reed established the Before Columbus Foundation, believing that "we could best serve the literature we championed by establishing new institutions." Rather than confronting "commercial literary institutions" and their supporting intellectual discourses of "standards" and "quality," Reed and his associates created an independent cultural apparatus committed to publishing and disseminating multicultural literature and thereby challenged "the literary industrial complex [to] face up to the important changes that have occurred in American literature since the 1960s." See Reed, *Airing Dirty Laundry* 117, 120.

42. Reed, *Airing Dirty Laundry* 271. John Domini, "Ishmael Reed: A Conversation with John Domini," in Dick and Singh, *Conversations with Ishmael Reed* 137. Judith Moore, "A Conversation with Ishmael Reed," in Dick and Singh, *Conversations with Ishmael Reed* 223. For a discussion of Reed's play with genre, see Weixlmann, "African American Deconstruction of the Novel in the Work of Ishmael Reed and Clarence Major," *MELUS* 17 (1991–1992): 63.

43. Robert B. Stepto, *From Behind the Veil: A Study of Afro-American Narrative* (1979; Urbana: U of Illinois P, 1991) xv. Frederick Douglass, *My Bondage and My Freedom,* ed. William L. Andrews (Urbana: U of Illinois P, 1987) 220–21.

44. Frances Smith Foster, *Witnessing Slavery: The Development of Ante-bellum Slave Narratives* (Westport, CT: Greenwood, 1979) 3, 23. Stepto, *From Behind the Veil* 207, 3.

45. William L. Andrews, *To Tell a Free Story: The First Century of Afro-American Autobiography, 1760–1865* (Urbana: U of Illinois P, 1986) 32–33, 65, 64. Gates, *The Signifying Monkey: A Theory of African-American Literary Criticism* (New York: Oxford UP, 1988) 218. James Olney, "'I was Born': Slave Narratives, Their Status as Autobiography and as Literature," in *The Slave's Narrative,* ed. Charles T. Davis and Henry Louis Gates, Jr. (New York: Oxford UP, 1985) 154. Andrews, *To Tell a Free Story* 65.

46. Nazareth, "An Interview with Ishmael Reed," in Dick and Singh, *Conversations with Ishmael Reed* 195. On the ways white racial identity was "naturalized" in American legal practice, see Ian F. Haney López, *White by Law: The Legal Construction of Race* (New York: New York UP, 1996).

47. Jean-Paul Sartre, "Why Write?" in *Criticism: The Major Statements,* ed. Charles Kaplan (New York: St. Martin's, 1975) 542, 544.

48. Douglass, *Narrative of the Life of Frederick Douglass, An American Slave, Written by Himself,* ed. Benjamin Quarles (Cambridge, MA: Harvard UP, 1960) 70–71, 162–63. Abdul JanMohamed, "Negating the Negation as a Form of Affirmation in Minority Discourse: The Construction of Richard Wright as Subject," *Cultural Critique* 7 (1987): 247.

49. Reed, *Shrovetide in Old New Orleans* 239–40. The article Reed is quoting about "white masters" is Robert Moss, "The Arts in Black America," *Saturday Review,* November 15, 1975.

50. Reed, *Airing Dirty Laundry* 270.

51. For critical commentary on Reed's use of HooDoo, see: Neil Schmitz, "Neo-HooDoo: The Experimental Fiction of Ishmael Reed," *Twentieth Century Literature* 20 (1974): 126–40; Chester J. Fontenot, "Ishmael Reed and the Politics of Aesthetics, or, Shake Hands and Come Out Conjuring," *Black American Literature Forum* 12 (1978): 20–23; Frank McConnell, "Ishmael Reed's Fiction: Da Hoodoo is Put on America," in *Black Fiction: New Studies in the Afro-American Novel Since 1945,* ed. A. Robert Lee (New York: Barnes and Noble, 1980) 136–48; James R. Lindroth, "Generating the Vocabulary of Hoodoo: Zora Neale Hurston and Ishmael

Reed," *Zora Neale Hurston Forum* 2 (1987): 27–34; Reginald Martin, *Ishmael Reed and the New Black Aesthetic Critics* (New York: St. Martin's, 1988) 63–108; and Darryl Pinckney, "Trickster Tales," in *Speech and Power: The African-American Essay and Its Cultural Content from Polemics to Pulpit*, ed. Gerald Early (Hopewell, NJ: Ecco, 1992), Vol. 1: 315–24.

52. I am alluding partly, of course, to the Derridean concept of the "trace." I discuss the connections between Derrida and Reed more fully elsewhere; see my "Ishmael Reed's Neo-HooDoo Slave Narrative," *Narrative* 2 (1994): 112–39. On the Derridean "trace," see Jacques Derrida, "Difference," in Derrida, *Speech and Phenomena and Other Essays on Husserl's Theory of Signs*, trans. David B. Allison (Evanston, IN: Northwestern UP, 1973) 129–60; and Derrida, *Of Grammatology*, trans. Gayatri Chakravorty Spivak (1967; Baltimore: Johns Hopkins UP, 1976). On the ways of "resolving" the problem of the "trace," see Derrida, *Of Grammatology* 55–57, 60, 56, 61, 62, 65; Rodolphe Gasché, *The Tain of the Mirror: Derrida and the Philosophy of Reflection* (Cambridge, MA: Harvard UP, 1986) 192; and Jean-Luc Nancy, "'Eating Well,' or the Calculation of the Subject: An Interview with Jacques Derrida," in *Who Comes After the Subject?* ed. Eduardo Cadava, Peter Connor, and Jean-Luc Nancy (New York: Routledge, 1991) 96–119.

53. For a discussion of the significance of Swille's dyslexia, see Spillers, "Changing the Letter" 56–57. As Spillers notes, having Swille dyslexic is Reed's parody on Stowe's Uncle Tom, who is dyslexic (or at least cannot tell the difference between a *q* and a *g*). See Stowe, *Uncle Tom's Cabin* 68–69. Stowe is herself perhaps making a comment on Josiah Henson's difficulty in learning to read. See Henson, *The Life of Josiah Henson* 64–65.

54. Cf. Theodore O. Mason, Jr., "Performance, History, and Myth: The Problem of Ishmael Reed's *Mumbo Jumbo*," *Modern Fiction Studies* 34 (1988): 107; and Byerman, *Fingering the Jagged Grain* 233.

55. James W. C. Pennington, *The Fugitive Blacksmith; or Events in the History of James W. C. Pennington* (3rd ed.; London, 1850) xii, 63–64, Douglass, *Narrative of the Life of Frederick Douglass, An American Slave, Written by Himself* 135–36. Henry Box Brown, *Narrative of Henry Box Brown, Who Escaped from Slavery Enclosed in a Box Three Feet Long, Two Wide, and Two and a Half High. Written from a Statement of Facts Made by Himself* (Boston, 1849) 59. For a list of other attempts by slaves to ship themselves north of slavery through the mail system, see Marion Starling, *The Slave Narrative: Its Place in American History* (1981; Washington: Howard UP, 1988) 170–71.

56. Reed is expanding on an important theme that former slaves had developed in their own writing and oral interviews. Having an intimate life story stolen from them was a situation more than one former slave feared. As former slave Thomas Hall, who was 81 years old when he was interviewed in North Carolina in 1937, put it poignantly to an interviewer from the Works Project Administration: "You are going around to get a story of slavery conditions and the persecutions of Negroes before the Civil War and the economic conditions concerning them since that war. You should have known before this late date all about that. Are you going to help us? No! You are only helping yourself. You say that my story may be put into a book, that you are from the Federal Writers' Project. Well, the Negro will not get anything out of it, no matter where you are from. Harriet Beecher Stowe wrote *Uncle Tom's Cabin*. I didn't like her book, and I hate her. No matter where you are from, I don't want you to write my story, because the white folks have been and are now and always will be against the Negro." Thomas Hall; in *Before Freedom: 48 Oral Histories of Former North and South Carolina Slaves*, ed. Belinda Hurmence (New York: Mentor, 1990) 45.

57. Cf. Gates, "[Review of Reed's *Flight to Canada*]" 80. According to Gates, Reed is writing about what Stepto called "narrative control"—"the possession of one's own story, be that our collective history or even one's very own autobiography."

58. Reed, *Shrovetide in Old New Orleans* 248.

59. C. W. E. Bigsby, *The Second Black Renaissance: Essays in Black Literature* (Westport, CT: Greenwood, 1980) 158.

60. Barbara Foley, *Telling the Truth: The Theory and Practice of Documentary Fiction* (Ithaca, NY: Cornell UP, 1986) 259. John M. Reilly, "The Reconstruction of Genre as Entry into Conscious History," *Black American Literature Forum* 13 (1979): 6. For studies of the relationship between Harriet Beecher Stowe's *Uncle Tom's Cabin* and Josiah Henson, see Thomas F. Gossett, *Uncle Tom's Cabin and American Culture* (Dallas: Southern Methodist UP, 1985) 107–9; and Robin W. Winks, "The Making of a Fugitive Slave Narrative: Josiah Henson and Uncle Tom—A Case Study," in Davis and Gates, *The Slave's Narrative*, 112–46. For a discussion of Stowe's relationship with other slaves and slave narratives, see Robert B. Stepto, "Sharing the Thunder: The Literary Exchanges of Harriet Beecher Stowe, Henry Bibb, and Frederick Douglass," in *New Essays on Uncle Tom's Cabin,* ed. Eric J. Sundquist (Cambridge: Cambridge UP, 1986) 135–53.

61. Reed, *Shrovetide in Old New Orleans* 74, 10. I have discussed Reed's use of Hoodoo more fully elsewhere; see my "Ishmael Reed's Neo-HooDoo Slave Narrative."

62. Michael Saturnin Laguerre; qutd. in Claude F. Jacobs, "Spirit Guides and Possession in the New Orleans Black Spiritual Churches" *Journal of American Folklore* 102 (1989): 46. Joan Dayan, "Voudon, or the Voice of the Gods" *Raritan* 10 (1991): 45, 35.

63. Maya Deren, *Divine Horsemen: The Living Gods of Haiti* (1953; New York: McPherson & Company, 1991) 73. Dayan, "Vodoun, or the Voice of the Gods" 50. Deren, *Divine Horsemen* 92, 228. Zora Neale Hurston, *Tell My Horse: Voodoo and Life in Haiti and Jamaica* (1938; New York: Harper & Row, 1990) 221, 252. Deren, *Divine Horsemen* 248–49, 30. Harold Courlander, *The Drum and the Hoe: Life and Lore of the Haitian People* (1960; Berkeley: U of California P, 1973) 75. Sheila S. Walker, *Ceremonial Spirit Possession in Africa and Afro-America: Forms, Meanings, and Functional Significance for Individuals and Social Groups* (Leiden: E.J. Brill, 1972) 98. Deren, *Divine Horsemen* 91.

64. Reed, *Shrovetide in Old New Orleans* 74, 3, 73, 75.

65. Cf. Gates, "[Review of Reed's *Flight to Canada]*" 79; Spillers, "Changing the Letter" 47; and Nazareth, "Heading Them Off at the Pass" 223.

66. Dayan, "Voudon, or the Voice of the Gods" 40.

67. For another instance of possessed writing, see Robin's explanation of his motive for rewriting Swille's will. As Robin explains to his wife Judy, when Africans first came to America "our gods came with us." He then "prayed to one of our gods" who came to him in a dream and told him that it was "okay" to dabble with the will: "The 'others' had approved" (170). In other words, Robin writes out the new will after he has been possessed by the gods. This possession not only enables him to write, but also promotes precisely the same kind of intersubjective relations Raven will enjoy once he too is possessed. As Robin explains to Leechfield, Swille was threatened by the acts of the fugitive slaves because the fugitives "were showing the other slaves that it didn't have to be that way. That the promised land was in their heads. The old way. *The old way taught that man could be the host for God. Not one man. All men.* That was the conflict between you and Swille. You, 40S and Quickskill threatened to give the god in the slave breath" (177; my italics).

68. Andrews, *To Tell a Free Story* 98–99, 103.

69. Douglass, *Narrative of the Life* 56, 105, 144, 115.

70. Andrews, *To Tell a Free Story* 143, 165, 164. Pennington, *The Fugitive Blacksmith* 22, 30, 78, 83.

5. Meditations on Story

1. William H. Chafe, *Civilities and Civil Rights: Greensboro, North Carolina, and the Black Struggle for Freedom* (1980; New York: Oxford UP, 1981) viii. Peter Collier and David

Horowitz, *Destructive Generation: Second Thoughts About the Sixties* (1989; New York: Summit Books, 1990). Maurice Isserman, *If I Had a Hammer: The Death of the Old Left and the Birth of the New Left* (New York: Basic Books, 1987) xiv. Michael Omi and Howard Winant, *Racial Formation in the United States from the 1960s to the 1980s* (New York: Routledge, 1996) 131–35. Isserman and Michael Kazin, "The Failure and Success of the New Radicalism," in *The Rise and Fall of the New Deal Order, 1930–1980,* ed. Steve Fraser and Gary Gerstle (Princeton, NJ: Princeton UP, 1989) 229.

2. Winifred Breines, "Whose New Left?" *Journal of American History* 75 (1988): 545. Tim Wohlforth, "The Sixties in America," *New Left Review* 178 (1989): 105. Isserman, "The Not-So-Dark and Bloody Ground: New Works on the 1960s," *American Historical Review* 94 (1989): 990. Cf. Morris Dickstein, "After Utopia: The 1960s Today," in *Sights on the Sixties,* ed. Barbara L. Tischler (New Brunswick, NJ: Rutgers UP, 1992) 13–23. David Farber, "Introduction" to *The Sixties: From Memory to History,* ed. Farber (Chapel Hill: U of North Carolina P, 1994) 1–10. A partial list of appreciative studies would include Chafe, *Civilities and Civil Rights* (1980); on SDS, James Miller, *"Democracy Is in the Streets": From Port Huron to the Siege of Chicago* (New York: Simon & Schuster, 1987); and Todd Gitlin, *The Sixties: Years of Hope, Days of Rage* (New York: Bantam, 1987); on 1968, Ronald Fraser, *1968: A Student Generation in Revolt* (New York: Pantheon, 1988); Farber, *Chicago '68* (Chicago: U of Chicago P, 1988); Charles Kaiser, *1968 in America: Music, Politics, Chaos, Counterculture, and the Shaping of a Generation* (New York: Weidenfeld & Nicolson, 1988); and David Caute, *Sixty-Eight: The Year of the Barricades* (London: Hamish Hamilton, 1988); and on general studies of the sixties, Doug McAdam, *Freedom Summer* (New York: Oxford UP, 1988); and Taylor Branch, *Parting the Waters: America in the King Years 1954–63* (New York: Simon & Schuster, 1988). Peter Collier and David Horowitz, eds., *Second Thoughts: Former Radicals Look Back at the Sixties* (Lanham, MD: Madison, 1989); Collier and Horowitz, eds., *Second Thoughts on Race in America* (Lanham, MD: Madison, 1991) ix. For other conservative explorations of the sixties, see Collier and Horowitz, *Destructive Generation: Second Thoughts about the Sixties;* and John H. Bunzel, ed., *Political Passages: Journeys of Change through Two Decades, 1968–1988* (New York: Free Press, 1988).

3. Manning Marable, *Beyond Black and White: Transforming African-American Politics* (London: Verso, 1995) 128–29. Harold Cruse, *Plural but Equal: A Critical Study of Blacks and Minorities and America's Plural Society* (New York: William Morrow, 1987) 7. Vernon E. Jordan, Jr., "Introduction," in *The State of Black America,* ed. James D. Williams (New York: National Urban League, 1980) i. Clarence Pendleton, Jr.; qtd. in Omi and Winant, *Racial Formation in the United States* 1. Derrick Bell, *Faces at the Bottom of the Well: The Permanence of Racism* (New York: Basic Books, 1992) 13. Shelby Steele, *The Content of Our Character: A New Vision of Race in America* (1990; New York: HarperPerennial, 1991) 54. Glenn Loury, "Beyond Civil Rights," *New Republic* (October 7, 1985): 25. Thomas Sowell, *Civil Rights: Rhetoric or Reality?* (New York: William Morrow, 1984) 119. Michael Eric Dyson, *Reflecting Black: African-American Cultural Criticism* (Minneapolis: U of Minnesota P, 1993) 248. Lerone Bennett, Jr.; in Studs Terkel, *Race: How Blacks and Whites Think and Feel About the American Obsession* (New York: New Press, 1992) 380. Loury, "Black Political Culture After the Sixties," in Collier and Horowitz, *Second Thoughts: Former Radicals Look Back at the Sixties* 148, 147. For the rise of black conservatives and neoconservatives in the eighties, see Charles Banner-Haley, *The Fruits of Integration: Black Middle-Class Ideology and Culture, 1960–1990* (Jackson: UP of Mississippi, 1994) 72–80. For the rise of the black middle class, see Joe R. Feagin and Melvin P. Sikes, *Living with Racism: The Black Middle-Class Experience* (Boston: Beacon, 1994).

4. Henry Louis Gates and Cornel West, *The Future of the Race* (New York: Alfred A. Knopf, 1996) 40–41. Cf. Richard M. Merleman, *Representing Black Culture: Racial Conflict and Cultural Politics in the United States* (New York: Routledge, 1995) 25–27; and Banner-Haley, *The Fruits of Integration* 109–20.

5. Sherley Anne Williams, "Some Implications of Womanist Theory," in *Reading Feminist, Reading Black: A Critical Anthology,* ed. Gates (New York: Meridian, 1990) 73. Williams, *Give Birth to Brightness: A Thematic Study in Neo-Black Literature* (New York: Dial, 1972) 233, 118–19.

6. Williams, "The Lion's History: The Ghetto Writes B[l]ack," *Soundings* 76 (1993): 255, 253. Williams, "[Interview with Shirley M. Jordan]," in Jordan, ed., *Broken Silences: Interviews with Black and White Women Writers* (New Brunswick, NJ: Rutgers UP, 1993) 286, 289. Williams, "[Foreword to 'Meditations on History']," in *Black-Eyed Susans / Midnight Birds: Stories by and about Black Women,* ed. Mary Helen Washington (New York: Anchor Books, 1990) 225.

7. Williams, *Dessa Rose* (1986; New York: Berkeley Books, 1987) ix. Hereafter all quotations from *Dessa Rose* will be taken from this edition and cited parenthetically in the body of the text. Since the specific form that names take are very important to this novel, I will retian Williams's practice and call Dessa Rose by only her first name, Adam Nehemiah by only his last, and Elizabeth Ruth Sutton by her pet name, Rufel. On naming in *Dessa Rose,* see Deborah E. McDowell, "Negotiating Between Tenses: Witnessing Slavery After Freedom—*Dessa Rose,*" in *Slavery and the Literary Imagination,* ed. McDowell and Arnold Rampersad (Baltimore: Johns Hopkins UP, 1989) 148–54; and Mary Kemp Davis, "Everybody Knows Her Name: The Recovery of the Past in Sherley Anne Williams' *Dessa Rose,*" *Callaloo* 12 (1989): 544–58.

8. See Williams, "[Interview with Shirley M. Jordan]" 289, where Williams talks about her editor's urging her to write an "Author's Note." "Meditations on History" was first published in *Midnight Birds: Stories of Contemporary Black Women Writers,* ed. Washington (Garden City, NY: Anchor, 1980) 200–248. (I will be using the updated edition of this anthology, cited in note 6 in this chapter). William Styron, *The Confessions of Nat Turner* (1967; New York: Vintage International Edition, 1992) [xi]. Critics who have written on Williams's revisionist strategies in her dialogue with Styron's *Confessions* include Mae G. Henderson, "(W)riting *The Work* and Working the Rites," *Black American Literature Forum* 23 (1989): 631–60; John C. Inscoe, "Slave Rebellion in the First Person: The Literary 'Confessions' of Nat Turner and Dessa Rose," *The Virginia Magazine of History and Biography* 97 (1989): 419–44; and Albert E. Stone, *The Return of Nat Turner: History, Literature, and Cultural Politics in Sixties America* (Athens: U of Georgia P, 1992) 367, 375–81.

9. Williams, "[Interview with Shirley M. Jordan]" 288.

10. Williams, "[Foreword to 'Meditations on History']" 225. Williams, "[Interview with Claudia Tate]," in Claudia Tate, *Black Women Writers at Work* (New York: Continuum, 1984) 213. Williams, "Returning to the Blues: Esther Phillips and Contemporary Blues Culture," *Callaloo* 14 (1991): 819. Regarding Black Arts theorists' attitudes towards literary form, see Madhu Dubey, *Black Women Novelists and the Nationalist Aesthetic* (Bloomington: Indiana UP, 1994) 9, 31.

11. Williams, *Give Birth to Brightness* 19–20, 243. Williams, "[Foreword to 'Meditations on History']" 225. Williams, "Some Implications of Womanist Theory" 69. Williams, "[Interview with Claudia Tate]" 213. For examples of Williams's Black Power poems, see Williams, "WITNESS," "the provision ground," and "Big Red and His Brothers," in *Some One Sweet Angel Chile* (New York: William Morrow, 1982) 69–76.

12. Williams, "[Interview with Shirley M. Jordan]" 289. Williams, "The Lion's History" 252.

13. Williams, *Give Birth to Brightness* 59. Williams, "The Lion's History" 248.

14. Williams, "Meditations on History" 230. Angela Davis, "Reflections on the Black Woman's Role in the Community of Slaves," *Black Scholar* (1971): 3–15. Herbert Aptheker, *American Negro Slave Revolts* (1943; New York: International Publishers, 1983).

15. Mona Gable; qtd. in Williams, "[Interview with Shirley M. Jordan]" 286. Williams, "[Interview with Shirley M. Jordan]" 289. Williams, "[Foreword to 'Meditations on History']" 225. I am here dividing the novel into two major sections, although it breaks down into five titled sections (six, if one counts the "Author's Note"). I am following Williams's own practice, since she also speaks of "Part I" and "Part II" of her novel. See Williams, "The Lion's History" 255.

16. Roger Abrahams, *The Man-of-Words in the West Indies: Performance and the Emergence of Creole Culture* (Baltimore: Johns Hopkins UP, 1983) 127. Williams, "Some Implications of Womanist Theory" 74.

17. Henderson, "Speaking in Tongues: Dialogics, Dialectics, and the Black Women's Literary Tradition," in *Changing Our Own Words: Essays on Criticism, Theory, and Writing by Black Women,* ed. Cheryl A. Wall (New Brunswick, NJ: Rutgers UP, 1989) 25; cf. 31–32.

18. Robert B. Stepto, *From Behind the Veil: A Study of Afro-American Narrative* (1979; Urbana: U of Illinois P, 1991) xv, 196. Gates, *Figures in Black: Words, Signs, and the "Racial" Self* (New York: Oxford UP, 1987) 249. Gayl Jones, *Liberating Voices: Oral Tradition in African American Narrative* (Cambridge, MA: Harvard UP, 1991) 178. Like Stepto, who shows how this basic "distrust" is always tempered by an equally "abiding faith" in literacy as a means of recording the black experience (196), and like Gates, who argues that African American writers in the Enlightenment "could become speaking subjects only by inscribing their voices in the written word" (*The Signifying Monkey: A Theory of African-American Literary Criticism* [New York: Oxford UP, 1988] 130), Williams also notes that "Afro-American literature" represents "the beginning of a new tradition built on a synthesis of black oral traditions and Western literate forms" (Williams, "The Blues Roots of Contemporary Afro-American Poetry," in *Chant of Saints: A Gathering of Afro-American Literature, Art, and Scholarship,* ed. Michael S. Harper and Stepto [Urbana: U of Illinois P, 1979] 123, 135).

19. Elizabeth Ammons, *Conflicting Stories: American Women Writers at the Turn into the Twentieth Century* (New York: Oxford UP, 1992) 5. See Anne E. Goldman, "'I Made the Ink': (Literary) Production and Reproduction in *Dessa Rose* and *Beloved,*" *Feminist Studies* 16 (1990): 314, 321, 324, 328.

20. Williams, "The Lion's History" 253. Williams, "[Interview with Shirley M. Jordan]" 289. Williams, "The Lion's History" 257. 258.

21. Williams, "The Lion's History" 257, 258. Stepto, *From Behind the Veil* 3–5. Cf. Williams, "The Lion's History" 245.

22. Williams, "The Lion's History" 258. Styron, *Confessions of Nat Turner* [xi].

23. Styron, *Confessions of Nat Turner* xv–xviii. Williams, "The Lion's History" 255. Williams, "Meditations on History" 239, 252. Williams, "[Interview with Shirley M. Jordan]" 288; cf. Williams, "The Lion's History" 255.

24. For a discussion of why Williams may have changed the date of the narrative, see Melissa Walker, *Down from the Mountaintop: Black Women's Novels in the Wake of the Civil Rights Movement, 1966–1989* (New Haven, CT: Yale UP, 1991) 28, 30.

25. Ishmael Reed, *Flight to Canada* (1976; New York: Atheneum, 1989) 173, 174. Not only does Nehemiah accept the categories and commercial advantages offered him within the field, but he also searches for further means of exploiting others in the pursuit of profits. When he learns that slaves are able to work "roots" in a manner that prevents conception, he think to himself that the "recipe for such a potion would be worth a small fortune—provided, of course, that one could hit upon some discreet means of selling it" (11). His first thought on learning about any cultural practice is how to market it for those who have the money to buy such knowledge. Like Browning Norton, his instinctual response is to take whatever the slaves have to offer and make a profit on it.

26. McDowell, "Negotiating Between Tenses" 148; cf. Davis, "Everybody Knows Her

Name" 547–50; and Henderson, "Speaking in Tongues" 25–26. Klaus Ensslen, "The Renaissance of the Slave Narrative in Recent Critical and Fictional Discourse," in *Slavery in the Americas,* ed. Wolfgang Binder (Würzburg: Königshausen & Neumann, 1993) 620. Elizabeth A. Meese, *(Ex)Tensions: Re-Figuring Feminist Criticism* (Urbana: U of Illinois P, 1990) 151.

27. Nehemiah Adams, *A South-Side View of Slavery* (4th ed.; Boston: Ticknor and Fields, 1860) 64–81, 206–7, 205.

28. Harriet Jacobs, *Incidents in the Life of a Slave Girl Written by Herself,* ed. Jean Fagan Yellin (1861; Cambridge, MA: Harvard UP, 1987) 73–74. Frederick Douglass, *Narrative of the Life of Frederick Douglass, An American Slave, Written by Himself,* ed. Houston A. Baker, Jr. (1845; New York: Penguin, 1982) 62. Jacobs, *Incidents in the Life of a Slave Girl Written by Herself* 68. Cf. Davis, "Everybody Knows Her Name" 558 (n. 3).

29. Williams, "[Interview with Shirley Jordan]" 288–89.

30. William L. Andrews, "Inter(racial)textuality in Nineteenth-Century Southern Narrative," in *Influence and Intertextuality in Literary History,* ed. Jay Clayton and Eric Rothstein (Madison: U of Wisconsin P, 1991) 305. Williams, "Meditations on History" 251. Williams, "The Lion's History" 246, 250–51.

31. Williams, *Give Birth to Brightness* 216.

32. Williams, *Give Birth to Brightness* 56, 35. Sterling Brown, *The Negro in American Fiction* (1937; Port Washington, NY: Kennikat, 1968) 31.

33. Keith Byerman, *Fingering the Jagged Grain: Tradition and Form in Recent Black Fiction* (Athens: U of Georgia P, 1985) 6.

34. Michelle Wallace, "Slaves In History," in *Invisibility Blues: From Pop to Theory* (New York: Verso, 1990) 145.

35. Elizabeth Fox-Genovese, *Within the Plantation Household: Black and White Women of the Old South* (Chapel Hill: U of North Carolina P, 1988) 100. Mary Boykin Chesnut, *Mary Chesnut's Civil War,* ed. C. Vann Woodward (New Haven, CT: Yale UP, 1981) 255. Jacqueline Jones, *Labor of Love, Labor of Sorrow: Black Women, Work, and the Family from Slavery to the Present* (1985; New York: Random House, 1986) 25–26. Fox-Genovese, *Within the Plantation Household* 349.

36. Davis, "Reflections on the Black Woman's Role in the Community of Slaves" 11. Aptheker, *American Negro Slave Revolts* 287, 289. For the account of the coffle uprising on which Aptheker drew, see J. Winston Coleman, Jr., *Slavery Times in Kentucky* (Chapel Hill: U of North Carolina P, 1940) 176–78. What I call "signifyin(g) on history" is a strategy I define elsewhere; see my "Daughters Signifyin(g) History: The Example of Toni Morrison's *Beloved,*" *American Literature* 64 (1992): 567–97, where I discuss how Toni Morrison constructs a scene of inspiration based on her reading of history and how she too resurrects historical women in order to revise their personal histories as well as to criticize the historiographical methods and ideologies responsible for propagating the characterization of the slave as an individual without community or agency.

37. Nancy Porter, "Women's Interracial Friendships and Visions of Community in *Meridian, The Salt Eaters, Civil Wars,* and *Dessa Rose,*" in *Tradition and the Talents of Women,* ed. Florence Howe (Urbana: U of Illinois P, 1991) 264. Meese, *(Ex)Tensions: Re-Figuring Feminist Criticism* 135. Doris Davenport, "[Review of *Dessa Rose*]," *Black American Literature Forum* 20 (1986): 340, 338. Patricia Ferreira, "What's Wrong with Miss Anne: Whiteness, Women, and Power in *Meridian* and *Dessa Rose,*" *Sage* 8 (1991): 18. For a discussion of the difficulties of interracial women's coalitions, see Davenport, "The Pathology of Racism: A Conversation with Third World Wimmin," in *This Bridge Called My Back: Writings by Radical Feminists of Color,* ed. Cherríe Moraga and Gloria Anzaldúa (1981; Latham, NY: Kitchen Table, Women of Color Press, 1983) 85–90. For general discussions of interracial women's friendships in American literature, see Elizabeth Schultz, "Out of the Woods and into the World: A Study of Interracial

Friendships between Women in American Novels," in *Conjuring: Black Women, Fiction, and Literary Tradition,* ed. Marjorie Pryse and Hortense J. Spillers (Bloomington: Indiana UP, 1985) 67–85; Minrose C. Gwin, *Black and White Women of the Old South: The Peculiar Sisterhood in American Literature* (Knoxville: U of Tennessee P, 1985); and Anna Maria Chupa, *Anne, the White Women in Contemporary African-American Fiction: Archetypes, Stereotypes, and Characterizations* (Westport, CT: Greenwood, 1990).

38. Meese, *(Ex)Positions: Re-Figuring Feminist Criticism* 151.

39. I will be focusing on the oral–narrative relations between Dessa and Rufel here. For a reading of how the two sections of the novel represent "two consubstantial systems of representation—one is verbal; the other, visual," see McDowell, "Negotiating Between Tenses: 150–54.

40. David Brion Davis, *Slavery and Human Progress* (New York: Oxford UP, 1984) 16. Orlando Patterson, *Slavery and Social Death: A Comparative Study* (Cambridge, MA: Harvard UP, 1982) 63.

41. Cf. Kenneth Burke, "What Are Signs of What?: A Theory of Entitlement," in *Language as Symbolic Action: Essays on Life, Literature, and Method* (Berkeley: U of California P, 1966) 362.

42. Cf. Wallace, "Slaves of History" 143; Davis, "Everybody Knows Her Name" 553–54; Barbara Christian, "'Somebody Forget to Tell Somebody Something': African-American Women's Historical Novels," in *Wild Women in the Whirlwind: Afra-American Culture and the Contemporary Literary Renaissance,* ed. Joanne M. Braxton and Andrée Nicola McLaughlin (New Brunswick, NJ: Rutgers UP, 1990) 339; Porter, "Women's Interracial Friendships" 263; Meese, *(Ex)Positions: Re-Figuring Feminist Criticism* 146; Marta E. Sánchez, "The Estrangement Effect in Sherley Anne Williams' *Dessa Rose,*" *Genders* 15 (1992): 30; Nicole R. King, "Meditations and Mediations: Issues of History and Fiction in *Dessa Rose,*" *Soundings* 76 (1993): 361; and Aldon N. Nielsen, *Writing Between the Lines: Race and Intertextuality* (Athens: U of Georgia P, 1994) 277.

43. Mikhail Bakhtin, *The Dialogic Imagination: Four Essays,* trans. Caryl Emerson and Michael Holquist, ed. Michael Holquist (Austin: U of Texas P, 1981) 286, 345.

44. Patterson, *Slavery and Social Death* 337. Eugene D. Genovese, *Roll, Jordan, Roll: The World the Slaves Made* (1974; New York: Random House, 1976) 97.

45. Audre Lorde, "An Open Letter to Mary Daly," in *Sister, Outsider: Essays and Speeches* (Freedom, CA: The Crossing Press, 1984) 66. Ashraf H. A. Rushdy, "Fraternal Blues: John Edgar Wideman's Homewood Trilogy," *Contemporary Literature* 32 (1991): 342.

46. Stepto, *From Behind the Veil* 211. James Alan McPherson, "Elbow Room," in *Elbow Room* (1977; New York: Scribner's, 1987) 241. Reed, *Flight to Canada* 9.

47. Mary Prince, *The History of Mary Prince, A West Indian Slave. Related by Herself* (London, 1831) 23.

48. The title of this section is obviously indebted to Trudier Harris's *From Mammies to Militants: Domestics in Black American Fiction* (Philadelphia: Temple UP, 1982). Walker, *Down from the Mountaintop* 31. For another reading of how Dorcas figures in the relationship between Dessa and Rufel, see Meese, *(Ex)Positions: Re-Figuring Feminist Criticism* 143–44.

49. Williams, "The Lion's History" 246.

50. Deborah Gray White, *Ar'n't I a Woman?: Female Slaves in the Plantation South* (New York: Norton, 1985) 55, 58. Fox-Genovese, *Within the Plantation Household* 291–92. Carby, *Reconstructing Womenhood: The Emergence of the Afro-American Woman Novelist* (New York: Oxford UP, 1987) 22. Patricia Hill Collins, *Black Feminist Thought: Knowledge, Consciousness, and the Politics of Empowerment* (Boston: Unwin Hyman, 1990) 68, 67. For the creation of the "Sambo" stereotype in the 1830s, see Mina Davis Caulfield, "Slavery and the Origins of Black Culture: Elkins Revisited," in *Americans from Africa: Slavery and Its Aftermath,* ed. Peter I. Rose

(New York: Atherton, 1970) 171–93; and George M. Frederickson, *The Black Image in the White Mind: The Debate on Afro-American Character and Destiny, 1817–1914* (1971; Middletown, CT: Wesleyan UP, 1987) 43–70. For discussions of the "cult of true womanhood," see Barbara Welter, "The Cult of True Womanhood: 1820–1860," *American Quarterly* 18 (1966): 151–74; and Carby, *Reconstructing Womanhood* 20–39.

51. Peter Novick, *That Noble Dream: the "Objectivity Question" and the American Historical Profession* (New York: Cambridge UP, 1988) 72–77. Genovese, *Roll, Jordan, Roll* 353. Charlotte Hawkins Brown, *"Mammy": An Appeal to the Heart of the South* (Boston: Pilgrim, 1919) viii. W. E. B. De Bois, *The Gift of Black Folk: The Negroes in the Making of America* (1924; New York, 1970) 188–89. Jessie W. Parkhurst, "The Role of the Black Mammy in the Plantation Household," *Journal of Negro History* 23 (1938): 349–50. For the nostalgia over "Mammy," see Kevin K. Gaines, *Uplifting the Race: Black Leadership, Politics, and Culture in the Twentieth Century* (Chapel Hill: U of North Carolina P, 1996) 70–72. For a comparison with how the "Uncle Tom" myth was revised in the 1920s, see Wilson Jeremiah Moses, *Black Messiahs and Uncle Toms: Social and Literary Manipulations of a Religious Myth* (1982; University Park: Pennsylvania State UP, 1993) 115. For the politics of "Mammy" representations, see Wallace, "The Search for the 'Good Enough' Mammy: Multiculturalism, Popular Culture, and Psychoanalysis," in *Multiculturalism: A Critical Reader,* ed. David Theo Goldberg (Oxford: Basil Blackwell, 1994) 259–68.

52. Genovese, *Roll, Jordan, Roll* 353. Barbara Christian, *Black Feminist Criticism: Perspectives on Black Women Writers* (New York: Pergamon, 1985) 5. Cf. Sondra O'Neale, "Inhibiting Midwives, Usurping Creators: The Struggling Emergence of Black Women in American Fiction," in *Feminist Studies / Critical Studies,* ed. Teresa de Lauretis (Bloomington: Indiana UP, 1986) 146–47.

53. Genovese, *Roll, Jordan, Roll:* 353. White, *Ar'n't I a Woman?* 55.

54. Du Bois, *The Souls of Black Folk* [1903], in *W. E. B. Du Bois: Writings,* ed. Nathan Huggins (New York: Library of America, 1986) 487, 539, 542, 541.

55. Styron, *Confessions of Nat Turner* 55, 58, 145–50. William Sidney Drewry, *The Southampton Insurrection* (1900; Murfreesboro, NC: Johnson Publishing Company, 1968) 27. Cf. Stephen B. Oates, *The Fires of Jubilee: Nat Turner's Fierce Rebellion* (New York: Harper & Row, 1975) 10–11. Lerone Bennett, "Nat's Last White Man," in *William Styron's Nat Turner: Ten Black Writers Respond,* ed. John Henrik Clarke (Boston: Beacon, 1968) 9. Styron, *Confessions of Nat Turner* 129–31. Cf. Thomas Gray, *The Confessions of Nat Turner* (Baltimore, 1831), reprinted in *The Southampton Slave Revolt of 1831: A Compilation of Source Materials,* ed. Henry Irving Tragle (Amherst: U of Massachusetts P, 1971) 306.

56. Williams, *Give Birth to Brightness* 28. Cf. Charles T. Davis, "The American Scholar, the Black Arts, and / or Black Power," in *Black Is the Color of the Cosmos: Essays on Afro-American Literature and Culture, 1942–1981,* ed. Gates (1982; Washington, DC: Howard UP, 1989) 31.

57. Octavia E. Butler, *Kindred* (1979; Boston: Beacon, 1988) 145. Frances M. Beal, "*Black Scholar* Interview with Octavia Butler: Black Women and the Science Fiction Genre," *Black Scholar* 17 (1986): 15. Randall Kenan, "An Interview with Octavia E. Butler," *Callaloo* 14.2 (1991): 496.

58. Williams, *Give Birth to Brightness* 20. Williams, "Returning to the Blues" 819.

59. Williams, "Returning to the Blues" 819. Cf. Williams, "[Interview with Claudia Tate]" 208–9. Douglass, *Narrative of the Life of Frederick Douglass* 57. Du Bois, *The Souls of Black Folk* 541. Williams, "Returning to the Blues" 821. Williams, "Blues Roots of Contemporary Afro-American Poetry" 124, 125.

60. Williams, "The Lion's History" 258. Jones, *Liberating Voices* 38.

61. Cf. Wallace, "Slaves to History" 141–42; McDowell, "Negotiating Between Tenses" 145; and Henderson, "(W)riting *The Work* and Working the Rites" 655. For an interesting

reading of "Mammy" as a *lieu de mémoire,* see Andrée-Anne Kekeh, "Sherley Anne Williams's *Dessa Rose:* History and the Disruptive Power of Memory," in *History and Memory in African-American Culture,* ed. Geneviève Fabre and Robert O'Meally (New York: Oxford UP, 1994) 219, 224.

6. Serving the Form, Conserving the Order

1. Jonathan Little, "An Interview with Charles Johnson," *Contemporary Literature* 34 (1993): 161. Charles Johnson, "Introduction" to *Oxherding Tale* (New York: Plume, 1995) xi. Johnson, "A Phenomenology of the Black Body," *Michigan Quarterly Review* 31 (1993): 605. Frantz Fanon, *Black Skin, White Masks,* trans. Charles Lam Markmann (1952; New York: Grove, 1967) 110. Johnson, "A Phenomenology of the Black Body" 606, 604, 608, 609, 610. Johnson, "Popper's Disease," in *The Sorcerer's Apprentice: Tales and Conjurations* (1986; New York: Penguin, 1987) 128. Little, "An Interview with Charles Johnson" 164. Johnson, "Popper's Disease" 130, 134.

2. Little, "An Interview with Charles Johnson" 161. Johnson, "Popper's Disease" 134. Johnson, *Being and Race: Black Writing Since 1970* (Bloomington: Indiana UP, 1988) 49.

3. Johnson, *Being and Race* 49. Johnson, *Middle Passage* (New York: Atheneum, 1990) 171, 149.

4. Johnson; in Studs Terkel, *Race: How Blacks and Whites Think and Feel About the American Obsession* (New York: New Press, 1992) 217. Johnson, "Introduction" ix–xv. Johnson, "A Phenomenology of the Black Body" 611.

5. Johnson, "Introduction" xvii. Johnson, *Being and Race* 122. I take the term "history-laden" from Margaret R. Somers and Gloria D. Gibson, "Reclaiming the Epistemological 'Other': Narrative and the Social Construction of Identity," in *Social Theory and the Politics of Identity,* ed. Craig Calhoun (Cambridge, MA: Blackwell, 1994) 44.

6. Peter Collier and David Horowitz, *Destructive Generation: Second Thoughts About the Sixties* (1989; New York: Summit, 1990) 15. Little, "An Interview with Charles Johnson" 173, 170–71. Johnson, *Being and Race* 65, 25. Cf. Collier and Horowitz, eds., *Second Thoughts: Former Radicals Look Back at the Sixties* (Lanham, MD: Madison, 1989); and Collier and Horowitz, eds., *Second Thoughts About Race in America* (Lanham, MD: Madison, 1991).

7. Little, "An Interview with Charles Johnson" 170–71, 167, Johnson, *Being and Race* 21. Unfortunately, Johnson's critique of Morrison's novel is sadly misguided, because he reads it through the filter provided by Stanley Crouch, a critic whose reading of Morrison is scandalously ill informed, considerably lacking in judgment, and thoroughly pusillanimous (and wrong, too). Like Crouch, Johnson wants representations of slavery not to be so depressing; he wants to see a fictional representation of slavery that does not register all African Americans as victims whose only agency is reaction to white oppression. Had he read Morrison's novel carefully and attended to its strategic representations of slavery and slaves, he would have found that it is not a tale of black victimage and reaction to white oppression. He would have seen that Morrison performs an almost magical feat in producing the most subtle and nuanced fictional treatment of a community of slaves in postures of resistance, accommodation, despair, and healing wisdom in American fiction. Yet, like Crouch, Johnson produces a reading of the novel that ignores its subtlety, eliminates its complexity, and demonstrates the reader's own desire to deny the history *Beloved* excavates. On *Beloved's* historical analogues, see Ashraf H. A. Rushdy, "Daughters Signifyin(g) History: The Example of Toni Morrison's *Beloved,*" *American Literature* 64 (1992): 567–97. For Stanley Crouch's reading of *Beloved,* see *Notes of a Hanging Judge: Essays and Reviews 1979–1989* (New York: Oxford UP, 1990) 202–9.

8. Johnson, *Being and Race* 83. Johnson, "Philosophy and Black Fiction," *Obsidian* 6 (1980): 59, 58. Little, "An Interview with Charles Johnson" 173.

9. Johnson, *Being and Race* 7. I adopt Todd Gitlin's distinction between "identity politics" and "commonality politics"; see Gitlin, "From Universality to Difference: Notes on the Fragmentation of the Idea of the Left," in *Social Theory and the Politics of Identity* 152–53, 156–57.

10. Johnson, *Being and Race* 23. Little, "An Interview with Charles Johnson" 169, 170.

11. Johnson argues that writers should create art that is "socially responsible," by which he means something like what John Gardner, his former teacher, called "moral fiction." "Where social responsibility comes into play is in the simple fact that whatever the work is, whatever the book is, whatever the product is, it's something that we interject into the public space. It's a public act. It's our human expression, and we are responsible for all our forms of human expression, all our deeds and actions, of which art is one." Nonetheless, he does not consider art "promoting or supporting certain political ideas" to be the sole means of producing socially responsible art. Little, "An Interview with Charles Johnson" 171, 173, 171. For Johnson's assessment of John Gardner's idea of "moral fiction," see Johnson, "A Phenomenology of *On Moral Fiction,*" in *Thor's Hammer: Essays on John Gardner,* ed. Jeff Henderson (n.p.: U of Central Arkansas P, 1985) 147–56; and Johnson, "Introduction" to John Gardner's *On Writers and Writing,* ed. Stewart O'Nan (Reading, MA: Addison-Wesley, 1994) vii–xvi.

12. Little, "An Interview with Charles Johnson" 169, 170. Johnson, "Popper's Disease" 134.

13. Ron Karenga, "Black Cultural Nationalism," in *The Black Aesthetic,* ed. Addison Gayle, Jr. (Garden City, NY: Doubleday, 1971) 33, 34. Hoyt W. Fuller, "Towards a Black Aesthetic," in Gayle, *The Black Aesthetic* 4. Caroyln F. Gerald, "The Black Writer and His Role," in Gayle, *The Black Aesthetic* 376. Sarah Webster Fabio, "Tripping with Black Writing," in Gayle, *The Black Aesthetic* 190.

14. Johnson, *Being and Race* 114. Johnson; in Terkel, *Race: How Blacks and Whites Think and Feel About the American Obsession* 216. Little, "An Interview with Charles Johnson: 168. Johnson; in Terkel, *Race* 216–18. Little, "An Interview with Charles Johnson" 167. Johnson has also tried to redefine "universality," noting that it is not "static" but "changing, historical, *evolving* and enriched by particularization." But his strategy for reconciling "universality with the particulars of Black life" is primarily perceptual, the application of the "epoche, or so-called 'phenomenological reduction' to experience," without being especially skeptical about how historical manifestations of power created the specific form of "universality" inhabiting the so-called Western tradition. See Johnson, "Philosophy and Black Fiction" 57, 56.

15. Louis Althusser, *Lenin and Philosophy and Other Essays,* trans. Ben Brewster (New York: Monthly Review, 1971) 161. Adam David Miller, "Some Observations on a Black Aesthetic," in Gayle, *The Black Aesthetic* 401. Ishmael Reed, "Can a Metronome Know the Thunder or Summon a God?" in Gayle, *The Black Aesthetic* 406. Gayle, *The Way of the New World: The Black Novel in America* (1975; Garden City, NY: Doubleday, 1976) 270. James T. Stewart, "The Development of the Black Revolutionary Artist," in *Black Fire: An Anthology of Afro-American Writing,* ed. LeRoi Jones and Larry Neal (New York: William Morrow, 1968) 6.

16. Stewart, "The Development of the Black Revolutionary Artist" 8. Christina Crosby, "Dealing with Differences," in *Feminists Theorize the Political,* ed. Judith Butler and Joan W. Scott (New York: Routledge, 1992) 137, 132. Michael Awkward, *Negotiating Difference: Race, Gender, and the Politics of Positionality* (Chicago: U of Chicago P, 1995) 8, 18. Stewart, "The Development of the Black Revolutionary Artist" 9. Gayle, *The Way of the New World* 379.

17. Larry Neal, "The Black Arts Movement," in *Visions of a Liberated Future: Black Arts Movement Writings,* ed. Michael Schwartz (New York: Thunder's Mouth, 1989) 65. Gayle, "Cultural Hegemony: The Southern White Writer and American Letters," in *Amistad 1,* Ed. John A. Williams and Charles Harris (New York: Random House, 1970) 23. Little, "An Interview with Charles Johnson" 169.

18. Awkward, *Negotiating Difference* 13–14. August Wilson, "I Want a Black Director," *New York Times* (September 26, 1990), sec. 1: 15.

19. Johnson, *Being and Race* 39, 40. For other versions of "Caliban's dilemma," see James Baldwin, *Notes of a Native Son* (1955; London: Corgi, 1965) 3; and Houston A. Baker, Jr., "Caliban's Triple Play," in *"Race," Writing, and Difference,* ed. Henry Louis Gates, Jr. (Chicago: U of Chicago P, 1986) 381–95.

20. Little, "An Interview with Charles Johnson" 165–66. Cf. Crouch, Role Models," in Collier and Horowitz, *Second Thoughts About Race in America* 63: "We must get back to the grandest vision of this society, which is that all exemplary human endeavour is the heritage of every person. . . . All people are heir to everything of wonder that anyone has produced, regardless of race, gender, and place."

21. Johnson, "Popper's Disease" 130. Little, "An Interview with Charles Johnson" 177. Paul Potter, "The Incredible War," in *The New Left: A Documentary History,* ed. Massimo Teodori (Indianapolis: Bobbs-Merrill, 1969) 248; originally delivered at the SDS Washington March of April 17, 1965. Nathan Glazer, "Individual Rights Against Group Rights," in *Ethnic Dilemmas 1964–1982* (Cambridge, MA: Harvard UP, 1983) 273; originally published in 1978. See Peter Clecak, *America's Quest for the Ideal Self: Dissent and Fulfillment in the 60s and 70s* (New York: Oxford UP, 1983) 76–79, for a description of neoconservative values and "the bourgeois ethos."

22. Edmund Husserl, *Ideas: General Introduction to Pure Phenomenology,* trans. W. R. Boyce Gibson (1931; London: Macmillan, 1970) 389. Husserl, *The Crisis of European Sciences and Transcendental Phenomenology: An Introduction to Phenomenological Philosophy,* trans. David Carr (Evanston, IL: Northwestern UP, 1970) 182–83, 254–55. Husserl, *Ideas* 346.

23. Johnson, *Being and Race* 44.

24. Johnson, *Middle Passage* 61, 76, 61, 65, 140, 61, 164. I have more fully discussed the Allmuseri's role in Johnson's short stories and novels about slavery elsewhere; see Rushdy, "The Phenomenology of the Allmuseri: Charles Johnson and the Subject of the Narrative of Slavery," *African American Review* 26 (1992): 373–94.

25. Little, "An Interview with Charles Johnson" 173. Johnson, "Introduction" xii. Husserl, *The Crisis of European Sciences* 76. Johnson, *Being and Race* 5.

26. Johnson, *Being and Race* 5, 6, 20, 39, 38, 39. Maurice Merleau-Ponty, *The Prose of the World,* ed. Claude Lefort, trans. John O'Neill (Evanston, IL: Northwestern UP, 1973) 133.

27. My use of "Africanist" here is indebted to but not synonymous with Toni Morrison's; see Morrison, *Playing in the Dark: Whiteness and the Literary Imagination* (Cambridge, MA: Harvard UP, 1992) 6–7.

28. Johnson, *Being and Race* 47, 48, 52. William Gleason, "The Liberation of Perception: Charles Johnson's *Oxherding Tale,"* *Black American Literature Forum* 25 (1991): 705, 707. Johnson, "Introduction" xv. Johnson; in Susan Stefani, "Johnson, Charles (Richard)," in *Contemporary Authors: A Bio-Bibliographical Guide to Current Writers,* ed. Hal May (Detroit: Gale Research, 1986), Vol. 116: 235. For other critics on the forms of *Oxherding Tale,* see Jennifer Hayward, "Something to Serve: Constructs of the Feminine in Charles Johnson's *Oxherding Tale,"* *Black American Literature Forum* 25 (1991): 689–90; and James W. Coleman, "Charles Johnson's Quest for Black Freedom in *Oxherding Tale,"* *African American Review* 29 (1995): 631–44.

29. Johnson, *Oxherding Tale* (New York: Grove, 1982) 143. I have silently corrected one word in this quotation ("White, if your nonwhite" in the original). All future quotations from *Oxherding Tale* will be taken from this edition and hereafter cited parenthetically in the body of the text.

30. Johnson, *Being and Race:* 5, 83. Baldwin, "Everybody's Protest Novel," in *The Price of the Ticket: Collected Nonfiction 1948–1985* (New York: St. Martin's, 1985) 33. Johnson, "Introduction" xiv.

31. Johnson presistently raises questions about parody and beauty. Cf. Johnson, "The Sorcerer's Apprentice," in *The Sorcerer's Apprentice* 167, 164–65.

32. Johnson, *Being and Race* 4; the second quotation is from André Malraux's *The Voices of Silence*. Hayden White, *The Content of the Form: Narrative Discourse and Historical Representation* (Baltimore: Johns Hopkins UP, 1987) 42. Johnson, *Being and Race* 47, 48.

33. This could be a remnant of Johnson's original conception for the book which was to have Andrew Hawkins be "over one hundred years old," telling "his tale at some time in the twentieth century." See Johnson, "Introduction" p. xvi.

34. Johnson, "Introduction" xvii. Little, "An Interview with Charles Johnson" 161, 162, 163.

35. Johnson, *Being and Race* 5–6.

36. Johnson, *Middle Passage* 180. Johnson, "Introduction" xvii. Johnson, *Being and Race* 45.

37. Cornel West, *Race Matters* (Boston: Beacon, 1993) 30.

38. Jacques Derrida and Jean-Luc Nancy, "'Eating Well,' or the Calculation of the Subject: An Interview with Jacques Derrida," in *Who Comes After the Subject?* ed. Eduardo Cadava, Peter Connor, and Jean-Luc Nancy (New York: Routledge, 1990) 115.

39. Johnson, *Being and Race* 29. As Ralph Ellison, in *Shadow and Act* (New York: Random House, 1964) 84, interprets Bland's idea, this form of thinking is effected socially through an elaborate scheme of taboos. "To wander from the paths of behavior laid down for the group is to become the agent of communal disaster." The presupposition of pre-individualistic thinking is that individual acts endanger the larger cultural community.

40. Johnson, "Introduction" xvii. Luce Irigaray, "Women on the Market," in *This Sex Which Is Not One,* trans. Catherine Porter (Ithaca, NY: Cornell UP, 1985) 170–91.

41. Cf. Gleason, "The Liberation of Perception 727 (n. 17); and Hayward, "Something to Serve" 690–701, who both note that while Johnson disrupts all other binaries in his novel, he does not dismantle the idealization and essentializing of *woman* as *Being*.

42. This phrasing of this belief is Ludwig Landgrebe's, although the sentiment changes in context. Landgrebe writes: "Thus is each of us thrown back upon himself as the 'subject' of his opinions, of his experience, upon this: he has to answer for them. He is therefore the subject of 'absolute experience'—absolute in the sense that what he acknowledges as his experience and allows to be determinant for his life depends upon himself and nothing else." See Landgrebe, "The Problem of the Beginning of Philosophy in Husserl's Phenomenology," in *Life-World and Consciousness,* ed. Lester E. Embree (Evanston, IL: Northwestern UP, 1972) 49. Cf. Johnson, "A Phenomenology of *On Moral Fiction*" 154–55.

43. Johnson, *Being and Race* 52. Little, "An Interview with Charles Johnson" 164. Johnson, *Being and Race* 7, 123. Johnson, "Philosophy and Black Fiction" 60. Johnson, "Introduction" xviii; I should note that Johnson talks about the work of "black male writers" and might not think that black women had the same difficulties or were accorded the same reception by commercial presses (he would be wrong in that case, I think).

44. In *Oxherding Tale,* Andrew repeats virtually verbatim what Johnson himself said about the historiographical tradition of Stanley Elkins and Eugene Genovese. Meditating on the pain of black life, Andrew thinks: "You needed little more proof than I'd received to believe that this world was, had always been, and might ever be a slaughterhouse—a style of being characterized by stasis, denial, humiliation, thinghood, and, as the philosophers said, 'relative being'" (70). Cf. Johnson, *Being and Race* 21: "Stanley M. Elkins and Eugene Genovese drove home the sense that black history was, and might always be, a slaughter-house—a form of being characterized by stasis, denial, humiliation, dehumanization, and 'relative being.'" Johnson first used this formulation in an earlier essay, in which he had included "slave narratives" and Harold Cruse's *The Crisis of the Negro Intellectual* among those documents driving home the sense that "black history was, had always been, and might always be a slaughterhouse." See Johnson, "A Phenomenology of *On Moral Fiction*" 153.

45. Johnson, "Introduction" xvi.

46. Johnson, *Being and Race* 65, 26, 45.

47. Johnson, "Introduction" xvii. For a description of the Nation of Islam's theology, especially the matter relating to the creation of white people from an original black people, see Malcolm X with Alex Haley, *The Autobiography of Malcolm X* (1964; New York: Ballantine, 1992) 187–94; and C. Eric Lincoln, *The Black Muslims in America* (Boston: Beacon, 1961) 76–78.

48. Andrew takes his most concerted stand against the Black Power tenets of George when he explores the costs of George's stark division in the domestic realm. Believing that "love conquered the illusion of race, this lifelong hallucination that *Thou* and *That* differed" (170), Andrew challenges George's politicization of interracial marriage (142). For other fictional accounts, social statements, and critical discussions of this topic, see John Oliver Killens, *'Sippi* (1967; New York: Thunder's Mouth, 1988) 396, 417–18; Killens, "The Black Mystique or Would You Want One of Them to Marry Your Daughter?" in *Black Man's Burden* (1965; New York: Pocket Books, 1969) 125–43; and Jonathan Little, "Charles Johnson's Revolutionary *Oxherding Tale*," *Studies in American Fiction* 19 (1991): 141–51.

49. Regarding slaves who commit violence against their masters, one could also argue that Andrew's punching Flo five times in the nose constitutes an act of violence against the master class, although it seems to me the novel doesn't make that sense of this scene. Rather, it seems more closely connected to the series of acts of violence against women in *Oxherding Tale*. For a discussion of this facet of Johnson's novel, see Hayward, "Something to Serve" 699–701.

50. At least one historian of the sixties has used the Buddhist term of "householder" to describe the afterlife of political activists. According to Todd Gitlin, when the forces of the New Left encountered the massive counterforces of the resurgent Right after 1968, when the movement for social change broke down and its participants lost faith in the values they were attempting to live out, they were likely to "retreat to private life—all the more so as they ascended toward what the Hindus call the householding stage of life." See Gitlin, *The Sixties: Years of Hope, Days of Rage* (1987; New York: Bantam, 1993) 420. Gitlin makes a mistake in seeing in "householding" the sort of defeatist apoliticism for Candide (he later equates "householding" to "cultivating our garden" [430]), since the householding stage is not one of retreat from politics to the pleasures of individualistic private life. According to one version of Buddhist teachings, there are four stages in life, and one can become a "householder" during the second of them. The first stage is that of *brahmacarin*—a student living a chaste life. The second is that of *grhasta*, which includes marriage and raising one's children. When one's own grandchildren reach the stage of *grhasta*, one can become a householder. The third stage is that of *vanaprastha* (literally, this means being stationed in forest; a hermit who is not wandering, working on spiritual salvation). At this stage one seeks *moksha*, meaning "enlightenment" or "liberation" (the title of the final chapter of *Oxherding Tale* is "Moksha"). The fourth stage, after one has gained *moksha*, is that of *sannyasin*, which is the position of a wandering ascetic. Buddha changed the order of these four stages of life, proclaiming that one did not need to go through the first two stages, and he claimed that *moksha* was available to anyone (and no longer limited to the grandfather of children in the stage of *grhasta*). It should be noted that *moksha* is a term from an earlier, pre-Buddhist, Aryan tradition and is rarely used in Buddhist tradition. I would like to thank my friend and colleague Jan Willis for sharing with me this information about Buddhist traditions.

51. For a reading of *Oxherding Tale* as a parody of slave narrative and novel of passing, see Fritz Gysin, "Predicaments of Skin: Boundaries in Recent African American Fiction," in *The Black Columbiad: Defining Moments in African American Literature and Culture*, ed. Werner Sollors and Maria Diedrich (Cambridge, MA: Harvard UP, 1994) 288–90.

52. Oliver Cromwell Cox, *Caste, Class, & Race: A Study in Social Dynamics* (1948; New York: Monthly Review, 1959) 327, 332, 335–36. On the ideology of race in the process of social class formation, see David R. Roediger, *The Wages of Whiteness: Race and the Making of the American Working Class* (New York: Verso, 1991); and Edmund S. Morgan, *American Slavery, American Freedom: The Ordeal of Colonial Virginia* (New York: Norton, 1975).

53. Barbara Jeanne Fields, "Slavery, Race and Ideology in the United States of America," *New Left Review* 181 (1990): 101, 110. Ernest Renan, "What Is a Nation?" trans. Martin Thom, in *Nation and Narration*, ed. Homi K. Bhabha (New York: Routledge, 1990) 11.

54. My discussion of passing, amnesia, and racial formation benefited from Eric Lott's essay on "racial cross-dressing" as an example of the "necessary *centrality and suppression* of 'blackness' in the making of American whiteness," from Ruth Frankenberg's work on "the social construction of whiteness," and especially from Michael Awkward's suggestive comments on texts of racial passing and texts of "transraciality." Lott, "White Like Me: Racial Cross-Dressing and the Construction of American Whiteness," in *Cultures of United States Imperialism*, ed. Amy Kaplan and Donald E. Pease (Durham, NC: Duke UP, 1993) 474–95; Frankenberg, "Whiteness and Americanness: Examining Constructions of Race, Culture, and Nation in White Women's Life Narratives," in *Race*, ed. Steven Gregory and Roger Sanjek (New Brunswick, NJ: Rutgers UP, 1994) 62–77; Frankenberg, *White Women, Race Matters: The Social Construction of Whiteness* (Minneapolis: U of Minnesota P, 1993); and Awkward, *Negotiating Difference* 19, 180–82.

55. Gleason, "The Liberation of Perception" 715. For studies of the economic effects of the transatlantic slave trade, see Philip D. Curtin, *The Atlantic Slave Trade: A Census* (Madison: U of Wisconsin P, 1969); Basil Davidson, *The African Slave Trade* (1961; Boston: Little, Brown, and Co., 1980); David Eltis, *Economic Growth and the Ending of the Transatlantic Slave Trade* (New York: Oxford UP, 1987); Joseph E. Inikori and Stanley L. Engerman, eds., *The Atlantic Slave Trade: Effects on Economies, Societies, and Peoples in Africa, the Americas, and Europe* (Durham, NC: Duke UP, 1992); Nathan Irvin Huggins, *Black Odyssey: The African American Ordeal in Slavery* (1977; New York: Random House, 1990); Herbert S. Klein, *The Middle Passage: Comparative Studies in the Atlantic Slave Trade* (Princeton, NJ: Princeton UP, 1978); and Edward Reynolds, *Stand the Storm: A History of the Atlantic Slave Trade* (Chicago: Ivan R. Dee Publishers, 1985). For studies of the construction of race in the early colonial slave codes and legal cases, see Oscar and Mary Handlin, "Origins of the Southern Labor System" *William and Mary Quarterly* 7 (1950): 199–222; Carl Degler, "Slavery and the Genesis of American Race Prejudice," *Comparative Studies in Society and History* 2 (1959–1960): 49–65; Winthrop D. Jordan, "Modern Tensions and the Origins of American Slavery," *Journal of Southern History* 28 (1962): 18–30; Jonathan L. Alpert, "The Origin of Slavery in the United States—The Maryland Precedent," *American Journal of Legal History* 14 (1970): 189–221; Whittington B. Johnson, "The Origin and Nature of African Slavery in Seventeenth Century Maryland," *Maryland Historical Magazine* 73 (1978): 236–45; A. Leon Higginbotham, *In the Matter of Color: Race and the American Legal Process: The Colonial Period* (New York: Oxford UP, 1978); Alden T. Vaughan, "The Origins Debate: Slavery and Racism in Seventeenth-Century Virginia," *The Virginia Magazine of History and Biography* 97 (1989): 311–54; and Ronald Takaki, *A Different Mirror: A History of Multicultural America* (Boston: Little, Brown and Co., 1993) 51–76.

56. Gitlin, *The Sixties* 85.

7. *Revising the Form, Misserving the Order*

1. Peter Collier and David Horowitz, *Destructive Generation: Second Thoughts about the Sixties* (1989; New York: Summit, 1990) 15. Thomas C. Holt, "Marking: Race, Race-Making, and the Writing of History," *American Historical Review* 100 (1995): 12. Holt discusses minstrelsy as both "racist discourse and performance" space for white identity (15–16). Cf. Alexander Sax-

ton, *The Rise and Fall of the White Republic: Class Politics and Mass Culture in Nineteenth-Century America* (London: Verso, 1990) 165–82; David R. Roediger, *The Wages of Whiteness: Race and the Making of the American Working Class* (London: Verso, 1991) 115–31; and Eric Lott, *Love and Theft: Blackface Minstrelsy and the American Working Class* (New York: Oxford UP, 1995).

2. Lerone Bennett, Jr.; in Studs Terkel, *Race: How Blacks and Whites Think and Feel about the American Obsession* (New York: New Press, 1992) 382. Collier, "Foreword" to *Second Thoughts About Race in America,* ed. Collier and Horowitz (Lanham, MD: Madison, 1991) xi. Noel Ignatiev and John Garvey, "Editorial: Abolish the White Race by Any Means Necessary," in *Race Traitor,* ed. Ignatiev and Garvey (New York: Routledge, 1996) 9–14. Nathan Glazer, "Affirmative Discrimination: For and Against," "Liberty, Equality, Fraternity—and Ethnicity," and "Individual Rights against Group Rights," in Glazer, *Ethnic Dilemmas 1964–1982* (Cambridge, MA: Harvard UP, 1983) 159–81, 209–32, 254–73. James R. Kluegel, "'If There Isn't a Problem, You Don't Need a Solution': The Bases of Contemporary Affirmative Action Attitudes," *American Behavioral Scientist* 28 (1985): 761–66. Kimberlé Williams Crenshaw, "Race, Reform, and Retrenchment: Transformation and Legitimation in Antidiscrimination Law," *Harvard Law Review* 101 (1988): 1348 (n. 66).

3. Thomas Sowell, *Civil Rights: Rhetoric or Reality?* (New York: William Morrow, 1984) 45. Shelby Steele, *The Content of Our Character: A New Vision of Race in America* (1990; New York: HarperPerennial, 1991) 11–25. Patricia J. Williams, *The Rooster's Egg: On the Persistence of Prejudice* (Cambridge, MA: Harvard UP, 1995). Derrick Bell, *Faces at the Bottom of the Well: The Permanence of Racism* (New York: Basic Books, 1992). Crenshaw, "Race, Reform, and Retrenchment" 1336, 1370. Cornel West, "The New Cultural Politics of Difference," in *Out There: Marginalization and Contemporary Cultures,* ed. Russell Ferguson, Martha Gever, Trinh T. Minh-ha, and Cornel West (Cambridge, MA: MIT P, 1990) 29.

4. Charles Johnson; in Terkel, *Race* 214. Johnson, "Introduction" to *Oxherding Tale* (1982; New York: Plume, 1995) xi.

5. Johnson, *Oxherding Tale* 118–19.

6. Evelyn Brooks Higginbotham, "African-American Women's History and the Metalanguage of Race," *Signs: Journal of Women in Culture and Society* 17 (1992): 253.

7. Johnson, *Middle Passage* (New York: Atheneum, 1990) 162. All quotations from *Middle Passage* will be taken from this edition and hereafter noted parenthetically in the body of the text.

8. Johnson, in "Introduction" to John Gardner, *On Writers and Writing,* ed. Stewart O'Nan (Reading, MA: Addison-Wesley, 1994) xiv, describes himself as "a philosophy student then oriented toward Marxism." Johnson, "Exchange Value," in *The Sorcerer's Apprentice: Tales and Conjurations* (1986; New York: Penguin, 1987) 27–40.

9. John W. Blassingame, *The Slave Community: Plantation Life in the Antebellum South* (1972; rev. ed.; New York: Oxford UP, 1979) 254. Eugene D. Genovese, *Roll, Jordan, Roll: The World the Slaves Made* (New York: Random House, 1976) 603. James M. Phillippo, *Jamaica: Its Past and Present State* (London: John Snow, 1843) 252. Genovese, *Roll, Jordan, Roll* 602, 603, 605. Lawrence W. Levine, *Black Culture and Black Consciousness: Afro-American Folk Thought from Slavery to Freedom* (New York: Oxford UP, 1977) 123–24. J. R. Pole, *Paths to the American Past* (New York: Oxford UP, 1979) 189. Sterling Stuckey, "Through the Prism of Folklore: The Black Ethos in Slavery," in *The Debate Over Slavery: Stanley Elkins and His Critics,* ed. Ann J. Lane (Urbana, IL: U of Illinois P, 1971) 261 (n. 42). Cf. Toni Morrison, *Beloved* (New York: Alfred A. Knopf, 1987) 190–91.

10. Frederick Douglass, *Life and Times of Frederick Douglass* (1892; New York: Collier, 1962) 104, 86, 105.

11. James Baldwin, *The Price of the Ticket: Collected Nonfiction, 1948–1985* (New York: St. Martin's, 1985) 88–89.

12. Morrison, *Beloved* 226. Douglass, *Narrative of the Life of Frederick Douglass, an American Slave. Written by Himself*; in *The Classic Slave Narratives,* ed. Henry Louis Gates, Jr. (New York: New American Library, 1987) 282.

13. Edmund S. Morgan, *American Slavery, American Freedom: The Ordeal of Colonial Virginia* (New York: Norton, 1975) 9.

14. Karl Marx, "Excerpts from James Mill's *Elements of Political Economy,*" in *Karl Marx: Early Writings,* ed. Quintin Hoare, trans. Rodney Livingstone and Gregor Benton (New York: Random House, 1975) 266, 267, 277.

15. Johnson, *Oxherding Tale* 82, 85–86, 88, 88–94.

16. Marx, "Excerpts from James Mill's *Elements of Political Economy*" 277.

17. Marx, "Excerpts from James Mill's *Elements of Political Economy*" 277.

18. Thomas Hobbes, in *Leviathian,* ed. C. B. McPherson (Harmondsworth, UK: Penguin, 1968) 119, makes the distinction: by "Desire, we always signifie the Absence of the Object," while "by Love, most commonly the Presence of the same." Cf. Kenneth Burke, *Attitudes Toward History* (1937; Berkeley: U of California P, 1984) 372. It is worth noting that the plantation where Andrew learns about desire is called "Leviathan."

19. Baldwin, *The Price of the Ticket* 375, 635.

20. Johnson, *Oxherding Tale* 101. Robert Smalls; in *Slave Testimony: Two Centuries of Letters, Speeches, Interviews, and Autobiographies,* ed. John W. Blassingame (Baton Rouge: Louisiana State UP, 1977) 375. Harry McMillan; in *Slave Testimony* 381. Jane Johnson; qtd. in Genovese, *Roll, Jordan, Roll* 468. Harriet Jacobs, *Incidents in the Life of a Slave Girl. Written by Herself,* ed. Jean Fagan Yellin (Cambridge, MA: Harvard UP, 1987) 37. Douglass, *Narrative of the Life of Frederick Douglass* 321. Morrison, *Beloved* 162.

21. Robert Hayden, "Middle Passage," in *Robert Hayden: Collected Poems,* ed. Frederick Glaysher (New York: Liveright, 1985) 48.

22. Morrison, *Beloved* 273.

23. Marx, *Economic and Philosophical Manuscripts*; in *Karl Marx: The Early Writings* 378, 375, 379.

24. Johnson, *Being and Race: Black Writing Since 1970* (Bloomington: Indiana UP, 1988) 39. Cf. Cyrus Colter, Gilton Gregory Cross, Fred Shafer, Charles Johnson, and Reginald Gibbons, "Fought For It and Paid Taxes Too: Four Interviews with Cyrus Colter" *Callaloo* 14 (1991): 897.

25. William L. Andrews, *To Tell a Free Story: The First Century of Afro-American Autobiography, 1760–1865* (Urbana: U of Illinois P, 1986) 290. William Wells Brown, *Narrative of William W. Brown, a Fugitive Slave. Written by Himself* (Boston, 1847) 103–4. Douglass, *Narrative of the Life of Frederick Douglass* 325, 326, 331. Robert B. Stepto, *From Behind the Veil: A Study of Afro-American Narrative* (1979; Urbana: U of Illinois P, 1991) xv. Andrews, "The Representation of Slavery and the Rise of Afro-American Literary Realism 1865–1920," in *Slavery and the Literary Imagination,* ed. Deborah E. McDowell and Arnold Rampersad (Baltimore: Johns Hopkins UP, 1989) 65.

26. James W.C. Pennington, *The Fugitive Blacksmith; or, Events in the History of James W. C. Pennington* (London, 1849) iv. Brown, *Narrative of William W. Brown* 71, 104. Pennington, *The Fugitive Blacksmith* iv, vii, 51. While Pennington is explicit about arguing how the "system" and its various written records validate slavery, many fugitive slave narratives implicitly attested to this same point by appending documents such as contracts, bills of sale, and such at the end of their personal narratives—to demonstrate the incongruous relationship between personal rights (those who can tell their own stories) and property rites (the transmission of chattel).

27. Johnson, *Oxherding Tale* 152–53. Cf. Johnson, *Being and Race* 5–6, 39.

28. Ishmael Reed, *Flight to Canada* (1976; New York: Atheneum, 1989) 82, 171.

29. Williams, *The Alchemy of Race and Rights* (Cambridge, MA: Harvard UP, 1991) 124, 114.

30. Nathan Irvin Huggins, *Black Odyssey: The African-American Ordeal in Slavery* (1977; New York: Random House, 1990) 36–37, 34. For the legal statutes of the early republic, see A. Leon Higginbotham, Jr., *In the Matter of Color: Race and the American Legal Process: The Colonial Period* (New York: Oxford UP, 1978). Winthrop Jordan, in *White over Black: American Attitudes Toward the Negro, 1550–1812* (1968; New York: Norton, 1977) 95, noted that the term "white" began to appear in the republic after about 1680. David Roediger, in *The Wages of Whiteness* 21, adds that the "term *white* arose as a designation for European explorers, traders and settlers who came into contact with Africans and the indigenous people of the Americas."

31. Homi K. Bhabha, in "DissemiNation: Time, Narrative, and the Margins of the Modern Nation," in *Nation and Narration,* ed. Bhabha (New York: Routledge, 1990) 310, notes that there is a crucial connection between a national amnesia and the re-creation of nationhood, between that "site of a strange forgetting of the history of a nation's past" and the beginning of a "nation's narrative."

32. Reginald Horsman, *Race and Manifest Destiny: The Origins of American Racial Anglo-Saxonism* (Cambridge, MA: Harvard UP, 1981).

33. Horsman, *Race and Manifest Destiny* 300. Roediger, *Wages of Whiteness* 21. For the self-delusion of the English settlers in Virginia as they constructed these racial identities of "whiteness," see Morgan, *American Slavery, American Freedom* 44–70, the chapter entitled "Idle Indian and Lazy Englishman." Cf. Theodore W. Allen, *The Invention of the White Race: Volume One: Racial Oppression and Social Control* (New York: Verso, 1994); and Abbot E. Smith, *Colonists in Bondage: White Servitude and Convict Labor in America, 1607–1776* (1947; New York, 1971).

34. Harold Cruse, *Rebellion or Revolution?* (New York: William Morrow, 1968) 122, 124, 116. It is also important to remember that Johnson has consistently argued for a "universality" that is "not static," but "changing, historical, *evolving* and enriched by particularization." See Johnson, "Philosophy and Black Fiction," *Obsidian* 6.1–2 (1980): 57. For a different reading of how appropriation works in *Middle Passage* as a method for examining identity, see Daniel M. Scott III, "Interrogating Identity: Appropriation and Transformation in *Middle Passage,*" *African American Review* 29 (1995): 645–55. For a different reading of Johnson's problematizing of racial categories, see Molly Abel Travis, "*Beloved* and *Middle Passage:* Race, Narrative, and the Critic's Essentialism," *Narrative* 2 (1994): 179–200.

35. Teresa Ebert, "Political Semiosis in/of American Cultural Studies," *American Journal of Semiotics* 8 (1991): 118. Johnson, "Introduction" to *Oxherding Tale* xi.

36. Johnson, "Philosophy and Black Fiction" 55.

8. Conclusion

1. Raymond Williams, *Marxism and Literature* (New York: Oxford UP, 1977) 212. Paul Gilroy, *Small Acts: Thoughts on the Politics of Black Cultures* (London: Serpent's Tail, 1993) 163, 134. James C. Scott, *Domination and the Arts of Resistance: Hidden Transcripts* (New Haven, CT: Yale UP, 1990).

2. Gilroy, "'After the Love Has Gone': Bio-politics and Etho-poetics in the Black Public Sphere," in *The Black Public Sphere,* ed. Black Public Sphere Collective (Chicago: U of Chicago P, 1995) 69. Manning Marable, "Race, Identity, and Political Culture," in *Black Popular Culture,* ed. Gina Dent (Seattle: Bay Press, 1992) 292–302. The term "subaltern public sphere" is taken from Steven Gregory, "Race Identity and Political Activism: The Shifting Contours of the African American Public Sphere," in *The Black Public Sphere* 157; Gregory is drawing on the

term "subaltern counterpublics" from Nancy Fraser, "Rethinking the Public Sphere," in *The Phantom Public Sphere,* ed. Bruce Robbins (Minneapolis: U of Minnesota P, 1993) 4.

3. Werner Sollors, "Introduction: The Invention of Ethnicity," in *The Invention of Ethnicity,* ed. Sollors (New York: Oxford UP, 1989) xv. Cornel West, "Black Critics and the Pitfalls of Canon Formation," in *Keeping Faith: Philosophy and Race in America* (New York: Routledge, 1993) 41. Hayden White, *The Content of the Form: Narrative Discourse and Historical Representation* (Baltimore: Johns Hopkins UP, 1987), xi. Roger I. Simon, "Forms of Insurgency in the Production of Popular Memories: The Columbus Quincentenary and the Pedagogy of Counter-Commemoration," in *Between Borders: Pedagogy and the Politics of Cultural Studies,* ed. Henry A. Giroux and Peter McLaren (New York: Routledge, 1994) 130.

4. Charles Johnson, *Oxherding Tale* (New York: Grove, 1982) 119. Johnson, *Being and Race: Black Writing Since 1970* (Bloomington: U of Indiana P, 1988) 47, 48, 52.

5. Robin D. G. Kelley, *Race Rebels: Culture, Politics, and the Black Working Class* (New York: Free Press, 1994) 21. Peter Kolchin, "Reevaluating the Antebellum Slave Community: A Comparative Perspective," *Journal of American History* 70 (1983): 579, 580, 581, 582, 601. Laurence Shore, "The Poverty of Tragedy in Historical Writing on Southern Slavery," *The South Atlantic Quarterly* 85 (1986): 148, 153, 155, 160, 162, 164, 154, 149 (n. 6).

6. Jonathan Little, "An Interview with Charles Johnson," *Contemporary Literature* 34 (1993): 173. Johnson, *Middle Passage* (New York: Atheneum, 1990) 66.

7. Edward Said, *Culture and Imperialism* (New York: Alfred A. Knopf, 1993) 221.

8. Michael Awkward, *Negotiating Difference: Race, Gender, and the Politics of Positionality* (Chicago: U of Chicago P, 1995) 14, 8. LeRoi Jones [Amiri Baraka], *Home: Social Essays* (New York: William Morrow, 1966) 246. Philip Brian Harper, "Nationalism and Social Division in Black Arts Poetry of the 1960s," *Critical Inquiry* 19 (1993): 239, 250–51. Stephen Henderson, *Understanding the New Black Poetry: Black Speech and Black Music as Poetic References* (New York: William Morrow, 1973) 183.

9. Michael Omi and Howard Winant, *Racial Formation in the United States from the 1960s to the 1980s* (New York: Routledge, 1986) 116–17, 92–93. Nathan Glazer, *Affirmative Discrimination: Ethnic Inequality and Public Policy* (1975; New York: Basic Books, 1978) 220. Cf. Thomas Sowell, *Civil Rights: Rhetoric or Reality?* (New York: Quill, 1984) 54–55, 118–19.

10. George Lipsitz, "The Possessive Investment in Whiteness: Racialized Social Democracy and the 'White' Problem in American Studies," *American Quarterly* 47 (1995): 369.

11. Paul Gilroy, *Small Acts* 105; and *The Black Atlantic: Modernity and Double Consciousness* (Cambridge, MA: Harvard UP, 1993) 105, has made some very suggestive comments on how slave autobiographies "blend and transcend key Western categories: narrative and documentary; history and literature; ethics and politics; word and sound" as an example of the "dialogic character of black expressive culture." He has also remarked that the "premium which all these black diaspora styles place on the process of performance is emphasised by their radically unfinished forms—a characteristic which marks them indelibly as the products of slavery."

12. Richard Ohmann, "The Shaping of a Canon: U.S. Fiction, 1960–1975," in *Politics of Letters* (Middletown, CT: Wesleyan UP, 1987) 80, 91. William Styron; in "Slavery in the First Person," *Yale Alumni Magainze* 31 (1967): 35. Styron, *The Confessions of Nat Turner* (1967; New York: Vintage International Editions, 1992) 125.

Index